Depression *to* Decolonization

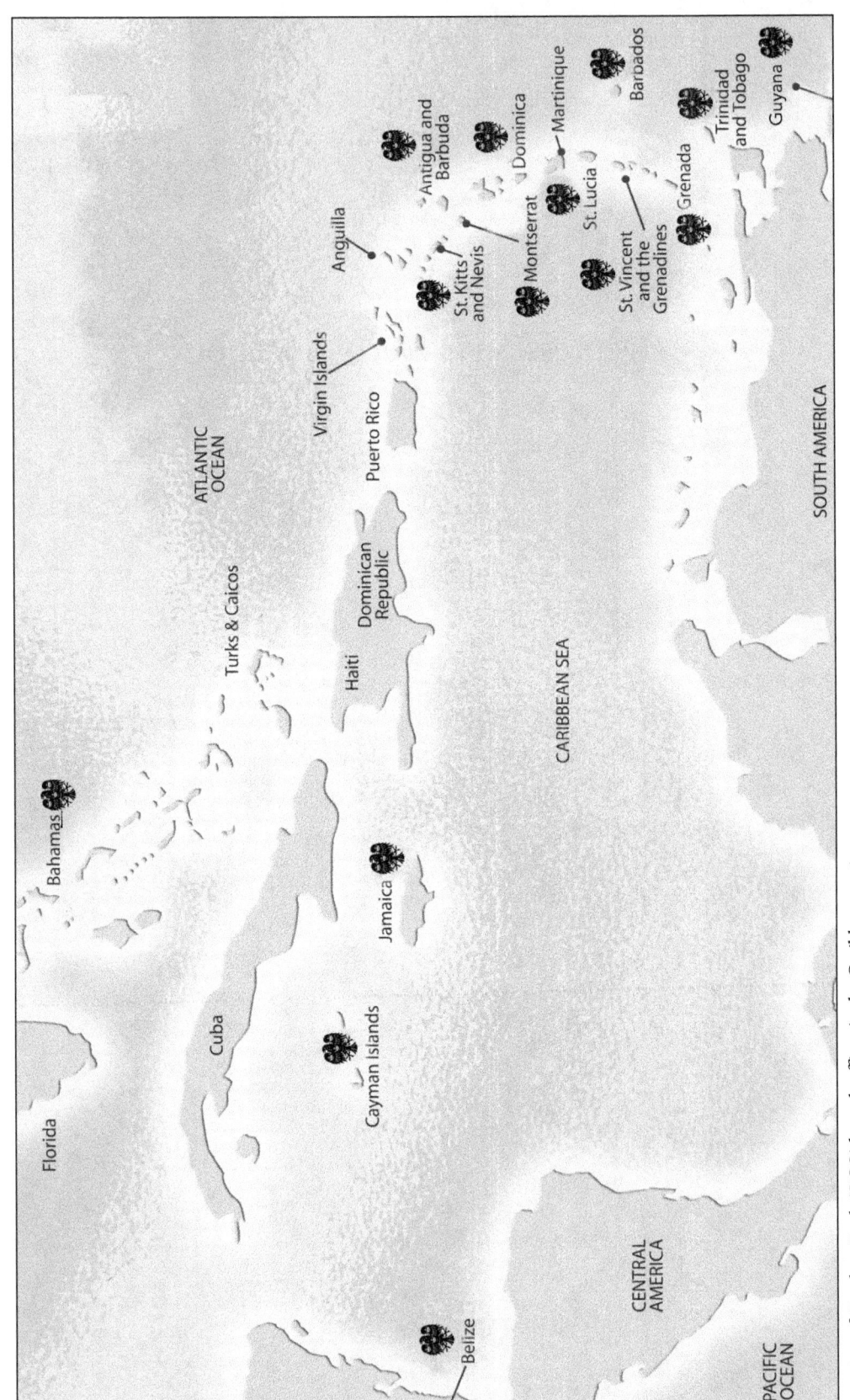

Location of Barclays Bank (DCO) branch offices in the Caribbean, 1962.

Depression to Decolonization

Barclays Bank (DCO) in the West Indies, 1926–1962

Kathleen E.A. Monteith

University of the West Indies Press
Jamaica • Barbados • Trinidad and Tobago

University of the West Indies Press
7A Gibraltar Hall Road   Mona
Kingston 7   Jamaica
www.uwipress.com

© 2008 by Kathleen E.A. Monteith

All rights reserved. Published 2008

12 11 10 09 08   5 4 3 2 1

Monteith, Kathleen E.A.

Depression to decolonization: Barclays Bank (DCO) in the West Indies, 1926–1962 / Kathleen E.A. Monteith.

p. cm.

Includes bibliographical references.

ISBN: 978-976-640-198-6

1. Barclays Bank (Dominion, Colonial and Overseas). 2. Banks and banking – West Indies, British – History. I. Title.

HG2998.B34 M76 2008   332.1'09729

Cover illustration: One of six tile murals at Barclays Bank (DCO)'s King Street, Jamaica, branch, depicting the regions where the bank had branch operations. By R.W. Baker, Royal College of Art, London, 1955.

Book and cover design by Robert Harris.
Set in Dante Regular 11.5/15.5 x 27
Printed in the United States of America.

Contents

List of Illustrations / *vii*

List of Tables / *xi*

Acknowledgements / *xii*

Explanation of Terms / *xv*

Abbreviations / *xvi*

Introduction / *1*

Chapter 1	Banking in the West Indies, 1836–1925: An Overview / *11*	
Chapter 2	The Depression Years: Bank Performance, 1926–1939 / *28*	
Chapter 3	Collusion and Competition: Challenges from the Canadian Banks, 1926–1945 / *54*	
Chapter 4	Financing Agriculture and Trade: Bank Products and Services, 1926–1945 / *75*	
Chapter 5	Regulation of Commercial Banking in the West Indies, 1926–1962 / *108*	
Chapter 6	Reform of the Currency System in the West Indies, 1930–1962 / *128*	
Chapter 7	Towards Independence: Bank Performance, 1940–1962 / *156*	
Chapter 8	Towards Independence: Branch Expansion, Competition and Product Diversification, 1940–1962 / *189*	

Chapter 9   Towards Independence: Staffing and Decentralization, 1940–1962 / *232*

Conclusion / *256*

Appendices / *267*

Notes / *277*

Bibliography / *329*

Index / *345*

Contents

List of Illustrations / *vii*

List of Tables / *xi*

Acknowledgements / *xii*

Explanation of Terms / *xv*

Abbreviations / *xvi*

Introduction / *1*

Chapter 1	Banking in the West Indies, 1836–1925: An Overview / *11*
Chapter 2	The Depression Years: Bank Performance, 1926–1939 / *28*
Chapter 3	Collusion and Competition: Challenges from the Canadian Banks, 1926–1945 / *54*
Chapter 4	Financing Agriculture and Trade: Bank Products and Services, 1926–1945 / *75*
Chapter 5	Regulation of Commercial Banking in the West Indies, 1926–1962 / *108*
Chapter 6	Reform of the Currency System in the West Indies, 1930–1962 / *128*
Chapter 7	Towards Independence: Bank Performance, 1940–1962 / *156*
Chapter 8	Towards Independence: Branch Expansion, Competition and Product Diversification, 1940–1962 / *189*

Chapter 9   Towards Independence: Staffing and
             Decentralization, 1940–1962 / *232*

             Conclusion / *256*

             Appendices / *267*

             Notes / *277*

             Bibliography / *329*

             Index / *345*

Illustrations

Figures

Figure 2.1   Barclays Bank (DCO), total operating profits, 1926–1939 / *33*

Figure 2.2   Barclays Bank (DCO), West Indian section, operating profits, 1926–1939 / *35*

Figure 2.3   London sugar prices, 1926–1939 / *36*

Figure 2.4   Barclays Bank (DCO), West Indian branch accounts, 1926–1934 / *39*

Figure 2.5   Barclays Bank (DCO), West Indian branch accounts: exchange, 1926–1934 / *39*

Figure 2.6   Barclays Bank (DCO), West Indian branch accounts: overdrafts and loans, 1926–1934 / *40*

Figure 2.7   Barclays Bank (DCO), West Indian branch accounts: discounts, commission and interest received, 1926–1934 / *41*

Figure 2.8   Barclays Bank (DCO), West Indian branch accounts: bills discounted and bills received, 1926–1934 / *42*

Figure 2.9   Barclays Bank (DCO), West Indian branch accounts: banknote circulation, 1926–1934 / *42*

Figure 2.10   West Indian sugar production and exports, 1926–1939 / *52*

Figure 6.1   Barclays Bank (DCO), note circulation in the West Indies, 1937–1942 / *140*

Figure 6.2   Currency notes in circulation, Jamaica, 1941 and 1942 / *144*

Illustrations

Figure 7.1	Barclays Bank (DCO), West Indian section, operating profits, 1940–1962 / *163*	
Figure 7.2	West Indian sugar production and exports, 1940–1962 / *165*	
Figure 7.3	Value of West Indian trade, 1940–1962 / *169*	
Figure 7.4	Barclays Bank (DCO), West Indian branch accounts: deposits, loans and advances, 1952–1962 / *177*	
Figure 7.5	Barclays Bank (DCO), West Indian branch accounts: ratio of loans and advances to deposits, 1952–1962 / *179*	
Figure 7.6	Barclays Bank (DCO), West Indian branch accounts: foreign currency transactions, 1952–1962 / *181*	
Figure 7.6a	Barclays Bank (DCO), West Indian branch accounts: foreign currency sales, 1952–1962 / *182*	
Figure 7.6b	Barclays Bank (DCO), West Indian branch accounts: foreign currency purchases, 1952–1962 / *182*	
Figure 7.7	Barclays Bank (DCO), West Indian branch accounts: cost as a percentage of gross operating profits, 1952–1962 / *185*	
Figure 7.8	Barclays Bank (DCO), West Indian branch accounts: interest paid on deposits, 1952–1962 / *186*	
Figure 9.1	Management structure of Barclays Bank (DCO), 1952 / *252*	

Plates

Plate 4.1	The Colonial Bank, Harbour Street, Kingston, Jamaica, 1887 / *78*	
Plate 4.2	The Colonial Bank, Harbour Street, Kingston (rebuilt after the 1907 earthquake) / *79*	
Plate 6.1	Banknote issued in British Guiana, 1934 / *136*	
Plate 6.2	Banknote issued in Barbados, 1937 / *138*	
Plate 6.3	Banknote issued in Barbados, 1949 / *140*	
Plate 8.1	Barclays Bank (DCO), Freeport City branch, Grand Bahama, 1960 / *191*	
Plate 8.2	Barclays Bank (DCO), Harris Promenade branch, San Fernando, Trinidad and Tobago / *192*	

Plate 8.3	Barclays Bank (DCO)'s branch at Arima, Trinidad and Tobago / *193*	
Plate 8.4	Barclays Bank (DCO), New Amsterdam branch, Berbice, British Guiana, 1957 / *195*	
Plate 8.5	The Bank of Nova Scotia, King Street branch, Kingston, Jamaica, 1960 / *200*	
Plate 8.6	Royal Bank of Canada, King Street branch, 1960 / *200*	
Plate 8.7	The Canadian Bank of Commerce, corner of King Street and Harbour Street, Kingston, c. 1962 / *201*	
Plate 8.8	The Bank of Nova Scotia, Bridgetown, Barbados, 1962 / *201*	
Plate 8.9	Barclays Bank (DCO), Half Way Tree branch, Kingston, Jamaica, 1957 / *209*	
Plate 8.10	Barclays Bank (DCO)'s newly rebuilt King Street branch, Kingston, Jamaica, 1955 / *209*	
Plate 8.11	Mural outside the King Street branch, 1955 / *210*	
Plate 8.12	Barclays Bank (DCO), Harbour Street branch interior, Kingston, Jamaica, 1961 / *211*	
Plate 8.13	Marine Square, Port of Spain, Trinidad and Tobago, showing the Barclays Bank (DCO) branch / *211*	
Plate 9.1	Jim Whiting, 1975 / *236*	
Plate 9.2	Barclays Bank (DCO) staff (with their wives), Jamaica, 1926 / *237*	
Plate 9.3	Barclays Bank (DCO) staff (and wives) Barbados, 1926 / *238*	
Plate 9.4	John Basford and his wife upon arrival in Jamaica, 1955 / *239*	
Plate 9.5	Barclays Bank (DCO) branch managers in Kingston, Jamaica / *240*	
Plate 9.6	Don Banks, 1956 / *241*	
Plate 9.7	Eldon Forrest, c. 1951 / *241*	
Plate 9.8	Barbara Duhaney, 1967 / *241*	
Plate 9.9	Augusta Payne, 1974 / *241*	
Plate 9.10	Barclays Bank (DCO) staff in Jamaica, 1952 / *242*	
Plate 9.11	Barclays Bank (DCO) staff in Barbados, 1952 / *243*	
Plate 9.12	Barclays Bank (DCO) staff at the San Fernando branch, Trinidad and Tobago, 1952 / *247*	

Illustrations

Plate 9.13 Barclays Bank (DCO) staff at the Half Way Tree branch, Kingston, Jamaica, 1957 / 248
Plate 9.14 Ena Evadne Leung-Walker, 1968 / 249
Plate 9.15 Dorothy Eve Reid / 249

Tables

Table 2.1	Barclays Bank (DCO), Operating Profits and Losses, 1926–1939 / *31*
Table 2.2	West Indian Section, Barclays Bank (DCO), Operating Profits, 1926–1939 / *34*
Table 2.3	British Government Loan Guarantee Scheme to the West Indies / *47*
Table 2.4	Direction of West Indian Trade, 1922–1937 / *51*
Table 3.1	Commercial Bank Branch and Sub-branch Distribution in the West Indies, 1926–1939 / *59*
Table 3.2	Banknote Circulation in the West Indies, c. 1933 / *60*
Table 3.3	Jamaican Bank Offices of Barclays Bank (DCO) and BNS / *62*
Table 4.1	Annual Average Sugar Exports from the West Indies, 1920–1929, 1930–1939 and 1946 / *81*
Table 4.2	Barclays Bank (DCO), Breakdown of Advances in the West Indies, 1948 / *82*
Table 4.3	Import and Export Trade, the West Indies, 1936–1938 and 1948 / *91*
Table 6.1	Circulatory Limits on Banknotes for the West Indies, 1942 / *147*
Table 6.2	Average Currency Notes in Circulation in Jamaica, 1946–1957 / *152*
Table 7.1	Barclays Bank (DCO), Operating Profits and Losses, 1940–1962 / *158*
Table 7.2	Territorial Spread of Barclays Bank (DCO), Loans and Advances, 1948 and 1949 / *164*
Table 7.3	Sugar Prices, 1937–1949 / *167*

Tables

Table 7.4	Sugar Prices, 1950–1962 / *171*
Table 7.5	Barclays Bank (DCO), West Indian Branch Accounts, 1952–1962 / *178*
Table 7.6	Barclays Bank (DCO), Interest Rates on Loans and Advances in the West Indies, 1952–1962 / *179*
Table 8.1	Number of Barclays Bank (DCO) Branches and Sub-branches in the West Indies, 1939–1962 / *190*
Table 8.2	Number of Branches and Sub-branches of Multinational Banks in the West Indies, 1962 / *199*
Table 8.3	Location of Branches and Sub-branches of Barclays Bank (DCO) and the BNS in Jamaica, 1962 / *202*
Table 8.4	Barclays Bank (DCO), Breakdown of West Indian Advances, 1952–1962 / *215*
Table 8.5	Total Bank Loans and Advances, Jamaica, 1946–1962 / *216*
Table 8.6	Total Bank Loans and Advances, Trinidad and Tobago, 1946–1962 / *217*
Table 8.6a	Bank Loans and Advances ("Other" Category), Trinidad and Tobago, 1954–1962 / *218*
Table 8.7	Barclays Overseas Development Corporation, Loans by Region, 1951, 1957 and 1961 / *224*
Table 8.8	Barclays Overseas Development Corporation, Loans in the West Indies, 1951 and 1957 / *226*
Table 8.9	Barclays Overseas Development Corporation, Loans by Applicant, 1957, 1961 / *227*
Table 8.10	Barclays Overseas Development Corporation, Loans by Category in the West Indies, 1951 / *229*
Table 9.1	Barclays Bank (DCO), Annual Salary Scales for British and West Indian Male Staff, 1946 / *245*

Acknowledgements

The primary research for this book was conducted during my tenure as a doctoral student at the University of Reading between 1992 and 1995. The book is not a commissioned work, and Barclays Bank plc has not imposed any conditions or restrictions on the use of the data other than a request not to identify clients of the bank named in its records. A wide range of material pertaining to the operations of Barclays Bank (DCO) in the West Indies was made available for my examination during a three-month period spent in the Barclays Bank Archives. I am grateful to Peter Emerson, then Head of Archives and Records Management, Barclays Bank plc for providing access to the records, and to Jessie Campbell, Senior Archivist, who was most helpful in identifying and retrieving the data. My extended visit was very pleasant, made so by her and the other staff members who provided a most congenial atmosphere in which to work. A University of the West Indies Mona Research Fellowship between 2000 and 2002 provided valuable leave from teaching, which allowed me to concentrate on important additional research for this book.

I am also very grateful to the staff of the following institutions for their courtesy and hospitality: the National Library of Jamaica, Kingston; the University of the West Indies Libraries at Mona, Cave Hill and St Augustine; the Barbados Archives, St Michael; the Bahamas National Archives, Nassau; the Institute of Commonwealth Studies, London. Frances Salmon and Glenroy Taitt of the West Indies and Special Collections Section of the University of the West Indies Libraries at Mona and St Augustine, respectively, were very helpful in my research.

I appreciate the time extended to me by Mrs Augusta Payne, Mr Donald Banks, Mr Eldon Forrest and Mr Maurice Clarke and their willingness to discuss their experiences of being among the first non-white West Indian staff members of Barclays Bank (DCO). Mrs Edna Ramsey also generously shared her reminiscences of being an early employee of the Bank of Nova Scotia in Jamaica. The information they provided has been most valuable to this work. George C. Money told me of his tenure as local director of the bank, for which I am grateful. I dearly appreciate the trust placed in me by Eldon Forrest, who willingly handed over personal material to me in the later stages of the preparation of the manuscript. I am also grateful for material given to me by Eric Armstrong of Barbados, who has been most supportive of the project, and I thank Mrs Margaret Banks for the loan of Barclays and NCB newsletters and magazines that are not in the libraries.

I am particularly grateful to Barry Higman for reading the thesis and providing valuable comments on how to go about converting it into this book. I thank him for encouragement and guidance in my academic and professional pursuits and for every so often enquiring, "How's the book coming along?" Similar queries and encouragement also came from Geoffrey Jones, who willingly read and commented on each draft chapter as the book progressed. I am grateful for his interest and support. I appreciate the encouraging comments and suggestions made by the two anonymous reviewers of the manuscript.

Advice and encouragement also came from friends and colleagues in the Department of History and Archaeology, University of the West Indies, Mona. I make mention of Roy Augier, Carl Campbell and Swithin Wilmot. Brian Moore, now at Colgate University, New York, and Maureen Warner-Lewis provided valuable information about areas and locales in Guyana and Trinidad and Tobago. Family members' moral support was not unnoticed, and is well appreciated. I make special mention of my parents, Basil (now deceased) and Dorothy Monteith, who have provided immeasurable nurturing. This book is dedicated to both of them.

Explanation of Terms

Throughout this work, the Barclays Bank (Dominion, Colonial and Overseas), which was formed following the merger of the Colonial Bank with the National Bank of South Africa and the Anglo-Egyptian Bank in 1925, is referred to as Barclays Bank (DCO). In 1954 the name was changed to Barclays Bank DCO, without the brackets, a shortened version of the original name.

The West Indies generally refers to the group of islands that form part of an archipelago which extends in a wide curve from near the southern tip of Florida in the United States of America to the north coast of South America. Included are islands which at one time fell under British, French, Spanish and Dutch imperial control. In this book the term West Indies alludes only to those islands and territories which were under British imperial control and where the Colonial Bank and Barclays Bank (DCO) established a branch network. These include the Leeward Islands of Antigua, St Kitts and Nevis, Montserrat, and Dominica; the Windward Islands of Grenada, St Lucia, St Vincent, Barbados, and Trinidad and Tobago; and Jamaica, the Cayman Islands, the Bahamas, British Guiana, and British Honduras. The last three are geographically situated outside the West Indies, but are close by and shared a similar political relationship with Britain.

Abbreviations

ACC	Antigua Chamber of Commerce
BBA	Barclays Bank Archives
BCCB	British Caribbean Curency Board
BG	British Guiana
BGSPA	British Guiana Sugar Planters Association
BMLA	Barbados Mutual Life Assurance
BNS	Bank of Nova Scotia
BOLAM	Bank of London and Montreal
BOLSA	Bank of London and South America
CBC	Canadian Bank of Commerce
CIBC	Canadian Imperial Bank of Commerce
CO	Colonial Office Papers
CSA	Commonwealth Sugar Agreement
D/A	Documents against acceptance
D/P	Documents against payment
FNCBNY	First National City Bank of New York
HBJ	*Handbook of Jamaica*
JIA	Jamaica Imperial Association
RBC	Royal Bank of Canada
UFCo	United Fruit Co. Ltd
WI	West Indies/West Indian
WISCo	West Indies Sugar Co. Ltd

Introduction

Barclays Bank (DCO) was one of the largest multinational banks of its time. Its history is linked with that of the Colonial Bank, which began operating in the West Indies in 1837.

Until fairly recently, most banking and management scholars maintained that multinational banking only began in the 1960s, when American banks expanded abroad in the wake of the emergence of the Eurodollar market and the tremendous expansion in American foreign direct investment. Subsequent research, however, by Geoffrey Jones, F.H.H. King, David Merrett and others has shown that British multinational banking networks were already in place in the nineteenth and early twentieth centuries.[1] This book adds to the growing body of business-history literature on multinational banking by examining Barclays Bank (DCO)'s operations in the West Indies between 1926 and 1962.

The Colonial Bank was one of the early British multinational or "overseas" banks, as they were called then, which emerged in the 1830s. The emergence and dominance of these institutions has been explained in the context of the considerable competitive advantages derived from British imperial expansion and dominance of the world political economy in the nineteenth century. The concept of nation-specific, or national, competitive advantages developed by Michael Porter has been shown by Geoffrey Jones to be useful in establishing why British banks were so prominent in multinational banking from the early nineteenth century through to the early twentieth century. Jones has shown that Britain's dominance of the world political economy in this period provided British businesses operating overseas with considerable nation-specific competitive advantages.[2] In the nineteenth century, the factor conditions were favourable, given the extent of British capital throughout the world economy. As a result, demand conditions for the services of British overseas banks were enhanced, given the importance of British trade and investment in the world economy. Ownership and firm-specific advantages stemmed from the fact that the banks were able to raise capital on the London stock exchange and from the well-established domestic banking system which provided a flow of trained personnel for these institutions. Jones also notes that political factors and the strength of the British empire provided prestige for the banks, thereby enhancing the demand for their services abroad.[3]

Following World War I, it became obvious that the original competitive advantages held by the British banks had begun to weaken. Factor conditions were less favourable. Depressed economic conditions, particularly in the late 1920s and 1930s, made it less desirable for banks to raise capital, since they were not generating sufficient profits. In addition, there was a noticeable decline in demand conditions with the weakening of British business abroad, especially among those active in the extractive sectors, resulting in a gradual erosion of the traditional customer base. This decline was to some extent aided by the growth in multinational activity by the United States: its considerable investments abroad often resulted in the loss of lucrative trade-finance business for the British banks, as it was transferred to American-owned banks.[4]

The decline in the relative importance of British business was matched by wider structural changes in the world economy which adversely affected the demand for trade-finance and foreign exchange services, both of which the British banks specialized in. The most striking change was the sharp fall in international trade that accompanied the shift in commodity terms of trade against primary producers, which usually translated into less business and more bad debts for the banks. This period also witnessed the beginning of a shift from sterling to US dollars in trade finance, accompanying the growth in American foreign

Introduction

Barclays Bank (DCO) was one of the largest multinational banks of its time. Its history is linked with that of the Colonial Bank, which began operating in the West Indies in 1837.

Until fairly recently, most banking and management scholars maintained that multinational banking only began in the 1960s, when American banks expanded abroad in the wake of the emergence of the Eurodollar market and the tremendous expansion in American foreign direct investment. Subsequent research, however, by Geoffrey Jones, F.H.H. King, David Merrett and others has shown that British multinational banking networks were already in place in the nineteenth and early twentieth centuries.[1] This book adds to the growing body of business-history literature on multinational banking by examining Barclays Bank (DCO)'s operations in the West Indies between 1926 and 1962.

The Colonial Bank was one of the early British multinational or "overseas" banks, as they were called then, which emerged in the 1830s. The emergence and dominance of these institutions has been explained in the context of the considerable competitive advantages derived from British imperial expansion and dominance of the world political economy in the nineteenth century. The concept of nation-specific, or national, competitive advantages developed by Michael Porter has been shown by Geoffrey Jones to be useful in establishing why British banks were so prominent in multinational banking from the early nineteenth century through to the early twentieth century. Jones has shown that Britain's dominance of the world political economy in this period provided British businesses operating overseas with considerable nation-specific competitive advantages.[2] In the nineteenth century, the factor conditions were favourable, given the extent of British capital throughout the world economy. As a result, demand conditions for the services of British overseas banks were enhanced, given the importance of British trade and investment in the world economy. Ownership and firm-specific advantages stemmed from the fact that the banks were able to raise capital on the London stock exchange and from the well-established domestic banking system which provided a flow of trained personnel for these institutions. Jones also notes that political factors and the strength of the British empire provided prestige for the banks, thereby enhancing the demand for their services abroad.[3]

Following World War I, it became obvious that the original competitive advantages held by the British banks had begun to weaken. Factor conditions were less favourable. Depressed economic conditions, particularly in the late 1920s and 1930s, made it less desirable for banks to raise capital, since they were not generating sufficient profits. In addition, there was a noticeable decline in demand conditions with the weakening of British business abroad, especially among those active in the extractive sectors, resulting in a gradual erosion of the traditional customer base. This decline was to some extent aided by the growth in multinational activity by the United States: its considerable investments abroad often resulted in the loss of lucrative trade-finance business for the British banks, as it was transferred to American-owned banks.[4]

The decline in the relative importance of British business was matched by wider structural changes in the world economy which adversely affected the demand for trade-finance and foreign exchange services, both of which the British banks specialized in. The most striking change was the sharp fall in international trade that accompanied the shift in commodity terms of trade against primary producers, which usually translated into less business and more bad debts for the banks. This period also witnessed the beginning of a shift from sterling to US dollars in trade finance, accompanying the growth in American foreign direct investment. Hence the competitive advantage of being a sterling-based bank with a head office in London diminished somewhat during the inter-war years, and was only partially restored with Britain's return to the gold standard in 1925. In addition, the City of London's role as the world's leading capital market declined as the Bank of England imposed informal restrictions on portfolio capital exports in the 1920s, followed by more stringent controls in 1932. Also, nationalist and anti-colonial sentiment, which manifested in the 1930s, grew in the post-war period and often led to a decline in receptivity which involved increased regulatory controls and discriminatory legislation.[5] Nevertheless, British multinational banks survived, and it was only after 1960 that they lost their prominence in international banking.[6]

This study of Barclays Bank (DCO) in the West Indies covers the period in which British multinational banks began to experience decline in many of their original competitive advantages. In spite of this decline, the analyses in the literature concerned with this period indicate that the banks generally held on to their market share in many of the regions in which they were established up to at least the beginning of the 1970s. This was particularly noticeable in the former colonial territories.[7] That British multinational banks were predominantly established in the empire, and the fact that they survived best in former colonial territories, suggests an "empire connection" with regard to their operations. It is this connection which is explored in this book with respect to Barclays Bank (DCO)'s operations in the West Indies in the period 1926 to 1962. Two central questions are addressed: To what extent did British colonialism provide competitive advantages for Barclays Bank (DCO) in its operations in the West Indies between 1926 and 1962? How well did the bank cope with the changing sociopolitical developments as the region moved towards political independence from Britain after 1940?

The operations of Barclays Bank (DCO) during the period 1926–62 are interesting to study for a number of reasons. When the bank began operating in the West Indies, it was primarily engaged in the provision of financing for the import/export trade. During the course of the period it gradually evolved into a retail commercial banking institution, broadening its range of products and services in the region. Therefore, the book also examines the bank's contribution to financial development and innovation in the region in this period under examination.

Between 1926 and 1962 there were significant developments in the social, economic and political environment of the region. Soon after the bank was established, the Great Depression occurred and lasted into the 1930s. The Depression affected the sugar industry in the region, which naturally had repercussions for the bank since its operations in the West Indies at the time were primarily centred on providing finance for the production and trade of sugar. The book examines the bank's ability to cope with and survive the drastic price reductions in the world markets for the commodities to which its business operations in the region were so closely bound.

After 1940 Barclays Bank (DCO) operated in a markedly different socio-economic and political environment in the West Indies. In many respects the Depression and World War II were catalysts for this change. As the labour riots which occurred towards the end of the Depression years were transformed into nationalist movements, there emerged an elite political/labour corps which readily organized workers into mass political parties and affiliate trade unions. It is true that the declaration of war against Nazi Germany in 1939 had dampened nationalist fervour for a while as West Indians and colonial peoples elsewhere rallied behind Britain. Yet the principles upon which the war had been fought found resonance among colonial peoples everywhere, including the West Indies, and contributed to further strengthening of a sense of nationalism among its people in the aftermath of the Allied victory in 1945.

With an increased sense of nationalism permeating throughout the West Indies, coupled with the decline in British power and influence and imperial will, along with the rising costs of empire and the pressures of international opinion, Britain committed to the decolonization of her empire.[8] Accordingly, beginning in Jamaica and extending to Trinidad and Tobago, universal adult suffrage was introduced in 1944. This essentially began the gradual decolonization process in the region, and by the late 1950s internal self-government was introduced, culminating in full political independence in 1962, first for Jamaica and Trinidad and Tobago, with others to follow in the years to come.

The tremendous growth in nationalistic feeling among the region's people and the call for self-government also reflected changes in the social fabric of West Indian societies. These changes included the emergence of an educated black middle class from the late nineteenth and early twentieth centuries, whose members not only had begun to demand more democratic forms of government but also had called for a sustained policy of economic development for the region.[9] Certainly, as the devolution of imperial power proceeded after 1944, many of the governments in the region introduced legislation designed to foster rapid commercialization and industrialization. This resulted in significant economic expansion and diversification after 1945 and particularly in the 1950s. Another aspect of this enquiry involves an assessment of the strategies and general policy adopted by Barclays Bank (DCO) with regard to its operations in view of these socio-economic and political changes.

The book is organized as follows. Chapter 1 is divided into three sections and provides a brief overview of the history of banking in the West Indies between 1836 and 1925. It discusses the establishment of the Colonial Bank, the predecessor of Barclays Bank (DCO), in the context of the emergence and expansion of British multinational banking, introducing the concepts which help to explain this phenomenon. It traces the establishment and demise of the early local West Indian banks, and notes the implications for the Colonial Bank of the establishment of Canadian banks in the region around the turn of the last century. The chapter ends with a brief discussion of the reincorporation of that bank as Barclays Bank (DCO) in December 1925.

Chapter 2 discusses the bank's performance between 1926 and 1945. It focuses on the impact of the Great Depression on the bank's profits and its ability to cope with the substantial fall in the price of sugar on the world markets in the period 1926–39. This chapter also establishes the position of the West Indian operations in the context of the bank's overall operations between 1926 and 1939.

Chapter 3 examines the competition from the Canadian commercial banks which operated in the West Indies during the period 1926 to 1945. It assesses the nature and the impact of this competition, given the presence of a collusive agreement among these banks, with a view to determining the extent to which the bank came under any significant threat to its position in the region in this period. In so doing, Barclays Bank (DCO)'s position in relation to the Canadian banks in the West Indian commercial banking market is established.

Chapter 4 examines the bank's products and services in the period

1926–45. The first section examines the customer base of the bank. The second examines the lending policy of the bank in this period and the circumstances in which the bank was prepared to be flexible and deviate from conventional banking practice. The third section discusses the alternative sources of credit that were available to peasants and small farmers and other individuals who were not accommodated by the bank.

Chapter 5 focuses on the regulation of commercial banks during the period 1926–62. The overall issue examined here is the extent to which the political relationship between the West Indies and Britain provided continued high receptivity for Barclays Bank (DCO) in the region in this period.

Chapter 6 discusses the reform of the currency system, which included the placing of the currency issue on a sterling exchange standard, and the impact that this had on the operations of Barclays Bank (DCO) in the West Indies.

Chapter 7 discusses the performance of the bank in terms of its profits for the period from 1940 to 1962, providing an assessment of the impact on its operations of World War II and the post-war economic expansion in the region.

Chapter 8 examines the strategies pursued by Barclays Bank (DCO) during the period 1940–62 in view of the sociopolitical and economic changes which occurred in the region during this period. This chapter focuses on the actions taken by the bank to improve its resource capabilities, competitive strategies and product diversification and innovation.

Chapter 9 examines other strategies in the area of staffing and the adjustments made in the organizational control of operations in the region during the period 1940–62.

This examination of Barclays Bank (DCO)'s operations in the West Indies ends at 1962. This date is significant, marking as it did the end of the colonial period. In that year and thereafter, political independence from Britain was achieved by a number of territories in the region. Jamaica and Trinidad and Tobago gained their independence in that year, followed in 1966 by Barbados and British Guiana. The territories of the Windward and Leeward Islands did not immediately become independent but entered into a status of voluntary association whereby they obtained internal self-government while the responsibility for defence and foreign affairs remained with Britain. Given these changes in the region, after 1962 Barclays Bank (DCO) entered a new era in terms of its operations. The post-1962 period merits more detailed examination and analysis than can be accomplished here. Certainly, in that period the bank was faced with a significantly changed political climate, as the various newly independent governments, particularly those in Trinidad and Tobago and in Jamaica, began to exercise greater supervision over the banking sector. They also pursued policies geared towards the creation of an indigenous financial sector. One of these policies included the requirement that all foreign institutions incorporate locally. Thus, Barclays Bank of Trinidad and Tobago and Barclays Bank (Jamaica) Ltd were formed in 1972, with local participation amounting to 25 per cent in each bank. In Trinidad and Tobago the parent bank's share was further reduced to under 50 per cent in 1981, and the bank's name was changed to Republic Bank Ltd. It was during this period that the bank withdrew from some of the territories in the region. In 1977 the bank sold its assets to the Jamaican government and was renamed the National Commercial Bank. In 1987 it sold its remaining shares in the Republic Bank. In Guyana, the bank ceased operations in 1987; the other branches in the region continued with the parent group.[10]

This book is one of a small number of academic business histories concerned with British multinational banking. The development of this area in business history over the past sixty years has been slow, mainly because banks in the past have been reluctant to allow access to their records for fear of breach of privacy of their clients' business activities and also for fear of potential bad publicity. As a result, early academic examinations of bank operations have been from a generalized perspective. This is true of the pioneering works on the history of British multinational banking by A.S.J. Baster, which trace the origins of the British banks which operated within and outside the British empire. Baster's work discusses the nature of the operations of these banks and outlines their advantages over their local rivals.[11]

Most of the banking histories which followed Baster's were commemorative pieces published or sponsored by the institutions themselves. Barclays Bank (DCO) began this tradition very early in its history with the publication of *A Banking Centenary: A History of Barclays Bank (Dominion, Colonial and Overseas), 1836–1936*.[12] This book was compiled and printed to mark the bank's one hundredth anniversary and was for private circulation among shareholders, customers and staff. The work outlines the early history of the three constituent banks before their amalgamation in 1925 and gives a general descriptive outline of the bank between that year and 1936. This publication was followed by *A Bank in Battledress: Being the Story of Barclays Bank (Dominion, Colonial and Overseas) during the Second World War, 1939–1945*, an account written primarily for the staff that recounts their activities during the course of the war. It can be regarded as a morale-boosting exercise in its recognition of the war's impact on the staff and on their daily work. It is particularly detailed about the branches in Britain, Africa, the Middle East and other areas directly affected by the war.[13]

The publication of *The DCO Story: A History of Banking in Many Countries, 1925–1971*, which followed, continued the tradition of commemoration within the Barclays group. This book is more comprehensive than the earlier ones and is therefore a useful reference for the bank's history in the various territories in which it was located. It contains valuable details about the formation of the bank, its organizational structure and the impact of the Depression on its operations. It also chronicles the post-war problems which the bank encountered, particularly those having to do with nationalism in the Middle East and Africa. However, because the book has a global perspective, it does not offer a comprehensive view of the bank's operations in any one territory or region.[14]

From Colonial to Republic: One Hundred and Fifty Years of Business and Banking in Trinidad and Tobago, 1837–1987, was the first and only commemorative history to focus exclusively on Barclays Bank (DCO)'s operations in a single West Indian territory. This work traces the history of the bank in Trinidad and Tobago from the establishment of the Colonial Bank in 1837 up to the time when it was renamed the Republic Bank. Essentially, the theme is one of continuity and adaptability to the changing social, political and economic circumstances in the region. A second commemorative booklet on the bank's history in the Caribbean was eventually published in 1991 with the title *Barclays Bank in the Caribbean*.[15]

In some respects, Deryck Brown's *History of Money and Banking in Trinidad and Tobago from 1789 to 1989* can be perceived as a response to *From Colonial to Republic*. To date it is the only major work concerned with the general topic of banking and currency development in the region. It begins in the pre-banking era, at the commencement of British colonization of Trinidad and Tobago, and traces the establishment and evolution of banking and currency development in the context of the social and political changes which occurred in that territory throughout this period. The focus is not solely on the commercial banks; reference is made to other types of banking institutions, such as the penny and cooperative savings banks, as well as to the popular financial institutions which catered to the masses. It ends with a discussion on the development of indigenous commercial banking, the localization of the foreign banks and developments in the capital market. The overall theme is the benefits which political independence has brought to banking and currency policy development in Trinidad and Tobago. It is more a popular than an academic history, probably because it was commissioned by the Central Bank of Trinidad and Tobago.[16]

This book, then, is the first detailed business history of a bank's operations in the West Indies. It is preceded by a "new wave" of scholarly banking histories in the 1980s and 1990s from which it has benefited tremendously. Notable among them is Geoffrey Jones's *British Multinational Banking, 1830–1990,* which examines British multinational banking in a global context, focusing on the banks' origins, strategies and performance. Jones's work has inspired many of the ideas and themes explored in this book.

A detailed examination of the performance and strategies of Barclays Bank (DCO) in the West Indies should provide a better understanding of the operations of what was one of the world's largest multinational banks, and should help to dispel some of the misconceptions about the role and operations of these institutions, particularly in a colonial environment. A few publications concerned with development, which have been critical of the role of foreign banks in the region, have not had the benefit of the banks' archival material. Most critical is the analysis offered by Maurice Odle in *Multinational Banks and Underdevelopment,* whose view is that the early multinational banks contributed to the underdevelopment of the region. According to Odle, they did so by preventing the development of local indigenous banking through collusion. In so doing, they stifled competition, which resulted in high prices to consumers for bank products and services. Odle also charges that the banks' discriminatory practices against indigenous borrowers and their bias against small-scale domestic agriculture and industry helped to sustain the region's economic dependency on the more advanced economies of the world.[17] To some extent, both Norman Girvan in *Foreign Capital and Economic Underdevelopment in Jamaica* and Owen Jefferson in *The Post-War Economic Development of Jamaica* concur with Odle's conclusion. However, Girvan and Jefferson state that the foreign banks played an important intermediary role in the post-war growth of the Jamaican economy, noting the strategic importance of their operations in determining the extent to which long-term capital inflows were channelled through industrial sectors, particularly mining and manufacturing, which in turn sparked secondary expansion and led to further economic development. At the same time, these authors note that substantial resources were channelled into consumption-oriented sectors with a high import content, and in this way the commercial banks contributed to patterns of expenditure and foreign exchange usage which were contrary to the requirements of the developmental process.[18]

Such criticisms are really based on the theoretical notion that commercial banks have the ability to promote or at least facilitate economic development. What is often overlooked by these critics is the importance of space and time and the fact that banking institutions, like everything else, have a history. The time and space in which these institutions existed to a large extent determined the nature of their operations, which evolve over time.[19] A history of Barclays Bank (DCO) in the West Indies based upon a detailed examination of its business records should result in a better understanding of the history of commercial banking activity in the region between 1926 and 1962.

Chapter One

Banking in the West Indies, 1836–1925
An Overview

Barclays Bank (DCO) was one of the world's oldest multinational banks. Its history in the West Indies is linked with that of the Colonial Bank, which was formed in London in 1836 and established branches throughout the West Indies in 1837. The establishment of the Colonial Bank was part of a worldwide phenomenon of British multinational enterprise in the nineteenth century. A multinational enterprise is defined as a firm which controls income-generating assets in at least two countries, with the acquisition and control of such assets involving foreign direct investment (hereafter FDI) by the firm.[1]

The term *multinational enterprise* was coined around 1960, when it was generally believed that the phenomenon was a post–World War II one, associated with the significant expansion in American FDI in manufacturing. While there was a great deal of international capital movement in the nineteenth century, until the 1970s scholars were of the view that this was primarily in the form of portfolio investment – that is, not involving managerial control and therefore not FDI. Since then, with the application of modern definitions of FDI, with their emphasis on management and control, it has been concluded that at least one-third of world investment in 1914 was indeed FDI.[2]

Western Europe accounted for 80 per cent of total world FDI in 1914, with British FDI accounting for 45 per cent. Much of British FDI was in the form of companies that were "free-standing"; that is, none of their equity was in the hands of domestic organizations, nor did they undertake production in their home country before investing abroad, being created specifically to conduct business overseas. Their organizational structure was simple: a head office, usually located in London, which controlled subsidiary operations overseas. This contrasted with the classic American model, wherein the multinational enterprise grew out of the domestic operations of the existing firm.[3]

No general estimates exist for the overall size of world FDI before 1914, but it is evident that multinational activity in the nineteenth century was dominated by FDI in natural resources such as copper, bauxite and foodstuffs, and in service-sector industries such as energy utilities, trading companies and banking. Multinational banking is therefore one of the oldest forms of multinational enterprise.[4]

A multinational bank can be defined as a bank which owns and controls branches, or affiliates, in more than one country, in contrast to banks that do not own and control branches or affiliates in more than one country but which engage in international banking transactions on behalf of customers. International banking has a long history, dating back to the Middle Ages when Italian banking houses such as the Bardi, the Peruzzi and the Medici provided trade financing and other loans beyond their borders. German and Dutch bankers became prominent in these activities in the sixteenth century. It is true that, in some instances, overseas branches were established, especially by Italian bankers. However, for the most part these bankers conducted their overseas business through partnerships and representational offices run by relatives.[5]

It was in the nineteenth century that multinational banking on a large scale emerged, with the establishment of the British overseas banks, as they were called then. These banks were all British-registered banks with a London head office and a branch network established overseas. Many were established in British colonies: in Australia, the West Indies, Canada, Asia and Africa. Branches were also established in British protectorates in the Mediterranean and in Latin America. By 1890 there were thirty-two banks with 710 branches and wholly owned agencies spread all over the world, reaching 1,286 by 1914.[6] These banks did not conduct domestic banking business in Britain, nor did they have equity links with British domestic banks. They were formed exclusively to undertake banking overseas, though their ownership and control were firmly based in Britain. They were therefore representative of that distinct form of British FDI, the free-standing firm of the nineteenth century.[7]

This nineteenth-century "first wave" in multinational banking can be explained in terms of the theoretical constructs which were developed in the 1970s to explain the "second wave" in multinational banking of the 1960s, which was dominated by American banks. The first theory was put forward by Herbert Grubel, who argued that a bank became multinational if it perceived that there were advantages in doing so. Others have refined this concept to include location-specific advantages and firm-specific-ownership advantages.[8]

Location-specific advantages can refer to the advantages of preserving an established customer's account by following that client abroad. It also refers to the business opportunities which a bank perceives it will derive from entering a particular market. Although the banks were not developed strictly to follow clients abroad – since many of these early banks were formed by merchants involved in overseas trade and business themselves – British dominance in world trade and investment during the nineteenth century meant that there was a substantial demand for the British overseas banks.[9] Britain's Industrial Revolution from the late eighteenth century provided the basis for its pre-eminence in the world economy in the nineteenth century. As a result of extensive growth in the textile, coal, iron and steel, engineering and shipbuilding industries, Britain by the mid-nineteenth century dominated total world exports in manufactured goods. From the 1850s, British capital exports increased to make Britain the largest foreign investor in the world. As industrialization spread and overseas trade expanded, London became the centre of the commercial world and as a result became more involved in the financing of foreign trade. The private and merchant banks were prominent in this development.[10] By the second half of the nineteenth century, this banking structure was considerably broadened with the emergence and growth of the British overseas banks, and by the turn of the century London was financing the bulk of the world's trade, shipping manufactured goods to the British overseas territories and other developing territories and shipping raw materials and foodstuffs to Britain in return.[11]

Britain's pre-eminence in the world economy conferred upon British institutions and organizations, including the British overseas banks, firm-specific-ownership advantages in terms of cost. London's position as the leading capital market for the raising of loans and stocks for the domestic market and for overseas investments helps to explain the establishment of these British overseas banks.[12] The emergence of the City of London as the centre of the world's financial and international payments system and of international trade also meant that the pound sterling became the common currency. Indeed, sterling was being used to finance two-thirds of the world's trade by the end of the nineteenth century.[13] The British overseas banks, with their capital base in sterling and with London as the centre of international finance, had immense cost advantages over other banks in terms of financing trade.[14]

In addition to the ability to establish branch networks overseas and internalize their transactions at minimum cost, firm-specific-ownership advantages included managerial competence and technological and marketing know-how. By the early nineteenth century Britain had a well-developed and well-established domestic banking system which afforded the overseas banks the blueprint for their management and organizational structures. The governance structures that were borrowed from the Scottish and Irish banking systems proved effective in the control of branch networks over large distances, and were ideal for the kind of trade-related business they were engaged in. This involved a London-based board of directors which made executive decisions on corporate strategy matters, including decisions on loans, staff recruitment and branches, and an overseas branch network headed by managers who were accountable to their boards. Governance was aided by a staff recruitment policy and socialization strategy which led to the creation of a specific corporate culture, which proved effective for monitoring and controlling the performance and behaviour of branch managers and staff located far from the metropolis in an era when transport and communications were still poor.[15]

Receptivity is another useful theoretical concept for explaining the emergence of multinational banking. Receptivity refers to the host country's regulatory environment – that is, the laws and regulations which may or may not encourage a bank entering a particular country or region. Britain's political influence throughout the world meant that in many countries and regions, particularly in the British empire, barriers to entry in international banking were low for British institutions, making receptivity very high.[16]

The Establishment of the Colonial Bank in the West Indies

As the Colonial Bank was one of the several British overseas banks established in this period, these theoretical concepts help explain its establishment in the West Indies in 1837. The follow-the-client theory, which maintains that a bank establishes branches overseas in order to maintain an established client account, is not strictly applicable to the Colonial Bank. Like many of its counterparts, the Colonial Bank was founded by a combination of British merchants and banking interests in London.[17] Indeed, the names of the first directors of the Colonial Bank included many who were closely identified with the West Indian–metropolitan trade. The first chairman of the bank was John Irving, who was to become the first chairman of the Royal Mail Steam Packet Company, which for many years was closely associated with West Indian shipping.[18] David Barclay, John Gurney Hoare, Abraham George Robarts and Samuel Gurney were all well-known banking figures who were among the Colonial's first directors. Others included J.A. Hankey, Charles McGarel and James Cavan, all active members of the West India Committee who had commercial interests in the West Indies.[19] A.S.J. Baster commented that the Colonial Bank could be considered "the child of the Committee of West India merchants".[20]

The perception that there were profits to be made best explains the decision to establish the Colonial Bank in the West Indies in 1837. Certainly, the full abolition of slavery in 1838 led to expansion in the West Indian economy and hence growth in demand for institutions to facilitate financial transactions.[21] With full emancipation, it was envisaged that planters would require much larger advances for working capital than could be obtained from British merchant firms. In fact, the founders of the Colonial Bank had noted that "demands for finance were becoming more and more extensive, and it [was becoming] necessary to find a financial organization which could provide wider local facilities than the merchants were organized to give".[22] In addition to having insufficient capital to meet planters' demands, British merchant firms not previously associated with the West Indies were reluctant to invest there, being drawn to the more lucrative East.[23] Also, it would also have been evident that business opportunities for a bank existed in the West Indies in the 1830s, given the thriving money-lending activities among local West Indian merchants. This was very much in evidence in Jamaica, where local merchants were becoming increasingly important as providers of capital to the sugar industry.[24] Indeed, Jamaica merchants appeared to have been able to establish a stranglehold on the market in bills of exchange.[25]

Other profitable opportunities lay with the expected expansion of the commercial sector and the required monetization of the economy once emancipation came into full effect. As former slaves would be earning money wages, there was expected to be a greater demand for consumer goods, which in turn would stimulate an expansion of the commercial and retail sectors in the region. In an assessment of the post-emancipation period of the Leeward Islands of Antigua, Barbuda, Montserrat, Nevis and St Kitts, Douglas Hall points to the immediate consequence of slaves becoming wage-earners and the purchasers of their own food and clothing; "that of an increase in the volume of imports of consumer goods, and a proliferation of small retailing establishments". Hall further notes that "the barrels of salted or pickled fish and beef, the barrels of meal, the bolts of osnaburgh and cheap cottons, and the hoes and machetes which had been previously solely consigned to estates, now passed to working class consumers through wholesale and retail dealers".[26]

The expanded commercial and retail sectors included not only the merchants in the large town areas who had seized the opportunity to expand their businesses, but also small dealers and itinerant traders who sought to capitalize on the increased demand.[27] Similar developments were witnessed in other West Indian islands, which led to an increase in imports to the colonies. For example, the value of imports to British Guiana between 1834 and 1839 increased by 88.8 per cent, from £637,186 to £1,203,192. Over the same period, imports of what can be defined as consumer items rose by 70.1 per cent.[28] Imports to Barbados in 1832 were valued at £48,610, with inward shipping tonnage of 79,005. By 1851 the value had risen to £787,977, with inward shipping tonnage of 96,381.[29] For Trinidad, the value of imports had increased from £307,075 in 1833 to £547,471 in 1851, representing an increase of 87 per cent. Inward shipping tonnage had risen by 66 per cent, from 37,403 tons, to 62,178 tons for the same period. For Jamaica, the value of imports had risen by 47 per cent from £765,400 in 1833 to £1,129,776 in 1851, with inward shipping tonnage increasing by 56 per cent for the same period, from 67,971 tons to 105,968 tons. Overall for the West Indies, the total value of imports increased by 47 per cent, from £3,205,523 to £4,737,295, between 1833 and 1851. Inward shipping tonnage for the same period increased by 37 per cent, from 473,091 tons to 651,698 tons.[30]

In addition to the expected expansion of the commercial sector, it was envisaged that with full emancipation public administration would expand, creating the need for banking institutions to facilitate financial transactions. Under slavery, most of the functions of social control had been in the hands of the slave proprietors. The state apparatus was simple and inexpensive because, in many ways, each plantation was a mini-state. The abolition of slavery changed all that, and as the direction of slaves was supplanted by the government of masters and servants, the judiciary and police force, of necessity, expanded. Education and hospital services, albeit on a rudimentary level, were introduced.[31]

The £20 million in compensation which was paid to slave owners for the loss of their slaves as a consequence of abolition is a much-repeated motivating factor for the establishment of banks in the West Indies in the 1830s. The basic argument is that the sums paid to estate and plantation owners resulted in a flow of money into the colonies which made a financial institution necessary.[32] But this could hardly have been a very important factor in the minds of the promoters of the bank in 1836, as by then it would have been clear that most of the slave compensation was being used to reduce previous indebtedness to British creditors, and that very little was entering the West Indies.[33] Kathleen Mary Butler has shown that the largest commercial collector of Jamaican compensation money, the London-based firm Mitchell and Co., collected a total of £93,900 from twenty-seven major Jamaica properties and a variety of small pens and coffee plantations. The Manchester house of W.G. and S. Hibbert and Co. received more than £59,500 from their Jamaica clients.

In all, £594,339 in compensation money was paid to twenty-four British merchants involved in trade with Jamaica.[34]

It would seem to have been more likely that the bank's promoters saw the compensation package as contributing to an improvement of the planters' creditworthiness, as outstanding debts were either paid off or reduced. This, in addition to the recovery in sugar prices on the London sugar market in the 1830s, would have signalled to the promoters that there was potential for profitable banking opportunities in the region.[35] Between the periods 1821–30 and 1836–45, the annual average price for West Indian sugar increased from 31s 10d to 37s 5d, largely as a result of decreased production following emancipation. As West Indian sugar supplies no longer exceeded British demand, less British colonial sugar entered the world market, so the world price had less of an influence on the price of West Indian sugar.[36]

In addition to the potential business opportunities that were to arise as a consequence of full emancipation, it is likely that the founders of the Colonial Bank saw the West Indies as a logical place to establish a bank, given the favourable British public policy. In the nineteenth century there were few prudential regulations and no exchange controls. Britain had a very liberal regulatory regime and was slow to develop formal controls over banks, a policy which was extended to its West Indian colonies.[37]

This is not to suggest that there were no objections to the establishment of the Colonial Bank in the West Indies. When news came of the bank's intention to establish branches throughout the region, it caused a great deal of consternation among local merchants. They strenuously opposed its establishment, framing their objections in quasi-nationalist language. For example, merchants in Barbados stated that the bank was "foreign" in origin and that it would use its note-issuing powers to displace the metallic currency in circulation whenever it found it profitable to do so.[38] A similar argument was raised by the promoters of the Bank of British Guiana, which had opened in early 1836. In a petition to the British government, they stated that the Colonial Bank would not operate in the interests of the colony and would drain it of capital, because the majority of the shareholders resided outside of the colony and could not identify with its interests. To emphasize this point, they pointed out that the directors having only allotted in the first instance £3,000 which had since been reduced to £2,000 shares out of £20,000 to the inhabitants of the West Indian islands generally . . . , and further that even the small portion of interest which the West Indian colonists may have in the possession of £2,000 shares can in no way be exercised to have any influence or control over the governing body which resides in London, 4,000 miles from the scene of its operations.[39]

The real issue was fear of loss of business to the larger and more organized British institution. The Bank of British Guiana's capital was a mere £300,000 sterling, compared with the Colonial Bank's £2 million, and – given the limited banking market in the colonies – merchants and promoters of local banks must have been afraid that their position would be usurped by the more powerful British institution.[40] Indeed, the secretary of the Colonial Bank, C.A. Calvert, acknowledged that his bank would more than likely impinge upon the business of established interests in the colonies.[41] It was perhaps this fear of intrusion that led some local indigenous commercial banks to wage a competitive battle against the Colonial Bank, which resulted in injudicious actions and contributed to their early demise.

Indigenous Commercial Banks in the West Indies: Their Emergence and Decline

In 1836 the Bank of Jamaica and the Bank of British Guiana were established in Jamaica and British Guiana, respectively.[42] They were followed by the Planters Bank in Jamaica in 1839 and the West India Bank in Barbados in 1840; branches of the West India Bank were opened in Trinidad and Tobago, St Kitts and Antigua.[43] These banks were short-lived: by 1848 both the West India Bank and the Planters Bank were liquidated. The other two banks lasted longer; the Bank of Jamaica's assets were taken over by the Colonial Bank in 1865, and the Bank of British Guiana's were absorbed by the Royal Bank of Canada (hereafter the RBC) in 1914.[44]

The precipitating factor which led to the demise of the Planters Bank and the West India Bank was the crisis that befell the West Indian sugar industry following the passage of the Sugar Duties (Equalization) Act in 1846. The West Indian sugar industry had been built and sustained by an import duty structure which gave colonial sugars preference over foreign-grown sugars in the British market from as early as the seventeenth century. This preferential treatment was part of an organized system under which British colonial trade was conducted and which gave practical meaning to the concept of mercantilism.[45] The Sugar Duties (Equalization) Act of 1846, like the repeal of the Corn Laws, was symbolic of the triumph of free trade in Britain in the early nineteenth century.[46] The passage of the act announced the British government's intention to reduce preferential duties so that by 1854 a single rate would apply to sugar of a given quality regardless of its origin. The act further stated that eventually all sugar would be imported into Britain free of duty.[47]

The act clearly indicated a "decisive shift in the policy of the British government towards the colonies".[48] The immediate consequence of this announcement was a drastic fall in the price of sugar on the metropolitan market, from 33s per hundredweight in 1846 to 27s per hundredweight in 1847. Prices continued to fall for the rest of the decade, reaching 23s per hundredweight in 1850.[49] The fall in prices and the panic which ensued led to a loss of confidence in West Indian sugar estates by British merchant companies and mortgage holders, which manifested in a drastic reduction of credit. This situation was aggravated by a financial crisis in Britain between August 1847 and August 1848, during which forty-eight merchant houses that dealt almost exclusively in West Indian produce collapsed, so affected were they by the precipitous drop in sugar prices on the international market.[50]

These events dealt a severe blow to the commercial banking sector – particularly to the local institutions, which were undercapitalized, overextended and generally mismanaged and therefore in no position to withstand the crisis. In a rather risky effort to secure business at the expense of the Colonial Bank, the local institutions had engaged in banking practices considered imprudent given the prevailing economic conditions of the period. These included advancing funds against land, houses and other property, and offering higher interest rates than the Colonial Bank. For example, in 1844 the West India Bank in Trinidad attracted a large number of accounts by offering 2.5 per cent interest on current deposit accounts. It also offered competitive rates of discount and exchange.[51] While the Colonial Bank charged a commission of 2 per cent on foreign exchange transactions, the West India Bank "shaded these margins to gain more of the exchange" business. The local bank discounted bills at 6 per cent per annum in comparison to the Colonial Bank's 8 per cent. This strategy was so effective that the Colonial Bank's Trinidad branch manager, William Rennie, was upbraided by Calvert, who wrote, "You ought to be the best judge whether by charging eight per cent whilst the West India Bank charges only six per cent you do not send them all the best customers."[52]

These very liberal banking practices meant that the West India Bank was particularly vulnerable to the uncertainties associated with the financing of agricultural production and trade. With sugar prices plummeting on the international market and the usual credit arrangements from British merchant houses drying up, estate and property values rapidly depreciated, and many planters were unable to service their debts to the banks. Matters came to a head when the West India Bank's London agents refused to accept its drafts in November 1847. By December the bank was forced to suspend cash payments in Trinidad, Barbados and the other colonies where it had branches.[53]

The Planters' Bank in Jamaica collapsed in 1848. It is evident from the bank's contemporary records that managerial incompetence contributed immensely to its early demise. Of over £180,000 in outstanding loans, £120,000 was due from borrowers engaged in agriculture. Only £41,140 of that was secured by personal bond, with a considerable proportion guaranteed by only three individuals, which in effect meant little real guarantee.[54] Between 1841 and 1846, receivables had increased from £127,482 to £207,763, before falling to £193,211 in 1847. In December 1847, the Planters' Bank had notes in circulation to the extent of £43,777 and deposits amounting to only £32,648. While the bank's total liabilities amounted to £78,425 and assets to £193,231, the drop in the price of sugar made collection of its receivables difficult, exposing it to potential liquidity problems in the event of unusually high withdrawals. This is exactly what happened: the continuous fall in sugar prices and planters' cries of ruin resulted in a loss of confidence, leading to heavy demands for redemption of the bank's currency notes, which it was unable to fulfil. To make matters worse, one of its managers absconded with some of the bank's funds, contributing to further loss of confidence and heavy withdrawals. The bank was forced to suspend payments. Its eventual liquidation came after the Colonial Bank and the government refused to come to its aid. When given the details, officials in the Colonial Office commented severely on the "rotten edifice" of the bank.[55]

Apart from having an inadequate capital base and poor management, the local banks lacked the organizational structures necessary for successful commercial banking in the West Indies in the nineteenth century. Geoffrey Jones has indicated that

> matters of information and control were at the centre of the organizational structures and many of the organizational problems of the "overseas" banks of the nineteenth century. The profitable and prudent operation of a bank required accurate information about clients, commodities, likely movements in exchanges and credit conditions in the City of London.[56]

This was precisely what was lacking for the local commercial banks in the West Indies, and, as noted by Deryck Brown, a local board of directors and very poor channels of communication meant deficiencies in intelligence on political, economic and financial trends in the metropolis. The local banks did not have access to regular intelligence reports from abroad about the international markets for colonial produce and British colonial fiscal policy. In contrast, the Colonial Bank's directors, located in London, had almost immediate access to information pertinent to the future market conditions for colonial produce – information that guided its policy in the region. By keeping abreast of House of Commons debates on the sugar question, it correctly anticipated changes in British fiscal policy with regard to the importation of colonial produce. In a communication to its branches, the Court of the Colonial Bank had noted:

> You will observe by the newspapers that the government have determined for the present not to make any alteration in the Sugar Duties. We may therefore calculate that nothing of the kind will be done for a year . . . and that consequently it must be considered as still impending.[57]

Branch managers were therefore advised from as early as 1842 to curtail credit and to make advances only to planters who were in good financial standing. They were advised to collect all outstanding bills discounted and not to extend credit for longer than three months. When it received information that the London agents of the West India Bank were refusing to accept its drafts, the Colonial Bank's secretary instructed branch managers "to lose no time in presenting for payment any notes or cheques on the West India Bank you happen to hold, thus taking the chance of getting paid before they determine on closing their doors".[58]

Another factor was that there was no real distinction between the "agent" and the "principal" with regard to the management of the local banks' operations, a situation that contributed to their imprudence. Theoretically, branch managers acted as agents for their principals, the boards, whose role was to exercise close control over lending and protect the interests of the shareholders. As Jones has pointed out, there were frequently conflicts in this relationship, when branch managers were tempted to engage in risky and irregular banking practices which ran counter to the stated policies of the directors.[59] Such was not the case with the local banks in the West Indies: the directors encouraged and condoned risky practices in the interest of acquiring more business. It can also be argued that the directors of the local banks were "too caught up and part of local circumstances",[60] being themselves members of the planting and merchant community in small societies where everyone knew each other, to remain neutral and prudent in the exercise of their duties.

The Entry of the Canadian Banks and the Formation of Barclays Bank (DCO)

For much of the second half of the nineteenth century the Colonial Bank dominated the commercial banking sector in the West Indies. The Bank of Jamaica, which had survived the economic crisis that followed the passage of the Sugar Duties (Equalization) Act, 1846, was eventually sold to the Colonial Bank in 1865. The International Bank made a brief appearance in 1864, opening a branch in Port of Spain, Trinidad, called the London and Colonial Bank. By March 1866, however, its shareholders decided to wind up the business of the bank, following a major shareholder's legal problems and the decision of the Committee of the Stock Exchange to strike the British and American Exchange Bank off its list because of violations committed by two directors.[61]

Although profitability returned to the West Indian sugar sector by the early 1850s, in the late nineteenth century a crisis loomed which had serious implications for the survival of the Colonial Bank in the region. In the twenty-five years after 1850, sugar prices were generally stable, and the emergence of corporate ownership improved the industry's creditworthiness, portending increased profitability for the banks. By the late nineteenth century, though, the stability that had been achieved in the West Indian sugar industry was disrupted by competition from European bounty-fed beet sugar. Lower production costs, combined with a hidden export bounty and the absence of British tariffs, resulted in massive amounts of beet sugar being dumped on the British market in the 1880s. The consequence was a plunge in prices on the international market from 25s 6d per hundredweight in 1877 to 11s 3d in 1900.[62] Between 1900 and 1914 sugar prices remained low, averaging approximately 10s per hundredweight on the London market, and it was not until the outbreak of World War I, when production of European beet sugar was severely disrupted, that they rose again, from 11s 7d in 1914 to 38s 5d in 1919. They reached an all-time high of 58s per hundredweight in 1920.[63] After 1920, however, sugar prices again nose-dived, following the recovery in European beet production and in the supply of cane sugar from other sources, particularly Cuba.[64]

Naturally, with the sugar industry being afflicted by declining prices, the Colonial Bank's profitability was severely affected. Real profits declined by as much as 42 per cent, from £98,637 in 1891 to £57,669 in 1902. The bank also faced significant depreciation in the value of its assets. In 1890, the market value of its capital was £1,080,000; this fell to £375,000 in 1898. Between 1900 and 1909 the market value of its capital averaged £538,700, and this only because substantial sums from profits were transferred to write down the cash value of investments.[65] And while profits rebounded during World War I, with real profits averaging £101,201, the bank registered a 56 per cent post-war decline in net profits, from £147,703 in 1919 to £65,409 in 1925.[66]

The situation became even more dicey for the Colonial Bank with the arrival of the larger Canadian multinational banks, which immediately posed a serious threat to its position in the region. In 1889 the Bank of Nova Scotia (hereafter BNS) entered Jamaica. It was followed by the RBC, which established its presence throughout the region between 1910 and 1916, and the Canadian Bank of Commerce (hereafter CBC). These banks, particularly the BNS and the RBC, established themselves very quickly, becoming a force to be reckoned with as they snared from the British bank both lucrative business accounts and those of the colonial governments.[67]

The Canadian banks had been attracted to the region because of its increased trade with Canada and the United States. Faced with unprofitable markets in Britain and Europe, West Indian sugar producers had found alternative markets to the north. In 1899 Canada included the West Indies in its preferential tariff without demanding reciprocal concessions. This entitled sugar from the region to be imported at 25 per cent below the current tariff. In 1900 this preference was raised to 33.33 per cent. Most of the West Indian territories signed mutual-preference agreements with Canada in 1912, which resulted in a significant increase in exports to Canada, from 3 per cent in 1896 to an average of 23 per cent between 1911 and 1922. Almost 72 per cent of West Indian sugar was sent to Canada in 1910.[68] Trade with the United States was also boosted. In 1898 the United States imposed countervailing duties on bountied beet sugar to the full value of the bounty. As a result, beet sugar was shut out of that market, and by 1900 almost three-quarters of West Indian sugar was being sold to the United States. Indeed, 83 per cent of Jamaican sugar was sold there in 1890.[69]

It was in this context, and under the chairmanship of William Maxwell Aitken (Lord Beaverbrook), that the Colonial Bank Act was amended to facilitate geographic diversification, and operations were extended to West Africa in 1917.[70] Lord Beaverbrook, who served as chairman of the Colonial Bank between 1915 and 1917, also recognized the need to form equity links with another bank, given the need for increased capital and the competitive pressures the bank was facing. In December 1917 a close "working arrangement" was established with Barclays Bank Ltd. This involved Barclays serving as principal banker to the Colonial Bank, directing all overseas business relating to those areas in which the Colonial Bank maintained branches. In 1918 a joint directorship was established, and Barclays purchased £40,000 worth of shares in the Colonial Bank. A further link was made in the same year when Barclays Bank Ltd acquired a domestic English bank, the London Provincial and South Western Bank, which also held shares in the Colonial Bank.[71]

Simultaneously, the British government was urging domestic banks to integrate with the overseas banks to increase Britain's economic power and viability, particularly as competition from Germany was expected in the period after World War I. F.C. Goodenough, who had been appointed chairman of Barclays Bank Ltd in 1916 and who was a strong believer in the empire, had urged that his bank should forge "a close working arrangement" with another bank that had branches abroad. He noted the "coming struggle for the markets of the world" and argued that the banks had a key role to play in this struggle, as well as in discovering new outlets for British manufactured goods. He believed that the establishment of a multinational branch network would be more effective than using correspondent agents.[72] Barclays Bank Ltd was one of the "Big Five" English joint stock banks to emerge from the amalgamation movement which occurred in the British domestic banking industry towards the end of the nineteenth century. Its interest in multinational banking was part of a general trend among the British clearers, which had begun to appreciate the merits of greater integration between domestic and overseas banks.[73]

Goodenough's vision of creating a multinational "empire" bank fitted well with the strategic objectives of the Colonial Bank at the time, and it came closer to reality when, in 1920, Barclays Bank Ltd acquired the Anglo-Egyptian Bank. Finally, between November and December 1925, the Colonial, the Anglo-Egyptian and the National Bank of South Africa, in which Barclays Bank Ltd had also acquired a majority share, were formally amalgamated, resulting in the creation of Barclays Bank (DCO), with total assets amounting to £69 million. The consequence was the creation of an institution which had operations in Egypt, Palestine, the Sudan, East and West Africa, Southern Africa, the Mediterranean and the West Indies.[74] The stockholders in the three constituent banks were offered a majority of the A shares, with Barclays Bank Ltd taking a controlling interest through the B shares. National Bank of South Africa shareholders received £1.483 million of the A shares; the remainder went to Barclays for its Colonial Bank shares of £0.3 million, and to Barclays and outside shareholders for the Anglo-Egyptian shares of £0.9 million. Barclays achieved over 75 per cent voting control through an additional investment of £0.5 million in B shares. Preference shares were also issued to existing shareholders to raise new capital.[75]

Summary

The first wave of multinational banking was dominated by the British overseas banks, which appeared in the 1830s. They were part of a phenomenon of nineteenth-century British multinational enterprise whose organizational structures in most cases were free-standing. Their emergence and dominance in the nineteenth century and part of the twentieth can be related to Britain's importance in the world political economy, which conferred on them significant advantages. Indeed, the establishment of Barclays Bank (DCO)'s predecessor, the Colonial Bank, in the West Indies in 1837 is best understood within the theoretical framework of advantages, which, although devised in reference to multinational banking in the 1960s, is equally applicable to the first wave of multinational banking in the 1830s.

Local indigenous commercial banks were also established in this early period, but these either failed or were eventually absorbed by the Colonial Bank and the Royal Bank of Canada, which entered the region, along with other Canadian banks, in the late nineteenth and early twentieth centuries. The indigenous banks were poorly managed or lacked sufficient capital with which to undertake commercial banking, or both. They also suffered from an inadequate organizational structure without access to regular intelligence about the international sugar market, which was vital for assessing risk in the provision of trade financing for this commodity.

The free-standing organizational structure of the British multinational banks was somewhat modified in the late nineteenth and early twentieth centuries, with British domestic banks engaging in equity shareholding in many of these overseas institutions. Barclays Bank Ltd, which bought majority shares in the Colonial Bank and two other overseas banks, formed Barclays Bank (DCO) out of the amalgamation of the three constituent banks. This amalgamation, which resulted in the creation of the largest multinational bank in the world at that time, was prudent and timely, given the competition from Canadian banks that the Colonial Bank had already begun to experience, and the problems associated with the international economy that the newly reconstituted bank was to face in the fifteen years following its creation.

Chapter   *Two*

The Depression Years
Bank Performance, 1926–1939

Barclays Bank (DCO) began operations in the West Indies just before the world economy was battered by the Great Depression. During this time, primary producers worldwide were affected by a drastic decline in commodity prices. Sugar was among the most seriously affected commodities, and, although the bank's main business in the region was the provision of financing for the sugar trade, its profitability was not seriously jeopardized. In fact, by the mid-1930s Barclays Bank (DCO)'s branch operations in the region had begun to exhibit a recovery, despite the long-lasting depression in sugar prices and the fact that the bank's business there remained predominantly linked with the sugar sector. Why was the bank's branch network in the West Indies able not only to withstand the most severe depression of the century, but also to show a recovery in profit levels while the world was still in its grip?

It has been shown for various parts of Europe and for Britain and Canada that banking structure, macroeconomic policy and performance, and lender-of-last-resort behaviour contributed in varying degrees to maintenance of financial stability during the Depression.[1] Appropriate business strategy and sound management have been identified as contributing immensely to the ability of British multinational banks to survive the Depression. The domestic banks' financial support of the overseas banks, whether through investment or mergers, along with the exercise of efficient management and organizational control, were all-important aspects of the strategies adopted in this period. Specifically, the banks utilized the inner reserves built up over the years in their published profits to continue to pay dividends, thereby preserving public confidence. Additionally, British multinational banks adhered to conventional banking practices, which meant that they were relatively free from bad risks. While they restricted their loan portfolios in their host countries – and, in so doing, reduced the risk of accumulating bad debts – they increased their holdings of British government securities, which allowed them to maintain some degree of profitability.[2]

As important as these factors undoubtedly are to the survival and stability of banks in general, they do not completely explain what could influence a bank's performance in a particular market. Certainly, it can be argued that the stability of Barclays Bank (DCO) in the West Indies was to some extent a function of the imperial ties which existed between Britain and the region. This chapter examines the bank's ability to remain viable in spite of the Depression's impact on the West Indian sugar industry. The chapter begins with the importance of the West Indian Section to the bank's total operations. It then examines the impact of the Depression on the bank's branch network in the region before accounting for the factors which influenced the reversal of the decline in the branch network's operating profits.

The Impact of the Great Depression: Barclays Bank (DCO)'s Performance

An understanding of Barclays Bank (DCO)'s worldwide performance can be gleaned from its profit and loss accounts. These accounts cover all the territorial sections of the bank's operations and are ledger accounts to which balances reflecting revenues, income, profits, expenses and losses are periodically transferred. They are therefore essentially repositories to which profit and loss are charged, and so the profits recorded are regarded as operational profits and do not represent real profits. These accounts provide an indication of the overall performance of the bank and its territorial sections in terms of the banking business generated for each year.

During the period 1926–39 Barclays Bank (DCO)'s operations worldwide experienced some fluctuation in profit levels. Nevertheless, the overall trend was upward (see Table 2.1 and Figure 2.1). Indeed, the bank's real profit performance was considerably stronger than its published profits, as it accumulated large inner reserves. During the period under review the bank was not faced with any major crisis that it was not capable of dealing with, as shown by the fact that it was not necessary for Barclays Bank Ltd, its parent bank, to provide any financial assistance.[3]

To some extent, the favourable performance of Barclays Bank (DCO) during this period was largely a result of its South African operations, as a high proportion of the bank's operational profits was derived from that section. In addition, the Circus Place Section, which contributed significantly to the profit levels of the bank, was responsible for the London end of the South African operations (see Table 2.1).[4] It can, in fact, be argued that Barclays Bank (DCO) was essentially a South African operation, and that the primary reason for its excellent performance during the Depression was the continued buoyancy of the South African economy.[5]

Nevertheless, the impact of the Depression was evident. While the bank registered an overall increase in profits of 43 per cent between 1926 and 1929, it was followed by a decline of nearly the same magnitude between 1929 and 1933. This trend was then reversed: the bank registered a continuous increase in profits of 140 per cent between 1933 and 1937 before registering a 33 per cent decline between 1937 and 1939 (see Figure 2.1).[6]

The West Indian Section's Performance

It is difficult to assess the performance of the bank in the West Indies from its operating profits because its figures for 1926 to 1935 were combined with those for West Africa and the Manchester and Liverpool offices in the Colonial Bank Section. Nevertheless, it can be inferred that the figures for the section up to 1935 are a reasonable representation of the performance of the West Indies, especially considering that a fair amount of the business conducted in the Manchester and Liverpool offices was directly related to the West Indian trade. Indeed, these offices

Table 2.1 Barclays Bank (DCO), Profit and Loss Accounts Showing Operating Profits and Losses (£), 1926–1939

Section	1926	%	1927	%	1928	%
South Africa	246,233	51.41	303,723	64.33	216,808	41.42
Circus Place	59,726	12.37	63,430	13.44	59,618	11.39
Colonial Bank	65,049	13.47	76,770	16.26	68,015	12.99
East Africa	0	0.00	(3,467)	−0.73	2,369	0.45
Anglo-Egyptian	57,539	11.92	14,742	3.12	20,515	3.92
Head Office	44,949	9.31	(1,504)	−0.32	134,828	25.76
Other[a]	7,331	1.52	18,414	3.90	21,251	4.07
Total	480,827	100.00	472,108	100.00	523,404	100.00

Section	1929	%	1930	%	1931	%
South Africa	279,532	40.45	126,049	30.40	137,747	28.60
Circus Place	65,339	9.45	62,283	15.02	65,044	13.50
Colonial Bank	62,396	9.03	31,767	7.66	6,233	1.29
East Africa	6,254	0.90	4,134	1.00	(5,818)	−1.21
Anglo-Egyptian	47,706	6.90	11,368	2.74	7,933	1.65
Head Office	199,363	28.86	171,034	41.26	257,674	53.48
Other[b]	30,482	4.41	7,952	1.92	12,967	2.69
Total	691,072	100.00	414,587	100.00	481,780	100.00

Section	1932	%	1933	%	1934	%
South Africa	136,097	32.09	79,145	19.55	312,622	46.32
Circus Place	67,641	15.95	85,242	21.06	104,259	15.45
Colonial Bank	6,211	1.46	23,476	5.80	23,671	3.51
East Africa	(1,976)	−0.46	(730)	−0.19	1,798	0.27
Anglo-Egyptian	(6,923)	−1.63	7,050	1.74	17,726	2.63
Head Office	204,481	48.22	175,119	43.26	186,734	27.67
Other[c]	18,519	4.37	35,524	8.78	28,147	4.15
Total	424,050	100.00	404,826	100.00	674,957	100.00

Table 2.1 continues

Table 2.1 Barclays Bank (DCO), Profit and Loss Accounts Showing Operating Profits and Losses (£), 1926–1939 *(cont'd)*

Section	1935	%	Section	1936	%
South Africa	368,967	52.93	South Africa	386,303	48.15
Circus Place	107,536	15.43	Circus Place	115,119	14.35
Colonial Bank	39,420	5.66	West Indies	71,620	8.93
East Africa	(2,462)	–0.35	W & E Africa	(15,469)	–1.93
Anglo-Egyptian	(4,440)	–0.64	Anglo-Egyptian	5,453	0.68
Head Office	126,601	18.16	Head Office	167,020	20.82
Other[d]	61,410	8.81	Other	72,254	9.00
Total	**697,032**	**100.00**	**Total**	**802,300**	**100.00**

Section	1937	%	1938	%	1939	%
South Africa	484,277	49.94	389,032	58.67	383,421	58.98
Circus Place	121,176	12.50	114,818	17.32	72,028	11.08
West Indies	146,680	15.13	30,319	4.57	45,780	7.04
W & E Africa	10,991	1.13	1,448	0.21	6,131	0.94
Anglo-Egyptian	16,449	1.70	(13,311)	–2.01	5,320	0.82
Head Office	115,234	11.88	95,328	14.38	108,966	16.76
Other[e]	10,645	1.13	45,426	6.86	28,432	4.38
Total	**969,701**	**100.00**	**663,060**	**100.00**	**650,078**	**100.00**

[a] St Martin's, New York, King William, Hamburg.
[b] St Martin's, New York, King William, Hamburg.
[c] St Martin's, New York, Gracechurch, Hamburg.
[d] In 1935, St Martin's, New York, Gracechurch, Hamburg, Palestine. In 1936, St Martin's, Manchester, Liverpool, New York, Gracechurch, Hamburg, Palestine.
[e] Oceanic House, Manchester, Liverpool, New York, Gracechurch, Hamburg, Palestine.
Source: Accounts and Board Meeting Papers, 1926–39, BBA 38/251.

The Depression Years: Bank Performance, 1926–1939

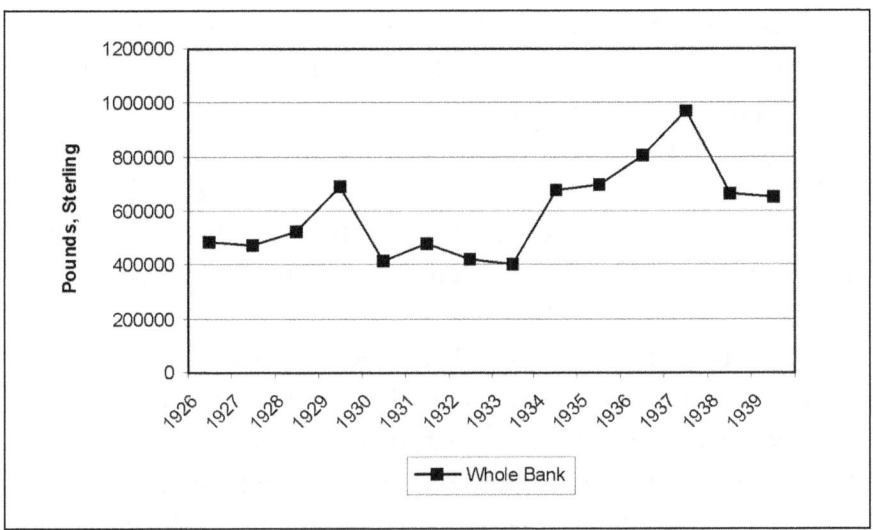

Figure 2.1 Barclays Bank (DCO), total operating profits, 1926–1939
Source: Accounts and Board Meeting Papers, 1926–39, BBA 38/251.

were specifically opened "with the object of getting closer in touch with the importers and exporters concerned with the overseas territories".[7] Also, the bank's operations in West Africa during this period were small compared with those in the West Indies, being restricted to the principal importing and exporting firms. In 1936, this section reported a loss of £14,420. In September 1937 the West African Section contributed £10,991, just 1.13 per cent of the bank's total profits. In 1938 and 1939, the section's share fell sharply, to £228 (0.03 per cent) and £1,657 (0.25 per cent), respectively. The Liverpool and Manchester offices also contributed insignificantly to the bank's profits as a whole during this period (see Table 2.1).[8]

Between 1926 and 1927 profits contributed by the Colonial Bank Section rose from £65,049 to £76,770, representing 16 per cent of the total profits of the bank in that year. After 1927, the section's profit level was in continuous decline until 1931, falling sharply to £6,233, or a mere 1.29 per cent of the bank's profits. Thereafter, this section's contribution to the bank's overall profit level increased substantially, reaching £39,420 in 1935. In 1936, when the West Indian figures were given separately from the West African, Manchester and Liverpool figures for the first time, the West Indian Section contributed £71,620, or 8.93 per cent of the bank's total profits, which was considerably better than the previously combined figures. In 1937 the West Indian Section contributed £146,680, or 15.13 per cent of the total profits of the bank. This figure seems anomalous, and it is difficult to explain the huge jump: although the figures for South Africa and the bank as a whole indicate substantial increases for that year, they were not of the same magnitude as that recorded for the West Indian Section. The recorded profit for the section in 1938 was £30,319, or 4.57 per cent of the total profits, and there was a slight increase in 1939, to £45,780, or 7.04 per cent of the profits (see Table 2.2 and Figure 2.2).

The performance of the West Indian Section as a proportion of the overall performance of the bank was relatively small and, at first glance, might be deemed insignificant. When viewed in relation to the performance of the bank's other sections during the same period, however, its importance is better appreciated. Certainly, during the three years following the reconstitution of the Colonial Bank as Barclays Bank (DCO) in 1925, the Colonial Bank Section contributed the second- and third-highest profits of the ten sections of the bank. This position fell to fourth

Table 2.2 West Indian Section, Operating Profits (£), 1926–1939

Year	West Indian Section	Percentage of Overall Profits
1926	65,049	13.47
1927	76,770	16.26
1928	68,015	12.99
1929	62,396	9.03
1930	31,767	7.66
1931	6,233	1.29
1932	6,211	1.46
1933	23,476	5.80
1934	23,671	3.51
1935	39,420	5.66
1936	71,620	8.93
1937	146,680	15.13
1938	30,319	4.57
1939	45,780	7.04

Source: Accounts and Board Meeting Papers, 1926–39, BBA 38/251.

The Depression Years: Bank Performance, 1926–1939

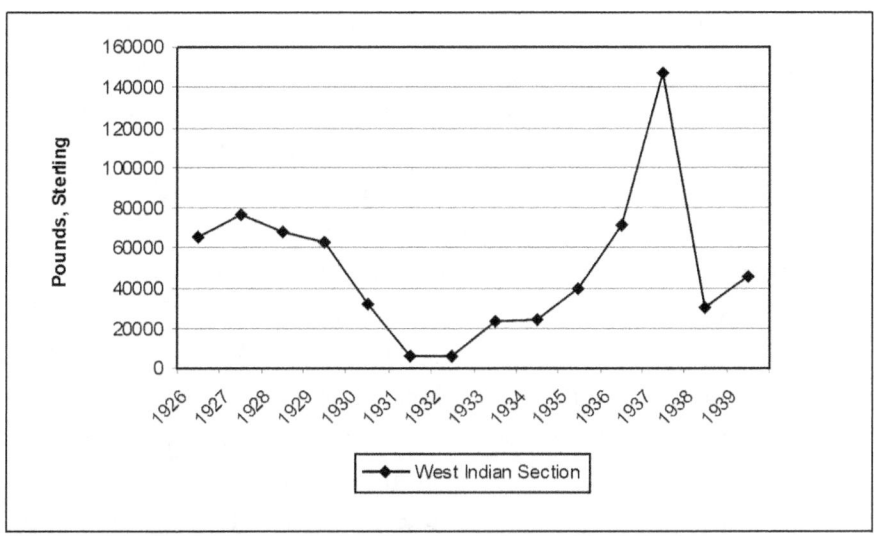

Figure 2.2 Barclays Bank (DCO, West Indian Section operating profits, 1926–1939
Source: Accounts and Board Meeting Papers, 1926–39, BBA 38/251.

and eventually to sixth in 1931, before reclaiming the fourth position in 1933. Following the separation of the figures for the West Indies from those of the other sections mentioned above, in 1936, the West Indies Section occupied fourth position after the South African, Head Office and Circus Place sections, out of a total of fourteen. The section held this position between 1936 and 1939, with the exception of 1937, when it rose to the number-two spot (see Table 2.1). Therefore, while its contribution in terms of profit levels to the bank as a whole was indeed relatively small, it was one of the more profitable sections of the bank. Notably, the West Indies Section was able to maintain its profit levels in relation to the growth in profits of the bank as a whole throughout the Depression and thus remained an important section of the bank.

The Depression and the West Indian Sugar Industry

The bank's performance in the West Indies between 1926 and 1939 was directly related to the Depression's effects on the region's export staples, since its main business there was providing trade financing for export crops. Practically all the principal West Indian crops suffered from falling prices during this period.[9] The impact on sugar was particularly severe because, despite significant diversification in agricultural production, sugar accounted for at least 55 per cent of the total average value of exports.[10]

The majority of the bank's business in the region during the inter-war period involved the provision of finance for the production and export of sugar.[11] In fact, the bank was virtually in control of the sugar trade: of a total of 350,000 tons of sugar produced in the region in 1930, clients of the bank were concerned with the production or manufacture of some 275,000 tons, or almost 80 per cent of total production.[12] Hence, the bank's profitability in the West Indies was to a large extent dependent upon sustained and increased production and export of sugar, which depended upon West Indian producers being able to recover their costs and make a reasonable return on their investment.

The fall in the price of sugar, therefore, was a particularly distressing development for the bank's operations in the West Indies.[13] Between 1926 and 1939 the price of sugar fell by over 40 per cent, from 12s 3d to 7s 4d per hundredweight. The sharpest drop occurred between 1926 and 1930, when the price fell by 50 per cent to 6s 7d per hundredweight (see Figure 2.3).[14] The slide continued thereafter, though more gradually, and it was not until 1934 that a degree of stability set in, before the price began rising again in 1936.

The fall in the price of sugar during the 1920s and early 1930s was primarily the result of overproduction and supply to the British market.

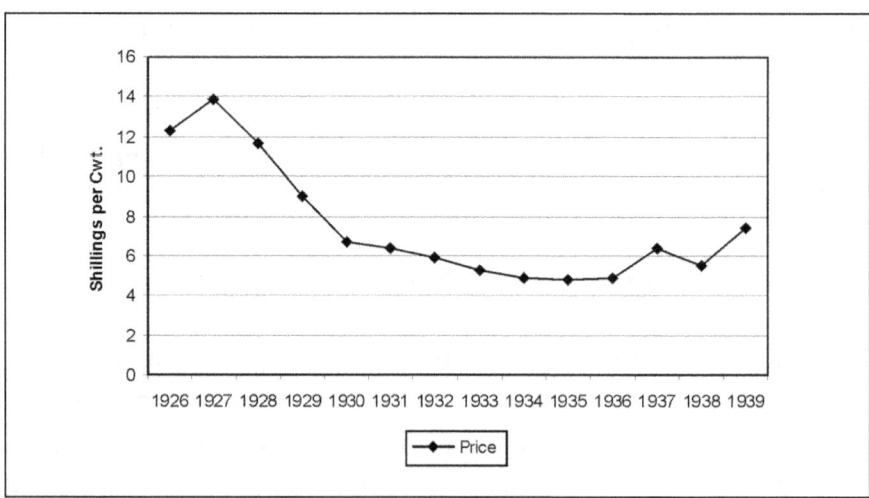

Figure 2.3 London sugar prices, shillings per hundredweight, 1926–1939
Source: Higman, *Abstract of Caribbean Historical Statistics*, table 19.

This was partially a result of the rapid return of beet sugar to the world market and of increased production made possible by technical improvements in the world cane-sugar industry. Primarily, however, it was a consequence of protectionist policies in some of the more substantial sugar-producing countries, which allowed producers to dump surplus sugar on the British market, the only remaining open market in the 1920s.[15] Owing to the treaties which linked sugar-producing countries such as Puerto Rico, Hawaii and the Philippines to the United States by a complete remission of duties, and because Cuban sugar was admitted to that market on preferential terms, a high price was guaranteed for the portion sold for internal consumption, enabling those producers to accept a lower price for the portion dumped on the British market.[16] As a result there was a substantial amount of sugar on the open market, particularly from Cuba and Java, where production had increased by over 50 per cent in the 1920s; by the period 1923–29 the accumulated surplus amounted to 3.5 million tons, with a surplus of 1.2 million tons in 1930 alone.[17] As the Jamaica Imperial Association noted in 1930, "though the West Indies [enjoyed] a preference in Britain, they were [doing so] in a dumped and demoralized market".[18]

Certainly, in 1929 and 1930 the situation became critical for West Indian sugar producers. Following the Wall Street crash in 1929, the price of sugar fell below a remunerative level for West Indian producers in 1930. The prevailing preference accorded to empire sugar in the British market was 3s 9d per hundredweight, which meant that the most efficient West Indian producers experienced losses of up to 2s per hundredweight at a price of 6s 7d per hundredweight, since the average cost of production was 12s $4^{1/2}$d per hundredweight free on board. Canada gave empire producers a preference of approximately 4s 8d per hundredweight. Although this preference was considerably higher than the British one, the open-market price for sugar in the Canadian market was so controlled that when the preference was added to it, the final price was only slightly higher than the British preferential price.[19] Therefore, even the largest and best-equipped producers in the region were finding it difficult to produce sugar profitably at the prevailing price. For example, the British Guiana Sugar Producers Association, composed of the largest British firms engaged in sugar production in the colony, indicated that if assistance was not forthcoming a number of their properties would eventually cease production and that there would be a suspension of further capital expenditure in the industry.[20] In St Lucia the two principal factories suffered serious deficits in 1929.[21]

In Jamaica, sugar producers kept their production costs below the average West Indian cost of production only by means of subsidies from the sale of by-products, particularly rum. The cost of production in Jamaica in 1928, including the cost of delivery on board ship but excluding any depreciation and interest on capital, was approximately £11 17s 6d per ton. This cost was determined by deducting from the expenses incurred in manufacturing one ton of sugar the amounts realized from the sale of the resultant by-products. On that basis, the cost was lower not only than the corresponding average throughout the West Indies but also than the cost of production for most other sugar-producing countries.[22]

Nevertheless, it was recognized that this advantage was likely to be temporary, as the loss sustained on sugar after taking into consideration the revenue from rum was approximately £1 7s 6d per ton (and the cost of production did not include provision for depreciation). Additionally, the market for rum was limited, and any further decrease in the price of sugar could not have been offset by increased revenue from rum sales. Although Jamaica's high-flavoured rum had found a ready and profitable market in Germany, where it was used to flavour potato spirits, this market collapsed in the financial crisis of 1931, and it would have been only a matter of time before Jamaica producers found themselves unable to cover their production costs.[23]

Impact on Branch Profits

Certainly, the dire market conditions of the late 1920s and early 1930s which were affecting the West Indian sugar industry had begun to make their mark on Barclays Bank (DCO)'s operations in the region. Gross operating profits of the bank's West Indian branches fell by 51 per cent between 1926 and 1932, from £134,278 to £65,280. While there was a small increase in net profits – some 13 per cent – between 1926 and 1928, it was followed by a 65 per cent decline between 1928 and 1932, in spite of a 46 per cent reduction in operational charges over the same period (see Figure 2.4).[24]

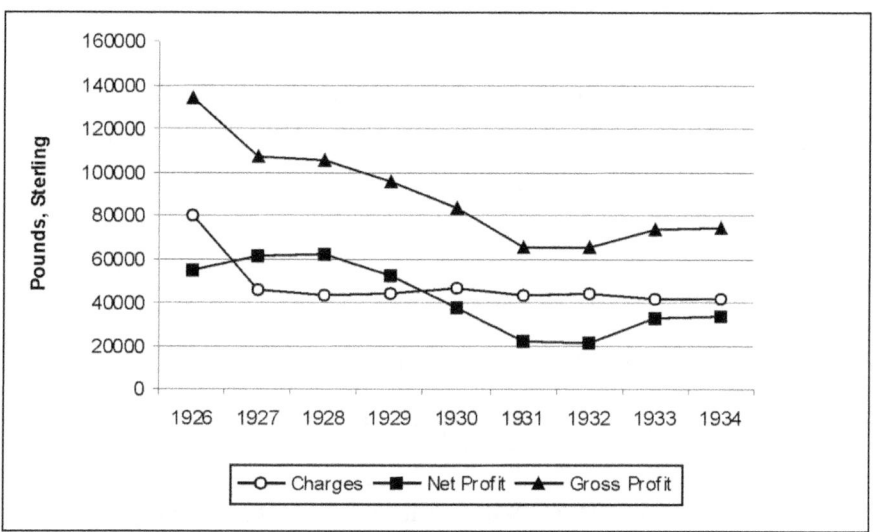

Figure 2.4 Barclay's Bank (DCO), West Indian branch accounts, 1926–1934
Source: West Indian Branches, 1926–34, BBA 38/202.

The foundation of this decline in profit levels was a general contraction in the level of business conducted by the bank's West Indian branch network. The most important source of profits was in exchange earnings, and this category of profits fell by 83 per cent between 1926 and 1934, with the sharpest drop, by 85 per cent, occurring between 1926 and 1931 (see Figure 2.5). Overdrafts and loans increased by 33 per cent

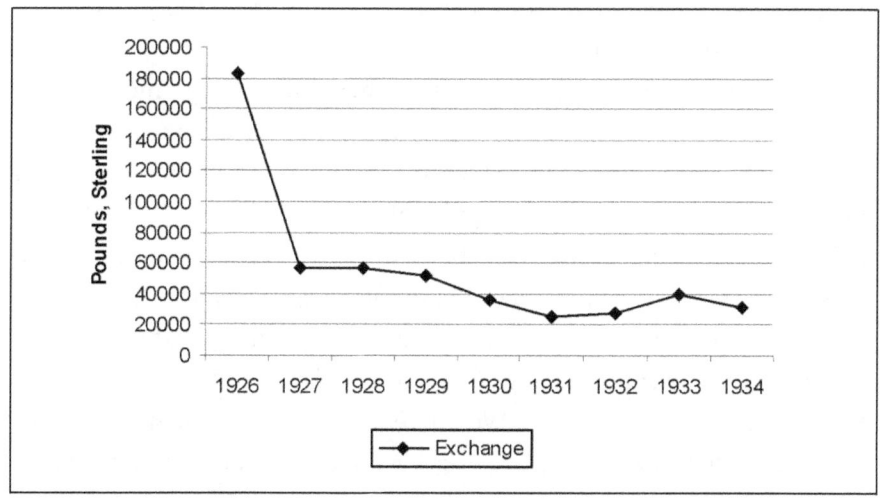

Figure 2.5 Barclay's Bank (DCO), West Indian branch accounts: exchange, 1926–1934
Source: West Indian Branches, 1926–34, BBA 38/202.

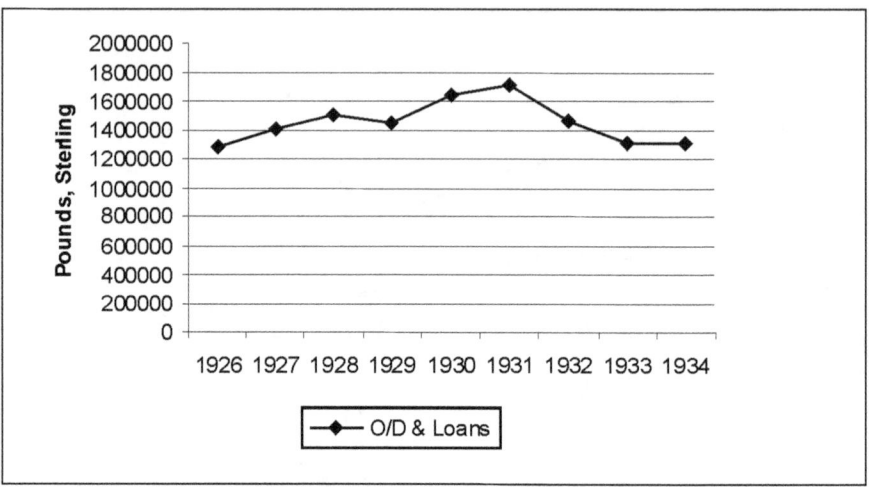

Figure 2.6 Barclays Bank (DCO), West Indian branch accounts: overdrafts and loans, 1926–1934
Source: West Indian Branches, 1926–34, BBA 38/202.

between 1926 and 1931, with a noticeable increase of 18 per cent between 1929 and 1931 followed by a reduction (see Figure 2.6). This was probably an indication that customers were finding it increasingly difficult to repay their loans when they became due, though the proportions that represented overdue loans and new loans is not known. It was reported that producers in Antigua were finding it impossible to repay loans due in 1930 owing to low prices and poor crops. As result there was a large carry-over of loans that should have been repaid from the proceeds of the previous year's crop.[25]

In commenting on the position of the bank in the West Indies at the time, the chairman, F.C. Goodenough, noted that the bank risked "if not a loss, at least a 'frozen loan' which represents the difference between production costs and the selling price of sugar".[26] Facing the likelihood of prices falling even further, the bank began to curtail its lending, and between 1931 and 1934 the level of overdrafts and loans was reduced by 23 per cent as a number of estates were refused further advances (see Figure 2.6).[27] The same strategy was adopted by the other banks in the region. Fred Clarke, owner of Worthy Park sugar estate in St Catherine, Jamaica, noted in his diary that, after having been a faithful customer of the Canadian Bank of Commerce for the preceding eight years, in July 1929 he was refused any further advances. Clarke was therefore forced to

The Depression Years: Bank Performance, 1926–1939

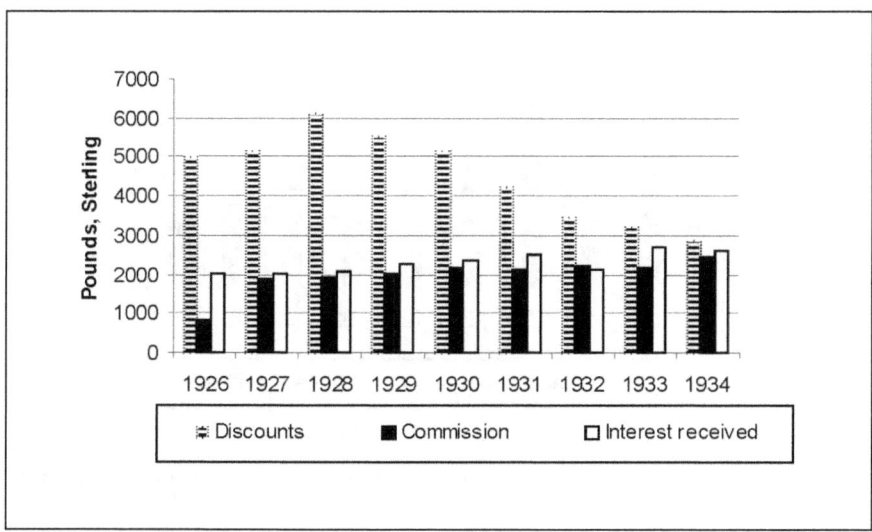

Figure 2.7 Barclays Bank (DCO), West Indian branch accounts: discounts, commission, interest received, 1926–1934
Source: West Indian Branches, 1926–34, BBA 38/202.

turn to the large mercantile establishment, Lascelles, DeMercado and Co. Ltd, which provided a crop loan of £5,000 at 6 per cent. In return, the firm was guaranteed permission to handle the Worthy Park crop for a commission of 2.5 per cent on foreign sales and 5 per cent on island sales, resulting in a further cost of £400 and £500 to Clarke. In 1930, the loan was renewed with the firm, but, as market conditions had worsened, the conditions included a second mortgage against the estate and all its stock as well as absolute control of all sales of sugar and rum.[28]

The cutbacks in loans and advances by Barclays Bank (DCO) meant that there was no appreciable rise in the level of interest received (see Figure 2.7). The overall contraction of credit also explains the general fall in the level of bills discounted over the period. After a slight increase, by 14 per cent, between 1926 and 1928, there followed a general contraction by 59 per cent between 1928 and 1934 (see Figure 2.8). Correspondingly, discount earnings fell by 52 per cent in the same period (see Figure 2.7). Also, a general decline by 12 per cent was exhibited in bills receivable between 1926 and 1929 (see Figure 2.8). The low level of bills discounted and received explains the general failure of commission earnings to increase appreciably during this period (see Figure 2.7).

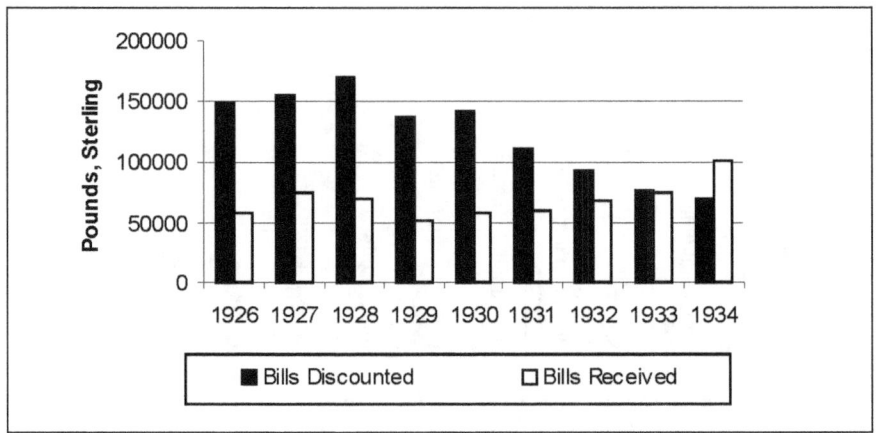

Figure 2.8 Barclays Bank (DCO), West Indian branch accounts: bills discounted and bills received, 1926–1934
Source: West Indian Branches, 1926–34, BBA 38/202.

Also indicative of the policy of curtailment in credit was the general decline in the level of banknotes in circulation after 1929. The level of circulation of the bank's notes for the period 1926–29 had increased by 18 per cent before dropping by 12 per cent between 1929 and 1930 (see Figure 2.9) – testimony to the general decline in the commercial sector owing to severe cutbacks in employment and wages. In British Guiana, for instance, total expenditure on labour was reduced by approximately 20 per cent between 1927 and 1930. The uncertainty regarding the sugar

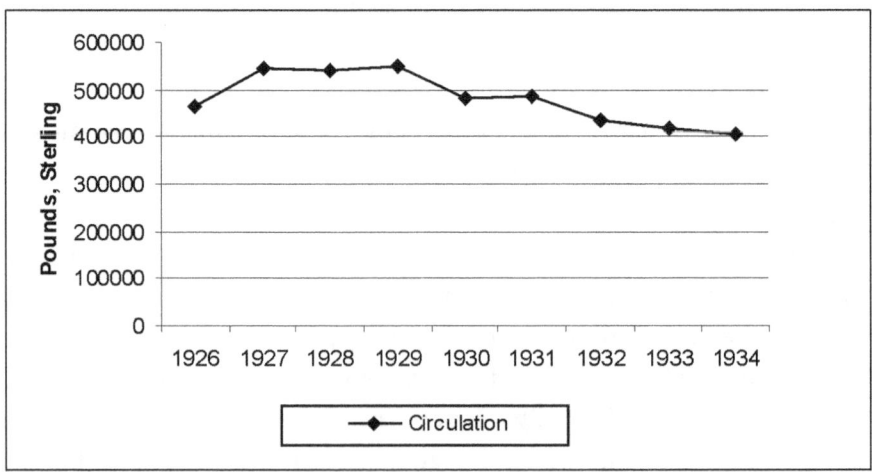

Figure 2.9 Barclays Bank (DCO), West Indian branch accounts: banknote circulation, 1926–1934
Source: West Indian Branches, 1926–34, BBA 38/202.

industry led to a reduction in the circulation of money, which brought on a general depression in trade and commercial business.[29]

Despite the severity of the situation facing the West Indian sugar industry, after 1931 the bank's branches in the region recorded some degree of recovery: net profits between 1932 and 1934 increased by £11,883, or 56 per cent (see Figure 2.4). After 1931 exchange earnings began to increase. By 1933 this category of income had also increased by 56 per cent, though it fell to £31,156 or by 23 per cent in the following year (see Figure 2.5). Though the level of bills discounted continued to fall, which explains the continuous fall in discounts earned in this period (see Figure 2.7), a substantial increase by 87 per cent in the level of bills receivable negotiated occurred between 1930 and 1934 (see Figure 2.8). The level of overdrafts and loans declined by 23 per cent between 1931 and 1934, from £1,715,667 to £1,315,951, which more than likely reflected a reduction in outstanding loans that had accumulated in the years leading up to 1931 (see Figure 2.6).

The recovery in profits occurred in spite of the continued drop in the price of sugar after 1930; and even though there was some recovery in the price between 1936 and 1939, it was still far below the highest level for the period 1926–39.

Government Guarantees and Imperial Preferences

The basis of the recovery in the profit levels in the bank's branch network in the West Indies was the return of some measure of profitability to the region's sugar industry after 1932. This was a result of the support the industry received in the form of government guarantees and, more important, the imperial preference schemes which came into being after 1932. Evidently colonialism conferred immense competitive advantages on Barclays Bank (DCO)'s operations in the region during the Depression years.

A patent manifestation of this advantage was the loan guarantees provided by the British government. The scheme came into being in 1930 following the Olivier Commission report, which noted the precarious position of the West Indian sugar industry; it involved the provision by the government of guarantees not exceeding £300,000 for potential losses on loans made by the bank to the industry. While the bank's stability was not solely dependent on government policy, it is obvious that these guarantees played a role in maintaining a higher level of business than would otherwise have been possible under the prevailing market conditions. The decision was reached in an atmosphere of uncertainty about whether preferences on West Indian imports were to be increased, given that the Labour government was not yet ready to adopt an all-out protectionist policy with respect to imports.[30] Indeed, the Chancellor of the Exchequer had previously issued a statement in which he noted that all duties and preferences on food, including sugar, would be removed. The Colonial Office was hard pressed to come up with a plan that would render some assistance to the region's industry which did not contravene the free-trade policies of the government of the day.[31]

Nonetheless, the political and social implications of the potential disintegration of the industry were not lost on officials in the Colonial Office. This was evident in a memorandum by Sir G.E.A. Grindle:

> [W]hile it may be that the sugar industry is to be wiped out, it is still incumbent on the Imperial government to do what it can to ease the process, to minimise the distress, and to safeguard against the inevitable calls on the Imperial Exchequer if the economic life of the sugar colonies is suddenly and abruptly terminated by cessation of cultivation . . . The Black and Coloured populations of the sugar colonies have a claim on us such as no other colonial producers have and it is not likely that we shall be allowed to forget it. Apart from considerations of humanity, there are strong political reasons to assist the people who would be deprived of their livelihood if sugar cultivation ceased . . . Hence it is politically and economically essential to ease the sugar industry's death agony, if it is moribund.[32]

As well as an admission of the government's neglect, the statement represented an acknowledgement of the moral obligation that followed upon the historical circumstances which had resulted in the mass of population being in the West Indian colonies in the first place. Further, it was a recognition that the livelihood of the majority of the people in the West Indies depended in large measure on the continued viability of the sugar industry, and that Britain's fiscal policies, which included subsidies to beet sugar at the expense of colonial cane sugars on which preferential duties had been removed, contributed in no small measure to the social and economic hardships being experienced. The statement also acknowledged the potential for political agitation which could lead to disruption in the economic and social life of the colonies – and which indeed did occur throughout the region in the form of strikes and labour riots, first in 1934 and then in 1937 and 1938.

In an effort to ensure some degree of continuity for the sugar industry, the Colonial Office drafted a plan to provide a loan to colonial governments which would form the basis of a revolving fund out of which the production of sugar would be financed from one year to the next. It was proposed that the loan should be interest-free to colonial governments, which would administer advances of £2 per acre to the cultivators at an interest rate of 1 per cent less than the current bank rate. It was envisaged that with the interest received, the colonial governments could build an insurance fund that would cover any losses, so as to keep the capital sum intact, and would enable eventual repayment of the loan. The total liability which the British government was willing to undertake amounted to approximately £650,000, apportioned in the following way: Mauritius, £315,400; Barbados, £70,000; Trinidad and Tobago, £65,748; British Guiana, £115,250; Leeward and Windward Islands, £67,500; Jamaica, £88,068.[33]

Following Cabinet-level discussions, however, the plan was revised, and a request was made for Barclays Bank (DCO) to participate in a scheme whereby the imperial government, through the respective colonial governments, would guarantee the repayment of loans made by the bank for the cultivation of sugar. The government's proposal also stipulated that as a condition of the guarantee, the rate of interest charged should not exceed 6 per cent. In the event of any loss through the failure of loans to be repaid, the British government would bear half the loss incurred, with the other half falling on the bank.[34]

Barclays Bank (DCO) welcomed the proposal but had reservations about the terms, as a number of the clauses ran against the grain of its general banking policy in the West Indies. The government's proposal had envisaged the provision of credit to small cane growers and peasants, with whom the bank dealt only indirectly through the large sugar factory companies, some of which were engaged only in the processing of cane sold to them by cane farmers.[35] For this reason, the bank considered the proposal of the government as being "too definite a risk to the bank and to the government". Indeed, Chairman Goodenough further pointed out that

> the extent to which cane farmers who are now selling to the factories at a loss who would come to the banks for advances is a matter of pure conjecture. Many of them are quite small peasant farmers . . . You will recognize that if the bank continues to make these advances, at the end of the Season, they may be only partially repaid, in which case the bank would be left in an entirely unsatisfactory position from a banking point of view. It might be possible to obtain certain forms of outside security, but these might not be proper banking securities. You will bear in mind the necessity for the bank to see these Seasonal advances repaid, having regard to its liabilities on current and deposit account.[36]

Clearly, the bank felt none of the moral obligation towards West Indian peasants and small farmers that had been accepted by Grindle of the Colonial Office, and saw the matter of providing guarantee loans from a purely business perspective. It was prepared to provide advances "in the usual way . . . taking the usual banking precautions as regards borrowers", which meant excluding the independent small cane farmers and peasants.[37] Effectively, the bank was able to impose its terms on the scheme. O. Barritt, manager in the Colonial Bank Section, argued that if small cane farmers were included in the scheme, the sum of £650,000 mentioned in the government's initial proposal would have been inadequate. The government's proposal had shown that of a possible 150,000 tons of sugar produced at £9 per ton, the maximum risk to the government at 15 per cent would have been £202,500. However, Barritt pointed out that it would be safer to contemplate a larger sum and proposed £400,000 as a more likely figure.[38] In arriving at that figure, Barritt noted that

> if for the sake of approximate calculation, we take it that 150,000 tons is financed at a cost of £9 per ton, we get an outlay of £1,350,000 for cultivation purposes, of which 15 per cent is £202,500, but it is doubtless safer to contemplate a larger sum in case the turnover from indirect to direct crop advances were greater than I have visualised. If by any development of the scheme, the whole crop were financed, the maximum risk of the government would be about £472,500, but as this is not conceivable, the maximum of £400,000 would appear to provide for every possible contingency.[39]

Eventually, the sum of £300,000 was settled on (see Table 2.3).[40] In place of the government's proposal, the bank suggested a scheme whereby for crop advances that were not repaid at maturity, the bank

Table 2.3 British Government Loan Guarantee Scheme to the West Indies

Territory	Average exports (tons), 1927–29	Percentage of total exports	Allocation of guarantees (£) by British government
Antigua	16,301	5.2	20,000
St Kitts	16,243	5.1	15,000
Barbados	60,427	19.0	60,000
British Guiana	108,249	34.3	100,000
Jamaica	43,925	14.0	40,000
St Lucia & St Vincent	4,410	1.4	5,000
Trinidad & Tobago	65,807	21.0	60,000
Total	315,362	100.0	300,000

Source: Government Loan Guarantees, CO 323/1113/21.

would be responsible for the first 70 per cent of the risk of repayment, the government and the bank would be equally responsible for the next 20 per cent, and the government would be responsible for the final 10 per cent.[41] The bank stated that it would be prepared to allow the payment by the government to carry over for a period of one year from the end of one season, so that any possible recourse might be made to covenants or securities, but that repayment would have to be made under the guarantees for any balance due from the government after that period expired. The crop advances made under these arrangements would be on a separate account and crop liens would be taken for them in the usual way.[42] This proposal was accepted by the government, the only modification being that the government and the bank were to share the last 30 per cent of the repayment of crop advances. The respective colonial governments were asked for their approval, with the understanding that the imperial government would guarantee half of any of the losses, provided that they did not exceed the amount apportioned to each colony. Under this arrangement, if only £7,000 were repaid of an advance of £10,000, the bank and the government would each suffer a loss of £1,500.[43]

The scheme did not preclude the involvement of other banks and lending institutions in the region. However, Barclays Bank (DCO)'s longevity in the region and its role as the premier financier of the region's sugar trade explains the government's willingness to be guided by it in the formulation of the scheme. The location of its headquarters in London was also to the bank's advantage, enabling it to keep in close contact with the Colonial Office regarding policy in the West Indies.

As important as the government loan-guarantee scheme was in minimizing the risks involved in providing loans to the industry during this period, it was ultimately Britain's return to protectionism in 1932 which assured the bank of continued profitable business in the region. That policy occurred mainly in response to the deepening of the Depression in 1931, which negatively affected Britain's balance of payments and contributed to increased unemployment. The adoption of a trade protectionist policy seemed to contradict the position taken earlier by the Chancellor of the Exchequer who had encouraged the Colonial Office to devise the loan-guarantee scheme. However, as Ian Drummond has explained, regarding Britain's imperial economic policy during the 1920s and 1930s, "there were two battling points of view; those of the laissez-faire free traders and the Imperial visionaries"; the latter believed that a return to protectionism was the best programme to pursue in the face of the severe economic problems facing Britain at the time.[44]

Britain had emerged from World War I severely weakened. Foreign investment had fallen by about 25 per cent, largely through the disposal of assets in the United States, and Britain's wartime debt to that country totalled $4.1 billion. Trade had suffered, and because of the wartime loss of former markets, British exports had declined by 35 per cent between 1913 and 1919.[45] The catastrophic fall in prices on the New York Stock Exchange in 1929, and the prolonged industrial and banking crisis in the United States which followed, reverberated around the world, resulting in a worsening of the economic crisis in Britain. Between 1929 and 1931 British industrial production fell by 16 per cent, while exports in 1929 still remained below that of 1913. Unemployment reached 2.5 million by the end of 1930. As foreign investors withdrew their gold from London and the British economy became overwhelmed by commercial and financial collapse, the decision was eventually taken to abandon the gold standard in 1931.[46]

Coming off the gold standard was only one of the steps taken in an effort to strengthen Britain's resistance to the impact of the Depression. Another was the abandonment of its free trade policy, which had characterized British international commercial practice for the previous seventy years. The passing of the Import Duties Act of 1932 and the implementation of the Ottawa Agreement of that same year marked Britain's decisive return to protectionism.

> The Import Duties Act of 1932 imposed a customs duty of 10 per cent on most imports, which was later increased to 20 per cent and higher, and the Ottawa Agreement vastly extended the imperial preferential tariff rates on colonial produce, which varied from 10 per cent to 33.33 per cent across a large proportion of British imports, with some commanding even higher rates.[47]

Colonial sugar was accorded a preference of £1 per ton. Further preferences were granted on a limited quantity of colonial sugar under what became known as the Colonial Sugar Preference Certificates system, which was renewed in 1935 and again in 1938.[48] By 1939, the preferential duty enjoyed by colonial sugar imported into the British market amounted to 40 per cent of the price received.[49]

The significance of the increased preferential rates on colonial produce as they related to Barclays Bank (DCO)'s operations in the region and elsewhere was acknowledged by the bank's officials.[50] Certainly, the reports of the ordinary general meetings after 1934 took on a more positive and optimistic outlook with regard to the region's industry, as the impact of the new direction in colonial policy was felt. This was revealed in the report for 1935:

> [T]hanks to the assistance afforded by the Mother Country through preferential duties, the sugar industry there are [sic] maintained during the past year; and estates have generally been able to meet their expenses . . . It will be appreciated that your Directors are in a unique position to feel the pulse of much of our Imperial trade, and it would be fair to say that in these Dominions, Colonies, Mandated territories, and other countries in due relation with Great Britain, the year generally has seen further progress towards a return to more normal conditions . . .[51]

This statement underscored the imperial thrust of the bank's business operations in the early twentieth century. It was also an acknowledgment of the importance of the "empire connection", in terms of British fiscal policy towards colonial produce, for the viability of its operations in regions under British control. An example was the Charley estates that the bank held in Jamaica. Barclays had inherited these estates through the Colonial Bank, which had acquired them in 1923 and had found it impossible to find a buyer because of their heavy indebtedness and the prevailing market conditions.[52] However, by 1936 the bank noted that the estates – amounting to 5,700 acres with a capacity production of 12,000 tons per annum – which had been running at a loss for a number of years, stood to return a profit of not less than £22,860, "thanks to the Ottawa Agreement". In that same year an agreement was made to sell the property to Tate and Lyle for £150,000, which not only repaid the original debt in full with interest but also left a surplus, out of which gratuities were paid to workers and a provision made to the original owner, James Charley.[53]

Similarly, the position of Worthy Park was much improved. Before his death in 1932, Fred Clarke had seriously contemplated selling his estate because he was having such difficulty in securing sufficient credit for its operations, but there had been no market. Thereafter, the position of the estate so improved, with gross profits increasing from £3,718 in 1933 to £7,131 in 1937 and £13,504 by 1940, that the Clarke sons were able to make significant improvements in the factory. Whereas a mere £715 was spent on factory improvements between 1933 and 1935, a total of £23,563 was spent between 1936 and 1940.[54]

The return to imperial preferences, coupled with the declining competitiveness of British manufactured goods in developed markets as a result of massive tariffs, resulted in the growth in importance of the empire in Britain's foreign trade during the inter-war years. Between 1930 and 1938 the empire proportion of total British exports and imports increased from 43 per cent to 50 per cent and from 29 per cent to 40 per cent, respectively.[55] This increase naturally included British trade with the West Indies, which came at the expense of West Indian trade with other nations, particularly the United States and, to a lesser extent, Canada. Between 1928 and 1933, imports to the region from Britain increased from 35 per cent to 44 per cent, before falling to 37 per cent in 1937. Imports from Canada declined from 19 per cent in 1928 to 13 per cent in 1937, and those from the United States declined from 24 per cent to 19 per cent for the same period. Exports from the West Indies to Britain between 1928 and 1937 also increased significantly, from 28 per cent to 48 per cent, while exports to Canada declined marginally, from 25 to 23 per cent. The drop in West Indian exports to the United States for

Table 2.4 Direction of West Indian Trade, 1922–1937

Year	Source of Imports (%)			Destination of Exports (%)		
	UK	Canada	USA	UK	Canada	USA
1922	31	18	32	34	26	27
1928	35	19	24	28	25	26
1933	44	14	13	45	24	7
1937	37	13	19	48	23	8

Source: Nash, "Trading Problems", 235.

the same period was more dramatic, from 26 per cent to 8 per cent (see Table 2.4).[56]

The redirection of West Indian trade towards Britain at the expense of the United States represented Britain's desire to reassert its interests in the region, in view of the growth of American imperialism there. The displacement of American trade with the West Indies was part of the "Visionaries" programme. Preferences would preserve and raise Britain's share of a growing trade in manufactured goods, and since the region was on a sterling exchange standard, preferences would support sterling rather than the American dollar. This was seen as important, since after 1914 the growing influence of the United States represented a real threat to Britain's position in the world economy, given the former's "unparalleled economic dynamism . . . spilling out . . . onto the world in the shape of trade and finance".[57]

A substantial portion of the increase in exports from the West Indies to Britain was represented by sugar, the production of which expanded tremendously in this period. The industry's growth in British Guiana was the most spectacular: total annual average production increased from 117,000 tons in 1929 to 196,000 tons in 1938.[58] Trinidad also experienced a huge expansion in exports during this period, from 81,600 tons in 1928 to 154,000 tons by 1936–37. Jamaica's sugar exports rose from 58,506 tons in 1932 to 117,946 tons in 1938.[59]

Overall, West Indian sugar exports increased by 121 per cent between 1926 and 1939, with the largest increase, 105 per cent, occurring between 1931 and 1937 (see Figure 2.10).

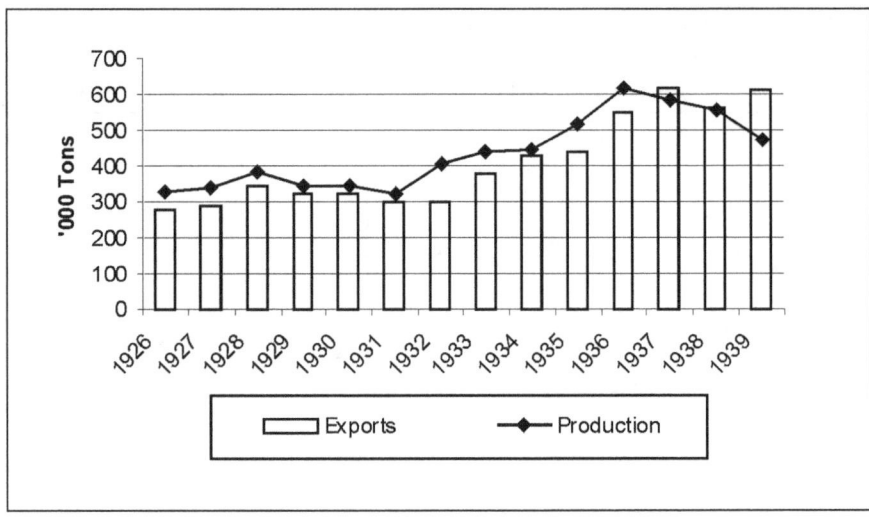

Figure 2.10 British West Indian sugar production and exports ('000 tons), 1926–1939

The slight dip in production between 1937 and 1939 was probably symptomatic of the widespread strikes and disturbances by sugar estate and other workers throughout the region in 1937 and 1938. Low wages and the lowering of living standards – a result of the sugar factories' retrenchment policies to reduce operational costs – were primary factors accounting for the strikes. Deep resentment and a growing sense of injustice, arising out of an awareness of their exploitation, was another factor; there is evidence which demonstrates that, in some instances, sugar workers knew that estate owners were making profits, having been guaranteed a minimum price.[60] Clearly the return to a state of "prosperous stability",[61] afforded by imperial government guarantees and preferences and made apparent by increased production, exports and profits, did not result in an easing of the economic hardships experienced by sugar estate and other workers in the region during the Depression years.

Summary

Barclays Bank (DCO) was extensively involved in financing the production and marketing of West Indian export crops during this period and was naturally affected by the Great Depression. Producers in the region found it increasingly difficult to cover their costs of production as the price of sugar fell drastically on the world market. As a consequence, many were unable to repay loans when they became due. This led to a general contraction in the commercial centres of the region – a result of the drop in demand for consumer items because less money was in circulation owing to the decline in money wages. A general contraction in business conducted by the bank also ensued. Nevertheless, some degree of recovery occurred during the period, as by 1933 profits at both the branch and sectional levels began to show an increase.

An important factor in this recovery was support from the British government in the form of a scheme of loan guarantees, which helped to minimize the bank's risks in providing credit to the sugar industry. Perhaps of greater importance was the extension of the imperial preferential tariff rate on colonial produce entering the British market in 1932. This had the immediate effect of increasing the returns on production and export of sugar from the West Indies since the commodity was assured of an expanded market and a profitable price under preferential rates of duty. The result was a tremendous growth in exports to the British market, which meant more profitable business for the bank.

Chapter Three

Collusion and Competition
Challenges from the Canadian Banks, 1926–1945

In addition to the Great Depression of the 1930s, Barclays Bank (DCO)'s performance in the West Indies was tested by the competition it faced from the presence of the Canadian multinational banks – despite the collusive agreements which existed between them. Critics of the multinational banks in the early twentieth century argue that through their collusive behaviour they contributed to the underdevelopment of the region. Maurice Odle, for example, has argued that collusion among the British and Canadian banks operating in the West Indies raised entry barriers which prevented the development of indigenous commercial banking, thereby severely limiting competition. He further argues that the artificial maintenance of a high price for credit helped to sustain the banks' discriminatory practices against indigenous borrowers and their bias against small-scale domestic-oriented agriculture and industry. Nugent Miller, while acknowledging that some degree of competition existed, implies that it was not significant enough to seriously threaten any of the incumbents' market share.[1]

Collusive agreements among rivals did not, however, necessarily mean the absence of price competition, and the argument that they instilled a non-competitive relationship does not take into consideration their terms – or the fact that from time to time they were broken.

Indeed, in Australia, the Bank of New South Wales demonstrated a penchant for breaking cartel agreements with the English, Scottish and Australian Bank during the 1930s.[2] Oligopoly theory posits that collusion may be largely dependent on the level of competition in an industry, where the firms have similar costs of operation. When costs begin to vary, higher-cost firms will become discontented and seek to renegotiate the agreement.[3] This chapter examines the nature of the collusive agreement between the Canadian banks and Barclays Bank (DCO) and scrutinizes the extent to which it precluded competition. It assesses the bank's regional performance in the context of competitive challenges to its position between 1926 and 1945.

Collusion with the Canadian Banks

While British fiscal policy played an important role in guaranteeing Barclays Bank (DCO) a relatively good performance in the West Indies in this period, its stability was also facilitated by the collusive agreements it entered into with the Canadian banks operating in the region. Collusive behaviour was a common feature among banks worldwide by the late nineteenth century. Many governments accepted it as a preventive measure against the potential economic dislocation which could arise from bank failure caused by unbridled price competition.[4] However, collusion among banks in any one market was designed largely to minimize competition and protect market share. It was a feature of the British domestic banking system, which by 1920 was dominated by the five largest banks. Collusive agreements on rates for loans and deposits were set through their control of the London Clearing House.[5] Collusive agreements among British multinational banks were prevalent by the 1930s and persisted well into the mid-twentieth century. Their terms included provision of adequate notification of the opening and closing of bank offices to the public, and mutual assent not to "poach" each other's customers.[6] The most significant aspect was the control of price competition, with the respective institutions concurring over borrowing and lending rates and other charges.[7] Such agreements were in place in South Africa, where the duopoly of Barclays Bank (DCO) and the Standard Bank of South Africa operated a wide-ranging cartel. Collusion was also evident in West Africa, where a rates agreement was in place between the Bank of British West Africa and Barclays Bank (DCO). This agreement was codified in 1945, in a document entitled "Cooperation between Banks in West Africa", and remained in force until 1957.[8]

Collusive agreements were also characteristic of the commercial banking system in the West Indies, though there were no formal written agreements before 1959. Evidence of collusion comes mainly from correspondence between branch managers and general managers at the bank's London head office, and from Sir Julian Crossley's diaries. There are also fragmentary indications that a formal written agreement existed in 1953 among the banks in the Bahamas. In 1959 an inter-bank agreement came into effect in Jamaica, and in 1961, the various banks were in the process of drawing up a standard agreement for the entire Caribbean.[9]

The primary focus of collusion among the banks in the West Indies, as in other regions, was the control of price competition. The rates agreement in existence between Barclays Bank (DCO) and the Canadian banks in the 1930s and 1940s covered rates of interest paid on savings and other deposit accounts as well as charges for overdrafts and other types of credit facilities. Changes in the rates charged to customers for various categories of business were subject to agreement among the banks.[10] The agreement on loan facilities involved a set range within which the banks were expected to work. For example, during the late 1920s, the banks' agreed-upon charge for overdraft facilities ranged between 6.5 per cent and 8 per cent, and was 6 per cent for other advances. In 1929, the bank's branch in Kingston, Jamaica, reported that it was able to charge 7 per cent, and sometimes 8 per cent, on overdrafts "when [it saw a] way to get it", while the sub-branches charged 7 per cent "whenever they [could]".[11] In effect, this meant that some amount of price competition was still possible within the set range agreed upon for loans and advances. The rates agreement also encompassed rates of exchange for buying and selling foreign currency (see Appendix A).

In early 1943 the Barclays Bank (DCO) head office in London was notified that the Canadian banks operating in Trinidad and Tobago and in Jamaica had departed from the framework within which all the commercial banks had been operating.[12] This was apparently a mark of their dissatisfaction with the new rates proposed by the British bank. Precisely which terms the Canadian banks found objectionable is not known;

however, it appears that they would have preferred an agreement more conducive to increased lending. The Canadian banks were particularly affected by a growth in deposits for which insufficient local profitable use could be found.[13] This had created an imbalance between loans and deposits, which led to funds being placed in lower-yielding assets, such as government securities.[14] Consequently, the Canadian banks favoured a general lowering of the lending rate. Apparently, this was the strategy they were pursuing in the West Indies during the early 1940s, following the breakdown in negotiations over the terms for a new agreement.[15]

The negotiations for the rates agreement among the banks were not public, and so it is difficult to assess the extent to which one had an advantage over the other or the amount of compromise that was finally reached in the process. The only available perspective is that of Barclays Bank (DCO), through the diary entries made by Julian Crossley, at the time one of its general managers. These indicate that the bank was able to exercise a great deal of influence. Following the news of the disruption to the agreement, A.T. Dudley, general manager of the bank's New York agency, who also had jurisdiction over the West Indies as local director, was sent to Canada to meet with the headquarters personnel of the respective banks to try to resolve the matter.[16] The initial meetings proved fruitless in the face of the Canadian bankers' tenacity. The RBC threatened that it would lose no opportunity to "make capital" out of any failure to reach an agreement on the terms for West Indian business.[17] Barclays Bank (DCO) maintained that this threat had little substance, given that the Canadian banks' proposed terms were less favourable to the public than its own,[18] and equally resolutely stated that it would take its own course, "whether or not the other banks [would] agree".[19]

The result was a two-month hiatus between the previous rates agreement and the eventual assent to a new one. This suggested that the respective banks were not only "playing a wait-and-see game", but also that the interval was used to engage in some amount of price competition. Indeed, Barclays Bank (DCO)'s response to the failure to reach an early settlement was to leave matters as they stood, while sticking by its proposed terms.[20] A new agreement was reached in March 1943, and Crossley noted, "Cable from Dudley, who is now back in New York, clearly indicates that we have called 'the bluff' of the Canadian banks, at least the Royal and the Commerce, and that they are now coming much more into line with our suggestions".[21]

By early April 1943, a return to "normality" was observed regarding the new arrangements, which presumably meant that the BNS "fell into line" and that Barclays Bank (DCO) was able to exercise price leadership over the business rates. The agreement was consolidated at a meeting between Crossley and the CBC's overseas branch superintendent in October 1943. Following this, Crossley boasted:

> [H]e appears to have a healthy respect for George's competitive powers. In the past he had been a close personal friend of Butt in Jamaica. He seemed definitely anxious to work together and to cooperate with us, and was entirely in agreement with our view about the limitation of the use of savings accounts and restriction of credit interest terms in the West Indies.[22]

No doubt, such influence would have resulted from a greater share of the West Indian market – though the only perspective available is Crossley's, unverified by an independent source. Nevertheless, it was acknowledged that from time to time Barclays Bank (DCO) found it difficult to exercise price leadership in some of the territories in the region, particularly Jamaica. For instance, a controversy arose in 1944 with respect to the minimum level of interest rates levied on overdraft accounts in Jamaica, when Crossley noted:

> We are now having another squabble with the other banks in Jamaica re our rates, this time on the Sugar Manufacturers' account which we regard as a quasi-government concern. There is no doubt that our minimum rates are too high, and I expect that we shall have to press the matter to a conclusion if we are to get our own way. We managed to do this quite successfully before and if they really see we mean business, I believe they will fall into line . . . although Jamaica is always an exception to the rule in the West Indies.[23]

Crossley's cautious note indicates that some compromise was forthcoming, and indeed, by December 1944 an agreement was secured for a reduction in the minimum rates charged for overdraft facilities.[24] Certainly, the fact that Barclays Bank (DCO) was able to price-lead all the time in some markets and not in others is evidence of the various levels of competitive pressure the bank experienced throughout the region.

Competition from the Canadian Banks

During the period 1926–39, Barclays Bank (DCO) remained generally dominant over the Canadian banks. In 1939 it maintained twenty-three branches and sub-branches in the region and was represented in all of the territories with the exception of Montserrat. In contrast, the RBC maintained thirteen branches throughout the region, and the BNS's thirteen were confined to Jamaica. The CBC maintained only three branches (see Table 3.1).

Barclays Bank (DCO)'s dominance in the West Indies was also evident in terms of its overall level of note circulation. The significance of the level of note circulation as an indicator of a bank's market share lies in the fact that a bank's currency notes are indicative of its level of business. For example, upon accepting a deposit from a customer, a bank accepts an obligation to honour cheques drawn on the account, for

Table 3.1 Commercial Bank Branch and Sub-branch Distribution in the West Indies, 1926–1939

Territory	RBC	CBC	BNS	Barclays Bank (DCO)
Antigua	1	–	–	1
Barbados	1	1	–	1
British Guiana	2	–	–	3
Dominica	1	–	–	1
Cayman Islands	–	–	–	1
Grenada	1	–	–	1
Jamaica	2	1	13	10
Montserrat	1	–	–	–
St Kitts	1	–	–	1
St Lucia	1[a]	–	–	1
St Vincent	–	–	–	1
Trinidad & Tobago	2	1	–	2
Total	13	3	13	23

[a]This branch was closed in 1939.
Source: Compiled from Currency, West Indies, Note Issues of Various Banks, CO323/1312/9; Quigley, "The Bank of Nova Scotia", 809; HBJ for 1910–19, 1920–36 and 1937–39; Yearbook of the Bermudas, British Guiana, and the British West Indies (for years between 1925 and 1940).

which banknotes are paid. Also, in discounting bills and promissory notes, a bank buys a right, due at a certain fixed future time, in return for which it gives the customer an immediate right to demand money in the form of banknotes.[25] In 1933, Barclays Bank (DCO)'s banknote circulation throughout the entire region was £449,936; its closest rival, the RBC, had in circulation £239,216 (see Table 3.2).

These facts, however, did not tell the true story of the British bank's position vis-à-vis that of the Canadian banks in certain West Indian territories. It was obvious that the Canadians had carved out a substantial market share by the 1930s, and in at least one market, Jamaica, the British bank had been overtaken by a Canadian rival, the BNS. In terms of total note circulation, in 1933 the BNS had captured at least 49 per cent of the commercial banking market, while Barclays Bank (DCO)'s share was 31 per cent. The RBC's and CBC's shares were 14 per cent and 6 per cent respectively. Viewed collectively, the Canadian banks held nearly 70 per cent of the commercial banking market in Jamaica in 1933, indicating a substantial erosion of the position of Barclays Bank (DCO) in one of the

Table 3.2 Banknote Circulation (£) in the West Indies, c. 1933

Territory	RBC	CBC	BNS	Barclays Bank (DCO)
Antigua	10,416	–	–	7,283
Barbados	25,625	13,808	–	53,142
British Guiana	64,943	–	–	95,973
Dominica	6,250	–	–	5,208
Grenada	7,438	–	–	19,030
Jamaica	39,697	15,169	137,634	85,860
St Kitts	11,458	–	–	10,417
St Lucia	645	–	–	9,977
St Vincent	–	–	–	12,285
Trinidad & Tobago	72,744	14,475	–	150,761
Total	239,216	43,452	137,634	449,936

Source: Compiled from Currency, West Indies, Note Issues of Various Banks, CO 323/1312/9.

region's more developed economies (see Table 3.2). Furthermore, the RBC had managed to firmly establish itself in Antigua, Dominica and St Kitts, where its level of business was either almost equal to or slightly higher than that of Barclays Bank (DCO).

Competition was evident between Barclays Bank (DCO)'s predecessor, the Colonial Bank, and the Canadian banks from the time of the latter's arrival in the late nineteenth and early twentieth century. In this earlier period much of the strategy involved establishing offices in areas where rival institutions were already sited or had plans to locate, in a bid to attract business. The intent was clearly manifested in the RBC's actions when it entered the region: between 1910 and 1916 it developed an extensive branch network. In addition to its office at Port of Spain, Trinidad, which it acquired in 1910 through its takeover of the Union Bank of Halifax, in 1912 and 1914 the RBC established itself in British Honduras and British Guiana through its acquisition of the Bank of British Honduras and the Bank of British Guiana, respectively. By 1916 branches were opened in Grenada, Antigua, Barbados, Nevis, St Kitts, Tobago, Dominica and Montserrat.[26]

For its part, while the BNS confined its operations to Jamaica, it rapidly expanded its branch network there, forcing the Colonial Bank to respond. Before the BNS entered Jamaica, the Colonial Bank maintained one branch there, at Kingston. With the objective of increasing its public profile, the BNS had by 1908 established six offices throughout the island. Further expansion followed, with ten offices established by 1918. In the meantime the Colonial Bank, forced to follow suit, also increased its offices to ten between 1908 and 1918 (see Table 3.3).

The CBC maintained only three branches in the West Indies – Jamaica, Trinidad and Barbados – in contrast to the BNS and the RBC, which were both influenced by their maritime origins and therefore were more focused on international trade.[27]

Branch expansion abated after 1926. In Jamaica, where branching had been most rampant, in 1926 – the year following the amalgamation – Barclays Bank (DCO) had ten offices and did not increase this number until after 1945. The BNS increased its number only from eleven to thirteen by 1939.[28] The RBC opened an office at Montego Bay in 1928.[29] Generally, however, branch expansion in the region halted until after 1945, undoubtedly owing to the Depression, which took its toll on the

Table 3.3 Jamaican Offices of Barclays Bank (DCO) and Bank of Nova Scotia

	Barclays Bank (DCO)		BNS	
Location	Opened	Closed	Opened	Closed
Kingston	1837	–	1889	–
Spanish Town	–	–	1916	–
Port Morant	1920	1923	–	–
Morant Bay	1916	1927	1916	1939
Golden Grove	1920	1921[a]	–	–
Annotto Bay	1916	–	–	–
Port Antonio	1910	–	1906	–
Port Maria	1912	–	1908	–
May Pen	1920	1924	1928	–
Mandeville	–	–	1907	–
Christiana	–	–	1930	–
Linstead	1920	1921	1920	1922
St Ann's Bay	1916	–	1911	–
Brown's Town	1920	1921	1920	–
Falmouth	1912	1933	–	–
Lucea	1916	1941	–	–
Black River	1921	1923	1911	–
Montego Bay	1912	–	1906	–
Savanna-la-Mar	1912	–	1908	–

Note: Some of these offices included agencies operated by the banks.
[a] Golden Grove re-opened in 1924 but closed again in 1925.
Source: Quigley, "The Bank of Nova Scotia", 809; *HBJ* (for 1910–1919, 1920–36, 1937–39).

profitability of multinational banks in general.[30] Furthermore, there were insufficient alternative economic activities which might have encouraged expansion. A number of light industries had developed, particularly in Jamaica and Trinidad, during the 1920s and 1930s. But the region's economy remained primarily agrarian, and the limited level of industrial activity could not be compared with developments in other regions – including Latin America, India, New Zealand and Australia – where developments had motivated a greater degree of bank branch expansion.[31]

The commitment to a branch presence certainly had not been abandoned, and the banks generally preferred to keep open a non-profitable branch, particularly in an area where a rival institution maintained a branch. Indeed, though consistent losses were incurred by a number of the Barclays Bank (DCO) Jamaica branches during this period, none were closed. For example, the Port Antonio and Port Maria offices incurred average losses of £365 and £452 respectively during the period 1926–34. The Falmouth sub-branch, though showing losses during the early 1930s, was reduced to an agency in Montego Bay in 1933 rather than being shut.[32] Although the closure of the Port Antonio and Port Maria sub-branches was approved in 1938, it was to be undertaken only if the BNS closed its branches at Morant Bay and Savanna-la-Mar. Furthermore, although the BNS's Morant Bay branch eventually closed in 1939, the two offices being considered for closure by Barclays Bank (DCO) remained open, despite having sustained losses. Only the Kingston branch was consistently profitable throughout the period.[33]

Visibility, as well as providing a physical infrastructure, was a significant aspect of the competition between the banks. Apart from the capital, Kingston, where the four banks had their main offices, Montego Bay in the parish of St James had three branches: Barclays Bank (DCO), the BNS and the RBC. Savanna-la-Mar in the parish of Westmoreland, Port Maria in St Mary, and St Ann's Bay in St Ann's all had a branch each of Barclays Bank (DCO) and the BNS. Barclays Bank (DCO) had two branches in the parish of St Mary, at Port Maria and Annotto Bay.

The campaign for deposits and lucrative business continued during the 1920s and 1930s, as shown by the banks' advertisements in local newspapers. In these, the BNS emphasized that it maintained savings departments at all its branches and displayed prominent signs indicating the interest paid on deposits.[34] In addition to making visits to landowners and businessmen,[35] the bank canvassed for deposits among small traders and grocery retailers, who were established all over the island.[36] Indeed, in its quest for such deposits the BNS had gone inland, establishing two offices in the parish of Manchester, at Mandeville and Christiana, one at Brown's Town in St Ann and one in Spanish Town in St Catherine, rather than staying in the port areas of major towns.

Though the RBC and the CBC lacked extensive branch networks in Jamaica, they were equally keen to solicit deposits.[37] One CBC advertisement read, "Daily opportunities are offered to the man with ready money. Accumulate a fund so that you may be able to take advantage of just such opportunities. Systematic deposits in a savings account will enable you to do this."[38] The CBC also targeted those with a "small salary", advising that "the need for careful saving is all the greater. Regular deposits of small sums in a savings account are a sure and safe way of accumulating a fund for future needs."[39]

Extensive branch banking in Jamaica, testimony to the intense competition for deposits, was not a feature in the other West Indian territories during this period. Competition in territories other than Jamaica was confined largely to the commercial centres of the capital and sometimes to one other major town. For example, in Trinidad and Tobago commercial banking was restricted to Port of Spain and San Fernando, where the RBC and Barclays Bank (DCO) each maintained a branch. The CBC had only one office at Port of Spain. In British Guiana, the RBC and Barclays Bank (DCO) had a branch each at Georgetown in Demerara and at New Amsterdam in Berbice, the colony's principal commercial centres. In Grenada, the RBC and Barclays Bank (DCO) maintained St George's offices and both were also present at Grenville.[40] In all the other West Indian territories where the banks were represented, each had just one office.

It may be argued that the apparent disparity in branch banking between Jamaica and elsewhere was a result of the BNS's regional policy. Quigley argues that this bank's aggressive quest for deposits was linked to its international reserve management strategy in the region. Deposits that were raised in Jamaica and not mobilized in local loans were transferred to the BNS's main secondary reserves from which settlements on New York and London drafts from any part of the bank's operations were made. Jamaican deposits thus to some extent facilitated the bank's ability to make loans in the Spanish Caribbean territories whenever deposits there were short. In this respect, the garnering of deposits by the BNS was an integral part of its strategy of minimizing the transaction costs of its operations in the Spanish Caribbean.[41] The disparity may also suggest that by the early 1930s the Jamaican economy supported more retail banking services than other economies in the region.

As trade finance was the primary focus of the banks, their main offices were concentrated in the capital towns of each of the territories in which they were present. This placed them close to the centres of the export-import trade and the general commercial life of the communities. It was therefore not unusual for rival banks to be located within walking distance of one another, as was the case in Kingston, where all four were sited near each other. Competition among the banks for all aspects of the West Indian trade, from small deposits to large-scale trade financing, was intense.

Competition was especially keen for the West Indies–Canada trade. It can be argued that the Canadian banks possessed a significant competitive advantage over Barclays Bank (DCO) in this area. The West Indies–Canada trade had been stimulated largely by Canadian preferences during the late nineteenth century, and, as a result, that country was an important purchaser of sugar and molasses before 1914. The annual value of exports from Barbados to Canada averaged 70 per cent between 1910 and 1914.[42] Trade between Canada and the West Indies intensified with the 1920 agreement, and, while the primary destination of West Indian exports throughout the 1920s and 1930s was Britain, a significant proportion went to Canada.[43] Antigua, St Kitts–Nevis, Dominica and Montserrat figured prominently in this trade: as much as 44 per cent of their total exports went to Canada.[44]

A plausible conjecture can be made here regarding the relationship between the significant level of exports to Canada and the RBC's market share in the Leeward Islands group by the 1930s. The RBC had by then made significant inroads in these colonies, retaining a collective 55 per cent share of commercial banking, compared with Barclays Bank (DCO)'s 45 per cent share. On the other hand, in Barbados, where 79 per cent of exports were sent to Canada, the RBC and CBC together had yet to usurp the position of Barclays Bank (DCO), though by 1933 these two banks had carved out a sizeable collective portion, 42 per cent (see Table 3.2).[45] An explanation for Barclays Bank (DCO)'s continued supremacy might lie in the relatively high proportion of British descendants resident in Barbados in contrast to the other British colonies in the region.[46] It is possible to argue that some degree of national affiliation prevailed in banking among the business community in Barbados. Certainly, the origins of most of the leading contemporary mercantile and commission firms in Barbados lay in British merchant houses that had collapsed in the nineteenth century and were then acquired by local British residents. A prime example is that of Gardiner, Austin and Co. Ltd, which had emerged as the island's largest sugar and molasses exporter by the 1930s. The company can be traced back to the London merchant firm Michael Cavan and Co., founded in 1797. In the 1830s the Barbadian branch separated from its parent company and became a local concern, run by descendants of the partners, who subsequently joined the company. One was John Gardiner Austin, from whom the enterprise eventually took its name. Another important undertaking was that of A.S. Cameron and Co., one of the foremost commission houses in the colony. The company had been formed by Alister Cameron, an English immigrant who had managed the holdings of Thomas Daniels and Sons, a London merchant house with a long history of business connections in the West Indian trade. When that company eventually folded, Cameron bought its largest sugar estates out of Chancery and formed his own business.[47] Both companies, along with four others of similar origin, combined in 1920 to form the Barbados Shipping and Trading Co. Ltd, which virtually controlled the export/import trade of Barbados.[48]

The competitive advantage which the Canadian banks had over Barclays Bank (DCO) with respect to the West Indies–Canada trade was particularly apparent in fruit exports. The fruit trade was also stimulated to a large degree by increased preferences in the late 1920s and early 1930s. A significant portion consisted of Jamaican citrus exports, with the number of oranges shipped increasing from just under 5 million in 1931 to about 14 million in 1933.[49] In 1934 a total of 79,196 boxes were exported, with Canada taking 52,815, representing 66 per cent of the total.[50] Only one credit relating to this trade was opened with the bank's auxiliary office in Montreal, Barclays Bank (Canada), as all the citrus trade with the West Indies was handled by the Canadian banks in the Montreal area.

Barclays Bank (DCO) had always been interested in the Canada–West Indies trade, which led to the establishment of Barclays Bank (Canada) offices in Montreal and Toronto in 1929. This was a chartered bank, jointly owned by Barclays Bank (DCO) and Barclays Bank Ltd. Canadian legislation required a certain amount of capital and reserves to be kept within Canada's boundaries, necessitating the establishment of a separate bank. Following the opening of these offices, advertisements in local handbooks and trade journals referred to Barclays Bank (DCO)'s long association with the trade and commerce between the West Indies and Canada, specifically drawing attention to the existence of the two offices in the Dominion for this purpose.[51] Nevertheless, the nationality of the Canadian banks continued to be an advantage over Barclays Bank (DCO) with respect to the West Indies–Canada trade, though it is noted that "an extreme lack of entrepreneurial flair" was responsible for Barclays Bank (Canada)'s failure to attract the accounts, including those of British companies operating in Canada.[52] Enquiries were made as to whether any of the bank's Jamaican customers who were fruit exporters could use their influence to secure a diversion of business to Barclays Bank (Canada).[53] This was found to be almost impossible, as at least 90 per cent of the trade was handled by Mutual Brokers (Montreal) Ltd, agents for Earl T. Robinson Ltd, whose bankers were the CBC.[54] Evidently, the CBC's extensive branch network in the Montreal area was a distinct advantage.[55] The only alternative left to Barclays Bank (DCO) was to approach the Canadian banks and suggest some form of mutual cooperation. With this in mind, John Caulcutt, general manager of Barclays Bank (DCO), wrote to H.A. Stevenson, general manager of Barclays Bank (Canada):

> It would be of mutual assistance if the Canadian banks in the West Indian Agreements would agree to those of our branches concerned being regarded as though they were your branches. Since we are the only Bank in these Agreements which has no branches in Canada, it does not seem unreasonable to ask the other parties to agree to this. Perhaps you will give the suggestion your consideration, and if you are in agreement, approach the banks concerned. If they are willing, the way will then be clear for negotiations between us as to mutual allowances and concessions.[56]

What became of this proposal is unknown. However, Barclays Bank (DCO) was not averse to exploring other means of attracting the Canadian end of the West Indian trade. Regarding sugar exports to Canada during World War II, Crossley noted that primarily through the influence of the powerful British sugar brokerage firm Czarnikows, Barclays Bank (DCO) in 1943 acquired some of this business that was largely controlled by the RBC. The RBC's dominance was perhaps related to the fact that Ran Noble, formerly of RBC, had been appointed Canada's sugar administrator in 1939.[57]

Competition was not restricted to the West Indies–Canada trade but was also evident in the West Indies–Britain and West Indies–United States trade. Early in the internationalization of their operations, the Canadian banks had established correspondent relationships with British and American banks to gain credit and foreign exchange facilities for their transnational banking operations. Soon afterward they began to establish their own offices. In 1910 the RBC opened its London branch in recognition of the main thrust of West Indian trade towards the British market.[58] The BNS and CBC also maintained offices in London and on the American continent while continuing their correspondent relationships with British and American banks.[59] Canadian banks' advertisements stressed their vast experience in trade facilities worldwide and called particular attention to their international offices and agents, especially in London and the United States.

In their quest for all aspects of the West Indian trade, the Canadian banks had no qualms about "poaching" prized accounts, even if this was undertaken through their correspondents. This was a strategy pursued by the BNS very early in its history in the West Indies. Upon its arrival in Jamaica, the BNS embarked upon a sustained attack on the position of the Colonial Bank. This involved the capturing of the accounts of the United Fruit Company (UFCo) in 1899 (which the Colonial Bank subsequently regained) and those of the colonial government in 1906. The UFCo was particularly prized, as the American company, being the largest concern in the growing and shipment of fruit in Central America and the Caribbean, was virtually in control of fruit exports to the United States from Jamaica. While the government accounts were of little pecuniary benefit to the bank, their possession carried some prestige and status in Jamaica's colonial society.[60]

This strategy continued in the late 1920s and was even conducted at the British end of the West Indian trade. In 1928, Barclays Bank (DCO)'s Liverpool office noted that for some considerable time they had received the bills for collection of North Shore Mills Ltd of Liverpool, drawn on the West Indies. However, this account was subsequently lost to Martin's Bank, an agent for the CBC in England. Martin's had approached the company and offered to collect bills at the same rate as that of Barclays Bank (DCO), but free of the commission normally charged.[61] This had prompted a Barclays Bank (DCO) officer to comment, "Does not this entitle us to take off the gloves at last and go all out for business which is legitimately ours, disregarding the objections of the Big Five?"[62] The "Big Five" referred to Barclays Bank Ltd, Lloyds Bank, the Midland Bank, the National Provincial Bank and the Westminster Bank, which had come to dominate English commercial banking through amalgamations which took place between 1870 and 1920. Largely through their control of the London Clearing House, a price cartel agreement had been put in place which limited competition to non-price competition. Though Martin's, a "second division" bank in terms of its size, was a member of the London Clearing House,[63] its actions indicate that it felt no obligation to honour this agreement with respect to facilities that it provided for clients engaged in international trade. Barclays Bank (DCO), an affiliate of one of the Big Five, Barclays Bank Ltd, was evidently peeved at this blatant disregard.

Poaching by the Canadian banks was not restricted to customers but targeted local staff as well. Competition for staff was particularly keen between the BNS and Barclays Bank (DCO) in Jamaica, and was a feature from the time of the BNS's entry in that market. Indeed, an appreciable changeover in staff had taken place at the expense of Barclays Bank (DCO) in favour of the other banks in Kingston between 1930 and 1934.[64]

While Canadian banks' strategies – including active solicitation of deposits, poaching of accounts and staff, and reliance on nation-specific advantages – contributed to the erosion of Barclays Bank (DCO)'s market share, the latter's managerial inflexibility was also an important factor. The bank's conservative business practices contrasted sharply with its rivals' more flexible approach. The Canadian banks were able to use the British bank's inflexibility to their advantage, as was most aptly demonstrated in Jamaica. For example, Barclays Bank (DCO)'s Kingston manager, R.V. Butt, noted in 1929 that

> everything is done to encourage the opening of current and deposit accounts, and every effort is made to retain them once we have them. You will recognize that we are up against very strong competition of the Canadian banks, and we are inclined to think that they are in some cases prepared to give accommodation that we will not.[65]

As evidence, Butt cited the case of two recently established motor car companies which had opened accounts with the BNS and the CBC. In his estimation, the accounts had not been worth having, given the companies' weak capital base for a business that was run mostly on credit. Furthermore, Butt noted that one of the companies, whose account the BNS then held, had been started by a former client of the bank with whom it had been forced to compromise upon a loan and who then, it was believed, had little appreciable means. The owner of the other company, with the CBC, was a former employee of a company that had previously been placed under receivership.[66]

Although the Canadian banks' more flexible attitude may have attracted what the Barclays Bank (DCO) manager considered to be less than desirable business, it also contributed to the loss of some of Barclays Bank (DCO)'s important accounts. This applied to two of the oldest and largest firms, whose activities included rum distilling and one of which had become particularly renowned for its fine blend.[67] The other was connected to a wealthy family that had made a fortune in Central America and held enormous interests in the Jamaican sugar and banana industries, not only as substantial property holders but also as significant produce agents and buyers. Its other commercial interests included the import/export trade and private banking.[68]

The precise circumstances which led to Barclays Bank (DCO) losing particular accounts are unclear. It appears that, generally, such losses resulted from the Canadian banks' competitiveness in terms of the level and type of security they were willing to accept for required accommodation, helped out by a fair share of incompetence on the part of Barclays Bank (DCO). The loss in 1934 of a valuable customer of fifty years' standing is instructive. The St Ann's Bay sub-branch received a request for a loan of £2,000 to facilitate the sale of rum which would have formed part of the security held by the bank. In all, seven lots of security were offered, including property and a life policy, to the total realizable value of approximately £14,000.[69] Upon referral to the Kingston branch, the manager requested an equitable letter of charge on three of the seven lots of security offered by the customer, as well as hypothecation of the rum, much to the surprise of the customer, who wrote to say:

> While I thank you for consenting to do so, I consider your terms excessive. While I wrote you that I would give the securities, I did not think you would require me to give them to you. Seeing that I possess them and furthermore

> I have been dealing with your Bank for over fifty years, I feel that I deserve some consideration. I have made arrangements otherwise to get the loan.[70]

Those arrangements were with the BNS, which was prepared to extend the loan on the strength of the customer's name alone.[71] It is not apparent whether the BNS was privy to Barclays Bank (DCO)'s terms. The customer obviously resented them, given his long and successful relationship with Barclays Bank (DCO), and was therefore motivated to seek alternative arrangements with the BNS. This case also indicates a degree of incompetence on the part of the manager, which the BNS was only too happy to exploit. By way of excuse, the manager stated, "If he had in any way notified me that he thought we were asking for too much security, I would naturally have reduced my requirements, but after all I took about one-third of what he asked me to do, and I really cannot see that I am to blame for losing this connection."[72] The Barclays Bank (DCO) head office management thought otherwise, and pointed out that a greater consideration of the matter by the branch manager should have led to the conclusion that it was not necessary to ask such a customer for the amount of security that was requested.[73]

Barclays Bank (DCO) also appears not to have adjusted as quickly as its competitors to the period's economic difficulties and circumstances. There was general complaint among the bank's customers that the institution was "too stiff" and "much more particular with [its] bills than the other banks", insisting upon the settlement of acceptances soon after the arrival of goods.[74] Customers also complained of being "over-worried by the bank because of the lack of reduction in advances", and as a result many of them transferred their business to other banks.[75] That complaint referred to difficulties which faced planters in meeting their debt repayments following losses occasioned by the hurricane in 1933, which destroyed much of the Jamaican banana crop.[76] It was noted that, in some of these cases, "the bank need have been under no misapprehension as to the safety of its advances, the security being ample and reasonably saleable, consisting for the most part of good properties".[77]

Indeed, routine calls by head office for reductions during this period had led not only to the prompt closing of well-secured accounts but also to the curtailment in the employment of the funds at the Kingston branch.[78]

The general inflexibility exhibited at the Kingston branch in the mid-1930s, and the consequences, prompted an immediate review of the way in which control on advances was exercised by the head office. It was noted that, while routine calls for reduction were generally expected to be acted upon, especially where the accounts exhibited some unfavourable feature, a degree of discretion was required from the branch manager. When attention was drawn to the absence of reduction on an account, it was expected that the branch manager, if he was satisfied with the safety of the advance and the position generally, would indicate to head office the circumstances accounting for the absence of reduction, whereupon such a case would be reconsidered.[79]

A review of the type of security considered suitable in the Jamaican market was also undertaken, as it was recognized that more flexibility was necessary. According to H. Richardson, an inspector and director of the bank, house and shop properties should be regarded as suitable as they were easily mortgageable, and therefore any advance secured in this way could not be described as "sticky". He further noted:

> One would not expect [borrowings] in a place like Jamaica and its sub-branches to be secured by marketable scrip, but rather that, as is the case so frequently in this country, local tradespeople would ask for limits against the security of their shops and premises and possibly other local properties which they own, and in this country it has been found, speaking generally, that such accounts are valuable to the Bank and they work quite satisfactorily. The Bank should be prepared to accept security such as the above-mentioned.[80]

Clearly, the quality of service offered by the banks had become an important issue by the 1930s, particularly in Jamaica, occasioned by the presence of alternative institutions offering the same service. The result was the development of a more discerning and critical clientele. Some of Barclays Bank (DCO)'s more valuable customers had, in fact, adopted "a most ungenerous view of the bank's administration generally". Consequently, the directors recognized the need for "treading delicately", especially when dealing with the more important customers. Director H. Richardson commented:

> On my visits to the West Indian branches, I have always made a point so far as is possible, of establishing contact with the business community, hearing

their views and generally getting their "feel" towards the various banking interests. In these small colonies a man's business is everybody's business and ungenerous treatment of one individual may engender a spirit of hostility to the bank concerned, and the matter become magnified out of all proportion to its importance, and it is important that this should be realized, as it doubtless is.[81]

In spite of these observations at management level in the mid-1930s, Barclays Bank (DCO) continued to suffer from a poor public image among the Jamaican business community in the early 1940s. Crossley reported that he "Saw Gingell, just back from New York. He seems to have heard some rather disquieting stories coming over on the boat from Jamaicans who told him some 'home truths' about the attitude to the Public adopted by our branch at Kingston."[82] Certainly, the business community continued to view the bank as being "aloof and unapproachable", which, the bank acknowledged, was having a negative impact on its business.[83]

Barclays Bank (DCO) was subjected to greater competition in Jamaica than in the other territories in the region, apparently because of the BNS's strategy with respect to the quality of service offered to the local business community. It is tempting to suggest that, as Jamaica was the only territory where all four banks were present, the greater choice of commercial banking institutions was a factor. However, the number of firms operating in a market does not necessarily influence the degree of competitiveness generated among the various institutions. Indeed, Barclays Bank (DCO)'s operations in Barbados and in Trinidad and Tobago, despite the presence of the RBC and CBC, were commended following an inspection tour in 1934, in contrast to the disappointment expressed with operations in Jamaica.[84]

Summary

Collusion contributed to Barclays Bank (DCO)'s relatively good performance in the West Indies during the period 1926–45. A collusive agreement on business rates, designed to minimize price competition, existed among the commercial banks active in the West Indies; however, its terms allowed for some price competition within the agreed-upon price range to be charged for overdraft facilities. Furthermore, although the agreements were long-standing, they were broken from time to time, and some price competition was engaged in as terms were renegotiated. The rigidity that is assumed to have been an essential part of collusive agreements among the banks of the time was not present in the West Indies.

In fact, despite a long-standing collusive agreement which limited price competition, the West Indian commercial banking market during the period under review was a much more competitive environment than has been previously thought. A significant amount of non-price competition involved the quest for deposits and lucrative business through the extension and maintenance of bank offices, even after they had ceased to be profitable in strict monetary terms. Other competitive methods used by the banks included the "poaching" of customers and staff and the advantages enjoyed by the Canadian banks with respect to the West Indies–Canada trade. Competition for business also involved flexibility in setting terms for credit facilities and in the types of business that a bank was willing to accommodate. The Canadian banks used this strategy to great advantage, as it brought into sharp contrast the more conservative practices of Barclays Bank (DCO) which drove away customers. By the 1930s the bank's public image was suffering, particularly in Jamaica, as a result of its inflexible attitude in banking practices and owing to indiscretion on the part of some branch managers. Indeed, it was in Jamaica that Barclays Bank (DCO) came under the greatest competitive threat, attributable mostly to the presence of the BNS. There, Barclays Bank (DCO) experienced a substantial loss in market share by the 1930s. The BNS's competitiveness in Jamaica had resulted in the business community in Jamaica placing on the agenda the issue of quality of service, which they identified with attitude and flexibility. The case of Jamaica in the 1930s clearly shows that non-price competition could erode a rival's market share regardless of the length of its history in the region.

Chapter   Four

Financing Agriculture and Trade
Bank Products and Services, 1926–1945

The products and services of the British multinational banks established in the nineteenth century were initially limited to the financing of the import/export trade, with very little provision for local industry. Nevertheless, over the course of the nineteenth century some amount of diversification in bank product and services was evident, spurred on largely by competition from local banks, as they became established, and from merchant houses. Economic growth and diversification in host countries and a general contraction in the presence of British firms abroad also encouraged the banks to diversify their products and services, resulting in their increased involvement in the domestic economies of their host countries.[1]

British multinational banks of the nineteenth and early twentieth centuries, however, were prepared to modify their bank product and services only so far.[2] Business historians generally agree that the lending policies of the British banks were highly selective and restrictive – that, in terms of the clientele they fostered, the banks engaged in a certain amount of discriminatory practice. What remains debatable is the basis for this discrimination; that is, whether it was racially motivated or based on the more benign factor of creditworthiness.[3] Most of the focus has been on British colonial Africa, where it has been found that the banks favoured the European, Levantine and Asiatic communities over Africans.[4] Chibuike U. Uche shows that black Africans believed they were racially discriminated against by the Bank of British West Africa, a belief which became the driving force behind the establishment of indigenous banks in West Africa.[5] Both P. Kennedy and M.H.Y. Kaniki state, without providing any substantive evidence, that the banks pursued a deliberate discriminatory policy against black Africans.[6] In contrast, D.C. Rowan has argued that discrimination was based on economic grounds, namely high risk due to sharp fluctuations in crop prices; a lack of liquid assets; low commercial reliability among black Africans and their lack of fixed capital assets; and the system of land tenure, which made it difficult to accept land as collateral. G.O. Nwankwo further argues that discrimination was inconsistent with profit-maximizing motives, suggesting as it does that banks would have turned down profitable business opportunities from locals in favour of less profitable ones from expatriate firms.[7] Uche suggests that the issue is more complex, arguing that "foreign banks' policies on lending to Africans varied according to the particular interests of their shareholders". He indicates that the Bank of British West Africa, though "initially keen to lend to Africans as well as Europeans", later denied African traders credit in the interest of preserving the barter trade and the British merchants' monopolistic position in the import/export trade.[8] Geoffrey Jones, in his broad survey of British multinational banking in the nineteenth and twentieth centuries, has indicated that while the banks based their lending decisions on commercial criteria, their assessments of risk and creditworthiness were also based on assumptions about ethnicity. Among these assumptions was that people of non-European ancestry in general lacked monetary and commercial responsibility.[9]

In this chapter the discussion is extended to the West Indies through an examination of the products and services offered by Barclays Bank (DCO) during the period 1926–45. The chapter begins with a brief overview of the products and services offered by the bank's predecessor, the Colonial Bank, in the nineteenth century. This is followed by a profile of some of the business entities that would have formed the bank's most important client base. The bank's credit facilities and arrangements are examined, including the degree to which the bank was prepared to be flexible. The chapter ends with a general discussion of alternative credit institutions and arrangements that were put in place or practised in this period.

Bank Products and Services in the Nineteenth Century: An Overview

Like other British overseas banks of the nineteenth century, the main focus of Barclays Bank (DCO)'s predecessor in the West Indies, the Colonial Bank, was initially the provision of financial accommodation to British merchant companies involved in the import/export trade. Banking services were also available to wealthy West Indian merchant companies and planters involved in procuring and shipping colonial produce and importing manufactured goods to the colonies.[10] In this early period, financial accommodation for the growing of export crops represented a relatively small proportion of the Colonial Bank's loan portfolio, this being mainly the business of British and local West Indian merchant companies.[11] The financial arrangement between the merchant and the planter involved the use of a credit system known as the consignee lien, or the commission system, which by the eighteenth century "had become an outstanding characteristic of the West India trade".[12] Through these credit arrangements with West Indian planters, British merchant houses always had a significant amount of investment in the economies of the region.[13] Under the commission system, British merchants advanced credit through banks to planters, for plantation supplies and wages necessary for the cultivation of the crops and for the general operation of the estates. The subsequent crop would automatically be consigned to the same merchant, who would arrange for its sale on the British market. Once the crop was sold, deductions were made for the supplies shipped to the estate on credit as well as for commissions, usually 2.5 per cent for the sale of the sugar. Further deductions included an additional 0.5 per cent, and 1 per cent for brokerage, if the merchant himself negotiated the sale, as well as charges for insurance and freight. After all deductions were made, the balance was either debited or credited to the estate's account.

The focus on financing trade and servicing the requirements of merchant companies involved in the West Indian trade reflected the underlying principles which governed conventional British multinational

Plate 4.1 The Colonial Bank, Harbour Street, Kingston, Jamaica, 1887. *Courtesy of the National Library of Jamaica.*

banking practices. British banking practice mandated that credit was made available only on a short-term basis. In the nineteenth and early twentieth centuries this was usually three months. It was expected that bank credit, particularly in the form of bills of exchange, was self-liquidating and represented real trading transactions.[14] The use of bills of exchange involved the granting of credit by the discounting bank. The British merchant, instead of waiting for money to arrive from the planter or merchant in the West Indies, might sell the bill to a bank at a discount. The British merchant would then receive prompt payment for his services and goods, while the planter in the West Indies would have a

Plate 4.2 The Colonial Bank, Harbour Street, Kingston, Jamaica, rebuilt after the 1907 earthquake. *Courtesy of the National Library of Jamaica. Colonial Bank, Kingston, 1887*

period of credit during which time it was hoped proceeds would be realized from the sale of his produce. Thus, what was known as the accepting and discounting of bills of exchange enabled the British merchant to be paid for his services and goods almost immediately after shipment, and the West Indian planter and merchant to receive credit.[15] In the event of an exporter in Britain sending goods to a wholesale or retail merchant in the West Indies, a bill requiring payment after a given period, normally sixty to ninety days, would be drawn by the exporter. The bill would be presented to the overseas customer, who would "accept" it, arranging payment before taking delivery of the shipping documents giving title to the goods in the case of bills drawn on a "Document against Payment" basis, or taking immediate delivery of the shipping documents upon acceptance in the case of bills drawn on a "Document against Acceptance" basis. The merchant in the West Indies could request a bank in Britain, through its branch in the West Indies, to pay the exporter in Britain, and in turn pay this bank in local currency in his own country.[16]

Related to the requirement that the credit advanced should be self-liquidating was the premium placed on what was considered suitable security. Generally, bills of exchange and bills of lading which represented goods in transit were the preferred forms of security – in spite of provision in the Colonial Bank Act of 1856 giving permission to hold mortgages on real estate for no more than two years.[17]

The Bank's Clientele in the West Indies

Over the course of the nineteenth century, the Colonial Bank extended credit for the growing of export crops; this development marked its gradual evolution from trade bank to retail bank. By the time of its reconstitution as Barclays Bank (DCO) in December 1925, its largest financial propositions involved accommodation for the cultivation of sugar cane and the manufacture and export of sugar, the region's major export commodity during this period.[18] This development, however, did not necessarily mean any significant departure from conventional banking practices, especially in terms of the banks' customer base. Despite the existence of a sizeable peasant and small-farmer class – mainly the descendants of African slaves brought to the region between the seventeenth and early nineteenth centuries – as well as a significant East Indian community, particularly in Trinidad and British Guiana, all of whom were engaged in the cultivation of sugar cane for processing and export, a substantial amount of land remained under the province of plantation agriculture.[19] Plantation land was not only under the auspices of the ruling merchant-planter elite, who during the late nineteenth and early twentieth centuries had usurped the position of the traditional planter class, but also under the control of British companies.[20] Indeed, these companies were responsible for a significant proportion of the production of the nearly 500,000 tons of sugar exported from the West Indies between 1930 and 1939 (see Table 4.1). In the main, they were also responsible for the increase by 28 per cent, to approximately 640,000 tons, exported from the region in 1946.[21] It was to this group that the bank gave the bulk of the finance for sugar production, as was noted in 1930 by O. Barritt, manager of the Colonial Section of the bank:

> [L]arger financial propositions are in respect of concerns for which the accommodation granted includes the growing of canes, purchase of canes from smaller farmers, the manufacture of the sugar, and in some cases general business purposes also. These clients are practically all large firms growing the bulk of the sugar themselves.[22]

Table 4.1 Annual Average Sugar Exports (Tons) from the West Indies, 1920–1929, 1930–1939 and 1946

Territory	1920–29	1930–39	1946
British Guiana	96,000	152,000	164,000
Trinidad & Tobago	63,000	108,000	110,000
Barbados	62,000	101,000	134,000
Jamaica	48,000	68,000	178,000
St Kitts	13,000	25,000	34,000
Antigua	15,000	19,000	17,000
St Lucia	4,000	6,000	6,000
St Vincent	200	1,000	–
Total	301,200	480,000	643,000

Sources: Higman, *Abstract of Caribbean Historical Statistics*, table 5/1; Stahl, *The Metropolitan Organization*, 39.

The wholesale and retail sectors in which many of these same large sugar-producing firms were engaged also accounted for a substantial proportion of loans and advances made by Barclays Bank (DCO). Table 4.2 provides a breakdown by category of loans and advances made by the bank as of September 1948, which, though three years beyond the period of discussion for this chapter, is still a fairly accurate representation. Loans and advances for agricultural purposes and to wholesalers and retailers together accounted for over half, 53.1 per cent, of the total disbursed by the bank. Retailers and wholesalers accounted for almost 30 per cent of total loans, indicating Barclays Bank (DCO)'s emphasis on financing trade. A significant proportion of loans and advances, 23.5 per cent, was provided to local governments and public bodies, including municipal bodies such as the gas, water and transport authorities. In contrast, "industries and manufacturers", which included a tobacco factory, newspaper publishers, and a knitting mill, accounted for only 8.86 per cent, whereas personal and professional loans accounted for a mere 4.5 per cent. Evidently, Barclays Bank (DCO), which by the 1930s had evolved into a retail banking institution in the West Indies, was still focused on financing trade.

Table 4.2 Barclays Bank (DCO), Breakdown of Advances (£) in the West Indies, 1948

Category	Secured	Unsecured	Total	% of Total
Agricultural	1,896,371	243,837	2,140,208	23.6
Retailers	963,871	431,571	1,395,442	15.4
Wholesalers	714,688	561,764	1,276,452	14.1
Personal/professional	303,574	105,196	408,770	4.5
Industry & manf.	436,768	365,654	802,422	8.86
Motor trade	226,118	7,893	234,011	2.58
Local govt., etc.	25,275	2,103,777	2,129,052	23.5
Mining	4,132	–	4,132	0.045
Brokers, private individual	217,029	713	217,742	2.40
Executive trust companies, building society	9,575	25,000	34,575	0.38
Cooperative societies	187	–	187	0.002
Other banks	–	559	559	0.006
Sundries	258,749	147,841	406,590	4.49
Total	5,056,337	3,993,805	9,050,142	100.0

Note: "Sundries" category included loans to religious bodies; "personal and professional" included loans to staff, architects and lawyers, and other private individuals.
Source: International Departments, General Managers' Office, BBA 11/551.

British Firms

The emergence of British corporate ownership of property in the West Indian sugar industry had begun in the late nineteenth century and continued into the early twentieth century. The opening up of newer plantation areas, particularly in the East, following the dismantling of long-standing policies which had given protection to West Indian produce in the metropolitan market, caused recurrent fluctuations in the price of plantation produce. As a result, many West Indian planters found themselves becoming heavily indebted, with many of the properties being acquired by their consignees owing to the heavy mortgages held against them.[23] It was through this avenue that many of the British merchant companies involved in the sugar trade became directly involved in the production of the commodity in the West Indies.[24] Many of them were also motivated to enter into the production of sugar as a result of the development of an intense competition within the trade during this period. The failure of a number of British merchant houses, and the fact that some of them transferred their investments to the more lucrative trade in the East as a result of the sharp drop in the sugar price in 1884 and 1885, led to a severe restriction of credit to the West Indian sugar industry.[25]

Subsequently, keen competition developed among the surviving companies and speculators who were prepared to buy commodities directly from producers and merchants in the producing areas. In fact, many planters generally abandoned the system of shipping produce on consignment, preferring to sell directly to merchants and other speculators on the spot.[26] In light of this development, the merchant houses which remained in the trade were also motivated to engage in production with a view to gaining better control of supplies of the commodity. To raise the capital necessary for such investments, several British merchants and commission agents organized themselves into what Stanley Chapman termed "investment groups", or business groups. The capital raised was then used to establish companies which managed the sugar-producing properties so acquired in the West Indies.[27] Undoubtedly, many of these companies were representative of the free-standing type of FDI which characterized many of the British multinational firms in the nineteenth century.[28]

In British Guiana, such companies included Booker Bros., McConnell and Co. Ltd; Sandbach, Tinne and Co.; and S. Davson and Co. Ltd. By the 1920s, Booker Bros., McConnell and Co. Ltd had emerged as the largest owner and controller of property in British Guiana.[29] The company's holdings in British Guiana were consolidated into three wholly owned subsidiaries: Bookers Demerara Sugar Estates Ltd, Corentyne Sugar Co. Ltd and West Bank Estates Ltd. The company also held half of the shares in Enmore Estates Ltd and in Ressouvenir Estates Ltd; and while it did not hold any shares in the local syndicate of Jones Estates

Ltd, one of its local directors did.[30] As a result of this substantial control and ownership of property, in 1945 Booker Bros., McConnell and Co. Ltd accounted for approximately 70 per cent of the total amount of sugar produced in British Guiana in 1945.[31] The company also had a majority participation in Inswood Sugar Estate Ltd, which oversaw the operations of the sugar factory of the same name, located in Jamaica.[32]

Initially, Sandbach, Tinne and Co.'s interests in British Guiana, which consisted of two sugar estates, Diamond and Providence, were managed by the company Sandbach, Parker and Co. Ltd, established in 1861. In 1891, a new company, the Demerara Co., was established to oversee the operations of its interests in the colony, which, in addition to its earlier acquisitions, by the early 1920s included the Ruimveldt and Leonora estates. In 1938, further reorganization of the company's interests in British Guiana saw the establishment of Demerara Company Holdings, which managed not only Sandbach, Tinne and Co.'s interests in that colony but also its various interests in Trinidad and Canada.[33]

S. Davson and Co. Ltd's sugar interests in British Guiana, which consisted of Blairmont, Bath and Providence sugar estates, were managed by the company Blairmont Factory Ltd.[34] These properties, along with those under the control of the Demerara Co., accounted for approximately 57,000 tons of sugar produced in 1945.[35]

British firms also owned considerable sugar-producing property in Trinidad and Tobago. The largest holding in 1930 was the Ste Madeleine, with 15,000 acres of land in cane, for which the Ste Madeleine Company had been established in 1913. The London merchant firm Henckell, Du Buisson and Co., which had a long association with the West Indies, was responsible for the flotation of this company. The Ste Madeleine accounted for 40 per cent of the total output of sugar in Trinidad in 1930.[36] Henckell, Du Buisson also floated the Gray's Inn (Jamaica) Central Factory Ltd in 1922 to take over the sugar estate and surrounding lands of the same name.[37] The Antigua Sugar Factory Company Ltd and the St Kitts (Basseterre) Sugar Factory Company Ltd were both established under the auspices of Henckell, Du Buisson and Co. Neither of these factories was involved in the cultivation of the cane that they processed but relied entirely on the cane they purchased from small farmers and the few estate owners still in existence.[38] Waterloo Estate, which accounted for 13 per cent of Trinidad's sugar production, was owned by Kleinwort, Sons and Co., while the British mercantile firms Furness, Withy and Co. Ltd and Prentice, Service and Henderson controlled the Caroni Sugar Estate Ltd.[39] Furness, Withy and Co. Ltd, based in Glasgow, became involved in the West Indian trade in 1920 through its acquisition of an old, established Scottish business, the Trinidad Shipping and Trading Co. Ltd, at Port of Spain. The company operated an extensive general and commission agency, representing a number of British and North American shipping lines, in addition to operating its own vessels, which sailed regularly between New York, Trinidad, Demerara and Surinam, calling at Grenada on both outward and return journeys. Furness, Withy also acted as agent for a number of British insurance companies and represented several British engineering and construction firms whose products it promoted in the region.[40]

While most of British FDI in the region's sugar industry during this period took the form of the free-standing firm, Tate and Lyle, the giant British sugar refining firm, in 1936 became the first modern British multinational enterprise in the industry. This company's operations in the West Indies as producers began then, as its business before that was confined to large-scale refining in Britain. Prior to that date, the only significant modern multinational that was involved directly in the sugar industry in the region was the giant American United Fruit Co. Ltd (UFCo), which acquired Bernard Lodge and Monymusk estates in Jamaica in 1929. In 1930 the two estates together accounted for just over 25 per cent of the total crop produced in the island.[41]

Upon its entry into Trinidad, Tate and Lyle established its first subsidiary, Caroni Sugar Estates (Trinidad) Ltd, following the incorporation of Caroni and Waterloo estates, which the company bought in 1936 and 1937 respectively.[42] Tate and Lyle held the absolute majority of 51.7 per cent of Caroni's ordinary capital, and United Molasses, 20 per cent. The rest was shared between the former owners of Caroni and the public, as the company was soon afterwards quoted on the London Stock Exchange.[43] This investment gave Tate and Lyle Ltd a vast control over sugar production in Trinidad and Tobago, as approximately 25,000 acres in cane belonged to the company in 1937. Local Trinidadian estates were responsible for the production of 15,000 tons of sugar in 1945.[44]

Tate and Lyle Ltd also made considerable investments in Jamaica in 1937. The Charley estates were under the control of Barclays Bank

(DCO) at the time of purchase by Tate and Lyle. Barclays had inherited them through the Colonial Bank, which had taken control of them in 1923. The estates comprised some 5,700 acres of land and had a production capacity of 12,000 tons of sugar per annum in 1936. With its purchase of the Charley estates, along with four other estates including Frome, all of which previously had been in the hands of Jamaican individuals, and with the acquisition of Monymusk from UFCo, Tate and Lyle formed the West Indies Sugar Co. Ltd (WISCo) in November 1937.[45] The company then owned some 29,500 acres of land in cane in Jamaica.[46] In 1945, Tate and Lyle through WISCo accounted for just over 33.33 per cent of the total output of sugar produced in Jamaica.[47] In 1946, foreign-owned sugar factories were responsible for the production of 67.2 per cent of total sugar produced in Jamaica.[48]

From Barclays Bank (DCO)'s point of view, the increased concentration of West Indian properties under British corporate control ensured an attractive customer base. Such companies brought a certain amount of creditworthiness to the properties, given their access to the London capital markets. They were therefore able to raise the necessary share capital for the reorganization and centralization of production on the properties, thereby making them more efficient and profitable.[49]

British firms not only were involved in plantation production but also operated substantial wholesale and retail businesses in the region. Some branched out into processing and light manufacture. In addition to its extensive holdings of sugar estates in British Guiana, Booker Bros. McConnell Co. Ltd in the 1930s operated a large general merchandise business.[50] This aspect of its business represented about 25 per cent of the entire commerce and industry of British Guiana. Indeed, the company's establishments practically dominated both sides of the thoroughfare on Water Street in Georgetown, where it conducted an extensive retail and wholesale trade in general groceries, provisions, wines and spirits, confectionery, clothing, jewelry, glass, china, toys and other curios. The company also operated a large hardware store providing estate supplies, ship chandlery, tools and domestic utensils.[51] Davson and Co. Ltd, in addition to the 5,000 acres of cane land it owned and its central factory at Blairmont, had by the 1930s diversified into industrial works, operating two large sawmills, a large foundry and engineering works devoted to the repair of sugar-mill machinery. The company was also engaged in lime-oil production, cattle rearing and an extensive wholesale and retail trade in hardware, groceries and dry goods in New Amsterdam.[52]

British capital played a prominent role in the Trinidadian oil industry, which underwent spectacular growth during this period. Although exploration had been undertaken as early as 1897, it was not until 1902 that the first oil well was drilled; as the strategic importance of the commodity grew – in response to the British government's plan to convert the navy to oil-powered ships in 1905, and following both world wars – official encouragement was forthcoming for the development of a colonial source. The result was rapid growth in the presence of British companies in the Trinidadian oil industry, companies that were responsible for the expansion in production.[53] In 1938, there were twenty-three companies operating there, the five major ones being Apex (Trinidad) Oilfields Ltd, Trinidad Leaseholds Ltd, United British Oilfields of Trinidad Ltd, British Controlled Ltd and Trinidad Petroleum Development Co. Ltd. The largest of these, Trinidad Leaseholds Ltd, was the only fully integrated oil company operating in the colonial empire, with its own oilfields, refineries, ocean transport facilities and retail markets. Other companies included Trinidad Central Oilfields Ltd, Trinidad Lake Petroleum Co. Ltd, Kern Trinidad Oilfields Ltd, Trinidad Consolidated Oilfields Ltd, Antilles Petroleum Co. (Trinidad) Ltd, which was Canadian-owned, Siparia Trinidad Oilfields Ltd and Petroleum Options (1925) Ltd.[54] Oil production expanded rapidly under the stimulus of the two world wars. In 1908 annual production totalled 47,000 barrels. This rose to 2,083,000 by 1920 and to 4,971,000 by 1926. Production totalled 9,419,000 barrels in 1930 and reached 20 million barrels in 1939.[55] Trinidad accounted for 44.4 per cent of the British empire's oil production in 1938; by 1946, the figure had risen to 65 per cent.[56]

A number of British mercantile firms which had remained involved in the West Indian trade concentrated primarily on the import/export trade. One such firm was the London-based firm of Thomson, Hankey and Co., which had a long-standing connection with the Windward and Leeward Islands, dating back to the eighteenth century.[57] This company maintained a branch of its business at St George's in Grenada, where it carried on a substantial wholesale business in provisions, hardware, liquor and lumber. Branches were also maintained outside the capital at

Grenville and at St Andrew, from where it controlled a large proportion of the export trade in cocoa and other produce from Grenada.[58] The Scottish mercantile and shipping firm of Thom and Cameron Ltd, which had been in existence from the early nineteenth century, maintained a business at Bridgetown in Barbados, shipping sugar and molasses and importing a wide selection of British and North American manufactured goods.[59]

West Indian Firms

In terms of their value as a customer base for the bank, the British firms involved in production and trade did not overshadow the West Indian firms and individuals involved in agriculture and commerce in the region.[60] Despite the British firms' extensive hold over sugar-producing property during the first half of the twentieth century, a significant amount of sugar-based plantation property remained in the control of local concerns, particularly in Trinidad, Jamaica and Barbados. Most of these properties were owned by merchants who operated commission agencies and acted as representatives for British, European and North American manufacturing firms whose goods they imported and sold in their wholesale and retail establishments. Many had acquired property using the profits from such business and took advantage of the depressed state of the industry in the late nineteenth and early twentieth centuries when the value of property was low.[61] Properties were also acquired as a result of the financial accommodation which many of them made to planters who did not qualify for loans from the commercial banks.[62] For example, Gordon, Grant and Co. Ltd of Port of Spain, Trinidad, had acquired substantial cocoa and sugar estates through defaulted payments on loans.[63] Esperanza and La Fortune, which were considerable sugar properties, were among those owned by this firm.[64] Woodford Lodge Plantation, which was among the largest sugar estates in the colony in the 1930s, remained under the control of Trinidadian interests.[65]

In Jamaica, Lascelles, DeMercado and Co. Ltd, a large mercantile and commission agency house located at Port Royal Street in Kingston, owned and controlled Vere sugar estate through its subsidiary, Vere Estates Co. Ltd. The company was also a large produce dealer, buying sugar, rum, coffee, cocoa and other produce for export. It represented a large number of European and North American companies, among which were the Royal Dutch West India Mail Steamship Co. Ltd; James Nourse Steamers, which operated between Calcutta and the West Indies; Tropical Steamship Corporation, which operated between New York and Jamaica; Nestle and Anglo-Swiss Condensed Milk Co.; Ogilvie Flour Mills Co. Ltd; Royal Typewriter Co. Inc.; Welch's Grape Juice Co.; Gerhard Mennen Chemical Co.; and Jamaies Baird Ltd. [66]

Other Jamaican merchants involved in the sugar industry included W.N. Farquaharson, who owned Holland and Rasheen estates in St Elizabeth, and H.V. Lindo, who owned United Estates.[67] Many of the properties that were acquired were reorganized and incorporated as limited liability companies. The capital that was raised was used to make technological improvements, which included the centralization of the production process, thereby increasing the efficiency of the factories that were established.

The commercial sector also included a number of West Indian commercial firms and wealthy merchants who operated on their own account and preferred to remain outside the ambit of agricultural production, specializing instead in the procurement and export of agricultural produce. Many of them were also wholesalers and functioned as representative agents for various British and North American manufacturing firms. One such individual was the very successful and wealthy merchant, J. Stephen Miller, from Christiana, Manchester, Jamaica, who had begun trading on his own account in 1907. By the early 1920s he had established the Jamaica Import and Export Co. at 22–28 Orange Street in Kingston, in addition to his principal business, Williamsfield Trading Co., in Manchester. Miller procured much of what he traded from small farmers and peasants, which included not only sugar and coffee but also cocoa, pimento, ginger cuttings, annatto seeds, orange oil, sarsaparilla, goatskins and hides. The business, which had an office and warehouse at Orange Street, also imported cotton piece goods and a variety of foodstuffs. In the late 1930s, this business was estimated to be worth at least £43,475.[68]

Some of the West Indian firms had their origins in the liquidated assets of collapsed foreign-owned merchant firms' holdings in the region. In Jamaica, the large general trading company Grace, Kennedy and Co. Ltd was born from the liquidated assets of the American firm

W.R. Grace and Co. Faced with the sharp recession that followed the post-war boom in 1918, which had caused several insolvencies, the company felt pressured to divest itself of its Jamaican operations.[69]

Many Barbadian firms were also established out of parent British firms in the late nineteenth and early twentieth centuries. An example of this was A. Cameron and Co. of Barbados, which was founded by Alister Cameron in 1891. Cameron had come to Barbados from England as an estate attorney to manage the holdings of the London firm Thomas Daniels and Sons but subsequently took over the company's Barbadian assets when they were liquidated in 1891. John Hadely Wilkinson, the son of a partner in the London firm Wilkinson and Gaviller, came to Barbados to take charge of the local branch of the firm in 1908. In 1920, the Barbados branch detached itself from the parent company and formed a partnership with an old, established Barbadian planter family named Haynes, giving rise to the large commercial concern Wilkinson and Haynes Co. Ltd. One other example was that of DaCosta and Co. Ltd, founded in 1868 by David Campbell DaCosta, a trader of Portuguese ancestry from St Vincent. The firm had begun out of the eighteenth-century Barbadian commercial house Barrow and Dummet.[70]

Other West Indian firms were started by immigrants to the region in the late nineteenth century. The founder of Joaquim Ribiero Ltd, a grocery and wine and spirits establishment, was a Portuguese native who arrived in Trinidad in 1882. Following Ribiero's death in 1910, the business was continued by his son of the same name and his son-in-law, who expanded the business into a large retail establishment, the Standard Grocery, as well as the Railway Bar and the Standard Hotel, both of which were popular among planters and other businessmen. Five branches of the business existed in Port of Spain apart from the main business at South Quay. The firm was also involved in buying and exporting produce and owned several cocoa plantations.[71]

William Fogarty Ltd, a wholesale and retail drapers and outfitters establishment located at Water Street in Georgetown, British Guiana, was begun by an Irishman who was initially a resident in Barbados. The business specialized in assorted dress materials and household fabrics and included the Philharmonic and the New Store, Fogarty's Corner, along with a shirt factory and a book and stationery store. William

Table 4.3 Import and Export Trade (Millions of Pounds Sterling), West Indies, 1936–1938 and 1948

Territory	Imports (total)		Exports (total)	
	1936–38	1948	1936–38	1948
Trinidad & Tobago	6.8	27.5	6.9	27.6
Jamaica	5.8	19.9	4.6	11.5
British Guiana	2.2	10.0	2.7	7.7
Barbados	2.1	6.4	1.5	3.0
Windward Islands	0.7	3.2	0.7	1.9
Leeward Islands	0.7	1.9	0.7	1.5
Total	18.3	68.9	17.1	53.2

Source: Nash, "Trading Problems", 224.

Fogarty also owned emporiums in Port of Spain, Trinidad, and Paramaribo, Surinam.[72]

Clearly, favourable demand conditions for Barclays Bank (DCO), with respect to both British and local West Indian firms, existed in the West Indies. The business activities of these firms were directly related to the region's foreign trade, which grew significantly during this period: the total value of imports to the region between 1936–38 and 1948 increased by 73 per cent and the total value of exports by 67 per cent (see Table 4.3). These increases testified to a flourishing import/export sector, which presented tremendous business opportunities for Barclays Bank (DCO).

Credit Facilities: Flexibility and Conservatism

In the early twentieth century, loans in the form of overdrafts and transactions involving various types of bills of exchange were used to facilitate the import of various types of manufactured goods and the export of agricultural produce. Usually, a portion of the negotiated loan would be allocated for the overdraft portion, and for the larger portion in bills of exchange. The most common type of bills included documentary bills, clean credit bills and bills for collection (d/a or d/p). Barclays Bank

(DCO) also provided credit by discounting bills. The provision of credit involving documentary bills entailed an arrangement whereby the bank undertook to pay the price of the goods being exported or accept a bill of exchange for the invoiced amount.

For example, a major Jamaican general produce and commission mercantile establishment was granted a £130,000 loan in September 1938. Of this total, £40,000 was allocated for overdraft facilities and the rest for various types of bills.[73] The bank, in return for the service, received a percentage commission. The security normally required for this type of credit was the documents to the goods, such as the bill of lading and invoices – thus, documentary bills.[74] Clean credit referred to credit given to a customer by the bank for the payment of bills of exchange drawn upon the customer for which there were no supporting documents attached.[75] Transactions involving bills for collection entailed an arrangement whereby bills of exchange drawn by an exporter, usually at a term, on an importer overseas, were brought by the exporter to the bank with a request to collect the proceeds. The bank would send the bills to its agent overseas where the importer was located and have them presented for acceptance, or payment, or both. The bank would then bring back the proceeds and credit the customer's account. If such a bill had documents of title attached, it was called a documentary bill; if not, a clean bill. The customer had to instruct the bank whether documents were to be released against acceptance by the importer – that is, document against acceptance (d/a) – or only against payment (d/p).[76]

Credit in the form of discounts entailed the discounting or purchase of bills of exchange drawn by the customer, usually an exporter on an overseas importer of the goods. By discounting the bill, the bank paid the face value of the bill less a discount, which was essentially its charge for the service.[77]

The most predominant type of security accepted by Barclays Bank (DCO) continued to be bills of exchange. These included bills drawn on reputable American and European manufacturing firms and on reputable local names and firms. The bank also accepted accommodation bills, wherein a person added his name to a bill to accommodate another person, thereby acting as a guarantor.[78] By the late 1920s the bank in the West Indies was also accepting life insurance policies, mortgages against real estate, and stocks and shares held in local and American businesses.[79]

Credit facilities advanced for the growing and processing of cane into sugar were referred to as crop advances. These covered expenses, including labour and plantation supplies, such as fertilizers and other necessary equipment, required on the estate for the duration of the season. They also covered the expenses associated with the marketing of the crop.[80] They were short-term in nature and were therefore expected to be recovered at the end of the crop season, which usually lasted six months, by which time it was expected that the crop would have been sold and the proceeds realized. Security for such advances included a lien held by the bank against the crop.[81] In addition, mortgages on factory, estates or both were sometimes required for such advances. The type of mortgage required was more often than not an equitable mortgage, which was created by a deposit of the deeds with or without a memorandum or by a memorandum of charge that gave the bank an equitable interest in the property.[82] If the mortgage value of the property plus the value of the crop was less than the crop loan required, the bank accepted additional security in the form of life policies and colonial government bonds.[83]

Credit facilities advanced for sugar production in the West Indies were predicated on the basis of what the price of the commodity would be at the time of sale. The hope was that sale would take place soon after shipment. Consequently, an element of risk was involved. The market conditions of the period which saw sugar prices plummeting, particularly in the late 1920s, made bank managers extremely cautious, and Barclays Bank (DCO) often requested considerable security for crop advances for sugar production. For example, a Trinidad client in 1928, on securing a crop advance of £100,000 for the 1928/29 season, was required to render as security first mortgages on sugar, cocoa and coconut estates and a lien on the sugar crop, which had a total value of £305,000.[84] The requirement for such extensive security was no different in Jamaica, where in 1936 a report was made on an account for which £46,000 had been advanced for the 1936/37 crop, along with a £9,000 loan repayable from crop surpluses at the end of the 1937/38 season. The proposed security consisted of the usual lien on the crop, which was estimated to value £48,659, along with mortgages against two sugar estates which together were valued at £15,000. In addition, a prior existing charge of £10,000 was postponed in favour of the bank, being available for any shortfall that might have arisen.[85]

Weather added to the risk factor involved in the provision of credit for crop production.[86] As hurricane and drought conditions were liable to cause shortfalls in projected yields, the likelihood always existed that the loans advanced against such crops would not be recovered entirely, or at all, at the end of a crop season. Given this uncertainty, some measure of flexibility was imposed upon Barclays Bank (DCO)'s lending terms in the event of such vicissitudes. In the event of a shortfall at harvest time, the bank was prepared in some cases to give what was termed a "policy" advance to cover the shortfall, in addition to the accommodation that was required for the forthcoming crop season.[87]

Generally, easier terms on loans were restricted to the British firms. One such company, a major owner of sugar-producing properties in British Guiana, in 1940 required financial accommodation amounting to £385,000 in the form of credits and overdraft. At least £350,000 of this loan was unsecured, with the remainder, £35,000, secured by produce.[88] A similar level of leniency was given to a significant British company in Jamaica in 1937, which was allowed to draw £20,000 in the form of clean drafts on sight on its parent company in London.[89] Its sister company in Trinidad was allowed £50,000 in the form of clean unconfirmed credit for twelve months, for which no security was required.[90] Such leniency, however, towards British companies engaged in the West Indian sugar trade was not a standard feature of Barclays Bank (DCO)'s operations: generally, some form of security was requested by the bank, even if it did not cover the full extent of the loan being granted.[91]

A degree of flexibility with regard to the terms on loans was also forthcoming for the large, well-established West Indian companies. Such was the case with a Jamaican company which maintained its account with Barclays Bank (DCO) from the time of its founding in 1922.[92] The company was involved in the heavy importation of foodstuffs, particularly rice, flour and salted and pickled fish, which were staples of the Jamaican diet. The company also imported other manufactured goods, representing at least thirty-two foreign manufacturing companies in the 1930s. In 1939, the company was allowed a loan totalling £46,500 in the form of an overdraft and documentary and clean bills, as well as indemnities for which no security was required. At the time of application, a current unsecured loan for £26,809 was due to run off at the end of September of that year.[93]

In general, credit facilities to the sugar industry in the West Indies were restricted to the production and marketing of the crop and were short-term, running for a maximum of six months, the duration of a crop season. However, on at least one occasion Barclays Bank (DCO) extended credit towards the purchase of property on a medium-term basis for three years. This occurred in Barbados in 1937, when a loan of £20,000 was advanced by the bank towards the purchase of a sugar estate comprising 450 acres and valued at £23,255. The deeds for the estate were required as security, and repayment of the loan was expected to be made on the basis of £4/5,000 per annum with full repayment by 1940. The bank retained the option of calling in the loan on demand and kept a close watch on the account with a review undertaken every six months.[94]

Similarly, a substantial sugar and banana plantation owner in Jamaica was given crop advances of £60,400 for the 1938/39 season and £53,000 for the 1939/40 season. On the strong recommendation of the branch manager, the Central Board sanctioned the proposal for the repayment of £18,000 of the total loan over a three-year period, with £7,000 repayable at the end of 1940, another £7,000 at the end of 1941 and the balance of £4,000 at the end of 1942. Security included mortgage against a sugar estate and factory in the amount of £45,000, equity in a banana estate in the amount of £14,000, a life insurance policy for which the surrender value was £2,500 and a lien against banana crops estimated at £44,000.[95]

Plantation owners were not the only recipients of medium-term loans in this period. Approval was granted in May 1941 for a "three to four year" £35,000 unsecured loan to a large dry-goods mercantile establishment in Kingston, Jamaica, whose average estimated surplus capital was £111,200 in January 1940.[96] This retail and wholesale business was the largest of its kind in Jamaica in the early twentieth century.[97]

This deviation in lending policy by Barclays Bank (DCO) in Barbados and Jamaica can be partly explained with reference to the customers involved. In the case of the Barbadian client, the bank's local adviser on West Indian operations recommended approval given the valuable connection between the company and the bank.[98] The client was among the most wealthy and influential property owners in Barbados. It also operated a major commercial business, importing general estate supplies, operated as a commission agent and manufacturers' representative for

British and North American firms and was a member of the island's largest trading conglomerate, often referred to as the "Big Six".[99]

The bank's willingness to accommodate the Jamaican clients is best understood within the context of the then prevailing competitive environment in the commercial banking market in Jamaica. As discussed in the previous chapter, Barclays Bank (DCO) was severely criticized in the early to mid-1930s for its stringent policy on loan facilities and security requirements that contrasted with its competitors' more flexible approach. Its rigidity had resulted in the loss of valuable clients to the Canadian banks, forcing the British bank to review and amend the way control on advances and loans was exercised. Barclays Bank (DCO)'s concern about the loss of clients to its rivals in Jamaica is exemplified by its acceptance of an unaudited balance sheet as testimony of the business transactions of a client who had requested loans and advances totalling £52,500 and US$20,000 on one account, and £11,397 on another – after the client declined to submit an audited balance sheet, in spite of the bank's repeated requests. The customer, who operated a substantial wholesale general mercantile business on Harbour Street in Kingston, importing a wide variety of dry goods from Europe and North America, responded to the bank's first request by stating that he was "quite satisfied that [the] accounts as then [set] out indicated a conservative estimate of the position, and that the additional expense was unnecessary". The branch manager, in imploring the London Committee of the Central Board of the bank to drop the matter, stated that ". . . to press the matter further might jeopardize the accounts . . . as Mr ———'s integrity is undoubted".[100]

The bank sometimes made accommodations for the purchase of an existing business. This was not a general feature in the loan portfolio of the bank in the West Indies, and such requests appear to have been considered only for highly regarded and reputable accounts. This was the case in 1939 when a major Jamaican commercial firm bought out a local retail rum business for £10,000. However, the terms of the loan granted for this transaction called for the loan to be repaid in six months. The average estimated value of this firm in June 1939 was £49,000.[101]

Barclays Bank (DCO) sometimes provided accommodation for the purchase of machinery, but again, this was more the exception than the rule – only one instance of this was identified in the bank's loan registers for this period. In 1936, in addition to crop loans for the period 1936/37 and 1937/38 amounting to £65,000, a Jamaican firm in control of a major sugar estate borrowed £40,900 in the form of discounts and other credits, £5,700 of which was "for the paying off on machinery bought by the company" for the estate and was expected to be paid back within six months.[102]

While long-term loans were not provided by Barclays Bank (DCO), from time to time short-term loans were "rolled over", giving the appearance of being medium- or long-term. For example, at the beginning of 1935 the body representing all the sugar-estate owners in Jamaica went into excess on its crop advance for 1933/34 by £14,000. This loan had been due to run off at the end of September 1934.[103] In June 1935 a loan of £225,000 in overdraft was negotiated by the organization for the 1935 crop. The amount outstanding at the time stood at £141,062, and it was proposed that an increase be granted to 30 November 1935.[104] In September it was realized that by the end of the 1934/35 crop season there would be a surplus over local requirements of about 6,000 tons of sugar. Consequently, credit facilities were required to enable the sugar manufacturers' representative body to export the surplus, and the bank was asked to carry about £25,000 until the end of the following crop season, when it was expected that the excess loan would be paid out of that season's sugar crop.[105]

Smaller accounts were not so fortunate. The failure to settle debts to the bank when they came due often resulted in the branch being instructed to recoup the debt through the sale of the security lodged. This was the ruling made when a small Jamaican retailer failed to reduce his loan by £750 by a certain date. The branch manager noted that the client in question had managed to repay only £250 at the appointed time and asked for leniency, stating that "this was absolutely all he can do and asks for . . . consideration of the fact that he has repaid £12,776 during the last two years". Though supported by the branch manager, and providing security in the form of American shares valued at £10,294, the customer was denied further accommodation, and the London Committee insisted upon a full reduction being effected by sale of the security held by the bank.[106]

The repercussions of World War II on overseas trade forced Barclays Bank (DCO) to modify its lending practices for its clients in the West

Indies. The irregularity in shipping services owing to submarine menace in the Atlantic, and the fact that fewer ships were in service because a number of them had been requisitioned for the war effort, resulted in frequent delays in the export of colonial produce. The situation worsened by 1942. For instance, the number of vessels visiting Barbados declined by approximately 40 per cent from 1941 to 1942.[107] The export of fancy molasses and sugar was particularly affected, as the carry-over from the 1941 crop amounted to approximately 65,000 puncheons, or 21,450,000 wine gallons, waiting to be shipped at the end of that year. At the end of 1942, as much as 50,000 puncheons of this quantity still remained on hand.[108] As a result, many of the bank's clients found it difficult to repay their loans when they became due, and faced severe loss.[109] Indeed, at the end of April 1940 a major Barbadian exporting firm had run up an excess of £81,210 on its overdraft as a consequence of its inability to ship its produce on time. The client had only managed to reduce this excess to £60,477 at the beginning of June.[110] The circumstances of the same firm were noted at a Central Board meeting of the bank in March 1943, in which attention was called to the firm's "top-heavy" position. Nevertheless, the board was considering advancing the firm a loan of £1,000,000, since it was expected that shipping facilities would become available in the near future.[111]

If Barclays Bank (DCO) demonstrated a fair degree of flexibility in its loan policies during this period, it was prepared to do so only within very narrow parameters, being informed by an assessment of the general creditworthiness of the clients. This explains why the bank provided very little accommodation to Barbadian plantation owners, since the relatively small size of most properties in that colony would have resulted in their being regarded as lacking sufficient creditworthiness. Barbados differed from the other West Indian territories in that British and other foreign corporate ownership was almost totally absent from its sugar industry.[112] This had to do with the steps taken by the planter-dominated legislature to safeguard planters' interests in the face of the economic crisis of the nineteenth century, steps that included passing legislation against the consignee lien system and voting to reject the adoption of the Encumbered Estates Act of 1854, opting instead for the English Chancery Court System.[113] Some indebted estates were kept in Chancery by their owners for years, whereas others were sold to local purchasers, some of whom were Barbadian merchants. While Barbadian merchants were in control of some property, however, the process of corporate ownership was slow in developing and did not really get underway until after 1935,[114] so that even though major corporate firms such as R. & G. Challenor Ltd, Manning and Co. and Wilkinson and Haynes had come into possession of large tracts of land by the mid-1930s, the rationalization and centralization of production in the Barbadian industry was generally slow in coming.[115]

It is not surprising that Barclays Bank (DCO), like its Canadian counterparts in the region, did not provide financial accommodation to the peasant and small farming communities in the region, since it was largely uneconomical and unprofitable to do so, even within the organizational framework of cooperative financial institutions. While the Colonial Bank had contributed to the working capital of the cooperative banks in British Guiana, with at least $7,584.90 (£1,580) being owed to the bank at the end of 1927, no further contributions were made by Barclays Bank (DCO) in the years that followed.[116] This contrasted with the policy it had adopted towards the indigenous agricultural sector in Palestine in this same period. In 1935 the bank became involved in the formation of the Agricultural Mortgage Corporation of Palestine "in order to provide a type of finance not readily forthcoming from the banks". Barclays Bank (DCO) lent funds on overdraft to this institution, providing 45 per cent of the Cooperative Bank's working capital during 1938.[117] In Cyprus, too, Barclays Bank (DCO) supported the Central Cooperative Bank established there in 1938. In fact, the bank specialized in this area in Cyprus, having provided the initial source of funds to the cooperative bank. The funds were advanced as an overdraft on the security of British government bonds and promissory notes of member cooperative societies.[118]

The reason Barclays Bank (DCO) was unwilling to lend working capital to the cooperative banks in the West Indies, in contrast with its policy in Palestine and Cyprus, was that it was not sufficiently remunerative for it to do so. It was argued that in Palestine, peasants had been subjected to excessive interest rates charged by moneylenders, and, in an effort to curtail this practice, the government had encouraged Barclays Bank (DCO) to participate in the establishment of the mortgage bank. Barclays Bank (DCO) was guaranteed a return on its investment of the working capital. This was not the case in the West Indies, where peasants and small farmers were in need of loans at very low rates of interest. In the essay on colonial development that he submitted to the bank in 1943, H.R. Smith, of the Port of Spain branch in Trinidad, explained:

> There are agricultural credit societies in various parts of the West Indies which make loans to farmers out of funds provided by the Government and members are collectively liable for the Society's borrowing, . . . it is self-evident that the bank could play no part in this arrangement. It is true that in Palestine loans are made by the bank to bodies analogous to Agricultural Credit Societies, but the system was initiated there to enable the peasants to evade exorbitant interest rates charged by money lenders, whereas in the West Indies it is necessary to provide money at rates which could not be accepted economically by private enterprise.[119]

In British Guiana, loans made by the government to the cooperative banks were repayable in 25 equal annual instalments, with loans up to 22 March 1920 bearing interest at the rate of 5 per cent per annum. After that date, the rate of interest was raised to 6 per cent per annum.[120] In 1938, it was reduced to 4 per cent, which was subsequently reduced to 3 per cent on loans made after 30 June 1944.[121] In 1927, the cooperative banks charged borrowers an interest rate of 12 per cent per annum.[122] Afterwards, the rate of interest charged on loans to members varied from 8 per cent to 12 per cent on loans made up to 30 June 1944; after that date all loans bore interest at a rate not exceeding 6 per cent per annum.[123]

Any confidence that Barclays Bank (DCO) might have had in the stability of the cooperative banks in British Guiana would have been undermined by the decision of the colonial government to suspend its contributions of working capital in 1928. This was a result of the worsened financial position of the colony, and it was not until 1940 that the government resumed its contributions to the cooperative banks. Until then, the cooperative banks were forced to rely solely on the sums previously granted by the colonial government along with subscribed shares by members.[124]

With the economic conditions as they stood at the time, participation by Barclays Bank (DCO) in the West Indian cooperative banks would have required a deviation from traditional banking practice which it clearly was not prepared to undertake. At least three of the cooperative banks failed to meet their repayment obligations at the end of 1927. The situation worsened in the early 1930s as the impact of the Great Depression rendered a number of borrowers unable to repay outstanding debts, which in turn meant that the cooperative banks were unable to repay loans due to the government and to Barclays Bank (DCO) when they became due. In 1933, members of the cooperatives owed loans amounting to $96,406.66 and interest amounting to $8,142.62, making a total of $104,549.28 (£21,781) outstanding. Of the total amount of loans outstanding, $80,212.85 (£16,710) represented loans in arrears, while the entire amount of interest was overdue.[125] Barclays Bank (DCO) was forced to settle by compromise on the remaining £5,780 that was due in 1933.[126] Indeed, in spite of "strenuous efforts to bring about a reduction in the arrears of loans and interest which had accumulated as a result of past transactions in 1933, of the $94,541.43 (£19,696) outstanding in 1938, $60,002.47 (£12,500) represented loans in arrears".[127]

The general attitude among the bank's personnel was that lending to small cane farmers and peasants was too risky, even through intermediary institutions such as state-controlled agricultural cooperative banks. Their participation in the provision of credit to the peasant and small farming class in the West Indies in this period was limited to acting in an advisory or administrative capacity. E.W. Lucie-Smith, Barclays Bank (DCO)'s local advisory director for the Jamaica operations and former manager of the Kingston branch, sat on the Jamaica Agricultural Loan Societies Board in 1928. This board dispensed loans to the various cooperatives in the island and also framed the rules for the control and supervision of the cooperative societies.[128]

While it is clear that economic criteria were an important factor in the decision to extend or deny credit to any particular class of persons, circumstantial evidence suggests that assessments of risk and creditworthiness were also based on assumptions about ethnicity. These assumptions were that non-whites in general lacked monetary responsibility and business acumen and therefore were unsuitable clients. Such an implication is certainly present in the explanation by R.V. Butt, manager of the Kingston branch in Jamaica, as to why an applicant's business was not desirable:

> The business was owned by a black man [who] was a clerk at ——'s garage, and bought out from the Receiver, put in by the Canadian Bank of

> Commerce, some of the old stock . . . He started in the garage that the firm occupied; we believe a few friends helped him, and his wife gave a Bill of Sale over her house and furniture for £1000 . . .We do not think that [this concern has] sufficient capital to swing a motor car business here, most of which is done on credit . . .[129]

The reference to the race of the owner of the business and to his former position as an employee in the same business indicates that his race and class were important factors in the bank's assessment of his creditworthiness. It suggests that the man's racial identity was used to reinforce the view that "the business was not worth having" and that blacks generally were not accommodated by the bank, and to have done so would have been an anomaly. As well, one can assume that the bill of sale that was offered as collateral and the "help from a few friends" were mentioned only to reinforce the branch manager's assessment of the garage owner's lack of creditworthiness.

Such discrimination was hardly unexpected, given the social and economic environment of the West Indies in this period. Having evolved out of the slave mode of production, West Indian agricultural and commercial sectors in the early twentieth century were highly stratified along racial lines. Agricultural and commercial business enterprises were predominantly in the hands of whites, and included Jews, who dominated the retail and wholesale sectors. Others included Lebanese, Syrian and Chinese migrants to the region in the early twentieth century, who were able to gain a foothold in the dry goods and haberdashery trade. While considered socially inferior to whites, the forementioned groups, because of their phenotype, were considered superior to blacks, coloureds and Indians. This had spawned ethnic stereotyping, consisting of the widespread belief that people of African and Indian ancestry were intellectually and morally inferior to those of European origin or descent.[130] As Brian Moore explains, the stereotyping covered not only

> social and cultural characteristics and attitudes, but also . . . economic behaviour and roles. Whites were reputedly endowed with the work ethic which made them the natural creators of wealth and leaders of industry. Blacks and coloureds by contrast were regarded as being indolent and improvident and therefore unsuited to independent economic enterprise.[131]

And even considered opinion also relegated blacks and coloureds below Indians, even if they occupied the same social and economic status. This prejudice was certainly evident in the essay that R.N. Escolme submitted to the bank's competition on the subject of post-war development in the colonies. Writing from Barbados, Escolme, who apparently worked at various branches in the region, commented that

> the East Indian and the Chinese understand the value of money and cut their cloth accordingly . . . But not so with the Negro population of these islands, they are too fond of the flesh pots . . . they lack the opportunism of the Indian or the Chinese. The Native say, from Barbados will go to Aruba, Curaçao or Maricaibo and make good money with the oil companies. He soon hankers to get back to Barbados. There he spends freely and showily until faced with no money, unemployment and the prospect of going away again.[132]

Escolme included in his indictment the West Indian black middle class: "Negro and Coloured lawyers, barristers, doctors and other professional men live up to their earning capacity. Good living appeals to them more than savings. They will have their wines and cigars."[133] Clearly, even if there was no official bank policy of discrimination on racial grounds, racial stereotyping was practised by bank employees and was apparently an important factor in determining an individual's creditworthiness.

Alternative Credit Institutions and Arrangements

Individuals and firms who were denied credit from the commercial banks had to seek alternative sources, some of which were state-sponsored financial institutions. Certainly, much of the sugar that was produced in Barbados in the early twentieth century was financed either by the commission merchant firms or by the state-owned Barbados Agricultural Bank.[134] The agricultural bank was established by the colonial government in 1908 with funds from a grant of £80,000 made by the British Treasury in 1902 to support the West Indian sugar industry, which at the time was in a state of crisis caused by severe competition from bounty-fed continental beet sugar on the international market. The adverse market conditions had made it difficult for many planters to cover their production costs, which caused the commercial banks to drastically cut back on loans to many sugar plantations which were still owned by local West Indian planters. Following the report of the Royal

Commission of Enquiry that had been established to examine the impact of the crisis, the British government granted financial assistance to the industry, which was used by many of the colonial governments to establish agricultural financial institutions to provide the credit that was no longer forthcoming from the commercial banks.[135]

A similar institution, the Agricultural Loan Bank, was established in Trinidad and Tobago. It began operating in 1925 following the passing of Ordinance No. 12, 1924, and was established to provide much-needed credit to local cocoa plantation owners who were being denied accommodation from the commercial banks. The Trinidadian cocoa industry, which was initially dominated by peasants, was by the early twentieth century controlled by the French creoles of Trinidad. By 1920, many of these planters found it increasingly difficult to obtain credit from the commercial banks as cocoa prices fell on the international market, largely owing to increased production and supply from the Gold Coast, Ecuador and Venezuela.[136] The agricultural bank was authorized to make loans of not more than £2,000 on first mortgages to owners of agricultural lands for the development, maintenance and improvement of their lands. These loans were repayable by equal annual or semi-annual instalments for a period of up to thirty years, and so, for the first time, some long-term credit was available to the agricultural sector in Trinidad. The second type of loan was short-term. It was a crop advance to landowners for the payment of labour and other expenses connected with the year's crop, or otherwise for the development, maintenance and improvement of their lands. This type of loan was not to exceed £1,000. Interest rates were determined by the board on a case by case basis, and the whole amount of the loan became repayable on 30 June of the year following the date of the advance. Interest rates were set at 7 per cent, which was 2 per cent above the rate charged on advances to the bank from the London capital market.[137]

Credit for Peasants and Small Farmers

The peasant and small-farming communities were also heavily involved in the production of agricultural produce for export, and generally had to rely on credit from the large companies in the industry to which they supplied cane. For example, in the 1930s, approximately 75 per cent of

Jamaica's sugar production was gleaned from cane cultivated by independent cane farmers. In Trinidad and Tobago, approximately 40 per cent of sugar-cane cultivation was in the hands of 18,000 tenant farmers, two-thirds of whom were of East Indian ancestry, and who cultivated lands owned by sugar factory companies or on properties owned by major landowners. These tenant farmers received credit from the large British sugar firms through the agricultural credit societies that they established, which had legislative support from government. In this way, the British sugar firms essentially acted as intermediaries; as Barritt, manager of the Colonial Bank Section explained, "the direct finance to the farmer [was] very small, the method being to finance the factories who [paid] the small farmer for his cane at a price based on the selling price of the manufactured sugar".[138] British firms, such as the Ste Madeleine Sugar Factory Co. in Trinidad, the St Kitts (Basseterre) Sugar Factory Co. Ltd and the Antigua Sugar Factory Co. Ltd, established agricultural credit societies to manage the advances they made to the small farmers who were under contract to supply them with cane for processing. In this way, as noted by Kelvin Singh, they "were able to retain their lien on crops, stock and moveable buildings through the medium of the societies, whose members were subject to unlimited liability".[139] The extent of the involvement of some of the factories in this system of advances is evident in the case of Trinidad, where the Ste Madeleine factory had by 1920 established twenty agricultural credit societies, with members of its managerial staff functioning as officers and trustees of the societies.[140] By 1939, there were fifty-nine agricultural credit societies in existence in the colony.[141]

Peasants and small farmers in the West Indies also received credit from commission and mercantile firms such as Geo. F. Huggins and Co. and Gordon, Grant and Co. Ltd, as well as from Indian and Chinese shopkeepers, who bought cocoa, nutmeg, mace and other produce from small farmers and peasants on behalf of the firms.[142] In 1909, the St Vincent Agricultural Credit and Loan Bank Ltd was established to advance credit to peasants cultivating cotton and other crops. This institution was not, strictly speaking, a cooperative, but it operated as such and offered financial assistance to small farmers and peasants. This privately owned institution was established with an authorized capital of $5,000, divided into shares of $1 each. Its capital was subsequently increased to $100,000 with shares of $1 each. It was closely monitored by the colonial government, being audited periodically by a government audit clerk.[143]

In general, however, government-sponsored financial institutions were the main source of credit for the majority of peasants and small farmers in the region, though in some colonies, government was slow to come to the aid of the peasantry in this way. For example, it was not until 1937 that provision was made for the establishment of the Peasants' Loan Bank in Barbados, when £10,000 was set aside in the government estimates of the budget for 1937/38.[144] In Jamaica, peasant loan banks were established earlier than in most other British colonies in the region. In 1905, the People's Cooperative Loan Banks were established. They were organized through the branches of the Jamaica Agricultural Society that had been formed to provide technical information and services. These banks were registered under the Industrial and Provident Societies Law, with the stated objective of "carrying on the business of banker and bill discounter, and to provide small farmers with credit". They were also authorized to deal in stocks, shares and bonds, debentures, mortgages and other securities, and to make advances for cooperative and industrial objects.[145] How effective these banks were is hard to assess, but it seems likely that they offered very little assistance, as by 1912 nearly all of them had failed, largely because of a lack of proper supervision and guidance. Following their failure, the Agricultural Loan Societies Law of 1912 was passed, providing for the establishment of an Agricultural Loan Board through which public funds were made available to the loan banks for lending to their members. The immediate recipients of loans were the owners and lessees of sugar crops and plantations which had been damaged by hurricane and drought between 1912 and 1917. In addition to government funding, the loan banks issued shares to the value of £5 and £1, payable by monthly instalments of 2s and 1s respectively. These banks served mainly the small farmers and met short-term credit requirements.[146]

Peasants and small farmers, and the working class in general, also devised and participated in alternative informal financial arrangements to obtain small amounts of credit. The "su su" among blacks, the "chaiteyi" among the Indians in Trinidad and Tobago, the "partner" in Jamaica, "meeting" in Barbados and "box" in Antigua were the dominant forms of credit arrangements made by the rural and urban working classes. These arrangements all operated on the principle that a core of participants agreed to contribute a specific amount weekly to a common pool, and at prescribed intervals, each contributor took a turn at collecting the total. On this basis, each participant in succession received and paid back his share of contribution and loan.[147]

Summary

Barclays Bank (DCO)'s customer base in the West Indies in the early twentieth century was largely determined by the nature of the society and the economy in which it operated. Its products and services were geared primarily towards providing credit facilities for agricultural production for export, and for the local commercial and retail business community that imported manufactured goods for wholesale and retail.

The bank generally adhered to conventional British banking practices, which meant that loans and advances were short-term and primarily for trade purposes, and against collateral which was considered easily convertible. At the same time, the bank exhibited a fair amount of flexibility in its lending policy in the West Indies, particularly during World War II when wartime conditions disrupted shipping, resulting in delays in the repayment of loans. In the interest of keeping the accounts of valued clients, the bank also provided loans for purposes other than the cultivation and marketing of crops and the financing of trade in general, and on occasion was willing to provide loans on a medium-term basis.

This flexibility did not extend to providing credit facilities to the peasantry and the small-farming and small-business communities, or to the middle classes. Generally, these groups had to rely on government and other financial institutions and arrangements that they devised themselves. While the bank's assessment of the general creditworthiness of potential clients was based primarily on economic criteria, there is evidence to suggest that race and ethnicity were also factored into the decision-making process. This is hardly unexpected, given the social and economic environment in which the bank operated. Drawing its clientele mainly from the white planter and mercantile business community, the bank catered primarily to the elite of West Indian society.

Chapter Five

Regulation of Commercial Banking in the West Indies, 1926–1962

Throughout the nineteenth and early twentieth centuries, Britain had a very liberal regulatory regime with few formal controls over banks. This policy was extended to its West Indian colonies. As there were few prudential regulations and no exchange controls, commercial banks in the West Indies, like those in the metropolis, were relatively free of restrictions on their day-to-day activities. It is true that the reform of the currency system that was undertaken during this period, which placed West Indian currency on the sterling exchange standard, imposed some restrictions and eventually led to withdrawal of the banks' long-held currency note-issuing privileges. The reform also brought the potential for some restriction on the banks' foreign exchange transactions. Nevertheless, there was virtually nothing in the regulations that could prohibit or influence the banks in their movement of funds and their allocation of credit. This only changed in the 1960s, when central banks were established as the various colonies became politically independent of Britain.

Britain did not, however, abrogate its duty with respect to financial stability and probity in the banking sector. On the contrary, these concerns were constant throughout the nineteenth and early twentieth centuries; the various clauses of the regulations that were implemented during this period and the subsequent amendments to them make this clear. In particular, a constant watch was placed on the currency note-issuing powers of the banks and the security arrangements for these notes in circulation. It is evident that the authorities' approach to bank regulation in the region was haphazard, but it is also clear that there was a strong tradition of regulation of the commercial banking sector prior to the 1960s.

In the early twentieth century Barclays Bank (DCO) in the West Indies continued to be governed by the principles of the Colonial Banking Regulations, which were first enunciated in the 1830s and applied to the early British multinational banks of that era. Therefore, it is useful to begin an examination of the regulatory regime with a review of the regulations applicable to the commercial banks in the nineteenth century. It is apparent that there was a haphazard approach towards the regulation of commercial banks in the West Indies, resulting in some degree of inconsistency. This continued into the twentieth century as the authorities adopted a reactive rather than a proactive approach towards bank regulation in the region.

This chapter opens with an examination of the regulatory environment of the commercial banking sector in the nineteenth century, beginning with the regulations that were applicable to the Colonial Bank and the local indigenous commercial banks. The regulations that were applicable to the Canadian banks operating in the West Indies are also examined, as are those that were passed into law in the various colonies during the early twentieth century. The chapter ends with an assessment of the clauses of the Jamaican Banking Law, No. 31 1960, passed as that island prepared for the establishment of the first central bank in the region, the Bank of Jamaica, in 1961.

The Colonial Banking Regulations

The Colonial Banking Regulations were promulgated largely in response to the rapid development of British overseas banking in the 1830s. While these regulations never had the force of law and were applied flexibly, they exercised a strong influence on the structures adopted by the banks. They were incorporated into royal charters that were granted to banks by the British government, and it was under these charters that many of the first British overseas banks, such as the Colonial Bank in the West

Indies, operated. Charters were regarded as seals of approval by the British government and provided some guarantee for the raising of equity, since early nineteenth-century English law did not confer on companies the privilege of limited liability.[1] These charters were issued only after the Crown Agents, on behalf of the Colonial Office and the Treasury, approved the fiscal soundness of the institution.[2]

Following the guidelines set out in the regulations, the charters specified a number of requirements. First, a company wishing to operate as a bank had to have at least half its capital stock paid up prior to commencement of business. Bank directors' business with their own institutions was prohibited from exceeding one-third of the total loans made by the bank, clearly indicating that banks were not to operate in a manner that would result in undue financial gain to those in charge of them. There was also a concern about placing the banks' capital in jeopardy, and so they were not allowed to hold or lend on their own stock nor to lend against land and other types of property. They were also required to submit half-yearly statements of their balance sheets to the government and have these published in local newspapers. Shareholders in banks were subject to double liability, which meant that in the event of default, they were responsible for up to twice the amount of their subscribed shares. It was therefore in the interest of shareholders to ensure that the institutions in which they had invested were prudently managed. Banks were limited to the business of "banking" and prohibited from engaging in any other type of economic activity. The banks were given limited periods of operation under their charters, which could be renewed only with the approval of the British Treasury.[3] This was to ensure that they complied with the regulations as set out in their charters, since violations could result in non-renewal of their charters.

In the nineteenth century the British government allowed many of the British overseas banks to issue their own currency notes. The charters stipulated that banknote issues were to be limited to the size of the paid-up capital of a bank, and that they should not be in denominations of less than £1 sterling or its equivalent. They had to be secured by a reserve fund equal to one-third in specie and by the general liability of the shareholders for the nominal amount of their subscribed shares. The Colonial Bank's charter of 1836 authorized the issue of banknotes payable only in colonial dollars, commonly referred to as "pieces of eight". These coins, along with English silver and gold coins and Spanish, Mexican and Colombian gold coins, known as doubloons, circulated freely, without any established exchange value among them, thereby restricting the usefulness of the banknotes. It was only after much representation by the Colonial Bank that an Order in Council fixed the doubloon at 64s sterling and the dollar at 4s 2d sterling, and made both legal tender. The bank was issued a supplementary charter in October 1838 authorizing it to redeem its currency notes in any currency that was legal tender in the West Indies.[4]

Charters also specified the geographical area in which a bank was allowed to operate. The royal charter governing the Colonial Bank specified the West Indies as its area of operation. The Treasury's view was that banks should confine their business to one region. The British government was particularly concerned about the security of the banknote issues, fearful that multi-regional banks would be unable to properly monitor and manage them, given the limited and unreliable communications, especially during the first half of the nineteenth century. It was not until after 1860 that significant developments occurred in communications technology, including cable telegraph systems and the application of steam to land and sea transport. The telephone was to emerge as an improvement on the telegraph at the turn of the century, and it was only after 1900 that British overseas banks were permitted to establish operations in more than one region. In 1916, the Colonial Bank's charter was amended to allow it to operate anywhere in the British empire, permitting its opening in West Africa in 1917.[5]

Regulations for the Incorporation of Banking Companies in the Colonies

The Colonial Banking Regulations were specific to the British overseas banks; apparently the possibility that indigenous banks might be established in the colonies by private individuals did not occur to anyone, in keeping with the lack of a decisive development policy towards the colonies in the immediate aftermath of slavery. In the event, a number of indigenous commercial banks in the West Indies were founded and operated, at least for a while, outside any form of regulatory framework.[6] As noted by Deryck Brown, "not all of these [institutions] were properly founded and organized, and very few of [them] were managed according to sound principles of banking".[7] It was not until 1840, after the Planters' Bank and the Bank of Jamaica, the earliest indigenous commercial banks in the region, were established and operating, that the Colonial Office sent out a despatch containing the "Regulations for the Incorporation of Banking Companies in the Colonies" prescribed by the British Treasury, by which colonial governments were to be guided in the framing of charters and legislative enactments for incorporating local banking companies.[8]

These regulations were sent out after the Jamaica government in 1839 sought to regulate the banks in the island by the Act 3 Vict. Cap. 46. This legislation provided that all companies carrying on business as bankers on 1 January 1841 make an annual return setting out, inter alia, the names and addresses of all members of the company, and submit a quarterly statement of the average amount of banknotes in circulation to the commissioners of stamp. An annual statement of the banks' assets and liabilities as well as the value of banknotes in circulation was required to be published in a newspaper in Kingston and a copy sent to the commissioners. It also made it compulsory for a bank to redeem its banknotes in coin on demand. Following objections raised to some of the clauses in the act, it was repealed, and new legislation was passed from which banks such as the Colonial Bank were exempt.[9]

Prior to the receipt of the regulations from London, the Bank of Jamaica in 1837 had obtained from the local legislature a charter similar to that of the Colonial Bank's, under Ordinance No. 3236. This was subsequently revoked by the secretary of state for colonies because the bank had violated aspects of the regulations, though the bank was able to continue operating as a joint stock company under a Deed of Settlement. The violations included the doubling of its capital without consent from the local legislature and the issuing of £1 currency notes payable in dollars, when there was no legal ratio between the latter and coins in circulation in the colony. Also, it was evident that the bank had overstepped the bounds of sound banking principles, having made an excessive note issue and advanced a significant portion against loans.[10]

The "Regulations for the Incorporation of Banking Companies in the Colonies" essentially mirrored the principles of the Colonial Banking Regulations, though, curiously, initially some of the clauses in the document were less stringent than those that pertained to the British overseas banks of that time. Accordingly, indigenous commercial banks needed a grant of an Act of Incorporation to operate and had to have the required amount of subscribed and paid-up capital before being granted one. Shareholders were subject to double liability in the event of failure. It was also stipulated that the amount of banknotes in circulation for any bank was not to exceed three times the amount of its paid-up capital plus the amount of deposits it held on behalf of its clients.[11] This was significantly less stringent than what was required of the Colonial Bank. Why this was so is not apparent in the records, and it was only in 1846 that this stipulation and others were amended and brought in line with what was required of chartered British overseas banks.

The 1846 revision also prohibited banks from holding shares in their own stock and making advances on the security of those shares. Discounts or advances against securities bearing the name of any bank director or officer, as drawer, acceptor or endorser, were not to exceed one-third the total advances and discounts of the bank. Also, for the first time the indigenous banks were not allowed to make advances against the security of lands, houses or ships except for the transaction of their business. Nor were they allowed to own ships or be engaged in trade except as dealers in bullion or bills of exchange.[12] They were to confine their transactions to discounting commercial paper and negotiable securities and other legitimate banking business.[13]

Both Richard Lobdell and Deryck Brown have stated that the clause prohibiting the acceptance of real estate as collateral contributed to the retardation of the development of the West Indian colonies. According to Brown, it "served as a fetter on the development of the sugar industry in the nineteenth century and may well have had the effect of . . . bringing about the accumulation and concentration of wealth in a few hands, in this case, the large corporate concerns that came to dominate the industry".[14] He and Lobdell are of the view that by prohibiting lending against mortgages, the regulations denied West Indian planters access to long-term capital, which they desperately needed for technological improvements to their sugar mills and estates. Brown further suggests that the Colonial Bank, by refusing credit to the French creole sugar planters on this basis and thereby displacing them in favour of the large British sugar companies, "appears to have been used as an instrument in the drive towards the anglicization of the Trinidadian economy".[15]

All of this is debatable. The issue, it seems, was what was economically feasible in the context of the prevailing market conditions and the lack of creditworthiness of many of the region's sugar planters. Lobdell himself had noted earlier in his article that, given the state of the international sugar market and the increasing indebtedness of West Indian planters, consignee merchant firms had begun to cut back on credit for investment purposes and to limit advances to the "barest necessities". Indeed, he noted that "only the financially strongest plantations after the emancipation could safely rely on this traditional source of credit for investment funds".[16] Therefore, even if the prohibition had not existed, it is hardly likely that the Colonial Bank's directors – whose first obligation was to their shareholders, and whose responsibility it was to ensure the profitability of the institution – would have acted differently from the consignee merchant firms.

Even if it had been allowed to lend against real estate and other property, the Colonial Bank, being a commercial bank, would have been averse to providing long-term investment capital, considering the nature of its operations. Commercial banks are distinctly different from investment and merchant banks. Their unique characteristic is that they offer par redemption of deposits on demand, which means that a high proportion of their assets are in the form of short-term demand deposits and reserves. Nineteenth-century commercial banks, whose primary business was providing short-term financing for agricultural production and trade, would have been subject to frequent seasonal patterns of demand for liquidity. The provision of long-term investment capital was fundamentally incompatible with their operations in the West Indies.

It is rather simplistic to view the Colonial Bank, in its operations in relation to the regulatory clause, as an instrument of the "anglicization project" in Trinidad and Tobago. The regulation was applicable to all the chartered British overseas banks, and not specific to the Colonial Bank in Trinidad. Also, it should be remembered that under similar circumstances significant amounts of property were transferred to the West Indian merchant-planter elite. They largely displaced the traditional planter class during the second half of the nineteenth century, not only in Trinidad and Tobago but also in other colonies, including Jamaica and Barbados. It is therefore best to view the clause prohibiting lending against real estate and other property in the context of the overall objective of the banking regulations as a whole, which was essentially to maintain financial stability in the sector by attempting to minimize the potential for bank failure.

The Colonial Bank Acts, 1856, 1898 and 1925

In 1856 the Colonial Bank's royal charter expired. No provision had been made for extending its operations beyond this date. This was mitigated by the passing of the Colonial Bank Act, 1856, by the British Parliament. Under this act the Colonial Bank remained a chartered bank but was established under the authority of the British Parliament, which would have to approve any future changes in its constitution and capital structure.[17]

The decision to extend the life of the Colonial Bank by an Act of Parliament rather than by issuing a supplementary charter must be seen in the context of the evolving ideology of *laissez faire* in Britain in the nineteenth century.[18] Regulators began to view the royal charter system as an offence against the principles of free trade, since it suggested the granting of special privileges to a few favoured banks. Jones notes that the British Treasury was anxious to relieve itself of certain responsibilities, such as having to give permission for increases in capital, for purchases of land and for the opening of branches in places not specified in original charters. Indeed, the granting of royal charters ceased after the passing of the Companies Act, 1862, which allowed banks to obtain limited liability with no special government controls. By the early 1880s the government had begun to issue a new "model charter" that every chartered bank was required to accept once its existing charter expired. This model charter relieved the Treasury of many of its original responsibilities and shifted other regulatory responsibilities to colonial governments.[19]

The Colonial Bank Act, 1856, introduced a number of features that, while imposing new requirements, relaxed other stipulations. The bank was now allowed to issue notes in the amount of £1 sterling and upwards. However, the bank's total liabilities were not to exceed £1.5 million, and it was required to keep specie and bullion in reserve to the value of at least one-third of the total of its banknotes in circulation in the West Indies. It was also allowed to accept mortgages on real estate or goods as security for loans and advances, but only for a period of two years. The latter clause was eventually withdrawn in 1898.[20] To facilitate increased supervision, the bank was also required to submit quarterly returns rather than half-yearly returns. If required, it was to allow government to inspect its accounts.[21]

Concern about financial stability was heightened in the 1880s and 1890s, following a spate of bank failures throughout the world. These failures, particularly that of the Oriental Bank Corporation in Ceylon in 1884, encouraged the British government to focus more carefully on the security arrangements for banknotes issued by British overseas banks.[22] This was reflected in the revised Colonial Bank Act of 1898, which required the Colonial Bank to deposit, with the Crown Agents for the colonies in London, securities amounting to the value of 25 per cent of its banknotes in circulation in the West Indies. In 1900, the Colonial Bank Act was further amended and repeated the above requirement, but also stipulated that the bank had to request permission from the British Treasury to increase the circulatory limit on its note issue in the West Indies.[23]

The Colonial Bank Act of 1925, which reincorporated the Colonial Bank in the West Indies as Barclays Bank (DCO), gave the British government even more powers with regard to the note-issuing powers of the bank. The act stipulated that the total amount of such notes was not to exceed £750,000. In addition, the Treasury reserved the right to request a reduction of the note issue to £600,000. The act also required the bank to seek Treasury's approval for any temporary increase beyond its maximum limit of £750,000.[24] All the notes issued by the bank were to be payable to bearers on demand at any of its principal branches as well as at the branch or agency from which they were first issued. They were to be expressed in dollars, in denominations of not less than $5 each or for multiples of that amount, and in current coin of not less than £1 or for multiples of that amount.[25]

With regard to the security requirements, Barclays Bank (DCO) was required to keep on deposit, with the Crown Agents in London or with trustees appointed by the Treasury, a fund consisting of coin or securities, or some of each, "equal to not less than one-third of the maximum amount of the notes in circulation in the West Indies and British Guiana ... up to £600,000 or less, and further security for the note issue equal to not less than 100 per cent of any excess issue over £600,000 up to £750,000". As a further disincentive to overextend on the issue of notes, the Colonial Bank Act, 1925, stipulated that the bank would be required to pay interest on the "aggregate amount of the note issue over and above £600,000 up to £750,000 at a rate calculated to leave the [bank] Company no more profit than will cover their expenses of issue . . .". The sum accumulated in this fashion would constitute a fund held by the Crown Agents or by trustees, out of which claims would be paid to note holders in the West Indies in the event of the bank becoming insolvent. The penalty for over-issuing on the prescribed amount entailed a maximum fine of £5 per day for every day during the period in which the over-issue continued, up to an amount not exceeding £1,000, and a further sum of £5 per day for every day during which non-compliance with the stipulation continued, and "for every complete additional sum of £1,000 of the nominal amount of notes issued in excess . . .".[26] The act also reiterated the 1908 Companies Act requirement to publish statements of accounts in a newspaper in general circulation in the colonies in which the bank operated.[27]

The Canadian Banks

Unlike the Colonial Bank Act, the Canadian Bank Act was not specific to Canadian bank operations in the West Indies but was applicable to the Canadian chartered banking system as a whole, which by 1890 extended into the region.[28] Indeed, as noted by Daniel Jay Baum, a general feature of Canadian bank legislation in the twentieth century was "a remarkable absence of any effort to regulate foreign activity".[29] Hence, while the Canadian Bank Act, which was originally passed in 1871, was amended in 1899 to permit these banks to issue and reissue banknotes outside of Canada, there was no requirement in the legislation regarding the provision of security specific to banknotes issued outside of Canada.[30] Under the act the Canadian banks were allowed to issue banknotes at their own discretion up to the amount of their paid-up capital; this provision applied to banks in the West Indies. Any issue in excess of the paid-up capital had to be backed 100 per cent by gold. The banks were also required to contribute a sum amounting to 1 per cent of their total note circulation towards the Canadian Bank Circulation Redemption Fund.

This fund was available to meet any deficiencies on the notes of an insolvent bank, in the West Indies as well as in Canada.[31]

Because Canadian banking legislation did not specifically address security for note issues in the West Indies, the Canadian banks were subjected to additional security requirements on their note issues in the region. It was in this area of regulation that a degree of haphazardness occurred – apparently as a result of incompetence and a lack of foresight by Colonial Office officials. In all the West Indian colonies, legislation was passed which required banks of issue to place on deposit, with the Crown Agents in London or with trustees in the respective colonies, securities to the full extent of the value of their notes in circulation.[32] The prescribed amount contrasted with the 25 per cent which was required of Barclays Bank (DCO), and in this regard, at least in theory, the Canadian banks were at a disadvantage in relation to the British bank. In practice, however, it appears that the legislation may have been intended as a barrier to the entry of less efficient institutions – perhaps local indigenous companies – to the commercial banking sector, rather than as an attempt at checking the operations of larger, more financially secure institutions such as the Canadian banks. One indication is that all the ordinances contained a clause which stated that the secretary of state for the colonies could dispense with the provisions specifying the level of security if he was satisfied that the notes of a bank were otherwise secure. Indeed, the security requirements of the Canadian banks were later reduced to 25 per cent of the value of their note issue in the West Indies.

Nevertheless, the application of security requirements for the Canadian banks was not uniform throughout the colonies. In Jamaica, security requirements for the banknotes issued by the BNS were never in place, apparently because the bank had received its licence to issue notes under the provisions of Law No. 38 of 1868, which did not stipulate any security requirements. The Banknotes Law of 1904, which was subsequently passed to regulate the issue of banknotes, required the establishment of a security fund by an issuing bank, but specifically exempted the BNS in Section 11, stating that it was "already lawfully issuing banknotes". Similarly, in Trinidad and Tobago, the Banknotes Ordinance of 1906 exempted banks with headquarters in other British possessions from security requirements – which, Brown notes, was specifically framed with the BNS in mind, following its opening in Port of Spain in

1906 (the bank closed shortly thereafter). The RBC also appears to have been exempted from security requirements in British Guiana. However, Banknotes Ordinance No. 1, 1914, chapter 51, section 4, stipulated a circulatory limit for that bank in the colony to be $500,000 (which was equivalent to about £100,000), and stated that if this were increased the bank would be required to deposit 25 per cent of the value of its notes in circulation as security. While the RBC was exempted from security requirements for up to £100,000 in British Guiana, it was not in Jamaica nor elsewhere in the region; neither was the CBC so privileged.[33]

A certain inconsistency also characterized regulations on circulatory limits. In some of the colonies legislation had been passed which gave the respective governments the power to impose specific limits on banknote circulation. No such provision was made in the Barbados law, and while provision was made for such an imposition in the St Lucia law under section 3 of ordinance no. 24, 1920, no limitation was imposed. The power to limit banknote circulation also existed in the Leeward Islands under Federal Act cap. no. 115, but it was not exercised.[34]

The reason that legislation limiting banknote circulation existed but was not imposed in some cases may be that, for some colonies, it was actually framed with future indigenous banks in mind and not necessarily applicable to the larger Canadian banks. Indeed, it appears that the Canadian banks, though they were given a circulatory limit of £100,000 when they applied for permission to issue banknotes, made their own note allocations within their overall limits as prescribed under the Canadian Bank Act. For instance, the RBC, following its establishment in the region, applied for and received a circulatory limit of $750,000 or £154,320 for its Trinidadian operations.[35] In 1933, this bank's circulatory limit for Trinidad was listed as being $2,000,000 or £416,666. It appears that individual colonies imposed no real circulatory limit on the Canadian banks, notwithstanding the British Guiana Banknotes Ordinance No. 1, 1914, which placed the RBC's circulatory limit at $500,000 or £100,000. Whereas in 1933 the circulatory limit for the bank's British Guiana operations was listed as $200,000 (about £40,000), its actual circulation was considerably more: $311,730, or £64,943.[36] Essentially, then, regardless of the existence of various pieces of colonial legislation, the Canadian banks in the West Indies, like the Colonial Bank and later Barclays Bank (DCO), made their own allocations within their overall legal limits related to their paid-up capital.[37] It was not until 1942 that a more equitable and uniform policy on circulatory limits and security requirements was implemented. This occurred in the context of the gradual reform of the currency system, which is discussed in chapter 6.

Legislation in the Colonies

Other aspects of bank regulation in the colonies in the early twentieth century amounted to an extension of the Companies Act.[38] As joint stock banks were in the main incorporated as public limited companies, they were subject to the provisions of the Companies Act, which related to all public companies. Under the Companies Act of 1862, all public companies including British domestic banks were obliged to deposit with the Registrar of Companies an annual profit and loss report and an annual balance sheet. In addition, section 131 and schedule 7 of the Act of 1929 included provisions specifically applicable to banks, including the obligation to publish half-yearly a statement of position in a prescribed form, and to exhibit this statement in every branch. The banks also had to have their balance sheets signed by the secretary or manager and at least three directors of the said banking institution.[39]

In the West Indies, colonial legislation generally followed the same principles. Most laws gave the respective governments the power to inspect the books of any banker and required the banks to publish annual or half-yearly statements of their assets and liabilities.[40] In addition, all the commercial banks had to pay annual registration licence fees as well as taxes levied on their notes in circulation. Licence fees ranged from as low as £30 to as high as £250 per annum. In British Guiana, the licence fee was particularly high, being a flat rate licence duty of $3,000 or £625 per annum. In Barbados, each bank paid a stamp duty of £75 annually under the Stamp Act of 1916 for licence to issue or reissue banknotes. All banks in St Lucia were liable to pay an annual licence fee of £50 under schedule to ordinance no. 123, 1916.[41] In Jamaica, commercial banks were liable to pay an annual licence fee of £150 under section 6 of Law of 1916. In addition, a tax of 1 per cent on the value of the note circulation was imposed under Law 40 of 1908 and increased to 3 per cent by Law 7 of 1916.[42] This was later reduced to a composition tax of 1 per cent of average quarterly note issues in circulation under the Stamp

Duty Further Amendment Law 12 of 1929.[43] In 1939, this tax was raised to 2.5 per cent, representing a 150 per cent increase over the previous rate.[44] These various levies were mainly pecuniary measures, though they could be considered regulatory as they would have acted as a deterrent to weakly based institutions entering the commercial banking market.

Clearly, legislation pertinent to the operations of commercial banking in the West Indies remained somewhat disparate. The main emphasis in regulations was on the provision of adequate security for banknotes in circulation, to protect the holders of such notes in the event of bank failure. In this regard, legislation was such that it discouraged weak financial institutions from circulating notes.

The prevailing view in the Colonial Office was that, as banking in the colonial empire was predominantly in the hands of large British and Canadian concerns with many years' experience, there was no need for specific legislation to monitor their business operations there.[45] This was clearly expressed in the advice from the Colonial Office to colonial governments, which stated that "in colonies which are fortunate enough to have banking facilities provided by larger British institutions or their equivalent, elaborate banking legislation . . . is probably unnecessary".[46]

At any rate, the requirements of the Companies Act, 1929, and the banking legislation of the Dominion states were considered sufficient for monitoring the British and Canadian banks. Canadian legislation was considered more than sufficient; its comprehensive nature was a result of central banking, which existed by the mid-1930s. The same was true in South Africa and Australia. Legislation pertaining to banking in these countries covered areas such as capital and reserve requirements, the relationship of cash to deposits, interest rates, accounts and returns as well as general inspection. In addition, banks were defined, and provision was made for their authorization. Legislation in the Dominion states also placed strict limits on the activities of deposit banks, some of which affected their ability to hold real estate and to invest in industry, and mortgage business was either prohibited or severely restricted.[47]

The Colonial Office argued against more comprehensive legislation on the grounds that the phenomenon known as "mushroom" banking had yet to develop in the West Indies.[48] The term *mushroom banks* referred to the indigenous banks that grew rapidly, almost overnight, and most of which were very weak, operating on a small capital base. The prevailing view was that comprehensive bank regulation was required only in the event of the proliferation of indigenous concerns. The bias in favour of larger concerns was evident in the advice sent out to the West Indies in 1949 by the secretary of state for the colonies, A. Creech-Jones, which read in part:

> On the other hand, it would appear that where banking operations are likely to be extended considerably to meet the increased demands of trade and commerce, local colonial governments should possess the necessary powers to exercise a reasonable degree of control over the companies conducting such operations . . . Where, however, it is felt that some measures are needed these could probably be confined to provisions dealing with the small bank, and in particular guarding against the "mushroom" bank.[49]

The development of mushroom banks was witnessed in Cyprus, Hong Kong and Palestine in the 1930s. In the 1920s, 37 banks operated in Palestine; by the middle of 1935 there were 113, with about 50 branches, many of which were reported to be based on grossly inadequate capital.[50] They were considered irresponsible because, in their quest to compete with the larger and better established banks, they undertook business which the more orthodox concerns refused to touch and offered rates and terms far more favourable than what was considered sound banking practice. As a result, their operations were precarious – and prone to cause instability in the financial sector, which the authorities were anxious to guard against.[51]

As this situation had yet to materialize in the West Indies, the Colonial Office's policy was to maintain a "watch", and to wait to introduce new provisions until the problem arose.[52] The banking crisis which occurred in Palestine in 1936 had certainly alerted the authorities to the possibility. Following that crisis, the Bank Ordinance, 1937, amending the principal Ordinance, was passed; it resulted in a compulsory diminution in the number of banks and an increase in their solvency and general soundness. The important provisions stipulated for new banks a minimum registered share capital of £p50,000, half of which had to be paid up within three months from the date of application. Existing banks were required to increase their registered share capital to £p25,000 and their paid-up capital to £p10,000 immediately, and within two years – that is, by October 1939 – to the prescribed minimum. Foreign banks were required to have capital of £100,000 and to publish annually in the press a statement of their assets and liabilities. Restrictions were placed on the use of the word *bank,* in titles where it was considered to be misleading and in regard to who was eligible to serve on boards of directors.

Following the implementation of this legislation, the number of banks in Palestine was gradually reduced. In October 1937 there were sixty-eight local banks. During December 1937 and January 1938, nineteen banks indicated that they did not intend to carry on business, followed shortly thereafter by eight more. Amalgamation further reduced the number by three, and two that had closed their doors were struck off the list of registered banks. This process continued until 1941, when the number of banks had fallen to thirty-two.[53]

The Banking Law, No. 31, 1960, and the Bank of Jamaica Act, No. 32, 1960

It was not until 1960 that a comprehensive banking law was passed which sought to regulate the operations of commercial banks. This was in Jamaica as that island prepared for full political independence from Britain. The Banking Law, No. 31, 1960, reflected concern for the maintenance of financial stability and the integrity of the banking system, and gave the government extensive regulatory power over commercial banks in the region for the first time.[54]

The law consolidated many provisions that were already in force. It specified that a licence from the Ministry of Finance must be obtained to carry on the business of banking. It provided for the publication of balance sheets and for the submission of returns to a government inspector of banks. The law also defined the terms *banking* and *banking business,* prohibited banks from engaging in certain classes of business, and restricted banking business to normal banking operations. Section 10 stipulated that a bank was not to engage in any trade other than the normal operations of a bank and the due performance of its function as a trustee, executor or administrator or as attorney for any such person. Banks were prohibited from acquiring land, except for their operations and for housing their employees, and in the ordinary course of banking operations and services including the satisfaction of debts owed to them.[55] These stipulations were intended to prevent companies from conducting business that was incompatible with what was normally understood to be banking operations and which was liable to lead to the fleecing of unsuspecting depositors.

Other provisions included minimum capital and reserve requirements. Section 5 stipulated a minimum subscribed capital of £100,000, half of which had to be paid up in cash at the time of the application for a bank licence. Section 6 required each bank to maintain a reserve fund into which, at the end of each year, 10 per cent of the net profits were to be transferred, until the reserves were equal to the amount of the authorized capital of each bank. Section 7 prohibited any bank from incurring liabilities exceeding twenty times the amount of its paid-up capital and reserve fund.[56]

All of these stipulations were really a safeguard against the development of the mushroom phenomenon and were hardly likely to be applied to the established banks such as Barclays Bank (DCO), whose authorized capital was raised from £15 million to £25 million in 1961. Its paid-up capital for that year stood at £17 million.[57] Certainly, neither Barclays Bank (DCO) nor the Canadian banks and, by then, City Bank and the Bank of London and Montreal (BOLAM) – all of which were part of big multinational conglomerates – were obliged to comply with these provisions. The law provided for this, stating in section 22 that the Minister of [Finance], ". . . upon the application of any bank not incorporated in Jamaica for exemption from provisions of sections 5, 6, 7, may after consultation with the inspector if he is satisfied that the financial position of that bank is sound, by order grant the application". At the same time, it was specifically stated that all banks which had head offices outside of Jamaica were required to maintain a principal office in Jamaica and appoint one of its officers as an authorized agent in the island.

This stipulation seems to have been aimed at the new multinational banks, particularly American, that were beginning to show an interest in investing in the island, and was not really applicable to the British and Canadian banks which had already established principal offices in the 1940s and 1950s.[58]

Of greater significance were the provisions which gave the Government of Jamaica, through the Bank of Jamaica, the means by which to impinge directly upon the operations of the commercial banks. In June 1961 the Bank of Jamaica, the first central bank established in the region, was opened, with power vested in it through the Bank of Jamaica Act,

No. 32, 1960. In addition to its duties of implementing policies consistent with monetary stability, maintaining the external value of the local currency and fostering the development of money and capital markets, the central bank was charged with regulating the money supply and controlling the volume of credit "so as to promote the fullest expansion in production, trade and employment".[59] Under section 11 of the law, all commercial banks were obligated to maintain cash reserves of not less than the average of 5 per cent of their total deposit liabilities at the Bank of Jamaica, which had the power to vary this percentage from time to time, up to a maximum of 15 per cent.[60] This meant that, for the first time, the commercial banks no longer had unlimited freedom to transfer funds out of the country for investment purposes.

In addition, the Bank of Jamaica was given the power to dictate lending policy to the commercial banks. It was able to prescribe the maximum amount of loans and advances that commercial banks could make for any period it might decide, and to apply this limit either generally or to specific classes of lending. Other pertinent provisions included the power to fix the bank rate and to conduct open market operations.[61] The central bank also assumed all the responsibilities of the island's currency board, including the sole right and authority to issue and redeem notes and coins. This provision did not abrogate the right of Barclays Bank (DCO) to issue its own banknotes, though by then that bank had ceased to issue notes in the territory.[62]

All of these stipulations were in keeping with the general notion of what was regarded as the role and function of central banks in modern economies. They were neither new nor revolutionary; the idea that central banks were responsible for the formulation and implementation of monetary policy had taken firm root during the inter-war period, particularly in the self-governing parts of the British Commonwealth and in parts of Latin America. It was only to be expected that as the territories in the West Indies attained political independence they would want to pursue a monetary policy which was perceived as being suited to their own domestic needs.[63] Nevertheless, in the context of the preceding period, during which the government played a relatively limited regulatory role, the Banking Law of 1960 and the law establishing the Bank of Jamaica marked a turning point in the history of commercial bank regulation in the region.

Summary

A strong tradition of regulation of the commercial banking sector, established in the early nineteenth century when British multinational banks began to make their appearance in the world, was maintained in the West Indies through the first half of the twentieth century. A desire for financial stability and probity was uppermost in the minds of the framers of the regulations, and this was reflected in both the Colonial Banking Regulations and those regulations that pertained to local indigenous commercial banks and the Canadian banks. Nevertheless, the regulation of the sector was subject to inconsistency and a certain degree of haphazardness. This was most noticeable in relation to the security requirements and circulatory limits on currency notes issued by the respective banks. The difference in imperial policy towards potential local commercial banks on the one hand and the British and Canadian banks on the other certainly contributed to the lack of uniformity. The general view was that since commercial banking was in the hands of sound British and Canadian institutions, there was no need for comprehensive regulation of the sector. Indeed, imperial advice to colonial governments was that they should introduce regulations only when it appeared that local banking institutions were likely to emerge.

Nevertheless, bank regulations for the West Indian commercial banking sector possessed modern features in terms of paid-up capital requirements, inspection and publication of financial statements. The overall concern was the protection of the interests of shareholders and depositors, and holders of currency notes issued by the banks and commercial banks. At the same time, commercial banks enjoyed a great deal of latitude with respect to their day-to-day operations. They could obtain the cash they needed from the local currency authority, and credit continued to be a matter for their own discretion. Nor were there legal requirements regarding capital and reserves which they had to observe in the respective colonies in which they operated.[64]

In general, then, for much of the period under review, commercial banks remained unfettered by government legislation as far as their overall operations were concerned. This remained so until the advent of central banking in Jamaica in 1961. It was also during this period that the long-held right of the commercial banks to issue currency notes came under significant challenge as the monetary system in the region underwent reform. This raises the question of the role that British colonialism played in facilitating a low level of government control over commercial banking in the West Indies, which is explored in the next chapter.

Chapter Six

Reform of the Currency System in the West Indies, 1930–1962

The reform of the currency system involved the establishment of a sterling exchange standard and entailed replacing the government currency note issue with new notes that were backed by sterling reserves held in London. The ultimate objective was the establishment of a common West Indian currency note issue, administered by a single regional currency board. This chapter examines the process of achieving that objective.

The monetary system in the West Indies has often been discussed in the context of the "economics" of the currency-board system – in other words, whether the system, by its very nature, hindered the economic development of the participating territories. This issue was much debated by monetary economists in the 1950s, with very little attention being paid to the actual reform and what it entailed.[1] This chapter demonstrates that the issues raised during the reform of the monetary system are significant as they reveal the change in the attitude and thinking of British and colonial government officials towards commercial bank operations. It was during this period that the position of the banks' currency note issue in relation to that of the colonial governments was raised. Circulatory limits on the banknote issues were imposed, which eventually led to their withdrawal altogether. In addition, the reorganization of the currency-board system generated the possibility of restrictions being imposed on the commercial banks' foreign exchange transactions. In this respect, the period is particularly significant, especially set against the background of the nineteenth century, when commercial bank operations in the West Indies were relatively free from government restrictions and control.

In some respects, the currency-board system in the West Indies can be viewed as the precursor to central banking. In this regard it can be likened to the early European central banks, which, when first established, were not assigned any supervisory role over other banks. As noted by Charles Goodhart, in their initial stages European central banks' functions were solely to bring order to a chaotic currency system and to centralize, manage and protect the metallic reserve of the country and improve the payments system. Goodhart continues:

> In any case, prior to 1900, most economic analysis of the role of central banks concentrated on the issue of whether the note issue should be centralized, and if and when centralized, how controlled by the central banks. Over time, these functions led these central banks to become the bankers' bank; and as commercial banks came to rely on the central banks for extra liquidity during times of crisis, the central banks assumed regulatory and supervisory roles over the banking system.[2]

This evolution was evident during the early twentieth century, particularly during the inter-war period, when governments across Europe instituted policies to manage their money supply that included exchange controls, various trade regulations and restrictions on movement of capital, all of which affected the operations of commercial banks.[3]

The currency-board system was essentially a money-changing accounting system. It had a specific function, that of maintaining the convertibility of West Indian currency to sterling and vice versa. It did not have control over the commercial banks' ability to create or restrict credit, nor did it have the power to restrict the banks' movement of capital in and out of the territories in which they operated.[4] And while currency boards themselves did not evolve into central banks, their functions were eventually assigned and assumed by the central banks when they were first established in the region.[5] In this regard, the reform of the currency system, which included the reorganization of the currency boards, can be seen as the preliminary step towards greater regulatory control over banking activity in the West Indies.

The Establishment of the Sterling Exchange Standard

The reform of the currency system and the establishment of the sterling exchange standard in the various West Indian territories in the 1930s has to be viewed in the context of the difficulty of maintaining stable exchange rates which plagued the international economy during the inter-war period. Following the end of World War I, most countries returned to a fixed gold parity with the hope of stabilizing their currencies. However, because of the high tariff walls erected by most nations, ostensibly with a view to protecting their reserves, many countries soon found it increasingly difficult to settle their international debt payments. The situation was aggravated by the depression in world commodity prices which began in the early 1920s, reached its lowest depths with the American stock market crash in 1929 and continued throughout the 1930s. These events forced all the major industrialized countries off the gold standard.[6]

Immediately after Britain left the gold standard in 1931, the pound sterling fell heavily in relation to other currencies that were still on a gold standard of exchange. So as not to be placed at a trade disadvantage, many other countries whose main export market was Britain sought to tie their currencies to sterling, to remain convertible and to ensure some measure of stability in the exchange relationship of their currencies. All these countries were encouraged to fix their currencies to the pound sterling and to hold some or all of their reserves in sterling. This development, in effect, created what became known as the Sterling Area, which represented one facet of the regional currency blocs into which the international community became divided during the 1930s as most nations pursued policies of increased protectionism and greater regulation of their financial transactions. This Sterling Area or Bloc included not only territories of the British empire, but also a large group of countries economically dependent on Britain, some of which were in Europe.[7]

In the British empire itself, the holding of sterling as a reserve asset and for transaction purposes had begun before 1913. The 1923 Imperial Economic Conference recommended that this practice should be increased, especially in light of the growth in importance of empire trade in Britain's foreign trade following World War I. Exports of British goods to the empire grew from 35 per cent in 1909–13 to 41 per cent by 1934–38, while net imports into Britain from the empire grew from 26.9 per cent to 41.2 per cent for the same periods.[8]

In the West Indies, however, up to the mid-1930s, the existing currency arrangements did not entail the holding of sterling as a reserve backing. Currency in the West Indies included government currency notes, which had been introduced for the first time in a number of colonies between 1900 and 1920. The first issue of government notes was made in the Turks and Caicos Islands immediately after the passing of the Currency Note Ordinance of 1902, and the second issue was in Trinidad in 1906. Though Jamaica passed the Currency Note Law 27 in 1904 authorizing the issue of government notes, it was not until March 1920 that the first set of notes, amounting to £17,500, was issued. The various commercial banks operating in the region also issued their own banknotes, and all of these currency notes, both governments' and banks', were legally based on British gold and silver coin as well as on US gold coins, all of which were unlimited legal tender. Cupro nickel coins in Jamaica and British copper coins in the rest of the West Indian territories were also in circulation. British silver coins in denominations of 5s, 2s, 1s and 6d were legal tender without limit, while 2s, 3d, 4d, 2d and 1½d were limited up to £2 in Jamaica. The copper coin was legal tender up to the limit of 1s, and was in circulation in all the West Indian territories except Jamaica. British coins were also legal tender without limit in all the territories but were not in circulation in the 1920s. In addition, in all the colonies the US gold eagle was legal tender at £2 and 1s, and its multiples at proportionate rates, without limit, and the subdivisions of the gold doubloon were legal tender without limit in Jamaica, but none of these coins was in circulation in the 1920s.[9]

With British silver being the principal metallic currency in circulation, the practical basis of the region's currency was effectively on a silver exchange standard, so token British silver coins of an unlimited amount formed the backing of the government and bank currency notes that were in circulation. Such notes were issuable and redeemable in either gold or silver coin, and the coin portion of the Note Guarantee Fund was held in either gold or silver. Notes presented for redemption were redeemable in silver.[10]

But British silver coin was not a wholly satisfactory basis for West Indian currency, as silver did not possess unlimited legal tender in Britain, and its intrinsic value was appreciably less than its face value. Accordingly, it was difficult to dispose of a large amount of silver coin at its face value, and this difficulty was aggravated by the fact that the supply of silver coin exceeded the demand, both in Britain and in other parts of the empire. It was easy, therefore, to envisage the problems that could occur if, in the event of a trade recession, the demand for West Indian currency notes declined and a substantial contraction of the issue became desirable. The fact that British silver was not readily disposable in Britain might hamper such a contraction, and it was conceivable that in such circumstances the exchange relationship with sterling would be disturbed. Conversely, a satisfactory expansion of the currency could be impeded owing to a lack of available silver coin to pay for the notes.[11]

In the context of the current world economic conditions, then, it became expedient for currency in the West Indies to be placed on a sterling basis to ensure its continued convertibility and stability. To ensure that fluctuations in the demand for currency were met with minimum difficulty, it was necessary to establish a direct link with sterling by means of what became known as the sterling exchange standard.

The essence of the sterling exchange standard was that the participating countries would hold external sterling assets to the full extent of local currency issues and would establish complete external convertibility of the local currency issue with sterling at a fixed exchange rate. The essential change involved the replacement of the existing government note issues with new notes which, instead of being in the form of "promises to pay" the amount of the face value, were inscribed "legal tender for the payment of any amount" and were backed by sterling reserves held in London. The new notes would then be issuable and redeemable in exchange for UK silver coin, with a limited legal tender up to 40s, as was the case in the United Kingdom, and exchangeable for the payment of sterling. This phase of the reform process was completed by the late 1930s. In Trinidad and Tobago, British Guiana, and the Leeward and Windward Islands where the dollar decimal system was in force, colonial dollars were established at a rate of $4.80 to the pound sterling. In Jamaica, the unit of currency was the Jamaica pound, which maintained parity with the UK pound.[12]

Government Note Issues in Relation to Banknote Issues

The reform of the currency system in the West Indies also involved the expansion of the government note issue. It was in connection with the contemplated reform of the currency system that a clear policy objective regarding the future relationship of commercial banknotes to the government currency note issue was first enunciated. The Currency Committee Report of 1923 recommended the introduction of government currency notes of higher denominations in the form of "legal tender for the payment of any amount", rather than being restricted to the low denominations of the older "promises to pay" issue. The purpose was to remove the commercial banks' monopoly on the issue of higher denominations, making the profits of such issues available to the various colonial governments.[13] The establishment of a common West Indian government note issue, managed by an amalgamated West Indian currency board similar to that established for West Africa, was also recommended as an ultimate objective of the reform process.[14]

This aspect of the reform process, however, was delayed for a number of reasons – including lack of consensus, as Jamaica clearly stated that it did not want to be part of a common West Indian government note issue. While Trinidad was not averse to the idea, its government questioned the financial benefits to be gained from such an arrangement, given the cost of administration. Perhaps more important was the refusal of the Treasury to redeem the surplus British silver coin then in circulation in the West Indies, given that there was no demand in Britain at that time and no prospect of a demand arising in the foreseeable future. So the reform of the system concentrated solely on replacement of the existing government note issues in the mid-1930s.[15] Attention was also given to the demonetization of US dollar currency and gold coins, such as the silver half and quarter dollars, along with the doubloon and Spanish silver dollar coins.[16]

Recognizing that the reform process had to be piecemeal, the

Colonial Office elected to carry on a constant review of the relative positions of the commercial banks' currency notes and the government issue, always bearing in mind the ultimate objective of the introduction of a common West Indian government note issue. This was expressed in an official memo that read, in part:

> I think our general policy should be to aim eventually at a single currency for the West Indies, that is a single note issue managed by a West Indian currency board with UK coin as subsidiary coinage. It is clearly impossible at present to bring such a system into operation at one step. I think our policy ought therefore to be to modernize the existing note issues and bring them into common form . . . to bear the general object in view where any question arises of renewing or revising the existing note issue privileges of the various banks . . . I think that if we pursue these various objects it may be found in a few years time that the various note issues can be amalgamated and the general object stated above achieved with a minimum of disturbance.[17]

So it was during the reform process in the 1930s that the future of the commercial banknotes in relation to the government note issue was raised for the first time. Nonetheless, Colonial Office policy remained ambivalent into the early 1940s. Throughout much of the nineteenth century, the official policy was to discourage governments from issuing currency notes, this being viewed as the prerogative of commercial banks. As a result, currency notes issued by the commercial banks in the West Indies were established as the principal medium of circulation.[18] This arrangement was satisfactory to the British government, as it left colonial governments free of the responsibilities of printing and distributing currency notes.

By the late nineteenth century this general attitude towards banknote issues was beginning to change. This was largely as a result of the collapse of the Oriental Bank Corporation in 1884 and the subsequent actions of the governor of Ceylon, who, fearing a financial panic in the colony, guaranteed the bank's note issue with colonial revenues and thus "saddled his administration with the liabilities of the bank's debacle".[19] Hence, government currency notes were introduced in the West Indies in the early 1900s. Notwithstanding this change in policy, commercial banknotes continued to be viewed as an important aspect of the currency system in the West Indies, providing a valuable service in the monetization of the region. Indeed, the importance attached to the banknote issue in the region was indicated by the fact that during periods of war, banknotes were made legal tender.[20]

Further evidence of the Colonial Office's ambivalence is the fact that, to avoid competition, the initial government currency note issues were restricted to denominations that were not covered by the commercial banks. In Trinidad and Tobago, British Guiana and the Leeward and Windward Islands, commercial banks issued notes in denominations of $5, $10, $50 and $100. Therefore, in Trinidad and Tobago, government note issues were restricted to denominations of $1,000, $2 and $1; in British Guiana, $2 and $1; and in the Windward and Leeward Islands, 10s and 5s.[21] In Jamaica the first set of notes were in denominations of 10s and 5s, while British Treasury notes in denominations of £1 and 10s, which previously had been in circulation, were placed on the same footing as current coin and were exchangeable for currency notes. Barclays Bank (DCO) and the Canadian banks operating in that colony issued notes in amounts of £1 and multiples thereof.[22]

As colonial governments contemplated the necessary legislative amendments required for the introduction of the new government currency notes based on sterling and sought the approval of the Colonial Office, it was evident that colonial officials believed that their currency notes should not continue to be at a disadvantage against those of the commercial banks. A clear indication of this position is reflected in the following statement from Barbados when the question of reform was first raised in 1929:

> As far as Barbados is concerned notes of such small denominations could not conveniently replace coin. Moreover, if there were material advantage in small denomination notes, the banks would have sought ere this authority for their issue. Ten shillings, if sterling, or $2^1/$_2$, if decimal coinage be adopted, seem to be the lowest denominations in which notes might be likely to be of service, while values of £1 sterling, or alternatively $5, or higher amounts than these would alone be certain of being useful as well as profitable. I do not think that competition with the banks should make the issue of such notes impracticable.[23]

The various colonial governments maintained this position in the mid-1930s. Trinidad also believed that if its government currency note issue was to be expanded, it should have similar denominations to that of the commercial banks.[24] The British Guiana government was equally

Plate 6.1 Banknote issued in British Guiana, 1934. Crossley and Blandford, *DCO Story*, vi.

explicit, arguing that "it would be unreasonable and contrary to the interests of the colony to regard the privileges presently enjoyed by the banks as perpetually preclusive of the profitable right which the colony possesses to issue its own notes of any and every denomination".[25] To rectify this position, British Guiana proposed to give the banks three years' notice, informing them that the government intended to issue its own currency notes of similar denominations to the banks', and pointed out that legislation for this purpose was already in existence. The government further noted that it was under no legal obligation to give notice to Barclays Bank (DCO) of such an intention.[26]

Two lines of argument ensued in the Colonial Office on this matter raised by British Guiana. Sydney Caine, a senior financial adviser in the Colonial Office, while not in favour of an immediate withdrawal of the banks' note-issuing rights, as proposed by British Guiana, favoured the introduction of higher-denominated government currency notes. As he saw it, pursuing such a policy with the new note issue was the first step in the gradual substitution of government note issues for banknote issues which would eventually lead to the introduction of a common note issue for the region.[27] But most of the Colonial Office officials concerned with the issue were not in favour of such action and remained unconvinced by Caine's argument. R. Burns, for example, argued, "I do not see that the introduction now of government notes of higher denominations will make a general West Indian issue any easier to attain at some future date. If these notes are necessary for that purpose they can be introduced much nearer the date of amalgamation."[28]

Another view had it that "to have a variety of paper currencies [was] a nuisance".[29] More important, it was argued that as "the banks in the West Indies [had] rights of note issue whose unconditional maxima [were] regarded as more than sufficient to cover the normal requirements of the territories", this left "an inconsiderable and uncertain margin for an expanded government note issue".[30] It was considered unwise to introduce a government note issue which, it was felt, could not hope to be competitive against the banks' note issue, given that government notes were legal tender only in the colony of issue, whereas the latter had a West Indian circulation. Given this advantage, it was further argued that the banks' note issue could "immobilize" the government issue, which colonial governments – some of them, particularly British Guiana, in a precarious financial position – could ill afford at that time.[31] Indeed, Burns expressed the view that "to balance this doubtful future gain we have the immediate risk of the issue being partly or wholly frozen out as Mr. Beckett suggests and I should not have thought that British Guiana's finances were such as to shoulder even the comparatively small loss on printing".[32] British Guiana was therefore advised not to pursue the suggestion it had put forward.[33]

One can argue that the basis of the reluctance to curtail or to withdraw the privilege of note issue from the commercial banks was confidence in the functioning of the banknote issue and the feeling that it could not be adequately matched by a government note issue at that time. It was also argued that there were no good grounds for depriving the banks of their rights of note issue and circulation and that, in any event, government notes would not be preferred over banknotes.[34]

There was also a valid concern about stability. It must be borne in mind that the reform of the currency system in the West Indies took place against the background of a phenomenal bank collapse, particularly in the United States.[35] The Colonial Office was reluctant to take any action that might have cast doubt on the stability and integrity of the major financial institutions in the region which could result in panic.

The wartime conditions of the 1940s also inspired caution about advancing the government note issue at the expense of banknotes. This concern was reflected in the response of the secretary of state to the

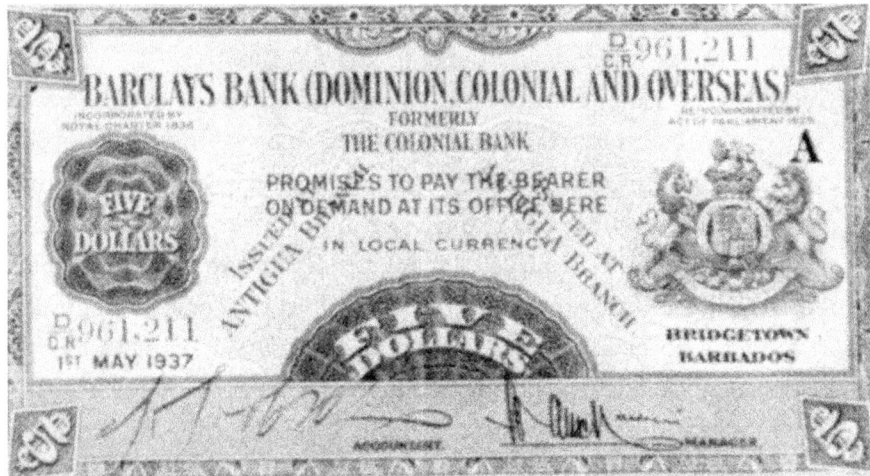

Plate 6.2 Banknote issued in Barbados, 1937. Crossley and Blandford, *DCO Story*, xiv.

Jamaica government's proposal in 1941 to instruct all heads of government departments to insist on the use of government currency notes for payments made on behalf of the government.[36] It was pointed out that while the long-term policy was that government notes would replace banknotes as the principal medium of circulation in the West Indies, "precipitate and enforced withdrawal of banknotes might, however, have serious financial consequences by shaking the public's confidence in all banks or in a particular bank".[37]

The fact was that the Colonial Office continued to see the banknote issue as being an important element of the West Indian currency system. The prevailing view was that in colonial regions where commercial development remained relatively basic and unsophisticated, metropolitan banking institutions such as Barclays Bank (DCO), which had wide experience throughout the world, were in a better position than colonial governments to manage the currency note requirements. Certainly, this was reflected in the security arrangements for the government note issue. As a reserve backing for the government currency issue, the currency commissioners of the respective colonies were required to hold a 100 per cent reserve made up of UK and Commonwealth securities held in a Note Guarantee Fund. In the case of Jamaica, the reserve backing constituted 110 per cent as a consequence of the subsidiary Jamaican coinage circulating in that colony. For this purpose, a Subsidiary Coinage Fund similar to the Note Security Fund, consisting of 10 per cent in reserves of the coins outstanding, was established.[38] The added require-

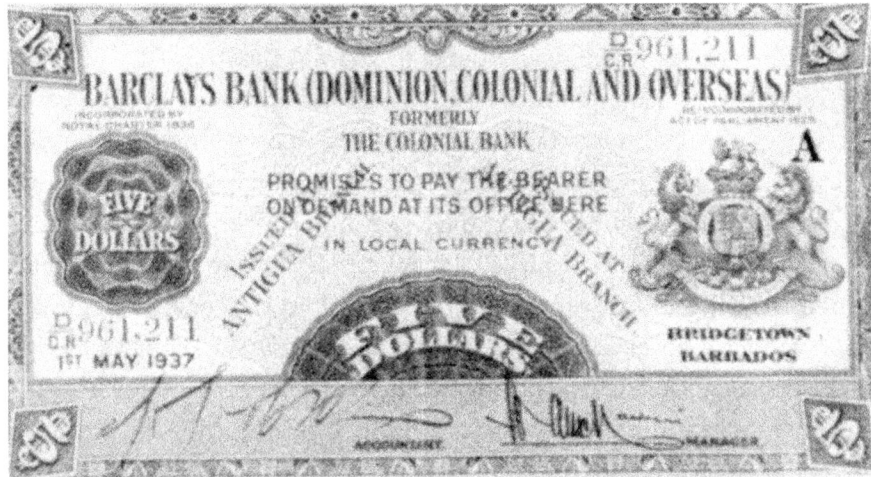

ment that currency funds were not to be invested in the stock of the local government was intended to ensure that, should there be economic difficulties in the territory, the holdings of the currency fund would not be diminished at a time when there might be substantial calls on it to redeem excess currency.[39]

In December 1938, Barclay's Bank (DCO) was granted permission by the Treasury for an increase on its limit of £750,000 to £1,000,000 for six months, to expire on 30 June 1939. In 1938, when the bank's request was being considered, it was acknowledged that there was little to prevent the expansion of the government note issue in the West Indies. Indeed, it was noted that conditions had changed in the recent years "in as much as the machinery for an expanded government note issue now [existed], and that no undertaking [had] been given to the banks that government notes [should] be only for $1 and $2, and that the silver position referred to in the Report of 1923 [had] been more or less cleared up".[40] Nevertheless, the Treasury official continued:

> On the other hand, it seems to me very unlikely that you will want the governments to issue such notes which would either be less popular than those of the bank's in which case the whole of any such issue would have to be redeemed after each seasonal peak, or would compete effectively with banknotes at all times, which would be contrary at least to the spirit of the arrangements under which the banks are allowed to issue.[41]

The statement clearly reveals the UK government's ambivalence towards currency reform in the West Indies, and the uncertainty about whether government currency notes would be accepted as the principal means of exchange.

Barclays Bank (DCO) applied for an increase in its circulatory limit because it expected that, as the build-up to war in Europe progressed, changes in the economic environment in the West Indies would result in an increased demand for banknotes. Changes in the West Indies in the late 1930s included a substantial increase in oil production in Trinidad and Tobago, as well as that colony's five-year programme of public works. In addition, record increases in sugar production in Barbados, British Guiana, and Trinidad and Tobago had brought about a swell in the wage bill, which contributed to an increased demand for currency notes.[42]

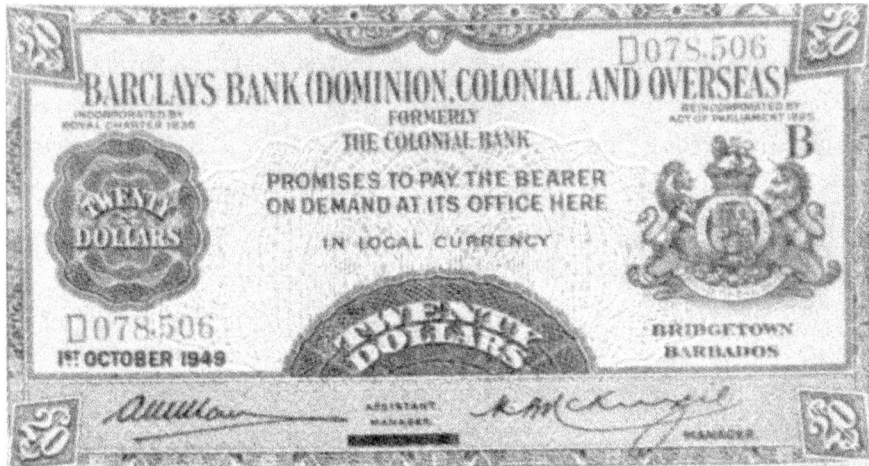

Plate 6.3 Banknote issued in Barbados, 1949. Crossley and Blandford, *DCO Story*, xiv.

Further expansion, particularly in connection with the construction of American naval bases in the West Indies, was to warrant additional increases and extensions of Barclays Bank (DCO)'s circulatory limit in the region. In 1939, the £1,000,000 limit was extended by twelve months to 30 June 1940, and thereafter a further increase, to £1,500,000 until 31 December 1941, was approved. This excess was subsequently increased to £1,750,000 and extended to 31 December 1942 (see Figure 6.1).[43]

In effect, the Colonial Office was caught unprepared in making

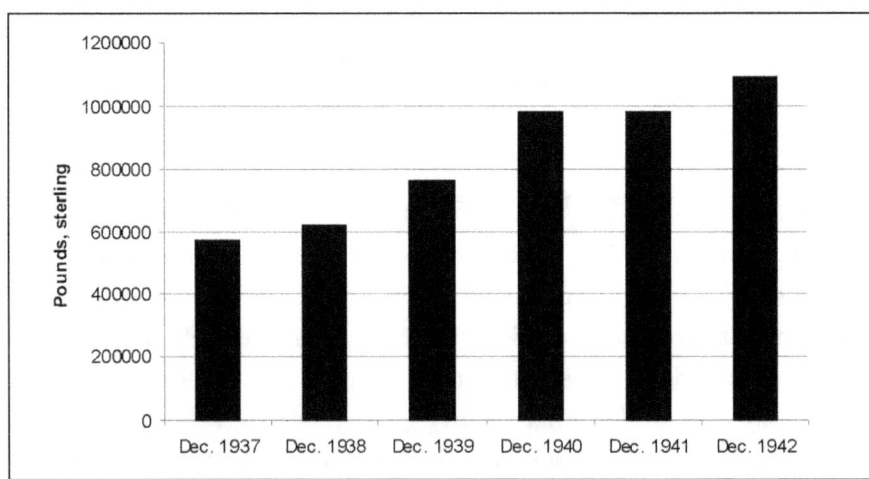

Figure 6.1 Barclays Bank (DCO), note circulation in the West Indies, 1937–1942
Source: Barclays Bank (DCO) West Indian Branches, Notes in Circulation, 14 July 1942, CO 852/359/2; Barclays Bank (DCO), Note Circulation in the West Indies and British Guiana, 31 December 1942, CO 852/359/3.

adequate arrangements to enable an expansion of the government note issue as opportunities presented themselves during the war. Following the initial approval of the increase on the bank's circulatory limit, J. Fisher of the Bank of England, in a letter to the Colonial Office in 1939, voiced his concern that the Colonial Office was not taking advantage of the circumstances on which an expansion of the government note issue could be based.

> It is not clear to me why the governments' legal tender note issues are limited to denominations of $1 and $2. I should have thought that if the increase in currency in circulation is to be regarded as permanent, (and if it is to expand further), the proper solution would be for the government to issue higher denomination notes and so provide for that part of the increased demand ... The modern tendency is towards decreasing and not increasing the note issues of commercial banks and I much doubt if section 19 (8) of the Colonial Bank Act of 1925 was intended to provide for what may well prove to be a permanent increase in the amount of Barclays note issue in the West Indies and British Guiana.[44]

Arrangements were subsequently made to send extra supplies of government currency notes to the West Indies. But delivery was severely delayed, mainly as a result of air-raid damage to the printing works in London, and the Colonial Office was left with no choice but to approve further increases in Barclays Bank (DCO)'s note issues.[45]

Local-Metropolitan Clash over Banking Policy

The approval of the increases to Barclays Bank (DCO)'s circulatory limit provoked a strong reaction from the government in Jamaica. On being informed that the bank had been granted a further increase in its circulatory limit in 1941, the Jamaica government replied to the secretary of state for the colonies, indicating that it intended to issue £1 notes and stating that the encouragement of the banknote issue was undesirable. Governor Richards suggested that

> it is perhaps desirable to bear in mind that with the introduction of a government [£1] note issue ... the encouragement of the banknote issue by Barclays and, or Canadian banks in business here is not desirable. From this angle it might perhaps be considered whether any purpose is served in continuing a general authority applicable to the West Indies as a whole.[46]

This response from Jamaica reflected the tensions that had developed in the early 1940s between the Jamaica government and the commercial banks over the whole question of the currency note issue. There was deep-seated resentment on the part of members of the government that the government issue had not yet been made the monopoly note issue in the colony. They also resented the fact that the higher security requirements for the government issue placed it at a disadvantage vis-à-vis the banknote issue, in spite of legislation which would have removed the discrepancy. Governor Richards pointed out that "it was one [position], which from the purely Jamaican standpoint, cannot but be regarded with some misgivings".[47]

Clearly, the colonial governments' attitude towards commercial bank note-issuing privileges had changed. One indication was the imposition in 1939 of a heavy tax of 2.5 per cent, which represented a 150 per cent increase over the previous rate on the banks' note issue in circulation. In addition, the Government of Jamaica took steps to introduce £1 government currency notes into circulation in August 1941. The stated objective of this two-pronged attack was that of "[restricting] the maximum issue of the commercial banks [by keeping] the royalty paid by banks on note issues at as high a premium to discourage issue".[48]

This strategy marked a significant departure from the previous terms of the relationship between Jamaica's commercial banks and the colonial government. While local taxes had always been levied on banknotes in circulation, they were intended to raise revenue, not to discourage the issuing of banknotes. In 1903, for instance, the Stamp Duty Law, No. 40, introduced a tax of 20s per £100 on the total notes in circulation. While this had been raised in 1916 to 60s, it was subsequently reduced back to 20s by the Stamp Duty Law, Further Amendment Law 1929. In fact, the stated reason for the reduction was to avoid infringing on the banks' £1 note issue.[49]

Further evidence of the cooling of the colonial government's attitude towards the commercial banks was the fact that the government's decision to introduce its own £1 note issue was taken without prior consultation with the banks. Seen as a deliberate breach of protocol, the snub indicated the government's level of resentment over the note issues. On top of that, the commercial banks were formally requested to use only government notes for payments on behalf of the government throughout Jamaica, notwithstanding that banknotes were also legal tender.[50]

The issuance of paper currency by the banks was an extremely lucrative undertaking, since very little was spent on the printing and distribution, and significant profits could be made from the currency depreciation fund securities held on their behalf by the Crown Agents. For example, on a note issue valued at £1 million, two-thirds of which was invested, the yield from the security fund would total £18,750 per annum (or 2.5 per cent per annum).[51] The Jamaica banknote issue tax of 2.5 per cent would obviously reduce the returns, and Barclays Bank (DCO) claimed it made only 1 per cent on its securities deposited against the notes following the imposition of this tax.[52] As a result of this, the Kingston manager had recommended to the bank's London general managers that it might be worthwhile to consider reducing its own £1 note issue, substituting for it the government issue of that denomination:

> As you are aware, the note tax has been raised since the war to 2½ per cent and it would appear to me that you may desire to consider reducing our own £1 issue to a minimum in order to reduce the tax payable as much as is possible, and utilize the government £1 notes.[53]

The combination of high duty levied on banknotes in circulation and the introduction of a £1 government note had the effect of significantly increasing the government notes in circulation at the expense of the banknotes. Between August 1941 and March 1942, banknotes in circulation declined by nearly 50 per cent, while government notes in circulation increased dramatically, by almost 160 per cent. Barclays Bank (DCO)'s note circulation in Jamaica during the same period declined by as much as 47 per cent (see Figure 6.2).

The impact that the Jamaican tax had on Barclays Bank (DCO)'s note issue led to an examination of whether colonial governments had the right to impose such taxes on that bank's note issue. The bank was particularly vexed about the high level of taxes it was paying on its note circulation not only in Jamaica but in Trinidad and Tobago as well. In that colony, where an ad valorem tax of 1 per cent per annum on the average note circulation of the banks had been imposed, Barclays Bank (DCO) had paid £25,000 between 1932 and 1943. This was in addition to the annual licence fee of £100 and a £50 fee payable for each branch in operation. In Jamaica, an estimated £20,000 in taxes on the British bank's note

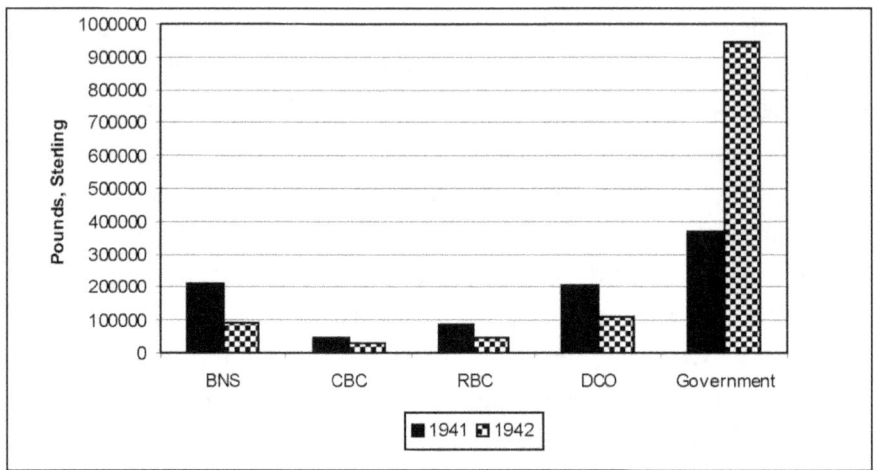

Figure 6.2 Currency notes in circulation, Jamaica, 1941–1942
Source: Chairman of the Board of Currency Commissioners, Jamaica, 10 April 1942, CO 852/359/4.

issue had been paid during the same period. The bank had paid a total of £12,500 for all the other islands and British Guiana.[54]

In its protest to the Colonial Office, Barclays Bank (DCO) argued that because its note-issuing privileges were derived from a British statute which prescribed the terms and conditions on which the issue could be made, the colonial governments had no legal basis on which to tax its note issue.[55] In addition, the bank contended that its excess note issue in the West Indies was made by an agreement with the Colonial Office that gave it the necessary statutory authority to meet an actual increase in demand for currency which supplies of government notes were unable to meet. It therefore objected to being "penalized" by the imposition of excessive taxation for a service which had the sanction of the Colonial Office.[56] The bank further stated that the Jamaica government's request that the banks use £1 government currency notes on behalf of the government throughout the island involved a principle with which it could not agree, especially as banknotes were legal tender in the island.[57]

Evidently, Barclays Bank (DCO) saw British colonialism as guaranteeing it some measure of protection from legislation that adversely affected its operations in the region. This explains the bank's appeals to the Colonial Office in the face of the hostile steps taken in Jamaica with regard to its note issue, and the premise upon which it based its argument. Theoretically, the bank was afforded some measure of a guarantee against hostile legislation. Given the terms of the colonial governments' relationship with the Colonial Office, colonial legislation emanating from the West Indies was subject to the terms of the Colonial Laws Validity Act, 1865. This Act read, in part:

> [A]ny colonial law which is or shall be in any respect repugnant to the provisions of any Act of Parliament extending to the colony to which such law may relate . . . shall be read subject to such Act . . . and shall to the extent of such repugnancy, but not otherwise, be and remain absolutely void and inoperative.[58]

While colonial governments were allowed some measure of legislative autonomy, the British government, through the Colonial Laws Validity Act, 1865, placed a check against colonial legislatures passing laws that were perceived to be repugnant to British imperial policy as embodied in the statutes passed by the British parliament. With respect to the note-issuing privileges of Barclays Bank (DCO) in the West Indies, theoretically, colonial legislation could not circumvent the provisions of the Colonial Bank Act, 1925, from which the British bank derived its operational powers in the colonies.

It soon became apparent, however, that there was a weakness in the Colonial Bank Act, 1925, regarding the interpretation of the provisions relating to the applicability of colonial legislation to Barclays Bank (DCO). Provision 35 of the Colonial Bank Act, 1925, stipulated that "a colonial legislature [did] not have the power to interfere with the constitution of the [Bank]" but went on to state that "nothing in [the] Act [exempted] the [Bank] from being otherwise subject to colonial law".[59] This meant that Jamaica, as well as Trinidad and Tobago, was legally permitted to introduce legislation regarding note issue to which the British bank would be subject so long as it did not interfere with its power to issue and circulate notes. Nevertheless, the question remained: with regard to the provisions of the Colonial Laws Validity Act, 1865, was colonial legislation that imposed a duty on the notes issued by the bank repugnant to the provisions of the Colonial Bank Act, 1925? This impasse became apparent as deliberations on the matter continued in the Colonial Office.

> It was expressed that as a colony, Jamaica could pass any legislation regarding note issues. That is to say, that apart from the complications raised by the

Colonial Bank Act, 1925, Jamaica could legally . . . pass an Act re saying no banks shall circulate banknotes in the colony and no person shall possess or pass a banknote. The field would then be free for a monopoly for a Jamaica or West Indian currency board note issue. But the Colonial Bank Act, 1925 seems to me to make it impossible for Jamaica to prohibit the circulation of the notes of the Bank to which it relates in Jamaica. On the other hand, I am not clear that there is anything in that Act to prevent Jamaica from raising a tax of three per cent, and for that matter five per cent or 50 per cent per annum on the notes of the Bank circulating in the colony.[60]

This was a question which the Colonial Office was unable to resolve by itself, since its legal advisers could not arrive at a proper interpretation of the Colonial Bank Act, 1925, so the matter was referred to the British attorney general.[61] Unfortunately for Barclays Bank (DCO), the attorney general was of the opinion that the power to issue banknotes and the conditions of the note issue were not a part of the bank's constitution. Accordingly, there was no legal basis for its appeal against taxes being imposed on its banknotes in circulation in the West Indies. After that decision, the bank finally dropped the matter in 1943.[62] Barclays Bank (DCO) therefore continued to be liable to pay taxes on its notes in circulation in Jamaica, as the colonial government did not consider it practicable to introduce legislation providing for a reduction in the rate of tax.[63]

A more satisfactory solution was found with the Trinidad and Tobago government. As it turned out, owing to an error in that colony's legislation, the bank had actually been exempted by local law from the tax payments on its note issue in that colony but had made payments on the basis of an improper interpretation of the local law.[64] Following negotiations with the Colonial Office and the Trinidad and Tobago government, the sum of £5,435, which had been paid under protest by the bank to the government in March 1942, was refunded, and the colonial government agreed to abandon its claim of £5,899 for the year ending March 1943. In addition, the government decided to reintroduce a fixed annual licence fee of £250 in respect of the note issue in place of the ad valorem basis of taxation.[65]

Changes in the Balance of Note Issues

The increased circulatory limit accorded to Barclays Bank (DCO) and Jamaica's objections to it can be regarded as a watershed in the currency reform process. Fisher's questioning of the Colonial Office policy on currency note circulation and the imbroglio sparked by Jamaica's banknote tax essentially forced the Colonial Office to act decisively. Accordingly, each bank was given a circulatory limit, and from 1 January 1943 the banks began to systematically reduce their notes, substituting government currency notes until the required limit was reached.

Barclays Bank (DCO)'s limit was £600,000, the statutory limit that had been specified in the Colonial Bank Act, 1925.[66] For the Canadian banks, global limits for the West Indies were arrived at by calculating the percentage reduction which would be required of Barclays Bank (DCO) based upon its average quarterly circulation for the period January 1937 to June 1942, and applying this percentage reduction to the Canadian banks' average note circulation for the same period. As Barclays Bank (DCO)'s average circulation for that period amounted to approximately £884,558, a 30 per cent reduction was required to bring it down to its prescribed limit of £600,000.[67] Therefore, a 30 per cent reduction was applied to the Canadian banks (see Table 6.1).[68]

The imposition of global limits on the Canadian banknote circulation introduced some uniformity and order to colonial legislation pertaining to currency matters. It also was a boon to Barclays Bank (DCO): despite the fact that the Canadian banks had been subjected to circulatory limits in some colonies, no global limit had previously been imposed on their note issue in the West Indies, whereas the British bank had been subjected to limits. In this respect, the imposition of a statutory limit as of

Table 6.1 Circulatory Limits on Banknotes, West Indies, 1942

Bank	Average Circulation 1937–1942 (£ sterling[a])	Global Limit (West Indies)
CBC	79,924	56,458
RBC	381,532	267,072
BNS	147,572	100,000
Barclays Bank (DCO)	884,558	600,000

[a]Amounts expressed in colonial dollars were converted to £ sterling using the rate $4.80 = £1.
Source: Fisher, Bank of England, to Colonial Office, 12 August 1942, CO 852/359/2.

1 January 1943 constituted a major curtailment of the note-issuing powers of the Canadian banks.[69]

This was the case especially for the BNS, which, from its inception in Jamaica, had operated without a limit and without having to comply with security requirements for its note issue. As of 1 January 1943, the BNS was required to deposit the equivalent of 25 per cent of its circulatory note issue limit with the Crown Agents – a requirement from which it had previously been exempted, unlike the other Canadian banks operating in the region. In this respect, the BNS arguably came off the worst, losing its privileged position under the new stipulations, and, accordingly, it initially opposed the new arrangements.[70] In addition to being piqued at having to comply with security requirements for its note issue, the BNS took umbrage at the imposition of a global limit, arguing that it was being placed at a disadvantage against the other three banks because it operated only in Jamaica. It complained that under the new legislation the bank could be subjected to unfair competition, as there was nothing preventing any of the other banks from concentrating their global limits in Jamaica and thereby undermining the BNS's operations there.[71]

The BNS was particularly concerned about Barclays Bank (DCO), its closest rival in Jamaica, and suggested that a specific limit be imposed on the British bank's note issue in that colony.[72] However, the BNS's concerns were regarded as mere "jibbing" by Colonial Office officials, who pointed out that it was highly unlikely that the bank would be subjected to unfair competition, given the prevailing high note-issue tax in Jamaica. Nevertheless, an undertaking was given which stated that if the BNS at any time had reason to believe other banks were concentrating their note issue in Jamaica they could make representation for a higher limit.[73]

The reduction to the stipulated limits of each bank began as of 1 January 1943 and was to have been completed by 30 June of that year, by which time the banks were expected to have reduced their circulation to an amount equal to or within their new limits.[74] However, the time allotted proved to be inadequate, and an extension for the withdrawal of the excess banknotes was given to 1 January 1944.[75] Even then, while Barclays Bank (DCO) and the BNS were able to meet this new deadline, the RBC and the CBC were unable to and were granted a further extension to 30 June 1944.[76]

The delay resulted mainly from the provision of inadequate amounts of government currency notes to replace the banknotes, which occurred because the authorities underestimated the level of demand. While they had built up reserve stocks of government currency notes equal to nearly 200 per cent of all currency notes (bank and government) in circulation in June 1942, this proved inadequate to cope with the demand which ensued during the second half of 1942 and 1943.[77] In Antigua the situation was even more complex. The Antigua government had approved an increase in the RBC's limit, to $150,000, in 1941, to cope with the demand resulting from the presence of the US bases in that colony. Upon being informed of the impending global limit being applied to the circulation of banknotes in the West Indies, the governor had written to say that he did not wish to see the limit curtailed as Antigua had no local issue of its own and was dependent on Trinidad and Tobago government notes, of which there was a shortage.[78]

The problem was compounded by the fact that the government issue had hitherto been restricted to low-denominated currency notes. It was not until the process of limiting the circulation of the banknotes was contemplated that the Colonial Office sanctioned the issue of high-denominated government currency notes. However, the authorities failed to provide adequate amounts of these notes. This proved to be a problem, especially in the territories where the construction of US naval bases was most extensive. The construction of the bases required a tremendous amount of labour, and the US military personnel preferred high-denominated currency notes for the payment of wages.[79] The difficulty was most acute in Trinidad and Tobago and British Guiana. As early as January 1942, reports out of Trinidad and Tobago were that the reserves of $5 government notes were inadequate to cope with the expected demand.[80] There was an even greater shortage of $20 government notes.[81] Under these circumstances the authorities had no alternative but to permit the banks to print new supplies of their banknotes for issue. This, of course, contributed to the swelling of the banknotes in circulation during the second half of 1942 and therefore prolonged the period of withdrawal of the excess during 1943.[82] The inadequate supply of high-denominated government currency notes continued to be a problem in the early months of 1943, so the banks had to reissue their own high-sum notes to meet the continued high demand, which contributed to the further delays in the reduction process.[83]

The hoarding of notes also prolonged the reduction process. The BNS had pointed out that 75 per cent of their outstanding circulation was in £5 denominations and that they suspected that many of these notes were being hoarded.[84] In February 1943, British Guiana seemed to confirm this:

> [While the] banks [are] taking [the] necessary steps to effect [the] desired reduction by issuing only currency notes . . . It is feared however, that required reduction of banknote circulation may not be completed by July 1, 1943, as outstanding banknotes are coming in very slowly. A fairly high proportion is in high denomination notes $20 and $100, part probably hoarded.[85]

The RBC and the CBC were particularly affected by the hoarding of banknotes. The two banks were the major holders of US army and navy accounts in the region and had made heavy wage payments on behalf of their clients. This meant that a significant amount of banknotes in the previous year had come into the possession of the labouring class, who were reluctant to deprive themselves of the novelty of holding such notes.[86]

Withdrawal of the Banks' Note-Issuing Privileges and the Establishment of the British Caribbean Currency Board

In effect, the imposition of circulatory limits on the banknote issue and the reduction process which followed were the preliminary steps in the withdrawal of note-issuing privileges from the banks. They were also prefatory to the ultimate objective of establishing a common West Indian note issue, managed by a central currency authority in the region.

Following the decision taken at the 1946 currency conference held in Barbados, the British Caribbean Currency Board (BCCB) was duly constituted in 1950, with its headquarters in Trinidad and Tobago. This body consisted of six members, five of whom represented the constituent territories – the Windward Islands, the Leeward Islands, Barbados, British Guiana, and Trinidad and Tobago (together known as the Eastern Group) – which had agreed to the introduction of a unified currency. The sixth member was the executive commissioner, who was appointed by the secretary of state for the colonies.[87]

The establishment of the BCCB in 1950 was not only an attempt to introduce economies in the organization of a currency system in the region. It should also be viewed in the context of the British government's desire to establish a federal government for the West Indies in preparation for the granting of independent status to the region. In effect, as noted by C.Y. Thomas, "the regional currency board established in 1950 gave functional reality to the idea of 'federation' ".[88]

The BCCB assumed all the liabilities, obligations and responsibility for the government currency notes which had been issued by currency authorities of the participating territories. In addition, the BCCB was given the sole right to issue currency notes and coin in the constituent territories. Legislation to this effect was enacted by the respective governments in 1950, and the note-issuing privileges of the commercial banks were rescinded. This was followed by the gradual retirement of the outstanding banknote issues, a process which began on 16 August 1951.[89] Legislation insofar as it related to currency notes came into effect on 1 August 1951, and currency notes were issued by the BCCB for the first time on 15 August 1951. Legislation relating to coin came into effect on 1 July 1955, with issues commencing on 15 November 1955. Individual government currency notes were demonetized with effect on 2 January 1955 in the participating colonies.[90]

Jamaica decided not to participate in the arrangement, preferring to maintain its own currency. This meant that the fully unified system which had been envisaged never materialized.[91] Nevertheless, some measure of a unified system involving Jamaica was instituted, as legislation enacted in the Eastern Group colonies made Jamaican currency notes legal tender at the rate of £1 to $4.80, effective from 1 October 1955. Similarly, BCCB currency notes were made legal tender in Jamaica at the rate of $1 to 4s 2d, effective as of the same date.[92]

Legislation withdrawing the note-issuing privileges from the commercial banks was enacted in Jamaica in 1954. The Bank Notes (Demonetization and Redemption) Law, No. 10, 1958, rescinded the legal tender status of banknotes in circulation in that colony. In addition, this law provided for the demonetization of all banknotes via an arrangement whereby the banks' liability for notes in circulation was transferred to the Jamaica government upon the banks' payment of the value in money of such notes to the accountant general.[93]

Table 6.2 Average Currency Notes in Circulation (£ Sterling) in Jamaica, 31 December 1946–1957

	1946–49	1950–53	1954–57
Government	2,836,832	3,975,813	6,722,992
BNS	42,880	24,995	0
RBC	8,020	4,686	0
CBC	5,754	2,977	0
Subtotal banknotes	56,674	32,658	0
Barclays Bank (DCO)	26,713	100,810	56,746
Total banknotes	83,387	133,468	56,746

Source: Compiled from *Report on Jamaica (Annual)* for the years 1946–58.

It should be noted that, while the note-issuing privileges of the Canadian banks in the West Indies were revoked by law in the constituent territories of the BCCB and Jamaica, that of Barclays Bank (DCO) was never abrogated.[94] This emphasized the distinctive position of the British bank, which was the result of the derivation of its operating powers and specifically its note-issuing privilege via the Colonial Bank Act, 1925. Consequently, no colonial statute could invalidate the note-issuing rights of the British bank. Indeed, it was acknowledged that while the Jamaica Law, No. 10 of 1958, referred to all banks that were "incorporated . . . under authority of an Act of the Imperial Parliament", it did not apply to Barclays Bank (DCO) because of the bank's special position under the British Colonial Bank Act, 1925.[95]

Nevertheless, Barclays Bank (DCO) at the request of the Bank of England voluntarily surrendered its right under charter to issue and reissue banknotes in the West Indies.[96] This decision can only be read as an indication that the bank recognized the changed environment in which it was operating and accepted the fact that the power to issue currency notes had become the prerogative of government.[97] This had also been recognized by the Canadian banks, and they had begun to reduce their notes as early as 1946.[98] This process was clearly evident in Jamaica, where between 1946 and 1951 the note issue of the three Canadian banks was reduced by 76 per cent.[99] While Barclays Bank (DCO) had substantially increased its note circulation between 1946 and 1950, after that the British bank evidently opted to reduce its note issue, as its total banknotes in circulation drastically declined, from an average of £100,810 for the period 1950–53 to an average of £56,746 for the period 1954–57 (see Table 6.2). In this regard, the legislation which was enacted rescinding the banknote issue served to formalize what had already begun to take place in the decade following the end of World War II.

Commission Charges and Exchange Business of the Banks

The expansion of the colonial governments' note issue at the expense of the banknote issue in the West Indies had implications for the exchange business of the banks. In fact, one of the main concerns raised by bank managers, when the intention to reform the currency system on the basis of a sterling exchange standard was announced, was the likelihood that their exchange business would be adversely affected.[100] The banks continued to voice objections in the 1940s, when discussion was renewed on the question of the commission to be charged by the currency boards for the issue and redemption of currency notes. Bank managers in the region urged that the banks should not be charged a commission as a general policy. They held that if a commission had to be charged, then the banks should be "granted preferential rates against the public in view of the facilities offered by the banks for the circulation of currency notes and the fact that banks now give preferential exchange rates to the government on providing Treasury cash remittances to London".[101]

The banks' opposition to the proposed commission charge for the issue and redemption of currency notes was related to the fact that their exchange business was intimately linked with their provision of trade finance. The commercial banks made considerable profits in the form of commissions charged for providing foreign money drafts that customers used to settle their bills in the course of their transactions. The banks had enjoyed tremendous leeway in setting the rates for such transactions. In the West Indies the rates were set through collusive agreements between Barclays Bank (DCO) and the Canadian banks. As currencies in the British colonies were either on par, as in the case of Jamaica and

Australia, or on a fixed rate of exchange with the pound sterling, the exchange operations between Britain and the colonies were limited to transferring funds. The exchange rate quoted by the Australian banks was regarded merely as the rate for the same currency in another place – in this case, London – and was expressed by saying that sterling in London stood at so many pence premium or discount.[102] Similarly, in Jamaica, where the colonial currency was established at par with the British pound, in 1942 the banks charged a premium rate of 0.5 per cent for telegraphic transfers and 0.25 per cent for demand (Jamaica on London) for every £100. In other parts of the West Indies where the colonial currency was based in West Indian dollars, the bank exchange quotations were expressed on a graduated scale, with different rates being quoted for categories of £1,000 to £1,999, £2,000 to £2,999, and so on, and a set rate established for transactions of £3,000 and upwards.[103]

Under the new arrangement the banks were required to conduct their trade finance business using government currency notes, for which they were now subject to a commission charge by the local currency board. When a bank required additional currency, it arranged for the required amount of sterling to be paid to the Crown Agent in London on behalf of the local currency board commissioners. In turn, the commissioners had to issue the required currency to the bank as soon as they were informed of the London payment. In the West Indies, the commission rate was established at 0.5 per cent of the value of all local currency redeemed and 0.44 per cent of the value of all currency notes issued. The banks would then apply their own commission charges to their customers for making these arrangements on their behalf.[104]

Theoretically, then, the currency-board system could severely circumscribe the banks' exchange business, because anyone could have sterling delivered in London by lodging the equivalent value in local currency with the currency board. However, in practice, the system as it came into operation in 1945 ensured that the banks' exchange business was protected. Indeed, this was the expressed policy of the Colonial Office, which noted that "there is no desire that the currency authorities should supplant the banks in the business of handling day-to-day transactions".[105] In compliance with this principle, transactions with the currency boards were limited to a minimum of £5,000 in the West Indies (£10,000 in the case of Trinidad and Tobago). Therefore, the currency boards hardly dealt with the general public, their customers being the banks and the local treasuries, and the exchange business of the commercial banks was maintained.[106]

Summary

Largely in response to the pressures of exchange instability and the need to protect commodity prices and the competitive position of colonial produce dependent on the British market, the region's currency was placed on a sterling exchange standard. This had implications for the commercial banks' operations in relation to their rights to issue currency notes and their foreign-exchange business. As the region's currency was placed on a sterling exchange standard, the future position of the banks' note issue in relation to the various governments' note issue was raised. It is clear that the Colonial Office was unwilling to sanction the immediate reduction and withdrawal of the banks' note issue, indicating that it had no clear-cut plan for the implementation of this policy. For their part, colonial governments were in favour of such action, and Jamaica took the initiative, promoting the circulation of the government currency notes at the expense of the banks' note issue.

The establishment of government currency notes as the principal medium of exchange during this period also had implications for the banks' foreign-exchange business. The banks were now obliged to conduct their trade finance business using government currency notes, in exchange for which they had to provide the required amount of sterling. For this they were charged a commission rate which was set by the colonial currency boards established in each colony. However, because the currency boards dealt only with transactions of £5,000 and over, the banks' exchange business was not adversely affected by the new arrangements. Therefore, although the reform of the currency system introduced changes which affected the banks' operations, the commercial banks continued to enjoy a relatively high degree of receptivity in the West Indies during this period.

Chapter Seven

Towards Independence
Bank Performance, 1940–1962

Barclays Bank (DCO) as a whole performed relatively well in the period 1940–62, with the West Indian Section continuing to make significant contributions in profits. In many respects World War II was a boon, for while trade was disrupted, the bulk purchasing and marketing arrangements that were put in place for colonial produce provided a measure of stability in the form of a guaranteed market and remunerative prices. This was particularly important for the sugar industry, which continued to be the region's mainstay and for which Barclays Bank (DCO) continued to be the major financier.

Post-war marketing arrangements, particularly the Commonwealth Sugar Agreement of 1951, provided continued preferential treatment in the British market and helped to ensure the profitability of sugar production for export. Perhaps even more important for Barclays Bank (DCO)'s operations in the West Indies was the growth in mining, manufacturing and tourism, particularly in the 1950s. Naturally, the increased economic activity and diversification resulted in increased levels of business, which generated substantial profits for the bank during this period. However, it was evident that profits were made at tremendous cost, indicating some inefficiency in the bank's West Indian operations. This chapter begins with an assessment of the bank's profits as a whole, and the position of its West Indian operations in relation to its worldwide operations, in the period 1940 to 1962. This is followed by an examination of the impact of World War II on West Indian trade, particularly the sugar trade, and its implications for the bank's operations. The chapter ends with a discussion on the post-war economic expansion in the West Indies and its impact on the bank's branch operations there for the period 1952 to 1962.

Barclays Bank (DCO)'s Sectional Performance

Barclays Bank (DCO) as a whole recorded a substantial increase in operating profits during the period 1940–62 (see Appendix B). Nevertheless, there was some fluctuation, particularly in the 1950s. Between 1956 and 1957, the South African Section, which continued to be the major contributor of the bank's profits, recorded a significant drop of almost 20 per cent, from £3,717,052 to £3,030,477. In addition, Circus Place, which continued to function as the London end of the South African Section, reported a decline by 13 per cent during the same period (see Table 7.1). The reason was the significantly lower prices in 1957 for maize, gold, copper and wool, which were among the principal exports from South Africa.[1]

Fluctuations in the bank's profit levels were also a result of political instability in the Middle East, particularly in Egypt, which had contributed significantly to total profits before 1957.[2] In 1957 this section suffered a massive decline, by 126 per cent, when profits fell from £497,041 to –£134,148 (see notes at end of Table 7.1). This decline resulted from the crisis over the Suez Canal, which culminated with the Egyptian government's sequestration of the bank's assets in that year.[3] The fall in profits was also a result of the escalating conflict between Jews and Arabs, which adversely affected the bank's Israeli operations – then called the Palestinian Section – following the creation and proclamation of the State of Israel on 14 May 1948. While profits were recorded for that section, which was renamed the Israel/Nablus Section, the situation worsened throughout the 1950s and the section exhibited tremendous losses (see notes at end of Table 7.1).[4]

Table 7.1 Barclays Bank (DCO), Profit and Loss Accounts Showing Operating Profits and Losses (£), 1940–1962

Section	1940	%	1941	%	1942	%
South Africa	393,255	43.00	370,211	32.50	397,988	32.00
Circus Place	87,053	9.000	66,431	5.80	52,618	4.20
West Indies	54,538	6.00	65,949	5.70	80,053	6.40
West Africa	(1,733)	-0.18	7,462	0.66	20,540	1.65
East Africa	7,164	0.70	11,282	1.00	38,468	3.23
Anglo-Egyptian	31,531	3.40	37,731	3.30	19,629	1.57
Other	66,783	7.18	57,479	5.04	52,912	4.25
Head Office	279,335	30.00	521,363	46.0	580,261	46.70
Total	917,926	100.00	1,137,908	100.00	1,242,469	100.00

Section	1943	%	1944	%	1945	%
South Africa	426,892	30.00	501,707	33.30	543,442	31.70
Circus Place	42,482	2.97	45,145	3.00	48,205	2.80
West Indies	94,492	6.60	97,723	6.50	89,208	5.20
West Africa	30,239	2.10	18,678	1.00	22,329	1.30
East Africa	30,211	2.10	14,148	0.90	15,199	1.00
Anglo-Egyptian	48,875	3.43	55,764	4.00	95,223	5.50
Other	69,544	4.90	43,773	3.00	77,226	4.50
Head Office	684,972	47.90	726,831	48.30	822,106	48.00
Total	1,427,707	100.00	1,503,769	100.00	1,712,938	100.00

Section	1946	%	1947	%	1948	%
South Africa	729,531	36.82	1,205,718	43.78	1,498,698	49.20
Circus Place	103,559	5.22	204,708	7.43	222,552	7.30
West Indies	107,446	5.42	172,069	6.24	181,095	6.00
West Africa	34,669	1.75	54,821	1.99	55,597	1.81
East Africa	11,197	0.56	33,960	1.23	68,686	2.25
Anglo-Egyptian	86,972	4.39	163,327	6.00	183,233	6.00
Other	85,895	4.34	174,019	6.32	142,352	4.67
Head Office	819,212	41.35	743,776	27.01	693,786	22.77
Total	1,978,481	100.00	2,752,398	100.00	3,045,999	100.00

Table 7.1 continues

Table 7.1 Barclays Bank (DCO), Profit and Loss Accounts Showing Operating Profits and Losses (£), 1940–1962 *(cont'd)*

Section	1949	%	Section	1950	%
South Africa	1,545,518	50.63	South Africa	1,477,236	51.45
Circus Place	219,904	7.24	West Indies	158,644	5.53
West Indies	177,876	5.82	West Africa	63,623	2.22
West Africa	99,236	3.25	Egyptian Control	274,350	9.55
East Africa	59,372	1.94	East Africa	112,459	3.91
Anglo-Egyptian	202,286	6.62	UK, NY, Hamburg	270,200	9.42
Other	113,406	3.71	Other	169,240	5.90
Head Office	634,789	20.79	Head Office	345,263	12.02
Total	3,052,387	100.00	Total	2,871,015	100.00

Section	1951	%	1952	%	1953	%
South Africa & Mauritius	1,674,575	41.32	2,115,656	49.25	1,638,460	42.98
Circus Place	440,058	10.85	341,808	7.95	300,882	7.89
West Indies	255,794	6.31	298,551	7.00	271,488	7.12
West Africa	184,978	4.56	146,976	3.42	225,859	6.00
East Africa	149,972	3.70	241,177	5.61	199,259	5.22
Egyptian Control	282,566	7.00	203,531	4.73	109,319	2.86
Israel, Nablus & Cyprus	153,155	3.77	146,710	3.41	103,213	2.70
Other	255,141	6.29	378,375	8.80	244,928	6.40
Head Office	656,465	16.19	422,395	9.83	718,510	18.83
Total	4,052,704	100.00	4,295,179	100.00	3,811,918	100.00

Section	1954	%	1955	%
South Africa	1,786,169	38.95	1,981,104	34.96
Rhodesia & Nyasaland	299,026	6.52	449,284	8.00
Circus Place	390,894	8.52	318,803	5.62
West Indies	225,004	5.00	309,639	5.46
West Africa	190,349	4.15	330,016	5.82

Table 7.1 continues

Table 7.1 Barclays Bank (DCO), Profit and Loss Accounts Showing Operating Profits and Losses (£), 1940–1962 *(cont'd)*

Section *(cont'd)*	1954	%	1955	%
East Africa	219,615	4.80	265,569	4.70
Egyptian Control	300,446	6.60	527,509	9.31
Israel, Nablus & Cyprus	101,072	2.20	149,818	2.60
Other	267,474	5.80	315,984	5.57
Head Office	804,953	17.55	1,017 985	17.96
Total	**4,585,002**	**100.00**	**5,665,711**	**100.00**

Section	1956	%	1957	%
South Africa	3,717,052	32.81	3,030,477	30.40
Rhodesia & Nyasaland	973,347	8.59	954,103	9.56
Circus Place	576,547	5.08	499,175	5.00
West Indies	623,587	5.50	714,801	7.16
West Africa	606,778	5.35	590,002	5.91
East Africa	577,901	5.10	462,532	4.63
Egyptian Control	939,699	8.34	275,471	2.76
Israel, Nablus & Cyprus Control	280,896	2.47	195,514	1.95
Other	703,812	6.21	719,759	7.21
Head Office	2,328,710	20.55	2,536,496	25.42
Total	**11,328,329**	**100.00**	**9,978,330**	**100.00**

Section	1958	%	1959	%
South Africa	3,659,640	33.40	3,141,417	33.60
Central Africa	890,155	8.11	533,293	5.70
West Indies	952,498	8.70	861,010	9.21
Ghana & Sierra Leone	313,322	2.85	205,185	2.20
Nigeria	365,579	3.33	262,741	2.81

Table 7.1 continues

Table 7.1 Barclays Bank (DCO), Profit and Loss Accounts Showing Operating Profits and Losses (£), 1940–1962 *(cont'd)*

Section *(cont'd)*	1958	%	1959	%
East Africa	573,320	5.22	354,328	3.80
Mauritius & Sudan	547,625	5.00	412,919	4.40
Israel & Mediterranean	281,934	2.57	139,782	1.50
Other	1,248,868	11.40	1,157,921	12.38
Head Office	2,130,493	19.42	2,277,824	24.40
Total	**10,963,434**	**100.00**	**9,346,420**	**100.00**

Section	1960	%
South Africa	4,258,197	34.00
Central Africa	731,589	6.00
West Indies	1,301,563	10.30
Ghana & Sierra Leone	377,753	3.00
Nigeria	511,158	4.00
East Africa	643,723	5.10
Mauritius & Sudan	493,916	4.00
Israel & Mediterranean	461,643	3.60
Other	1,387,523	11.00
Head Office	2,414,553	19.00
Total	**12,581,618**	**100.00**

Section	1961	%	1962	%
South Africa	4,974,751	36.00	3,676,218	27.30
Central Africa	809,569	5.80	821,949	6.10
West Indies	1,189,701	8.60	851,829	6.30
Ghana & Sierra Leone	442,398	3.20	–	–
Ghana	–	–	195,715	1.50

Table 7.1 continues

Table 7.1 Barclays Bank (DCO), Profit and Loss Accounts Showing Operating Profits and Losses (£), 1940–1962 *(cont'd)*

Section *(cont'd)*	1961	%	1962	%
Sierra Leone	–	–	143,254	1.10
Nigeria & Cameroons	317,418	2.30	650,414	4.80
East Africa & Seychelles	602,209	4.40	459,646	3.40
Mauritius & Sudan	389,895	2.80	864,580	6.40
Israel & Mediterranean	605,677	4.40	658,046	4.90
Other	1,677,476	12.20	1,505,599	11.10
Head Office	2,801,232	20.30	3,652,825	27.10
Total	**13,810,326**	**100.00**	**13,480,075**	**100.00**

Note: "Other" for 1940–49, includes Ocean House, Manchester, Liverpool, New York, Gracechurch and Palestine; for 1950, Mauritius, Cyprus, Israel, Gibraltar and Malta; for 1951–57, Ocean House, Gracechurch, Liverpool, Manchester, New York and Hamburg; for 1958–59, Circus Place, Ocean House, Gracechurch, Northumberland, Liverpool, Manchester, New York and Hamburg; for 1960–62, Old Broad Street, Ocean House, Gracechurch, Northumberland, Liverpool, Manchester, New York and Hamburg. For 1950–57, "Egyptian Control" figures include those for Mauritius and the Sudan, with breakdown for 1956 and 1957 as follows: for 1956, Egypt, £497,051; Mauritius, £107,693; the Sudan, £334,955. For 1957, Egypt, -£134,148; Mauritius, £105,581; the Sudan, £304,038. The Israel/Nablus figures for 1951–58, separated from the Cyprus figures, were as follows: £73,412; £27,788; £11,032; -£5,906; £13,641; -£40,513; -£93,418; -£22,295.

Source: Accounts and Board Meeting Papers, BBA 38/251.

The West Indian Section's Performance

The West Indian Section maintained an almost constant increase in its profit contributions to Barclays Bank (DCO). Between 1940 and 1950, the operating profits generated by the West Indian Section increased by 191 per cent. By 1955, a further increase by 95 per cent was recorded, which was followed by a spectacular increase by 320 per cent between that year and 1960. This was followed by a 34 per cent decline between 1960 and 1962, which was largely attributable to significant increases in operating costs (see Table 7.1, Figure 7.1, Appendix B).

In relation to Barclays Bank (DCO) as a whole, the West Indian

Towards Independence: Bank Performance, 1940–1962

Figure 7.1 Barclays Bank (DCO), West Indian section, operating profits, 1940–1962
Source: Accounts and Board Meeting Papers, 1940–62, BBA 38/251.

Section contributed an average of 6 per cent of total profits over the period 1940 to 1962. Again, while seemingly minuscule, when viewed in the context of the performance of the other sections of the bank's multinational operations, this contribution becomes more significant. Between 1940 and 1948, the section contributed, on average, the fourth-largest amount of profits for the bank out of a total of thirteen sections. It maintained this position between 1949 and 1954, during which time the number of sections increased to fifteen. Its importance in the bank's multinational network grew significantly during 1955 and 1962, when it contributed the third-largest amount of profits.(see Table 7.1).[5]

The importance of the West Indian Section was even more evident in terms of the territorial spread of loans and advances throughout the bank's multinational network (see Table 7.2). For 1948 and 1949, the only two years for which statistics of this kind are available, the West Indies accounted for 10 per cent of total loans and advances made by the bank, placing third behind the South African Section's 64 per cent and the Egyptian Section's 11 per cent for the same years. The West Indian Section owed its continued fair performance largely to the relative stability of the West Indian sugar industry during World War II and the economic expansion which occurred in the post-war period. The following sections discuss these developments in relation to the bank's performance in the region.

163

Table 7.2 Territorial Spread of Barclays Bank (DCO), Loans and Advances (£), 1948 and 1949

Territorial Grouping	Annual Average Loans & Advances, 1948–49	Percentage
South Africa	57.2 million	64.00
Egypt, Sudan, Libya & Eritrea	9.7 million	11.00
West Indies	8.9 million	10.00
United Kingdom	4.7 million	5.00
East Africa	4.2 million	5.00
Palestine	2.8 million	3.10
West Africa	861,000	1.00
Mediterranean	670,000	0.70
Port Louis	200,000	0.15
New York	45,000	0.05
Total	**89,276,000**	**100.00**

Source: Central Board, Analysis of Loans and Advances as at 30 September 1948 and 1949, BBA 11/551.

West Indian Trade and World War II

According to Havinden and Meredith, the overall volume of British colonial trade declined during World War II, with export levels of many of the primary products of the British empire lower in 1945 than in 1938. West African exports of cocoa, palm kernels, palm oil and groundnuts had all declined, as had tea and sugar exports from Ceylon and Mauritius; for the West Indies, sugar, cocoa and bananas, the principal agricultural exports, also declined.[6] Trinidadian cocoa fell primarily because of a severe labour shortage, and Jamaican banana production suffered from the Panama and leaf spot diseases. In addition, a hurricane in 1944 destroyed over 90 per cent of the trees on the island.[7]

Sugar production and exports for Trinidad and Tobago also declined. Between 1937 and 1945 exports plummeted by 59 per cent, from 143,000 tons to 59,000 tons. Exports from British Guiana fell by 27 per cent, from 182,000 tons to 133,000 tons.[8] As with the cocoa industry in Trinidad and Tobago, a chronic shortage of labour was largely responsible for the decline. Thousands of estate workers and cane farmers deserted the industry to seek better remuneration at the American naval bases that were constructed in these colonies between 1941 and 1944.[9] According to Brereton, only 16,700 labourers worked in the Trinidadian sugar industry in 1943, compared with some 25,000 in 1939. This was in contrast to the 30,000 employed on the naval bases, which, Brereton notes, was a considerable amount, given that the size of the labour market was only 200,000.[10] Similarly, in British Guiana the number of workers employed on sugar estates had fallen from 34,000 in 1938 to 25,000 by 1945.[11]

Overall, though, West Indian sugar exports were relatively stable during World War II, recording an annual average of 490,000 tons between 1940 and 1945 (see Figure 7.2). Sugar exports from Jamaica rose substantially for that period, by 45 per cent, in effect making up for some of the fall-off in production and exports from Trinidad and Tobago and British Guiana.[12] This relative stability was facilitated in large part by the food bulk-purchasing arrangements instituted by the British government during the war – arrangements that were not altruistic. Similar arrangements were made for other foods and commodities, including wheat, meat, wool, copper, sisal, rubber, and tin. The primary objective was to prevent a rapid escalation in prices by maintaining adequate supplies in Britain before and during the war.[13]

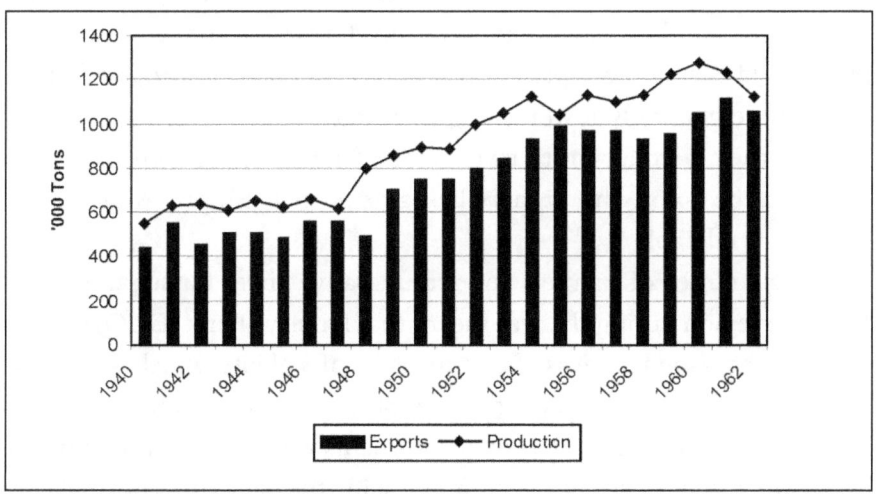

Figure 7.2 West Indian sugar production and exports ('000 tons), 1940–1962
Source: Complied from statistics from Higman, *Abstract of Caribbean Historical Statistics*, table 5.1, Sugar Production 1700–1983; and Commonwealth Economic Committee, *Plantation Crops* (for the years 1950, 1952, 1954, 1956, 1960, and 1963).

State control of colonial exports was an important mechanism that helped to reduce Britain's deficit with the United States during the war. By ensuring the provision of supplies to Britain during the war and boosting exports to dollar areas, the bulk purchasing and marketing arrangements contributed to the accumulation of sterling balances, which were used to supplement British foreign exchange reserves. It was, further, considered important that these arrangements continue in the immediate post-war period to help relieve the pressures on Britain's sterling and balance-of-payments problems.[14]

As early as 1936 a subcommittee in the Ministry of Food was created with responsibility for ensuring the maintenance of adequate food supplies in wartime, and plans were made for the control of the most important imports. In the case of sugar, a committee under the aegis of a sugar commission was established in 1939, and from July of that year, the structures of the "sugar division" in the ministry were put in place. The sugar division was responsible for making purchases not only for Britain but also on behalf of Canada and other territories, including non-producing colonies.[15] Under this arrangement, West Indian sugar production surplus to local needs was marketed under bulk-purchase contracts negotiated with the ministry. Prices were negotiated for a year at a time and were fixed after considering the cost of production and what was regarded as a reasonable return. Overall, prices paid by the British Ministry of Food for sugar exports from the West Indies rose steadily, from 11s 3d per hundredweight in 1939 to 17s 3d per hundredweight by 1945. While generally lower than prices in the London and New York market, they were far more favourable when compared with London prices in the 1930s, the highest being 7s 4d per hundredweight (see Graph 2.3 and Table 7.3).[16]

The guarantee of markets and remunerative prices for sugar exports from the region during the war meant that Barclays Bank (DCO)'s operations in the region were assured a measure of stability, which otherwise would have been absent in wartime conditions. Indeed, bank officials felt that while "settlements between governments were sometimes arranged by methods which had the effect of depriving the bank of its normal revenue", payments were made at agreed intervals irrespective of whether shipment had actually taken place. This, together with guaranteed markets for West Indian produce, ensured producers a full measure of pro-

Table 7.3 Sugar Prices (Shillings per Hundredweight) 1937–1949

Year	British Ministry of Food	London Average	NY Average
1937	–	6s 4d	11s 7d
1938	–	5s 5d	9s 4d
1939	11s 3d	7s 3d	9s 11d
1940	n/a	n/a	10s 6d
1941	n/a	n/a	13s 9d
1942	n/a	13s 3d	16s 6d
1943	n/a	13s 3d	16s 7d
1944	n/a	n/a	16s 7d
1945	17s 3d	21s 3d	19s 0d
1946	19s 6d	27s 3d	25s 7d
1947	24s 3d	31s 7d	30s 4d
1948	27s 3d	30s 3d	28s 2d
1949	27s 3d	29s 3d	9s 2d

n/a = not available

Note: The New York prices are those quoted for Cuban centrifugals 96 CIF ex-duty.
Source: Commonwealth Economic Committee, *Plantation Crops* (1950), 17, 18; (1952), 19.

tection, which in turn meant the bank was less likely to incur bad debts due to the circumstances of war.[17]

Certainly, in general the West Indian sugar industry exhibited a relatively good performance during the war (see Appendix C). A review of the available accounts as presented in the various commissions of enquiry into the performance of the sugar industry during the war demonstrates the relative profitability of the companies involved in the production and export of sugar during this period. The Antigua Sugar Factory, which was owned and controlled by the British firm Messrs. Henckell Du Buisson, recorded a 128 per cent increase in profits before taxation between 1938 and 1945, with total dividends paid averaging £11,000 (see Appendix D).[18] For Jamaica, where profit data are for only 1939 to 1943, the sugar companies were relatively profitable, though there was some fluctuation. Average net profits from cane and sugar production was £86,154. When combined with rum production, the return was even better, with an average of £199,542 (see Appendix E). Perhaps even more telling evidence is that provided by the Worthy Park Estate, whose operating profit at the outbreak of the war in 1939 was barely £40,000, but by 1946 had reached £150,000.[19] In Trinidad and Tobago the four major sugar companies, which included the Ste Madeleine Sugar Co. Ltd, Caroni Ltd, Trinidad Sugar Estates Ltd and the Woodford Lodge Estates, together indicated increases of 10 and 30 per cent in profits from 1944 to 1945 and from 1945 to 1946, respectively (see Appendix F).

Overall, the total value of West Indian exports rose by 71 per cent between 1940 and 1945 (see Figure 7.3). Contributing to these values were exports of oil from Trinidad and Tobago and bauxite from British Guiana, both of which had become important strategic commodities as a result of the war. Following heavy capital investments between 1938 and 1942 to upgrade its refining capacity and to develop plants to produce high-grade aviation fuel, Trinidad and Tobago's output of oil reached 20 million barrels by 1941 and by 1943 accounted for 80 per cent of the colony's total value of exports.[20] Similarly, British Guiana's bauxite production peaked in 1943 at 1,901,393 tons, having increased by over 40 per cent from 376,368 tons in 1938.[21]

Much of Barclays Bank (DCO)'s business in the region involved the provision of financing for the importation of foods and other manufactured goods. Like other parts of the empire, the import trade of the West Indies experienced decline during the war years, mainly owing to the lack of adequate shipping and shifts to war production in Britain.[22] The Japanese attack on Pearl Harbour and the entry of the United States, which was followed by a vigorous enemy submarine campaign, further increased the scarcity of shipping and therefore foodstuffs and other manufactured goods. For instance, the average number of vessels calling at Jamaican ports with cargoes declined from 1,459 between 1936 and 1938 to 341 between 1941 to 1945 – a drop of 76 per cent. The recorded average weight in cargoes carried by these vessels fell by nearly 90 per cent for the same periods. Similarly, for Barbados, the annual average dropped from 1,115 between 1936 and 1938 to 733 between 1939 and 1945, and the average weight in cargoes fell by 59 per cent.[23]

Not surprisingly, despite the imposition of price controls on basic food items, the price of many manufactured goods, including food, rose steeply during the war.[24] By 1943 consumer prices in the British

Caribbean had risen by approximately 65 per cent over their 1939 levels, with annual average inflation rates varying from 13.2 per cent in Trinidad and Tobago to 16.7 per cent in British Guiana.[25] The inflation prevalent in the West Indies was reflected in the value of imports, which rose by 75 per cent between 1940 and 1945. The total value of West Indian trade increased by 72 per cent between 1940 and 1945 (see Figure 7.3; see Appendix G). This meant a significant amount of revenue for a bank whose business was essentially that of financing trade, and helps to explain the continued rise in its operating profits during the war period.

Post-war Economic Expansion

West Indian trade boomed in the immediate post-war period: the total value of trade increased by over 600 per cent between 1946 and 1962. The value of exports rose by 125 per cent between 1946 and 1950, and by 247 per cent between 1950 and 1962. Import values rose just as spectacularly, by 100 per cent and 225 per cent for the same time periods (see Figure 7.3).

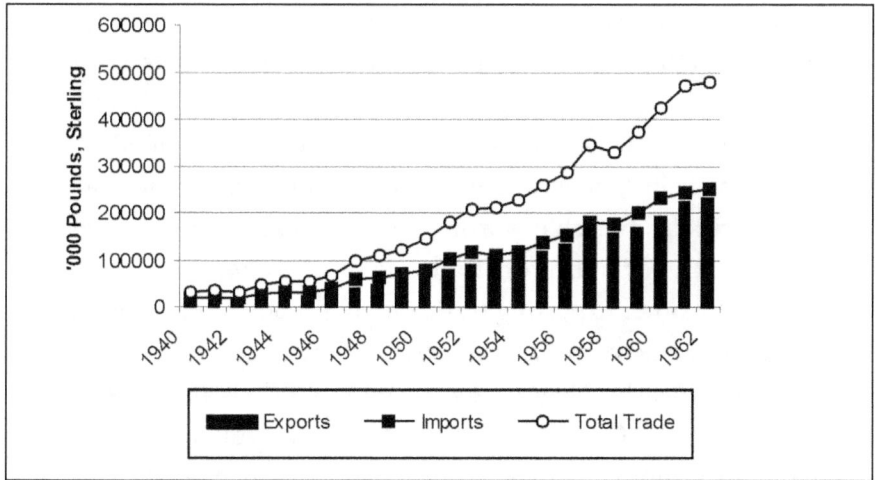

Figure 7.3 Value of West Indian trade ('000 pounds sterling), 1940–1962

Source: Compiled from *The West Indies Year Book, 1947–48*; *The West Indies and Caribbean Year Book* (for the years 1951, 1952, 1955–56); Colonial Office, *An Economic Survey of the Colonial Territories, 1951*, 208–9; *Barbados: Report for the Years, 1956 and 1957*, 32; HBJ, 1947–1948, 249–25; HBJ, 1950, 265–82; HBJ, 1953, 208–9; HBJ, 1957, 224–25; HBJ, 1959, 292–93; HBJ, 1963, 344; *Annual Report on Jamaica: For the Year 1947*, 27. For Barbados, statistics are absent for 1958. For British Guiana, statistics are available only for 1943 to 1962.

Sugar exports accounted for a significant portion of the total value of West Indian trade, as production and exports rose substantially, by 89 and 86 per cent, respectively, between 1946 and 1962. The arrangements that were put in place in the post-war period were largely responsible since they provided a guaranteed preferential market for West Indian produce and therefore a great deal of security and stability in the West Indian sugar industry.

The bulk purchasing arrangements that had been put in place during the war continued until 1953, when the Commonwealth Sugar Agreement of 1951 (hereafter the CSA) came into effect.[26] The CSA came about primarily as a result of lobbying by the British West Indian Sugar Association, which had been formed in 1942. The objective was to safeguard the interests of the region's sugar industry. While sugar continued to be in short supply immediately following the end of World War II, by 1951 world production had escalated to the point where prices had begun to fall. In addition, the British Labour government had negotiated what became known as the "Black Pact" with Cuba to secure cheap sugar for the British domestic market, which had undercut West Indian sugar.[27] Therefore, the objectives of the CSA were twofold: to prevent excess supplies on the international market, thereby preventing the forcing down of prices to unreasonable levels; and to assure markets for certain fixed quantities at guaranteed prices.[28]

Under the CSA, which was extended to 1959 and remained in place until 1967, the British government agreed to purchase, in each calendar year, quantities from each exporting territory up to a total of 1,568,000 tons. Any deficiency in exports from any of the other territories could be made up by other exporting territories in proportion to their respective overall agreement quotas. The quota allocated to the West Indies in 1951, described as the Negotiated Price Quota (hereafter NPQ), was 640,000 tons.[29] The CSA also stipulated that exportable surplus sugar from the Commonwealth was limited to 2,375,000 tons. This was referred to as Free Quota sugar, and the West Indian portion was limited to 900,000 tons. Free Quota sugar differed from NPQ sugar in that there was no agreement with regard to price, so Free Quota sugar was sold at world market price, in addition to the tariff preference in the United Kingdom and Canada. The Canadian preference was $1.00 per 100 lb and the British tariff preference was £3 15s per ton. The NPQ prices negoti-

Table 7.4 Sugar Prices (Shillings per Hundredweight) 1950–1962

Year	NPQ	UK Non-Commonwealth (average)
1950	30s 6d	40s 0d
1951	32s 10½d	50s 1d
1952	38s 6d	45s 3d
1953	42s 4d	31s 6d
1954	41s 0d	29s 2d
1955	40s 9d	32s 1d
1956	40s 9d	33s 11d
1957	42s 2d	50s 10d
1958	43s 10d	32s 8d
1959	45s 1d	27s 5d
1960	44s 5d	29s 0d
1961	45s 1d	26s 7d
1962	45s 9d	24s 7d

Source: Commonwealth Economic Committee, *Plantation Crops* (1952), 19; (1956), 43; (1958), 37; (1963), 46; (1964), 74.

ated annually were generally well above the free market price during 1951–62; it was only in 1950–51 and 1957 that drought conditions and the Suez Canal crisis, respectively, caused the world market price to rise much higher than the NPQ (see Table 7.4).[30]

West Indian sugar was also subject to the International Sugar Agreement (hereafter the ISA), the first of which was signed in 1937, but the agreement was never operative as a result of the war. A second agreement was negotiated at the United Nations Sugar Conference in London, August 1953, and until 1958 the CSA quotas were also the limit for total net export entitlements under the ISA. In 1959, the ISA quota was stipulated at 2,500,000 tons. This was later increased to 2,575,000 tons for 1960 and 1961.[31] After the Commonwealth "Overall Agreement" quota of 2,375,000 tons was divided into the NPQ of 1,568,000 tons, which was guaranteed for the British market, and a Free Quota of 807,000 tons, the surplus 125,000 tons, which was known as the International Quota, could only be exported to non-preferential markets.[32]

The agreements, particularly the CSA, theoretically limited West Indian sugar exports but in effect enabled production to continue at a more viable level, by providing "certain security with respect to outlets and prices for sugar". As actual exports of West Indian sugar in 1950 were approximately 725,000 tons, the CSA, when it first came into effect in 1953, allowed for some expansion to take place in the region's industry.[33] In fact, sugar exports rose by 25 per cent between 1953 and 1962 (see Figure 7.2).

Overall, West Indian sugar exports increased steadily by 119 per cent between 1945 and 1962. Sugar exports from the region, which averaged 508,000 tons per year during the war, had increased to an annual average of 658,000 tons between 1945 and 1953, and increased again to 980,000 tons between 1953 and 1962 (see Figure 7.2). Jamaica and British Guiana, with increases by 221 and 133 per cent, respectively, contributed the most to these increases.[34]

The Cuban revolution and the subsequent nationalization of that country's sugar industry, which led to the US embargo on Cuban exports, also provided a fillip to the West Indian industry. In 1960 the United States began providing temporary quota allocations for West Indian sugar on an ad hoc basis. The following year a permanent quota of 80,000 tons for that market, with the West Indies being eligible to share in the shortfalls of other suppliers, was granted. As a result, in 1962 the basic quota together with shortfalls allowed the region to export 160,000 tons to the United States alone.[35]

Trade in other agricultural products, especially bananas, also expanded in this period. During and after World War II, the banana industry was protected by the British Ministry of Food bulk purchasing scheme at prescribed prices, though no produce was actually exported. The fruit was guaranteed a protected market in the United Kingdom in the post-war period by a £7.10 per long ton tax on fruit from outside the Commonwealth. This had encouraged the resuscitation and development of the industry in Jamaica and the Windward Islands.[36] In Jamaica, banana production and exports rebounded, increasing from a mere 1.8 million stems exported in 1945 to 10.0 million by 1962, though this was a far cry from previous export figures that reached nearly 30 million in 1937.[37] As for the Windward Islands, bananas had become the major export crop by the 1950s, with Dominica, St Lucia and Grenada together exporting 888,000 stems in 1952. By 1957, these islands along with St Vincent accounted for exports of 4,108,000 stems.[38]

The vibrancy of the West Indian agricultural sector meant that it remained an important recipient of financing from Barclays Bank (DCO). In the late 1940s, this sector accounted for an average of 27 per cent of total loans and advances made by the bank.[39] By the 1950s, however, its proportion had fallen to an annual average of 9 per cent,[40] primarily because of the significant growth in importance of the manufacturing and service sectors. The following section discusses these developments and their impact on the bank's West Indian operations.

Industrialization by Invitation

The Moyne Commission, which was established to enquire into the causes of the West Indian labour disturbances of the 1930s, found the underlying factor to be high unemployment and underemployment, which had contributed to gross poverty among the majority of the West Indian population. The commission's report, which was published after the war ended, stopped short of recommending any fundamental economic reform, opting instead for palliative measures such as improved health care, housing, education and wages. But as unemployment became even more acute in the immediate post–World War II period, attention turned to the much-heralded Puerto Rican model of industrial development, which had begun in 1947. Sir W. Arthur Lewis, the St Lucia–born economist, emerged as the best-known proponent of the model for the English-speaking Caribbean. The fundamental tenet of the model was the offer of generous incentives, primarily in the form of tax-free periods, for the establishment of foreign subsidiary companies in the areas of manufacturing. Accordingly, beginning in the late 1940s practically all of the West Indian territories passed incentive legislation designed to encourage not only foreign entrepreneurs but local investors as well. Most of the foreign investment to the region was attracted to Jamaica, Trinidad and Tobago, and the Bahamas, and as a result a skewed pattern of development across the region, which had been evident before, became even more pronounced in the 1950s.[41] In Jamaica, incentive legislation included the Pioneer Industries (Encouragement) Law, 1949; the Industrial Incentives Law (1956); the Export Industry

Encouragement Laws (1956); and the International Business Companies (Exemption From Tax) Law.[42] All these pieces of legislation provided import duty and income tax concessions to local and foreign investors to promote the development of a viable manufacturing sector. And Jamaica's manufacturing output rose appreciably, from £7.9 million in 1950 to £30.4 million in 1960, taking precedence over agriculture, construction and mining. Manufacturing areas included food and beverages, which grew by 7.9 per cent, tobacco products (by 5.5 per cent), furniture and fixtures (by 7.1 per cent), and chemical and chemical products (by 5.8 per cent). Legislation also targeted specific industries and included the Textile Industry (Encouragement) Law in 1947, and the Cement Industry (Encouragement and Control) Law in 1948. The greatest increases were registered for textiles and garments (by 10.7 per cent) and cement and clay products (by 11.3 per cent). Metal products increased by 9.6 per cent, and other types of manufactures by 8.8 per cent.[43]

In Trinidad and Tobago, industrial development was encouraged through the passing of the Aid to Pioneer Industry Ordinance and the Income Tax (In Aid of Industry) Ordinance in 1950. By 1963 ninety-nine pioneer industries were in operation, representing capital investments of approximately US$85 million, and forty more were expected with an estimated investment worth US$173 million. The main manufacturing industries were those concerned with the processing of agricultural products, which, in addition to sugar and rum, produced gin and other cordials as well as citrus-fruit juices and the famous Angostura Bitters. Significant development also took place in the manufacture of textiles and garments, the production of building materials, foodstuffs, fertilizers, paints and industrial chemicals, and the processing of dairy and fish products.[44] During the 1950s manufacturing became an important sector in Trinidad and Tobago's economy, contributing an average of 12.5 per cent to total gross domestic product.[45]

The 1950s witnessed the rapid expansion of the extractive sector, which also benefited from incentive legislation. In 1950 bauxite production in Jamaica had barely started, but by 1960 the island had emerged as the world's largest producer of that commodity, following heavy investments by the US companies Reynolds Metal Company of America and Kaiser Bauxite Company and the Canadian company Jamaica Bauxite Ltd, whose name was changed to Alumina Jamaica Ltd in 1952 and changed again to Alcan Jamaica Ltd in 1962. By then bauxite and alumina exports were valued at £27.4 million, accounting for just under 50 per cent of the island's visible exports in that year. In 1961 these export values had increased to £30.4 million.[46]

In Trinidad and Tobago, while land production of oil had peaked in 1958 at 38 million barrels, marine exploitation was expanded, and by 1963 approximately 1.8 million acres of marine leases had been granted. By 1966, there were 250 marine wells producing 47,500 barrels per day. The island also expanded its oil-refining capacity after 1948, when new terms allowed for the importation of crude oil duty-free. In addition, takeovers and mergers in the industry fuelled major expansion programmes. British Petroleum, Shell and Texaco, with the latter leading in refining capacity after 1956, undertook substantial expansions that resulted in tremendous increases in production. In 1965 Texaco alone was responsible for the production of 70,000 barrels and the refining of 345,000 barrels per day. Shell's refinery at Point Fortin by then was producing 50,000 barrels of high-octane gas, kerosene and jet fuels per day. Overall, between 1951 and 1960 the manufacture and export of petroleum products accounted for 31.3 per cent of Trinidad and Tobago's gross domestic product.[47] By 1960, petroleum products were valued at £81.9 million, representing 80 per cent of the total value of exports from the colony.[48]

Tourism emerged as a major sector in this period, primarily in Jamaica and the Bahamas, with growth in this industry following the model that had been established for manufacturing. In Jamaica tourist arrivals rose from 75,000 visitors in 1950 to 227,000 in 1960, representing a 200 per cent increase, which helped to encourage the growth in accommodation on the island's north coast. The Hotel Aids Law helped in this direction, providing for duty-free import of building materials and equipment as well as income tax relief.[49] In the Bahamas, similar legislation virtually transformed that territory in the 1950s, into a holiday resort and tax haven for very wealthy British and American tourists.[50] As a result, a tremendous expansion programme in hotel accommodation and other real estate was undertaken there. In addition, a number of offshore companies, mostly American, were attracted to the Bahamas owing to the tax-deferment facilities which allowed them to build up profits earned by their operations outside the United States.[51] Similar developments, though not yet as spectacular, had begun to occur in the Cayman Islands in 1962.[52]

Comparable legislation was enacted in the Eastern Caribbean, which witnessed an appreciable growth in the hotel and tourist sector.[53] With the exception of Trinidad and Tobago, though, these colonies' economies remained primarily agricultural. Barbados, for example, remained totally dependent on the production and export of sugar and its by-products of rum and molasses, which together accounted for 97 per cent of total exports.[54] St Kitts/Nevis and Antigua also remained heavily dependent on sugar production and exports, while St Vincent, in addition to sugar, relied on bananas and arrowroot. Grenada's economy centred on the production of cocoa, nutmeg and other spices.[55]

British Guiana's economy, too, remained centred primarily on agriculture, in spite of developments in bauxite mining which led to its being the world's third-largest producer by 1960. In that year, exports totalled £26.5 million, of which sugar accounted for £12 million and rice £3 million. Bauxite exports accounted for £6 million. It is true that this sector, dominated by the main bauxite mining plant, the Demerara Bauxite Co. Ltd, a subsidiary of Aluminium Ltd of Canada and Reynolds Metal, whose mining site was at Kwakwani, Rio Berbice, had contributed to the expansion of the commercial and retail sectors.[56] Nevertheless, significant investment was deterred by a climate of political uncertainty, largely owing to Cheddi Jagan's socialist government and its subsequent dissolution following the suspension of the constitution in 1953 by the British government. The political uncertainty certainly contributed to a significant outflow of funds from the colony.[57]

Overall, the conventional economic indices clearly indicated a positive trend, and with the emergence of tourism and manufacturing, and the expansion of the bauxite and petroleum sectors in some territories, per capita incomes increased. In Jamaica, where the greatest economic expansion occurred, the gross domestic product (hereafter GDP) rose from £70 million in 1950 to £231 million in 1960, with national per capita income increasing from £48 to £128.[58] Trinidad and Tobago's national per capita income doubled during the 1950s, reaching approximately £207 by 1961. Nassau, in the Bahamas, recorded a national per capita income of £250 for 1959.[59] Smaller per capita incomes were recorded for those islands whose economies remained primarily agricultural. British Guiana's national per capita income was £100 in 1960, while Barbados's was £91, Antigua's £75, St Vincent's £56, St Lucia's £53, Grenada's £53,

Dominica's £60 and that of St Kitts/Nevis, £68.[60] In spite of the disparity in economic development across the region, the growth and expansion which occurred created immense business opportunities for commercial banking and contributed to the coffers of Barclays Bank (DCO).

Impact on Banking Business, 1952–1962

Practically all categories of Barclays Bank (DCO)'s business in the West Indies increased between 1952 and 1962, with the most important component being its loans and advances portfolio. Between 1952 and 1962 total loans and advances increased from £27.8 million to £68.9 million, representing an increase of 148 per cent (see Figure 7.4). This category of the bank's business, in terms of the interest received, accounted for an average of 48 per cent of total gross profits over this period. Between 1952 and 1957 interest received on loans and advances increased from £378,579 to £461,437, or by 22 per cent, with its most extensive increase, 147 per cent, occurring between 1957 and 1962, rising from £461,437 to £1,141,178 (see Table 7.5).

Increased interest rates levied on loans and advances also contributed to the profits accruing from this aspect of the bank's business.[61] In 1955 interest rates increased from 5.38 to 6.37 per cent for overdrafts, and from

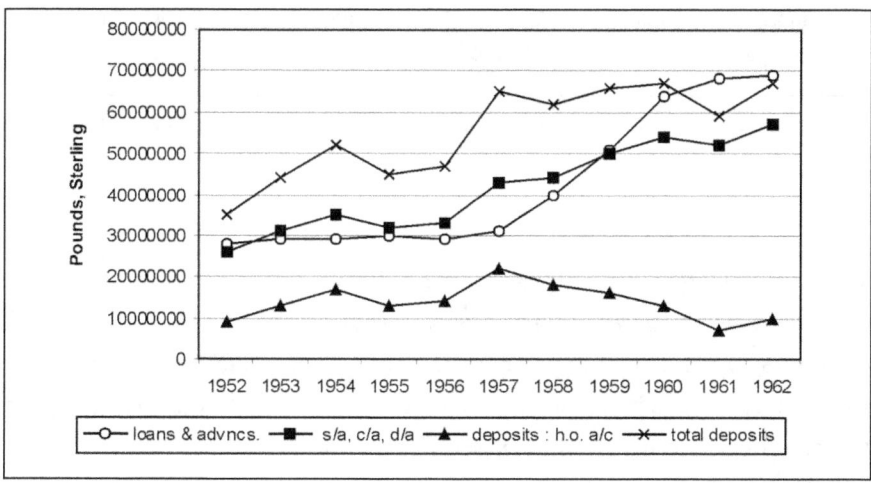

Figure 7.4 Barclays (Bank DCO), West Indian branch accounts: deposits, loans and advances, 1952–1962
Source: Amalgamated Results, Statistics and Review, September 1952–62, BBA 29/171, BBA 29/173, BBA 29/155.

Table 7.5 Barclays Bank (DCO), West Indian Branch Accounts (£), 1952–1962

	1952	(%)	1957	(%)	1962	(%)
Gross Profits						
Interest received						
on current accounts	378,579	(51.00)	461,437	(38.00)	1,141,178	(55.00)
on head office account	103,009	(14.00)	367,953	(31.00)	446,037	(21.40)
on sundries	–		–		6,198	(0.20)
Discount	6,146	(0.80)	7,944	(0.70)	9,010	(0.40)
Exchange	211,505	(28.40)	271,775	(22.60)	250,562	(12.00)
Commission	43,044	(5.80)	92,351	(7.70)	222,418	(11.00)
Total gross profits	**742,283**	**(100.00)**	**1,201,460**	**(100.00)**	**2,075,403**	**(100.00)**
Expenses						
Interest paid	95,651	(20.24)	266,784	(30.40)	678,486	(41.30)
Rents, rates, taxes &						
insurance	32,824	(7.00)	103,645	(11.80)	167,576	(10.30)
Repairs & maintenance	10,128	(2.10)	17,134	(2.00)	13,824	(0.80)
Salaries, wages &						
allowances	251,337	(54.10)	402,977	(46.00)	599,518	(36.50)
Other	74,289	(16.56)	85,366	(9.80)	184,620	(11.10)
Total expenses	**464,229**	**(100.00)**	**875,906**	**(100.00)**	**1,644,024**	**(100.00)**
Net profits	**278,054**		**325,554**		**431,379**	

Source: Amalgamated Results, Statistics and Review, September 1952–1962, BBA 29/171, BBA 29/173, BBA 29/155.

5.04 to 6.38 in 1956 for bills discounted. Between 1960 and 1961 interest rates were again increased, from 6.25 to 6.92 per cent for overdrafts, and from 5.18 to a hefty 8.019 per cent for bills discounted. Overall, interest rates on overdrafts increased by 26 per cent, and on bills discounted by 25 per cent between 1952 and 1962 (see Table 7.6).

Interest rates were raised as the bank became concerned about its liquidity. By the late 1950s the liquidity position of Barclays Bank (DCO)'s global operations was considerably reduced, since there was no commensurate increase in the level of deposits with its expanded loans port-

Table 7.6 Barclays Bank (DCO), Interest Rates on Loans and Advances in the West Indies, 1952–1962

	1952	1953	1954	1955	1956	1957	1958	1959	1960	1961	1962
Overdrafts	5.36	5.30	4.98	5.38	6.37	6.02	6.28	5.57	6.25	6.92	6.74
Bills	5.86	6.74	5.52	5.04	6.38	5.69	6.14	5.54	5.17	8.02	7.31

Source: Amalgamated Results, Statistics and Review, September 1952–1962, BBA 29/171, BBA 29/173, BBA 29/155.

folio. By 1960, total loans and advances by the bank's multinational operations had increased by £53 million over the previous year to reach a record figure of £301 million, with deposits at £616 million. This meant that the bank's ratio of loans and advances to deposits was 0.5:1 in 1960,[62] exceeding the 0.3:1 ratio traditionally considered prudent in banking circles.[63]

Commenting on the situation, the chairman of the bank in his 30 September 1960 report to the board of directors explained that, "In those areas where our lending [has] been exceptionally heavy and quite disproportionate to the business, we have been obliged to raise our rates charged, as well as our rates offered for deposits in order to exercise some corrective influence."[64] In the West Indies, the ratio of loans and advances to deposits averaged 0.7:1 for the period 1952–62 (see Figure 7.5). Between 1957 and 1962 the increase in loans and advances made by West

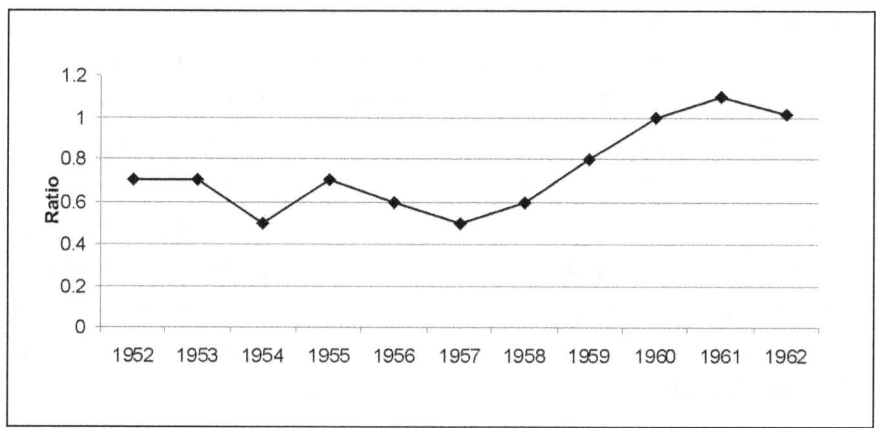

Figure 7.5 Barclays Bank (DCO), West Indian branch accounts: ratio of loans and advances to deposits, 1952–1962
Source: Amalgamated Results, Statistics and Review, September 1952–62, BBA 29/171, BBA 29/173, BBA 29/155.

Indian branches was sharpest, by 119 per cent (from £31 million to £69 million). Total deposits, which included those held on account at the head office, had increased by a mere 3 per cent, from £65 million to £67 million, over the same period (see Figure 7.4).

The raising of deposits was an integral part of Barclays Bank (DCO)'s operations, not only for the purpose of maintaining liquidity but also as a source of profit. As a result, a considerable portion was remitted to the London head office for investment in short-term securities. This aspect of the bank's business was the second most important area of profits, averaging 22 per cent of gross profits for the period 1952 to 1962. Between 1952 and 1957, the level of deposits remitted for investment increased by 153 per cent, from £8,888,992 to £22,473,703. Thereafter, the amount remitted declined significantly, by 56 per cent (see Figure 7.4).

Both domestic and international factors account for the change in the level of deposits remitted to London between the 1952–57 and 1957–62 periods. In the immediate period following the end of World War II, Barclays Bank (DCO), like other British multinational banks, was highly liquid, given the restrictions on imports and consumption that were imposed. This led to an accumulation of deposits.[65] With domestic demand dampened, and in the absence of a domestic market in liquid assets, the banks built up significant balances at their respective head offices. The domestic demand for credit was further dampened with the increase in lending rates during the early 1950s, particularly between 1954 and 1956.[66]

Between 1952 and 1956, advances increased by only 3.5 per cent, from £27,814,618 to £28,790,852, whereas balances at head office increased substantially during the same period. At the same time, the proportion of West Indian deposits held at the head office to deposits held in the West Indian branches increased, from 33 per cent in 1952 to 53 per cent in 1957. The significant decline in the level of deposits remitted from 1957 and onwards was largely a consequence of the growth in demand for credit in the West Indies (see Figure 7.4).[67] As noted earlier, it was between 1957 and 1962 that the increase in the amount of loans and advances by Barclays Bank (DCO) was sharpest. It was during this period that Barclays Bank (DCO)'s ratio of loans and advances to deposits in the West Indies increased from 0.5:1 in 1957 to 1.02:1 in 1962. (see Figure 7.5).[68] To meet the demand, the bank was permitted to draw on its overseas resources to finance the loans and advances made during this period. Therefore, rather than being a net exporter of capital from the West Indies during the period 1957–62, Barclays Bank (DCO) was a net importer of capital. Indeed, in Jamaica, Girvan notes, commercial banks by 1961 had become overseas borrowers to the tune of net £13 million, which represented 24 per cent of their total liabilities.[69]

Another important source of profit for the bank was the revenue, referred to as exchange in the bank's accounts, which was generated from foreign exchange transactions. Overall, this category of business contributed 21 per cent of total profits for the period 1952–62. In the period 1952–55, its annual average was 26.6 per cent of total profits, before falling to 17.6 per cent between 1956 and 1962 (see Table 7.5).

The revenue from foreign exchange transactions was the result of the difference between the bank's charges for providing foreign currencies in the form of trade bills, banker's drafts, telegraphic transfers, traveller's cheques and other instruments of credit, and the price at which it bought these instruments when they became payable abroad.[70] Therefore, a rapid turnover in foreign exchange transactions in the form of purchases and sales was important from the standpoint of profit earnings. Overall, between 1952 and 1962, the sale of foreign currencies by Barclays Bank (DCO) in the West Indies rose by 111 per cent, while purchases increased by 95 per cent over the same period (see Figure 7.6).

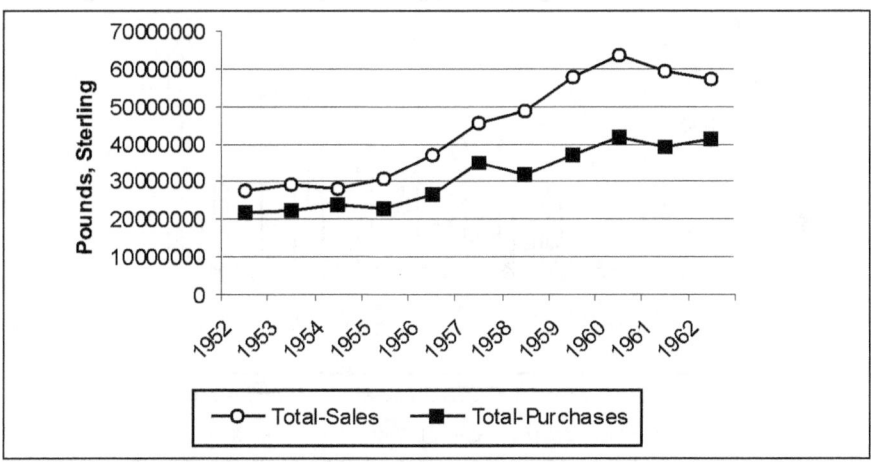

Figure 7.6 Barclays Bank (DCO), West Indian Branch accounts: foreign currency transactions, 1952–1962
Source: Amalgamated Results, Statistics and Review, September 1952–62, BBA 29/171, BBA 29/173, BBA 29/155.

Most of these transactions were in sterling, reflecting the region's general trade direction, which was still overwhelmingly tied with the United Kingdom.[71] Sterling accounted for an average of 76 per cent of total sales and purchases, whereas US dollar currency transactions accounted for an average of 15 per cent of total sales and 20 per cent of total purchases during the period 1952–62. Canadian dollar currency transactions accounted for an average of 8 per cent of total sales and 3 per cent of total purchases (see Figures 7.6a and 7.6b).

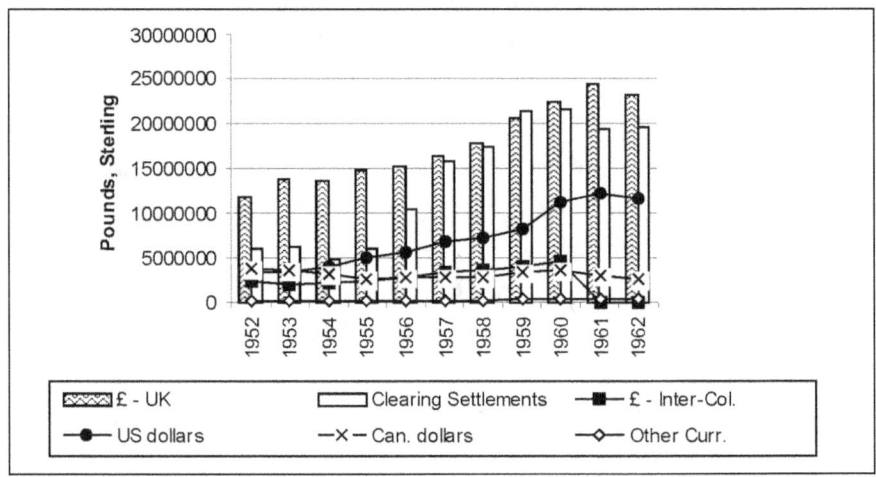

Figure 7.6a Barclays Bank (DCO), West Indian branch accounts: foreign currency sales, 1952–1962

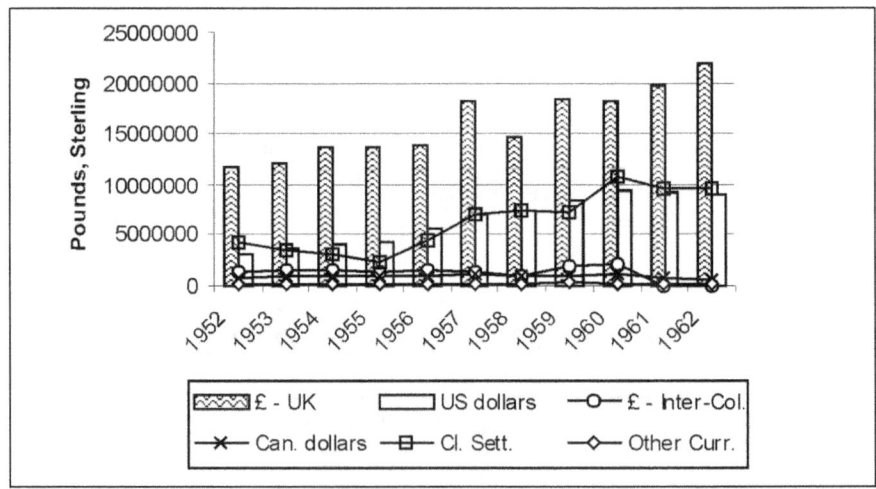

Figure 7.6b Barclays Bank (DCO), West Indian branch accounts: foreign currency purchases, 1952–1962
Source: Amalgamated Results, Statistics and Review, September 1952–62, BBA 29/171, BBA 29/173, BBA 29/155.

Overall, profits from foreign exchange transactions grew modestly, by 18 per cent, from £211,505 to £250,562, between 1952 and 1962. The most substantial increase occurred from 1956 to 1957, when profits increased by 28 per cent. A number of factors were accountable for this relatively modest growth over the period in spite of the rapid turnover in sales and purchases of foreign currencies. First, instead of having their trade bills, which were drawn on London, being remitted in sterling, a number of the large sugar-producing companies opted to have their money remitted by telegraphic transfer in local currency. At least one bauxite company in British Guiana had begun this practice in the early 1950s.[72] Branches that were heavily reliant on this aspect of the business were severely affected by this practice. For example, the manager of the Port Maria branch in St Mary, Jamaica, in commenting on the impact of this practice by one of the major sugar companies operating in that parish, noted that "we have had no negotiations on [their] bills since last year . . . and should this continue, we feel it would be difficult to show a profit for the succeeding half year".[73] The May Pen branch in St Catherine also felt the impact of the practice and registered a 50 per cent decline in exchange revenue, from £6,446 in 1960 to £3,235 in 1961.[74]

The downturn in general trading conditions between 1961 and 1962 was another factor contributing to the decline in revenue from foreign exchange transactions. Dry-goods merchants, finding trade conditions dull, experienced a top-heavy position in their stocks from the early part of 1958 and so curtailed their importation of goods, which resulted in a reduction in the bank's foreign exchange sales and earnings.[75] A major Jamaican wholesale merchant company reduced its foreign exchange transactions with the bank by £200,000 in 1961.[76]

Perhaps the most important factor was the evolution of "street" transactions in foreign currency, particularly in sterling.[77] This phenomenon manifested itself in the late 1950s, particularly in Jamaica, where it was reported that a number of business houses sold sterling to other companies, bypassing the services of the commercial banks. It was noted that a long-standing and valuable client of Barclays Bank (DCO) who was involved in sugar production and trade received £100,000 in sterling currency from a well-known American multinational firm and a local firm in 1958.[78] It is not clear why this practice arose, but it appears that it was less expensive than going through the banks. It might have also been a matter of convenience, as companies were often affiliated with one another by having the same parent company. The Savanna-la-Mar branch in Westmoreland found that its normal exchange profits had dropped by some £650, mainly because a certain company had arranged with an affiliated company operating in Jamaica to obtain the equivalent of £170,000 in local currency rather than going through the bank.[79] As the local director for the West Indies pointed out,

> [E]ven if [the banks] quoted par for buying Sterling this would not result in the business being handled by the banks, as in many cases business houses having Sterling to sell also are associated with others who want Sterling and nothing less than also selling Sterling at par would meet the case.[80]

In spite of exchange rates being lowered, the practice of street foreign-exchange transactions continued, much to the bank's distress.[81] This was evident in the report of the manager of the main branch at Kingston in 1961, who noted that "the question of street exchange continues to be a vexing one as most of our customers indulge in this habit some time or another and we feel that a great deal of business which would be profitable to the bank is being side-tracked".[82] In view of this, consideration again was given to reducing the spread of exchange rates in the hope that the street exchange would decline.[83]

Commission revenue arose from the fees charged for services regarding the negotiation of local trade bills, for issuing letters of credit and accepting drafts drawn under letters of credit. Revenue from safe custody services, as well as fees charged for the upkeep of ledgers and those charged for the issue of guarantees and indemnities, were also referred to as commission. In general, then, commission profits reflected the level of the various categories of the business conducted by a bank. Commission received by the Barclays Bank (DCO) West Indian branches showed a 416 per cent increase between 1952 and 1962, underscoring the tremendous growth of the bank's business in the region in this period. Overall, profits in the form of commission contributed an annual average of 8.5 per cent of total profits (see Table 7.5).

Discount earnings contributed the least of all categories, an annual average of 0.6 per cent, to total profits (see Table 7.5). These profits were really the interest retained by a bank at the time that a note acceptance or a bill was discounted and the proceeds given to the customer. In

Towards Independence: Bank Performance, 1940–1962

effect, discount earnings were to some extent a reflection of the level of bills in the system. The low proportion of this category of profits suggests that the use of local bills as an instrument of credit was on the decline in the West Indies.

Operational Costs

While a significant amount of operating profits was generated by Barclays Bank (DCO)'s West Indian operations during the period 1952–62, it was done at a tremendous cost. Gross profits increased by 180 per cent and net profits by only 55 per cent for the same period. This occurred because the costs incurred with the increased business were perpetually high, rising by 254 per cent between 1952 and 1962, accounting for an average of 72 per cent of gross profits (see Figure 7.7).

Salaries accounted for the highest proportion of the total expenses, averaging 45 per cent, and increased by 139 per cent between 1952 and 1962 (see Table 7.5). This was a result of both a tremendous increase in the number of employees and increases in emoluments made in an effort to recruit and retain staff, since other sectors, especially the civil service, offered more attractive salaries. Increases were also made in response to the dramatic rise in the cost of living. In April and October 1958, approval

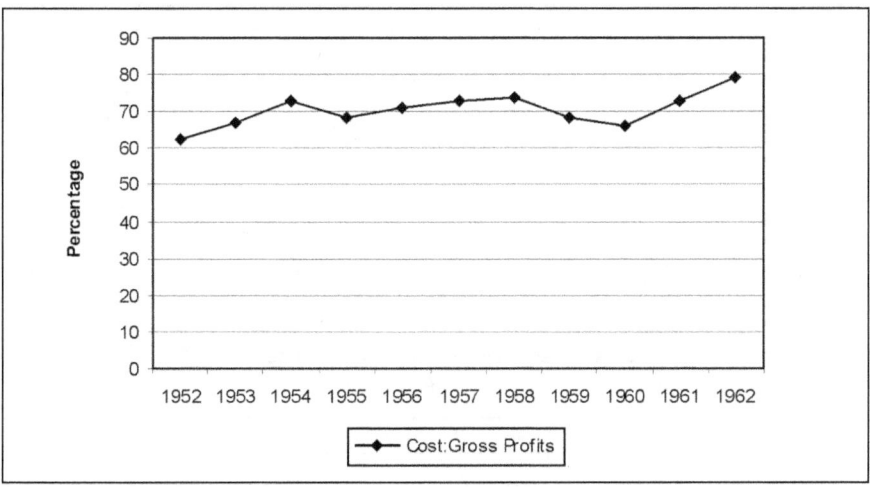

Figure 7.7 Barclays Bank (DCO), West Indian branch accounts: cost as a percentage of gross operating profits, 1952–1962

Source: Amalgamated Results, Statistics and Review, September 1952–62, BBA 29/171, BBA 29/173, BBA 29/155.

was given for increases of £175 per annum for senior married men in Nassau, where the cost of living was especially high, and territorial allowances were increased by £10 to £250 per annum for all staff. In addition, increases ranging from £20 for bachelors to £45 per annum for senior married officials with children were approved. All of this added up to an increase of approximately £50,000 in salaries from 1957 to 1958, with a further jump by nearly £100,000 between 1959 and 1962, following approval granted in June 1960, March 1961 and August 1962.[84] These increases, particularly those made in 1961, were largely responsible for the fall in net profits from 1961 to 1962.[85]

The interest paid on deposits was the second-largest proportion of the costs incurred by the bank in the West Indies, averaging 27.5 per cent between 1952 and 1962 (see Table 7.5). Both the number of accounts and the level of deposits were responsible: the level of deposits rose from £26 million in 1952 to £57 million in 1962, and the number of accounts grew by over 300 per cent in the same period. In addition, with a view to improving its liquidity position, the bank increased interest rates on deposits, which added to the costs incurred in attracting deposits. Interest rates paid on current credit balances were increased by 53 per cent; those on savings accounts were increased by 82 per cent, while rates paid on deposit accounts were raised by 287 per cent (see Figure 7.8).

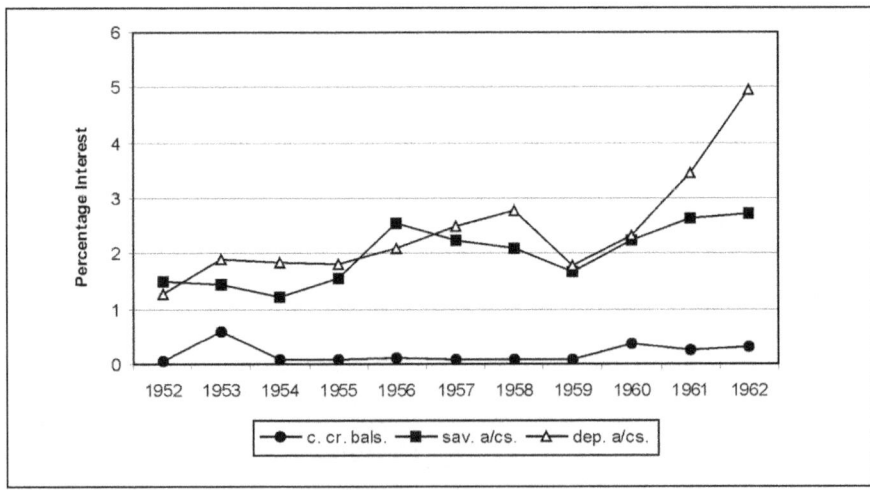

Figure 7.8 Barclays Bank (DCO), West Indian branch accounts: interest paid on deposits, 1952–1962
Source: Amalgamated Results, Statistics and Review, September 1952–62, BBA 29/171, BBA 29/173, BBA 29/155.

This area of cost rose from 20.6 per cent of total expenses in 1952 to 41.3 per cent in 1962, which was a much higher proportion than the rise for salaries. In fact, salaries as a proportion of total costs declined from 54.1 per cent in 1952 to 36.5 per cent in 1962 (see Table 7.5), which was achieved largely through the substitution of British staff for West Indians and the increased employment of women.[86]

Other expenses included rental for buildings and utility rates, as well as taxes and insurance, which accounted for an average of 10 per cent of total cost of operations. These costs rose mainly on account of the establishment of more offices throughout the region. Costs such as repairs and other office expenses, postage, stationery, legal charges and travel expenses amounted to approximately 12 per cent. The most significant increase in this category occurred in 1955, when stationery costs rose from £16,800 to £38,700 as a result of changes in the indenting system of the bank. In addition, extensive repairs and improvements to buildings were undertaken in view of the increased customer base, and also in response to the increased competition in the commercial banking sector.[87]

Summary

Barclays Bank (DCO)'s West Indian operations remained an important section of the bank's business in the period 1940–62. This was clearly evident in the almost constant growth in the level of operating profits that the section contributed to the bank as a whole. The section's importance was particularly significant given the difficulties, resulting in losses, in the other territorial areas of operations.

The increase in profits of the West Indian Section during this period was helped by the continuation of the imperial preferential marketing arrangements. By providing for a guaranteed market and remunerative prices for the region's agricultural produce, particularly sugar, the bulk purchasing arrangement during and after World War II ensured a measure of profitability for producers, which in turn gave the bank profitable business. The CSA of 1951, which succeeded the bulk purchasing arrangement in 1953, provided continued protection of colonial produce in the British market, thereby ensuring growth and profitability in the region's sugar industry.

As important as these imperial preferential marketing arrangements were, however, it was the business opportunities which arose from the expansion of other sectors in the region in the 1950s which were largely accountable for the swell in Barclays Bank (DCO)'s profits in this period. These areas included the further expansion of the petroleum industry in Trinidad and Tobago and bauxite mining in British Guiana and Jamaica, as well as the development and expansion of the manufacturing and tourism sectors, primarily in Jamaica, Trinidad and Tobago, and the Bahamas. This latter stemmed primarily from the implementation of the Puerto Rican economic model adopted by the various governments throughout the West Indies; and while the economic expansion which followed was uneven across the region, it was sufficient to generate significant business opportunities for banking. Indeed, all categories of Barclays Bank (DCO)'s business underwent significant increase in this period.

The increase in business conducted by the bank in this period came at a high cost. Operational costs accounted for a fairly high proportion of the gross profits recorded by the West Indian branches. Interest paid on deposits, and salaries and allowances accounted for the highest proportion of costs. Other significant costs included those associated with the extension of the bank's representation throughout the region. This, along with other responses, formed part of the strategies adopted by Barclays Bank (DCO) to deal with the changed social, economic and political environment, and are the subject of discussion in the following chapter.

Chapter Eight

Towards Independence

*Branch Expansion, Competition and
Product Diversification, 1940–1962*

This chapter examines the strategies adopted by Barclays Bank (DCO) in response to the economic expansion in the West Indies between 1940 and 1962. They included improving its resource capabilities in terms of representation, which was necessary if the bank was to take advantage of new business opportunities that had arisen as a result of new developments in the service and industrial sectors. Other strategies were adopted in response to increased competitive challenges from its rivals in the region. The chapter concludes with a discussion of the bank's diversification in products and services.

Branch Expansion

The most obvious reflection of the impact of economic expansion was the tremendous growth in the number of branches established by Barclays Bank (DCO). Between 1940 and 1962 its branches in the West Indies increased from twenty-three to eighty-seven (see Table 8.1).[1] Most of this increase occurred in Jamaica, Trinidad and Tobago, and the Bahamas, where the most significant economic expansion occurred – obviously in response to perceived business opportunities. This was aptly demonstrated by its decision to establish representation in the Bahamas,

Table 8.1 Number of Barclays Bank (DCO) Branches and Sub-branches in the West Indies, 1939–1962

Territory	1939	1955	1962
Antigua	1	1	1
Barbados	1	1	1
British Guiana	3	5	9
Dominica	1	1	2
Grenada	1	1	2
Jamaica	10	12	27
St Kitts	1	1	1
St Lucia	1	1	3
St Vincent	1	1	2
Trinidad & Tobago	2	11	21
Bahamas	–	3	15
Cayman Islands	1	1	1
British Honduras	–	2	2
Total	23	41	87

Source: Amalgamated Results, Statistics, and Review of the Periods Ending 30 September 1953 to 1961, BBA 29/173, BBA 29/155; HBJ 1939, 183; HBJ 1955, 223; HBJ 1962, 330; The West Indies and Caribbean Year Book, 1962, 48, 77, 151, 201, 249, 307, 361, 379, 391.

British Honduras and the Cayman Islands in the 1950s. Initially, the bank was motivated to enter the Bahamas because of oil companies' interest in the area. However, after 1945 its main interest rested on developments in tourism and the business opportunities which stemmed from this sector. This was evident in the thinking of A.C. Barnes, then vice chairman of the bank, who noted during a scouting trip to the region in 1946 the presence of a considerable number of very wealthy British, American and Canadian winter residents who owned or leased homes for the season. Following his trip, the bank's first Bahamian office was opened in Nassau on Bay Street in October 1947.[2]

At least four more sub-branches were added by 1958, all on account of the increase in tourism and the attendant expansion in the commercial sector throughout the 1940s and 1950s. Much of this development was

Plate 8.1 Freeport City branch, Grand Bahama, the Bahamas. *DCO Quarterly Magazine* (May 1960).

spearheaded by tax concessions which applied not only to the industrial and commercial sectors but also to personal income. The bank opened offices on New Providence Island, and close to exclusive residential areas at Coral Harbour and Palmdale and near luxury shopping facilities at Lyford Cay.[3]

Barclays Bank (DCO) was also encouraged to extend offices to the Bahamian Out Islands, where tourism was burgeoning. Bank offices were established at West End, Elbow Cay and Hopetown on Grand Bahama; at Marsh Harbour on Great Abaco Island; at New Plymouth on Green Turtle Cay; and at Frances Town on Andros. All these areas offered expanded tourist accommodation including clubs, guest houses and small hotels, as well as blocks of cooperative apartments built specifically for the executive staff of multinational corporations.[4]

Growth in tourism encouraged expansion to the Cayman Islands, though developments there in the 1950s were nowhere near as spectacular as in the Bahamas. A sub-branch to the Kingston, Jamaica, branch was opened in March 1953 at George Town, Grand Cayman.[5] It was upgraded to a full branch in 1957.[6]

In British Honduras the establishment of the Corazol Sugar Factory and ensuing development of the sugar industry provided the incentive for the opening of a branch at Belize in September 1949. In 1953 a sub-branch was established at Stann Creek, the second largest town in the colony, as the citrus industry developed there. British Honduras was also attractive to commercial banking because American land developers were showing an interest in it in the 1950s.[7]

Plate 8.2 Barclays Bank (DCO) Harris Promenade branch, San Fernando, Trinidad and Tobago. Republic Bank Ltd, *From Colonial to Republic*, 129.

An expansion programme was also undertaken in Trinidad and Tobago, where the number of branches increased from just two in 1939, at San Fernando and Marine Square, to twenty-one by 1962 (see Table 8.1). A significant number of branches were opened in the burgeoning commercial centres of Sangre Grande and Tragarete Road. In the capital, Port of Spain, additional branches were established in 1954, at Frederick Street and at the Harris Promenade, located at 55 High Street in San Fernando; the latter proved to be well placed, as its business continually increased throughout the 1950s.[8]

The expansion of the oil industry encouraged the extension of branches to the rural areas of Fyzabad, Pointe-a-Pierre, Point Fortin and Siparia, where Apex Trinidad Oilfields, Trinidad Leaseholds Ltd, and United British Oilfields of Trinidad (UBOT), a subsidiary of Shell Oil Co., operated drilling stations. Indeed, the expansion of the oil industry during this period had resulted in a tremendous increase in wages disbursed, rising from $22 million in 1949 to $100 million by 1962.[9] Therefore, as the bank undertook a major drive for deposits during the 1950s, such areas became important targets for new branches.

Branches were also opened in rural agricultural areas, including the sugar-producing areas of Couva, Tunapuna, and Chaguanas, which was also noted for rice cultivation. Offices were opened at Arima and Princess Town, where settlers were engaged in the cultivation of vegetable gardens, cocoa, coffee and other tropical fruits.

The greatest expansion of the bank occurred in Jamaica, where the number of offices increased from ten in 1939 to twenty-seven by 1962 (see Table 8.1). Much of this expansion involved the opening of branches in the urban and suburban areas of Kingston and St Andrew. In Kingston, expansion in the manufacturing and commercial sectors prompted the establishment of branches in the vicinity of the growing industrial complex at Industrial Estate on Spanish Town Road. The expansion in retailing and wholesaling in Kingston also encouraged the establishment of branches on Harbour Street and West Queen Street, as the main one at King Street came under pressure owing to increased commercial activity in the Kingston metropolitan area.[10] Branches were also established at Windward Road, Half Way Tree and Cross Roads, areas which were expanding commercially as well as being close to the growing middle-class residential areas in St Andrew such as Vineyard Town, Hagley Park, Richmond Park and Kencot.[11]

Plate 8.3 Barclays Bank (DCO)'s branch at Arima, Trinidad and Tobago, opened in 1953. Republic Bank Ltd, *From Colonial to Republic*, 131.

Developments in the bauxite and alumina industry in the 1950s encouraged the extension of branches to the rural towns and surrounding areas, where the retail and other commercial sectors responded accordingly. For example, in the parish of St Ann, where Reynolds Jamaica Ltd conducted mining operations, branches were established at Ocho Rios and Brown's Town. Reynolds Jamaica was operating mining works at Ewarton in St Catherine in 1956. This encouraged the bank to establish a branch at Linstead, a town which expanded greatly when the company erected a £12 million plant in 1958.[12] Branches were established at Mandeville, Porus and Christiana in the parish of Manchester, where the Aluminium Company of Canada had established mining operations, and at Santa Cruz in St Elizabeth and Christiana in Manchester, where the Kaiser Bauxite Company was based.[13] A branch was established at Old Harbour in the parish of St Catherine, just three miles from Old Harbour Bay, where Alumina (Jamaica) Ltd, a subsidiary of the Canadian Aluminium Company, had constructed Port Esquivel, which was connected by rail to its Shooter's Hill plant in Manchester.[14]

Branches were also extended to rural interior towns in the sugar- and banana-producing areas. In the parish of Clarendon, branches were established at May Pen and Lionel Town and at Chapelton, which by this time had developed into an important distributive retail trading area. Clarendon during this period contained three important sugar factories, namely New Yarmouth and Vere, both operated by the Tate and Lyle subsidiary West Indies Sugar Co. Ltd, and Bog Estate. The towns of Port Maria and Annotto Bay in St Mary underwent commercial expansion as a result of increased banana production. Branches were established at Spanish Town, which was in the vicinity of the Caymanas Estate, Bernard Lodge and Inswood sugar factories in St Catherine.[15]

The rapid development of the hotel and tourist sector on the north coast of Jamaica encouraged the establishment of branches at Port Maria, Ocho Rios and Montego Bay. Developments at Montego Bay in the 1950s were particularly promising from a banking point of view. This was noted by one bank official on a visit to the resort town in 1959:

> The hotels are extremely prosperous and swing well into credit. There are only 1,200 beds in Montego Bay and it is absolutely full for the short season . . . [The] Tryall development which was being carried out by rich Texans, making an 18 hole golf course, club rooms and beach houses, and were sell-

ing off about 300 plots to rich Americans to build holiday homes. They are asking and getting about £10,000 per acre. It is astonishing how many crazy rich people there are in the world![16]

There was also a fair degree of branch expansion by the bank in British Guiana, where the number increased from three in 1940 to nine by 1962 (see Table 8.1).[17] While significant investments had been made in British Guiana before 1939 by Canadian bauxite-mining companies, the election of a socialist-oriented government led by Cheddi Jagan, its subsequent dissolution and the suspension of the constitution by the British in 1953 resulted in uncertainty that deterred any further investments. In fact, this situation had contributed to an outflow of funds from the colony after 1953.[18] Branch expansion was therefore confined primarily to the urban areas, encouraged by the resultant increase in commercial activity spawned by developments in the agricultural and mining sectors. New branches were established at Regent Street and High Street, joining the long-established main branch at Water Street in Georgetown. A branch was also established on Main Street, which was an elite residential area containing grand homes with well-manicured lawns and included one entrance to the governor's residence. A branch was also established at Kitty, which was a semi-rural suburban area just outside of Georgetown, and at Anna Regina, a rural agricultural community on the Essequibo River. A second branch was established in New Amsterdam, at Springlands, on the Corentyne River bordering Suriname. This rural

Plate 8.4 New Amsterdam branch, Berbice, British Guiana. *DCO Quarterly Magazine* (October 1957).

area was heavily populated by settlers of East Indian ancestry who were either rice and livestock farmers or labourers on the sugar plantations in the area.[19]

The least expansion occurred in the Windward and Leeward Islands and Barbados, which was not surprising given the absence of any significant development outside of the agricultural sector. In Dominica, the growth of the banana industry led to the opening in Portsmouth in 1957 of a sub-branch to the main branch at Roseau,[20] whereas in the other Windward Islands, the Leeward Islands and Barbados, increased representation was limited to the establishment of agencies. Agencies were established at Hastings and Speighstown in Barbados to take advantage of business opportunities in tourism. Similarly, an agency was established at Vieux Fort in St Lucia, linked to the main branch at Castries, and the Nevis agency opened in 1958, linked to the main branch in St Kitts.[21]

Agency versus Sub-branch and Branch

The establishment of an agency rather than a branch or a sub-branch was an important strategic method utilized by commercial banks when circumstances did not justify more permanent representation in a particular area or territory. The idea behind the establishment of an agency in a particular area or territory was that, while some amount of business existed that was worth tapping into, it was not sufficient to warrant the establishment of a more permanent presence which would require the expenditure of fixed capital. In reference to the agency that was operated at Nevis, it was noted in 1962:

> Owing to the island's poor economy the expansion of our business has been slow and it appears that the up-grading of the agency to sub-branch status will not be warranted for some time to come . . . we do not consider that further increased representation is warranted unless more visits could be made at little additional cost.[22]

Operating an agency rather than a sub-branch or a full branch was one way banks kept their transaction costs to a minimum. The agency was, in effect, an extension of a sub-branch or branch.[23] The business that was contracted by agencies was on behalf of the particular parent branch or sub-branch, and therefore the profits and expenses incurred were reflected in that branch or sub-branch's accounts. Indeed, the operation of an agency entailed staff, usually a clerk, from the principal branch travelling out to rented premises. Such premises could very well be located in strategic locations; the one at Fyzabad shared accommodation with a rum shop located underneath a dance hall.[24] Costs were also kept to a minimum as the agencies were usually only open only for limited hours on certain weekdays. For example, the Scarborough agency in Tobago was open only two days per week, at which time the staff was flown in from the main branch at Marine Square in Port of Spain.[25] Some operated even less frequently, such as the one at Nevis in 1962, which was opened twice a month on a Friday, presumably timed to coincide with workers receiving their pay packets and thus enhancing the bank's savings-deposit business.[26] Agencies were particularly convenient for the transaction of ephemeral business such as that which took place at trade shows and exhibitions. For example, Barclays Bank (DCO) operated an agency at the Agricultural and Industrial show in Jamaica on 19 and 20 November 1953, and another at the Trinidad Trade Fair during April 1954.[27]

The bank's practice of operating agencies was not novel to this period. However, the earlier custom was to use local commercial firms to conduct basic banking business on the bank's behalf. For example, with the closure of the sub-branch at Scarborough that the Colonial Bank had maintained between 1914 and 1919, Miller's Stores was contracted to conduct banking business on its behalf. Similarly, Messrs J.E. Kerr and Co. operated as an agent for the Colonial Bank in Montego Bay for many years. This early practice of establishing agencies was similar in principle to correspondent banking, wherein foreign and overseas banks acted as correspondent agents for British domestic and other foreign banks which did not have branches in the particular country.[28] After the bank was re-incorporated as Barclays Bank (DCO) in 1926, the agencies that were established were under the direct control of a sub-branch or branch of the bank.

Where warranted, agencies were upgraded to sub-branch and eventually to full branch status. Several of the branches established by the bank in the West Indies had their origin as agencies to branches and sub-branches already in existence.[29] Such a change in status involved a significant change in the operational relationship between the respective offices. Sub-branches, while offering a full banking service and maintaining an independent accounting system from that of the parent branch, were still subordinate to that branch. This meant that the sub-manager in charge was accountable to the manager of the parent branch in all matters, including the approval of loans and advances. Even though it was thought that there was sufficient profitable business to justify the upgrading of an agency to a sub-branch, the level of risk was believed to necessitate continued supervision by the parent branch. With the upgrade to the status of a full branch, the manager became accountable to either the head office or to the local controlling office.[30]

Competition and Collusion

The extension of its branch and agency network in the region, while responsive to increased business opportunity, was also a major aspect of Barclays Bank (DCO)'s competitive strategy during this period. Competition among the various banks became more intense as the number of branches among them increased, from 52 in 1939 to 187 by 1962 (see Tables 3.1 and 8.2).

Like Barclays, the Canadian banks extended their branch network in the region during this period. Barclays Bank (DCO)'s main rival continued to be the RBC, which increased its number from thirteen to forty-five by 1962. The RBC extended its operations to St Lucia and St Vincent, where Barclays Bank (DCO) until then had been the only commercial bank.[31] It also operated a one-day-per-week agency at Mango Creek in southern British Honduras. This made it the only competitor bank to be represented at almost every point in the region where Barclays Bank (DCO) was established.[32] The only territories where the two were not in competition were Montserrat, where Barclays Bank (DCO) remained unrepresented, and Tobago, Nevis and Grand Cayman, where the RBC was not present. In Jamaica, the RBC increased its number of offices from two to six. In addition to its Montego Bay branch and its main branch at Duke Street in Kingston, the bank established four more branches in Kingston and St Andrew, some of which were close to the British bank.[33]

Competition was keen between the RBC and Barclays Bank (DCO) in

Table 8.2 Number of Branches and Sub-branches of Multinational Banks in the West Indies, 1962

	RBC	CIBC	BNS	DCO	BOLAM	Chase	CityBank
Antigua	1	0	1	1	0	0	0
Barbados	2	1	1	1	0	0	0
British Guiana	11	0	0	9	0	0	0
Dominica	1	0	0	2	0	0	0
Grenada	2	0	0	2	0	0	0
Jamaica	6	6	27	27	2	0	1
Montserrat	1	0	0	0	0	0	0
St Kitts	1	0	0	1	0	0	0
St Lucia	1	0	0	3	0	0	0
St Vincent	1	0	0	2	0	0	0
Trinidad & Tobago	7	2	2	21	2	0	0
Cayman Islands	0	0	0	1	0	0	0
British Honduras	1	0	0	2	2	0	0
Bahamas	10	3	1	15	1	1	2
Total	45	12	32	87	7	1	3

Source: *Royal Bank of Canada, Annual Report, 1962*, 43; Amalgamated Results, Statistics and Review, 1953–1961, BBA 29/171, BBA 29/173, BBA 29/155.

the Bahamas, where the Canadian bank, having been established since 1908, enjoyed first-mover advantages. The RBC held an excellent franchise among the Bay Street retail and commercial business sector and was in control of the majority of the colonial government accounts and at least half of the hotel and tourist business.[34] In spite of this head start, Barclays Bank (DCO) – while able to capture only a "fringe" of the lucrative Bay Street business – was able by the 1950s to garner a substantial portion of the commercial banking market. This was a result of the timing of its entry into the market, which coincided with the major expansion of the tourist industry on the islands, allowing it to gain a sizeable segment of the growing hotel and tourist market.[35]

The BNS continued to be Barclays Bank (DCO)'s main rival in Jamaica, where it increased its number of branches from thirteen to twenty-seven by 1962. Many of these branches were located in the same

Plate 8.5 The Bank of Nova Scotia, King Street branch, Kingston, Jamaica, 1960. *Courtesy of the National Library of Jamaica.*

Plate 8.6 Royal Bank of Canada, King Street branch, Kingston, Jamaica, 1960. *Courtesy of the National Library of Jamaica.*

Plate 8.7 The Canadian Bank of Commerce, Corner of King Street and Harbour Street, Kingston, Jamaica, c. 1962. *Courtesy of the National Library of Jamaica.*

Plate 8.8 The Bank of Nova Scotia, Bridgetown branch, Barbados, 1962. *West Indies and Caribbean Year Book, 1962.*

Table 8.3 Location of Branches and Sub-branches of Barclays Bank (DCO) and BNS in Jamaica, 1962

Barclays Bank (DCO)	Bank of Nova Scotia
1. King Street, Kingston	King Street, Kingston
2. Harbour Street, Kingston	Duke Street, Kingston
3. West Queen Street, Kingston	East Queen Street, Kingston
4. Industrial Estate, Kingston	Princess Street, Kingston
5. Windward Road, Kingston	Victoria Avenue, St Andrew
6. Cross Roads, St Andrew	Cross Roads, St Andrew
7. Half Way Tree, St Andrew	Half Way Tree, St Andrew
8. Montego Bay, St James	Hagley Park Rd, St Andrew
9. Savanna-la-Mar, Westmoreland	Liguanea Plaza, St Andrew
10. Lucea, Trelawny	Savanna-la-Mar, Westmoreland
11. Falmouth, Trelawny	Claremont, St Ann
12. St Ann's Bay, St Ann	Discovery Bay, St Ann
13. Brown's Town, St Ann	St Ann's Bay, St Ann
14. Ocho Rios, St Ann	Brown's Town, St Ann
15. Linstead, St Catherine	Ocho Rios, St Ann
16. Port Maria, St Mary	Linstead, St Catherine
17. Annotto Bay, St Mary	Port Maria, St Mary
18. Mandeville, Manchester	Highgate, St Mary
19. Christiana, Manchester	Oracabessa, St Mary
20. Porus, Manchester	Mandeville, Manchester
21. Santa Cruz, St Elizabeth	Christiana, Manchester
22. May Pen, Clarendon	Black River, St Elizabeth
23. Chapelton, Clarendon	May Pen, Clarendon
24. Lionel Town, Clarendon	Clarke's Town, Clarendon
25. Spanish Town, St Catherine	May Pen, Clarendon
26. Old Harbour, St Catherine	Spanish Town, St Catherine
27. Morant Bay, St Thomas	Port Antonio, Portland

Source: HBJ 1962, 330.

parish as Barclays Bank (DCO)'s. Of the twenty-seven branches established by BNS in Jamaica, fourteen were in the same vicinity as those of Barclays Bank (DCO) (see Table 8.3). Nevertheless, Barclays Bank (DCO) continued to maintain an excellent franchise in Jamaica, and Montego

Bay remained one of its strongholds, where it controlled approximately 80 per cent of the hotel business.[36]

The BNS was far less of a threat outside Jamaica, though it had established branches in Trinidad and Tobago in 1956 and in Antigua in 1962. A branch was also opened in Nassau, Bahamas.[37]

The CBC also underwent moderate expansion throughout the region during this period, opening a branch in Nassau in 1957.[38] A second branch was opened in Barbados and three more in Trinidad and Tobago. In Jamaica, it opened branches at Half Way Tree, Ocho Rios, Port Antonio and Montego Bay, and an agency at Buff Bay in Portland, which offered competition to Barclays Bank (DCO)'s Annotto Bay agency.[39] The CBC's competitive capabilities were enhanced when in 1961 it merged with the Imperial Bank of Canada to form the Canadian Imperial Bank of Commerce (hereafter the CIBC). Prior to the merger, Barclays Bank (DCO) acted as a correspondent agent for the Imperial in the region, with the Imperial representing its interests in Canada following the closure of its subsidiary office, Barclays Bank (Canada).[40]

This relationship ended following the CBC/Imperial merger. The move had come as a surprise for the Barclays Bank Ltd representatives on the Imperial's board, and after failing to get a withdrawal of the CIBC from the region, Crossley was forced to resign from the board of the Imperial Bank of Canada.[41]

Developments in the region's economy also attracted the Bank of London and Montreal (hereafter BOLAM). The BOLAM was the result of a collaboration between the Bank of London and South America (hereafter BOLSA) and the Bank of Montreal. This collaboration was part of BOLSA's overall strategy to modify its functional and geographical specialization as a result of its decline in Latin America, where it faced stiff competition from American banks. It was particularly affected by the increasing demand for dollars – a currency that it was grossly short of – to finance trade, which helps to explain the entry of the BOLAM into Nassau in 1958.[42] A Kingston branch was opened in 1959, followed by branches in Port of Spain and San Fernando in 1960.[43]

The economic expansion in the region attracted American multinational banks. The First National City Bank of New York (hereafter City Bank), which had extensive branches in Latin America, opened in Nassau in 1959,[44] and in Kingston the following year.[45] It was joined by the Chase Manhattan Bank (hereafter the Chase), which opened in the Bahamas in 1960.[46]

The entry of these banks to the region was part of the beginning of the phenomenal "second wave" in multinational banking, which occurred after 1960 and was dominated by American banks. This "wave" coincided with the tremendous growth in American worldwide foreign direct investment.[47] However, whereas the advent of American multinational banks had precipitated the loss of considerable market share held by British multinational banks in Latin America,[48] this was not the case in the West Indies. It appeared, in fact, that the American banks found it difficult to combat the excellent franchise already established by Barclays Bank (DCO) and the Canadian banks. The American banks arrived between the late 1950s and early 1960s, well after the main thrust of the expansion of the incumbent banks. As well, the lack of experience and proficiency in the region by some of them appears to have been a handicap. The lack of experience was largely the result of American legislation which had the effect of limiting not only the development of American multinational banking but also branch banking in the United States, so that most American domestic banks confined their operations to their home state. Further, most states restricted banks to a single office. It was only in 1913 that the Federal Reserve Act allowed nationally chartered banks with over $1 million in capital to establish foreign branches. At that time, only six American banks had branches abroad, and only a handful of national banks had branches. Even in 1960, most American banks could not branch freely in their home state.[49]

This lack of experience affected personnel, which was evident in the Chase early in its history in the region. While on a tour of the islands, one of Barclays Bank (DCO)'s directors commented on the lawyer and ex-governor of the US Virgin Islands who headed the Chase operations in Nassau, saying that he "knew nothing about banking". He further noted that the American bank had "burnt their fingers in a big way here and are possibly letting their commercial business run down and are devoting their energies to the provision of local service for their very rich clients who come to Nassau for holiday".[50]

City Bank had far more experience than the Chase, having opened its first overseas branch in 1914, at Buenos Aires, Argentina, followed by an extensive retail branch network in Latin America and Cuba.[51] City Bank was limited, however, by the hold that Barclays Bank (DCO) and the Canadian banks had over the domestic banking market in the West Indies and the Bahamas, and so confined its operations to corporate banking, servicing the needs of American multinational firms. This helps to explain the very limited branch network of both American banks in the region (see Table 8.2).

Most of the competition for banking business, then, continued to be between Barclays Bank (DCO) and the Canadian banks. Barclays employed a variety of strategies to fend off this competition, including the establishment of first-mover advantages in particular areas and regions not yet cornered by a rival. This strategy was evident in its branch expansion programme in the Bahamas, where it targeted the Out Islands. As a result, it was able to establish total control of the lumber industry which subsequently developed at Abaco and Green Turtle Cay. In 1960 the bank noted that there were "signs of continuing development [in] Abaco . . . and we have reason to believe that we are obtaining a far more substantial share of the new development than are our competitors".[52]

Barclays Bank (DCO) also targeted areas where it believed further business opportunities would arise in spite of the established presence of a rival bank. For example, at its Brown's Town sub-branch in St Ann, business had been slow during the first five months after its opening in 1958, no doubt due to the BNS's well-established franchise there. Brown's Town was always a bustling market town with a fairly sizeable residential middle class. In the late 1950s Barclays Bank (DCO) saw indications of "a slow but steady increase" in business in general, which was expected to rise further with the resumption of full-scale operations by the bauxite companies.[53] Indeed, the town was to witness further commercial development on which both banks thrived for many years.

Another strategy for Barclays Bank (DCO) was to target areas where it perceived there was a need for banking services that a rival bank was not meeting. This was evident in the case of its Santa Cruz agency in the parish of St Elizabeth, where the volume of business had increased considerably, apparently at the expense of the BNS's branch at Black River. Initially, the BNS's Black River branch serviced that entire community and the surrounding areas of Lacovia and New Market. Subsequent developments in the surrounding areas made it feasible to establish an agency at Santa Cruz, which appeared to be more convenient for residents of Lacovia and New Market. Barclays Bank (DCO)'s Mandeville branch manager commented:

> We have acquired five current accounts from them [BNS] and are paying close attention to this area as it appears to be a thriving agricultural area with wonderful prospects for cattle rearing. We shall be opening three days per week from next month as we are now convinced that the neighbouring villages of Lacovia and New Market prefer to use the facilities at Santa Cruz rather than at Black River.[54]

Establishing and maintaining personal contact and visibility, even if that meant modifying an agency's standard operating procedure, constituted another important competitive strategy. This was evident in the bank's approach to competition with the BNS in the Christiana-Spauldings area in the parish of Manchester. Recognizing the business opportunities which existed in the town of Spauldings, which was not far from Christiana, where the BNS maintained a sub-branch, Barclays Bank (DCO) proposed a change in the operations of its Christiana agency, which operated under the control of the Mandeville branch. This entailed the agency being modified to function as "a 'one man subbranch' with a resident sub-manager subject to snap checks from the parent branch". It was felt that with "someone living on the spot in Christiana, he might well work up a business in Spauldings as well".[55]

The luring away of customers by offering better terms for banking services was yet another useful competitive strategy. It was through this method that Barclays Bank (DCO) was able to siphon off a small fraction of the Bahamian government business from the RBC. It did so by suggesting that it would be cheaper for the government to route its dollar business through the bank's New York agency, where the finer exchange rates would result in considerable savings. It also pointed out that "the dollars are periodically sold for sterling which is then remitted to the Crown Agents who allow four per cent per annum on the balance remaining in their hands".[56]

Another strategy that Barclays Bank (DCO) employed was to solicit their existing clients for introductions to individuals who the bank thought were likely to make excellent clients. For example, Crossley noted that, during a meeting with an important client who had substantial real estate business in the Bahamas, it was mentioned that a certain "lady . . . [who had] immense interests . . . [in] the Bahamas . . . and so could be a very valuable client . . . was promised to [be brought to the bank for introduction when she came to London in the summer]".[57]

Yet another productive strategy was to act as an agent for banks that were not established in the region. In this way, Barclays Bank (DCO) had much of the business of the Bank of Montreal, Chase Manhattan and City Bank before they were established, along with that of the First National Bank of Miami, the Imperial Bank of Canada, and Lloyds Bank. Barclays Bank (DCO) also took advantage of its extensive multinational network, accessing the banking business originating out of the Barclays group.[58]

The bank also utilized nation-specific advantages arising out of the legacy of British colonialism. This was particularly evident in its thinking with regard to its competition for savings deposits in the 1950s. Recognizing the potential savings business that could arise out of remittances made by West Indian immigrants in the United Kingdom, deputy chairman A.C. Barnes, on a visit to the region between December 1957 and January 1958, noted that this was one particular source which the bank was in a better position to tap than the Canadian banks. He observed the savings potential of the thirty thousand Jamaicans who had migrated to the United Kingdom by 1958:

> If every man remitted £100 a year, this would mean £3,000,000 per annum and I would not put this figure as anything out of the way having due regard to the size of some of the remittances coming through. This is where Barclays Bank Ltd are helping through their branches, but we should be sure we get as much of this business as possible.[59]

The need for work among unskilled West Indians and the demand for labour in Britain in the aftermath of World War II had led to substantial migration to the United Kingdom in the 1950s and early 1960s. Estimates put this migration somewhere between 230,000 and 280,000 between 1951 and 1961, and so Barnes's estimate of potential savings remittances was not unrealistic. Some £34,000 in new money in savings accounts was recorded at the Mandeville branch for the March to September 1961 period alone, and most of it originated in the remittances made by West Indian immigrants in the United Kingdom.[60] Other branches in Jamaica, as well as in St Lucia and St Vincent, raised substantial deposits in this way.[61]

The extent to which nation-specific competitive advantages continued to operate in favour of the Canadian banks during this period is not clear. It seems likely that the Canadian banks were able to capitalize on them, at least with regard to certain business. The banks were able to make arrangements with corporations in Canada before their establishment in the region, and apparently that was how they were able to capture the accounts of the Canadian bauxite companies which invested heavily in the region in the 1950s.[62]

A worthwhile and rewarding strategy of Barclays Bank (DCO) was to offer specialized convenience services to customers in return for a major portion of their banking business. This was evident in its approach to win some of the business of the bauxite-mining companies. The bank maintained two agencies on the compound of an American bauxite company operating in Jamaica, which were specifically for the convenience of workers at the mines to readily cash their salary cheques. In return, the company put through the bank all its remittances from its home office, thereby providing it with considerable foreign exchange business which had previously gone to its competitors.[63]

Another important aspect of the competition among the commercial banks had to do with the provision of amenities which facilitated the comfort of their clients. For example, the manager of the Cross Roads branch of Barclays Bank (DCO) noted that its new branch building that was under construction in 1961 would boast "better banking facilities . . . with more parking accommodation for cars", compared with the BNS's premises located a few yards away.[64] Building design and interior decor of commercial buildings, particularly of banks and other financial institutions, symbolized prestige, profitability and, importantly, stability, and thus were believed to play an important role in attracting and retaining clientele. Therefore, while many of Barclays Bank (DCO)'s branches were renovated or rebuilt because of the need for more space as a result of the increase in business, a great deal of attention and importance was also paid to design and decor.[65] Indeed, Barclays Bank (DCO)'s branch manager at Half Way Tree was genuinely of the opinion that the fact that the number of current accounts held there in 1961 was stagnant was partly a result of "the much more attractive appearance of [our] com-

Towards Independence: Expansion, Competition and Diversification, 1940–1962

petitor's [branch]".[66] Extensive renovation and refurbishing – involving the expenditure of over £365,000 – were carried out on the premier King Street branch in Kingston in 1955. Upon its completion, one of the directors on tour of the region opined that it was "probably the nicest branch in the bank, [with its] famous tile murals on the external wall", though "these were unfortunately difficult to see and probably ought to have been placed inside the building".[67]

Plate 8.9 Barclay's Bank (DCO), Half Way Tree branch, Kingston, Jamaica, 1957. *Courtesy of the National Library of Jamaica.*

Plate 8.10 Barclay's Bank (DCO), newly rebuilt King Street branch, Kingston, Jamaica, 1955. *Courtesy of the National Library of Jamaica.*

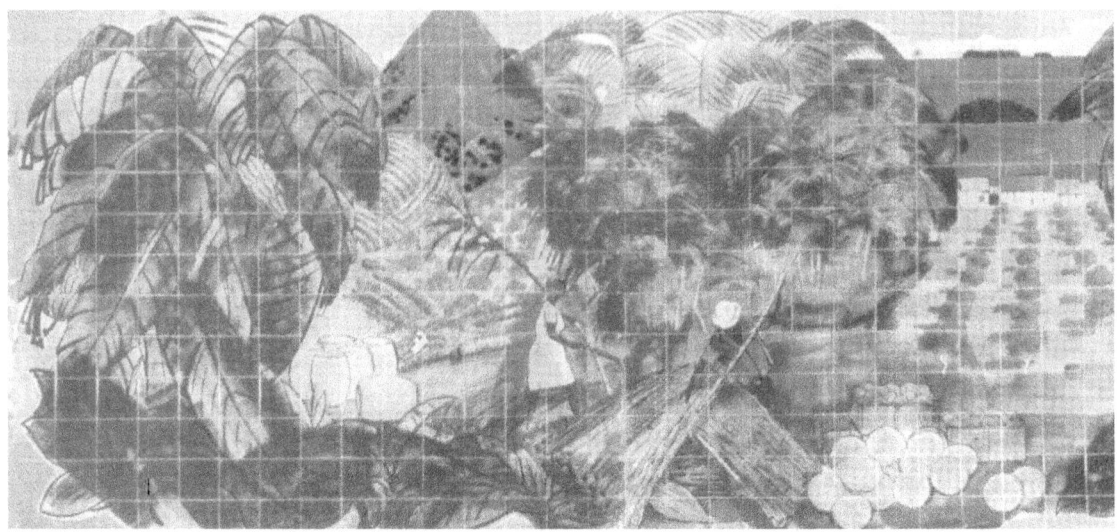

Plate 8.11 One of six murals that appeared on the outside of the King Street branch of Barclays Bank (DCO), 1955. *Courtesy of the National Library of Jamaica.*

These murals depicted the six regions – namely the West Indies, the Mediterranean, the Gold Coast, East Africa, the Rhodesias, and South Africa – where the bank had branches. The building itself, which was four storeys tall and covered approximately 10,000 square feet, boasted interior marble walls and a wooden counter made of the finest mahogany, sapodilla, and mahoe. A distinctive chandelier was suspended in the centre of the dome of the banking hall of the branch.[68] Barclays Bank (DCO) was also particularly proud of its Salvatori branch at Port of Spain, Trinidad.[69]

Such images suggested efficiency and professionalism in the provision of quality service. Barclays Bank (DCO) was appalled to learn that its Canadian competitors had introduced all-electric adding machines in their savings departments before Barclays, since this could convey the impression that the British bank was not as efficient and technologically advanced as its Canadian counterparts.[70] The bank's concern was clearly evident in the comments of George Money, the local director for the region, who noted:

> [W]e feel strongly that we must also be much more ready to adopt a fully mechanized system at the larger branches in order to provide a service which will not only be, *but seem to be,* the equal of or better than theirs. It is rather galling that even if we mechanize at our larger offices now, we shall in the eyes of the public be bringing up the rear instead of leading the way.[71]

Towards Independence: Expansion, Competition and Diversification, 1940–1962

Plate 8.12 Barclay's Bank (DCO), Harbour Street branch interior, Kingston, Jamaica, 1961. *West Indies and Caribbean Year Book,* 1961

Plate 8.13 View of Marine Square, Port of Spain, Trinidad and Tobago, showing the Salvatori building housing the Barclays Bank (DCO) branch. Republic Bank Ltd, *From Colonial to Republic,* 125.

The low liquidity experienced by Barclays Bank (DCO) in the region in the late 1950s, which was discussed in the last chapter, affected its ability to compete effectively with the other commercial banks in the West Indies. As the bank was compelled to reduce the amount of credit available to customers, it lost valuable clients to competitor banks.[72] Money noted that

211

the competition from the other banks is particularly aggressive, and it would appear that the Sterling funds and allied currencies available to the other banks for lending are not yet exhausted. As a result pressure from the bank's borrowing customers for increased facilities continued and in many cases Barclays Bank (DCO) was compelled to refuse on the grounds of our over-lent position.[73]

The main branch at King Street reported the loss of an American radio-engineering company, regarded as an important and valuable account, to the BOLAM as a result of its refusal to grant increased lending facilities.[74] The bank was particularly regretful at losing a valuable hotel account in the Bahamas to the BNS, because of its inability to finance a three-year loan. Reflecting on this loss, a senior director stated that "I think we made a mistake here in spite of our over-lent position."[75] The bank's overextended position also prevented it from acquiring new business. For example, the Linstead sub-branch in Jamaica reported the loss of new advance business to the tune of some £10,000 within a three-month period in 1961.[76]

Despite the competitive climate in the West Indian commercial banking market during this period, the practice of collusive agreements continued. Such agreements, like the ones made prior to 1940, were concerned with controlling price competition, with the ultimate objective being the maintenance of the stability and profitability of the commercial banking sector. The collusive agreements between Barclays Bank (DCO) and the other commercial banks represented an important aspect of its strategy. It can be argued that collusive agreements, by minimizing price competition, functioned as an important regulatory mechanism, helping to lessen the potential for a particular bank to become unstable through excessive price competition, which could have threatened the stability of the entire industry.

There was, however, a difference between the collusive agreements made among the banks in the post-war period and those made before 1940. Rather than seeking a comprehensive agreement applicable to the entire region, the approach in the post-war period was to make agreements applicable to individual territories. This was more than likely a response to the rapid economic changes which occurred in some of the territories in the 1950s, and the consequent emergence of a greater degree of disparity among the regional economies. In the Bahamas, where tourism and offshore banking were becoming the hallmarks of the economy, there was a formal written agreement between the banks by 1953. Written into it was an agreement to remove restrictions against paying interest on non-residents' deposits.[77] The banks also found feasible to have an agreement applicable solely to Jamaica, the most diversified of all the economies, with growing tourism and manufacturing sectors and vibrant agricultural and commercial sectors. The Jamaica agreement, known as the Inter-Bank Agreement, was drawn up in 1959 between the respective commercial banks, though City Bank, which began operating there in 1961, was not a signatory.[78]

The Jamaica Inter-Bank Agreement of 1959 covered every aspect of pricing in banking. This included rates of interest paid on savings and other deposit accounts, minimum rates of interest charged for advances and loans, ledger fees and a variety of commission charges for bills for collection, life insurance premiums, foreign exchange transactions, credits and guarantees.[79] Special rates were agreed upon for government current account deposits and on government loans and advances, as well as for foreign exchange transactions on behalf of the government and the bauxite companies. Special lending rates were also agreed upon for customers whose loans were secured by a deposit with the lending banks, and for finance companies. The terms of the agreement prohibited the "poaching" of customers with better terms regarding charges. No signatory bank was to open accounts for any customer of another signatory bank on better terms with regard to operating charges than the competitor bank had been charging. The agreement further required that when an account was transferred from one bank to another, the transferee bank was to satisfy itself as to the operating charge previously collected, before accepting the account. This stipulation also applied to loans and advances. No signatory bank was to open accounts for customers of another bank on better terms with regard to rates of interest or discount than the competitor bank had been charging. The agreement included a similar provision with regard to checking the customer's previous bank before accepting the account.[80]

The existence of agreements among the commercial banks in a single territory did not rule out reaching common ground on certain issues across the region. For instance, in the matter of street foreign-exchange transactions, which was affecting all the banks, an agreement was reached in 1957 for a reduction in the rates for sterling on London by 0.06 per cent to take effect on 1 January 1958.[81] This may have been a prefatory step towards a return to a regional agreement, as there is evidence that in 1961 attempts were being made for the drawing up of a standard agreement for the entire Caribbean. Apparently, one was put in place and operated up to the end of 1962, but it was rescinded in Jamaica, which had become politically independent of Britain in that year. Nonetheless, it was clear in Jamaica that a cartelist banking structure was the preferred modus operandi, since it fitted well with the priority of bank stability and protection of depositors. Accordingly, the government, through the central bank, the Bank of Jamaica, in consultation with the banks, through the Bankers' Committee, determined the areas and details of collusion and general banking policy for the island.[82]

Bank Products and Services

An important aspect of Barclays Bank (DCO)'s business strategy in the post-war period was the expansion of its products and services, all of which were indicative of its further transformation into a retail banking institution. This was clearly reflected in structural changes in the bank's loans and advances portfolio that indicated a response to the changes in the region's economy. Whereas in the period 1926 to 1945 the bulk of the bank's credit facilities were for agriculture and particularly for the sugar trade, by the early 1950s there was a shift to other sectors of the region's economy. The data garnered from the bank's half-yearly amalgamated reports for the period 1952 to 1962 show a significant decline in the level of advances to the agricultural sector and a steep rise in the level allocated to non-agricultural sectors. In 1952 the non-agricultural sector accounted for at least 87 per cent of all advances made by the bank in the region. By 1962 this had increased to 91 per cent. Advances made to the agricultural sector, of which sugar was the greatest recipient, fell to 11 per cent in 1952 and to 7 per cent by 1962 (see Table 8.4).

The way the bank's data were reported makes it difficult to distinguish among the non-agricultural categories for which accommodation was provided. Nevertheless, it is possible to get some idea from official data concerning the commercial banks as a whole, published by the governments of Jamaica and Trinidad and Tobago. These data are useful, since

Table 8.4 Barclays Bank (DCO), Breakdown of West Indian Advances (£), 1952–1962

Categories	1952	(%)	1956	(%)	1962	(%)
Sugar	1,228,009		1,118,090		2,178,327	
Other agric	325,820		241,241		299,704	
Subtotal	**1,553,829**	**(11.0)**	**1,359,331**	**(10.0)**	**2,478,031**	**(7.0)**
Gold, tin, diamonds	0		0		4,651	
Merchandise	716,520		97,573		429,981	
Trade bills	71,731		0		6,562	
Acc. bills & prom. notes	126,455		75,016		44,129	
Guarantees	3,106,054		3,627,358		9,560,402	
Subtotal	**4,020,760**	**(29.4)**	**3,799,947**	**(27.4)**	**10,045,725**	**(29.0)**
Blank advance	2,862,491		3,217,060		11,444,315	
Stocks & shares	755,444		705,441		817,272	
Mortgages	4,281,647		4,585,182		9,584,200	
Subtotal	**7,899,582**	**(58.0)**	**8,507,683**	**(61.2)**	**21,845,787**	**(62.0)**
Earmarked credit balances	125,066	(0.9)	121,508	(0.8)	287,055	(0.8)
Miscellaneous	99,107	(0.7)	77,619	(0.6)	444,999	(1.2)
Total advances	**13,698,344**	**(100.0)**	**13,866,088**	**(100.0)**	**35,101,597**	**(100.0)**
Total overdrafts[a]	14,116,294		14,924,764		33,887,323	
Total	**27,814,638**		**28,790,852**		**68,988,920**	

[a] No distinctions were made for overdrafts in these records.

Source: Amalgamated Results, Statistics and Review, 1952–1962, BBA 29/171, BBA 29/173, BBA 29/175.

it was in these two islands that the greatest level of economic diversification occurred in this period. It can also be assumed that these data are fairly representative of Barclays Bank (DCO)'s loan portfolio, given the bank's sizeable share of the commercial banking market in the two colonies. For Jamaica, the returns for 1946–52 were broken down into three categories, namely agriculture, industry, and commerce and other. During this period the share of loans and advances for agriculture fell

Table 8.5 Total Bank Loans and Advances (%), Jamaica, 1946–1962

Categories	1946	1948	1950	1952	1962
Agriculture	25	22	16	14	7.8*
Industry	14	18	16	28	14.3
Commerce & other	61	60	40	36	29.7*
Other	–	–	14	22	–
Personal & professional	n/a	n/a	n/a	n/a	13.9
Mining	n/a	n/a	n/a	n/a	9.9
Building, construction & hotels	n/a	n/a	n/a	n/a	9.1
Credit & financial institutions	n/a	n/a	n/a	n/a	2.1
Entertainment	n/a	n/a	n/a	n/a	0.8
Government and other public bodies	n/a	n/a	n/a	n/a	2.8
Land development	n/a	n/a	n/a	n/a	3.4
Other	n/a	n/a	n/a	n/a	5.3

*For the period 1946–52, the returns on bank loans and advances were broken down into only three categories, "Agriculture", "Industry" and "Commerce", with "Commerce" combined with "Other" for 1946–48. The returns for 1962 are broken down into several categories, and it is assumed that "Distribution" was what had been called "Commerce".

Source: Girvan, *Foreign Capital*, 184–85.

from 25 per cent to 14 per cent, whereas that to industry increased from 14 per cent to 28 per cent. The commerce and other category accounted for a steady average of approximately 58 per cent. A delineation in the statistics between commerce and other categories reveals commerce accounting for 38 per cent and "other" for 18 per cent in 1950 and 1952.

A further breakdown of the data for Jamaica in 1962 showed 11.5 per cent of total loans and advances allocated for the agricultural sector, with distribution accounting for 29.7 per cent. Industry accounted for 17.9 per cent, and mining for 9.9 per cent. A significant 13.9 per cent was allocated for personal and professional consumption (see Table 8.5). It should also be noted that for 1962 "Agriculture" does not include sugar, rum and other related industries which were included under the category of "Industry". "Industry" in 1962 included (1) sugar, rum, etc., 3.7 per cent; (2) food, drink, tobacco, 2 per cent; (3) textile, leather and footwear, 2 per cent; (4) other industry, 6.3 per cent. If we exclude "sugar, rum, etc." from the returns for industry and include them with agriculture, this category would account for 9.3 per cent of total loans and advances, and industry would account for 10.6 per cent. When the latter is combined with mining, building, construction and hotels, this total amounts to 29.1 per cent of total loans and advances made in 1962.

For Trinidad and Tobago, whereas industry (which, it is assumed, included manufacturing) accounted for an average of 16 per cent of total loans and advances made between 1946 and 1952, between 1954 and 1962 its share had increased to an average of 48 per cent (see Table 8.6). Agriculture, in contrast, declined from 12.75 per cent for the period 1946–52 to 7 per cent for 1954–62. Other sectors accounted for a substantial proportion: 71 per cent between 1946 and 1954 and 45 per cent between 1954 and 1962 (see Table 8.6a). The breakdown for this category

Table 8.6 Total Bank Loans and Advances, Trinidad and Tobago, 1946–1962

Year	WI$ (thousands)	Industry (%)	Agriculture (%)	Other (%)
1946	9,624	14	26	60
1948	17,610	24	9	67
1950	18,974	12	5	83
1952	28,082	14	11	75
1954	31,399	55	9	36
1956	40,399	51	8	41
1958	44,796	48	8	44
1960	82,976	48	8	44
1962	113,940	36	4	60

Source: Compiled from Central Statistical Office, *Annual Statistical Digest*, no. 12, 192.

Table 8.6a Bank Loans and Advances ("Other" Category), Trinidad and Tobago, 1954–1962

Year	WI$ (thousands)	Non-distribution (%)	Distribution (%)	Personal & Professional (%)	Non-personal & Non-professional (%)
1954	28,434	23	38	14	25
1956	37,228	26	30	17	27
1958	41,115	24	28	14	34
1960	76,658	19	33	18	30
1962	108,769	15	23	16	46
Average		21	30	16	32

Source: Compiled from Central Statistical Office, *Annual Statistical Digest*, no. 12, 192.

is available only for the 1954–62 period, and even then, the delineation is limited to distribution and non-distribution, personal and professional, and non-personal and non-professional.

Evidently, a significant amount of product diversification occurred in the banks' loan portfolios, and, indeed, the increased level of loans and advances to personal and professional categories and to industry attest to a greater level of involvement in the domestic economy.[83]

Modifications in the bank's products and services in this period were apparent in relation to the types of security accepted for credit facilities. Crop liens for loans made to the agricultural producers and exporters continued to be the main acceptable form of security, but it was clear that the bank had begun to exercise some flexibility with regard to loans for some crops. For example, it was willing to make loans against title deeds with a letter of undertaking to rice growers in British Guiana.[84]

Equitable mortgages, which, prior to 1945, were being accepted on a small scale, became more widely acceptable after 1945. Over 80 per cent of the total number of loans made at the Cayman branch were made against equitable mortgages over land. At the Nassau branch approximately one-third of total advances were secured by mortgages.[85] Overall, mortgages accounted for the largest proportion of loans and advances made during the period 1952–62, averaging 35 per cent of the total. The increased acceptability of this form of security can be explained by the relatively high property value on retail and wholesale establishments and on factory space. As well, the marketability of these properties was high as a result of the rapid expansion of these sectors, which made mortgages against them less risky.

A high proportion of the credit facilities were also made against guarantees. At Nassau at least one-third of the total value of loans and advances made were secured against guarantees.[86] Overall, an average of 28 per cent of non-agricultural loans were made against this form of security. As guarantees are a type of personal security which involve the right of action against the individual giving the security, facilities against them before 1940 were generally restricted to the large multinational companies and a few extremely wealthy individuals. The increased acceptability of this form of security after 1940 and particularly in the 1950s was an indication of the increased creditworthiness of clients, which was reflective of the general profitability of businesses in this boom period.

The acceptability of stocks and shares as security also increased, though not to the same extent as mortgages and guarantees. An average of 5 per cent of total non-agricultural loans were made against stocks and shares during the period 1952–62. This was a considerable increase over the 2.40 per cent and 0.05 per cent made available in 1948 and 1949 respectively.[87] Loans made available against stocks and shares were usually advanced to individuals from the professional class and to stockbrokers.[88] The increased acceptablity of stocks and shares as security was a response to the expanded new issue markets for government and corporate securities, particularly in Jamaica and in Trinidad and Tobago. As the large sums required for expenditure on the development plans were not available from ordinary sources, the colonial governments not only tapped the colonial and London capital markets but also entered the New York market for the first time. The expansion of the new issue market reflected both the increase of the corporate form of enterprise and greater reliance on public equity capital rather than on retained earnings alone.[89]

New areas of service included securities management and stocks and shares arbitration facilities, provided by trustee departments that were established at several of Barclays Bank (DCO)'s branches.[90] Many of these evolved to become nominees companies by the early 1960s. For example, the Barclays (Jamaica) Nominees Co. Ltd, established in 1962, grew out of the King Street branch trustee department.[91] These companies' primary function was to hold the legal titles of stocks and shares that were transferred to the bank as security by the borrowing customer. They also facilitated the transfer of property for customers who were domiciled abroad.[92]

The most significant development of the trustee business occurred in the Bahamas, a natural outgrowth of the area's fast development as a tax haven and the consequent attraction of significant "offshore" funds from individuals and corporations who wanted to avoid certain fiscal measures in their country of residence.[93] Because of the tremendous increases in the flow of such funds to the Bahamas, the Barclays (Nassau) Nominees Co. Ltd, which was established in 1950, was transformed into the Bahamas International Trust Co. Ltd (BITCO Ltd) in 1952.[94] BITCO was not a wholly owned subsidiary of the bank but was established in association with other foreign financial institutions located in London, New York and Canada. The staff, which was initially recruited from the original trustee departments of the bank, had to resign from Barclays Bank (DCO) before being appointed at BITCO. Barclays Bank (DCO)'s initial investment amounted to £78,000, in 5,200 shares of £10 each at a premium of £5 per share. This represented a holding of 26 per cent of the capital, which consisted of authorized capital of £1,000,000 in 100,000 shares of £10 each, of which 20,000 were issued and paid up in full at a premium of 50 per cent.[95] In February 1958 BITCO established a wholly owned subsidiary, the Bahamas International Trust Co. (Freeport) Ltd, which was incorporated with an authorized capital of £100,000.[96]

In addition to the services provided by a nominees company, trust companies offer services that include the acceptance of current and time deposits in foreign currency which was either on-lent or redeposited without being converted into the local medium of exchange; management of securities and property holdings of companies and individuals; provision of a registered office, company officers, directors and nominee shareholders; preparation of accounting and financial reports; filing of statutory returns with local authorities; holding of annual general meetings and preparation of company minutes; provision of escrow services with regard to property transactions; investment management;

custodian trusteeship of funds managed by someone else; and trust facilities for the pension funds of multinational corporations.[97] The extent of the services provided by BITCO is not known, but the fact that a separate company was created to deal with this aspect of the business suggests that it probably offered a wide range of services.[98]

Barclays Overseas Development Corporation

Credit facilities provided by Barclays Bank (DCO) continued to be short-term, repayable within three to six months. Loans and advances to the burgeoning industrial sector represented working capital for local manufacturing firms for the purposes of settling wages and importing raw materials and other capital goods necessary for production. As was customary, loans and advances to the agricultural sector were for a maximum of six months, while those made to other sectors had a three-month term. In general, Barclays Bank (DCO), like other commercial banks during this period, shunned the provision of long-term credit.

Nevertheless, Barclays Bank (DCO) found it necessary to establish a wholly owned subsidiary for the purpose of providing medium- and long-term credit. This came about in the context of increased public attention to colonial economic development: the empire played a much more important role in Britain's foreign trade during and after World War II as Britain's competitiveness with other industrial nations declined.[99] Social and economic conditions in the British colonies also attracted considerable public attention in Britain following the labour riots and strikes which had broken out in the West Indies and West Africa in the 1930s.[100] The publicity accorded the colonies in the British popular press, which was severely critical of British colonial policy, according to D.J. Morgan "helped change the political atmosphere in which colonial development was approached in Westminster and Whitehall".[101]

As the Colonial Office became more focused on a colonial economic policy and programme for economic development, attention turned to the lending and investment policies of the British overseas banks operating in the empire.[102] In view of the level of capital that was required for colonial economic development, the banks came under sharp criticism for their policy of exporting a high proportion of the deposits raised in the colonies to London. They were accused of not meeting the developmental needs of the economies in which they operated, instead being primarily concerned with the provision of short-term finance, to the detriment of their host countries' needs.

Indeed, the statistics supplied by the banks to the Colonial Office indicated that at the end of December 1943, the proportion of deposits invested in the respective colonial regions were as follows: less than 5 per cent in Northern Rhodesia, West Africa, Aden, Gibraltar, Malta and the Bahamas; 5 to 10 per cent in Nyasaland, Transjordan, the Leeward Islands and Fiji; 10 to 20 per cent in Barbados, British Guiana, Trinidad and the Windward Islands; 20 to 33 per cent in Ceylon and Mauritius; and over 33 per cent Cyprus, British Honduras, Jamaica and Palestine.[103] The banks argued that the high proportion of the bank deposits sent to London was partly the result of the decrease in outlets for investment during World War II, and that they had found themselves receiving deposits which under normal circumstances would not have been deposited with them.[104] They also maintained that their relatively low level of investment in their host economies was due entirely to the lack of opportunity "of a kind that the banks were willing to make within the framework of their traditional policy". At any rate, the banks saw their institutions first and foremost as deposit institutions and their service essentially as safekeeping, and did not regard their function as being to "redistribute the savings of the community within which they operated".[105] These arguments were found acceptable by Colonial Office officials, and thereafter, in spite of the initial severe criticism, agreed that the banks could not be expected to play a primary role in creating investment opportunities in the colonies.[106]

The fact is that Barclays Bank (DCO) was experiencing increased demands for long-term capital finance. These demands had materialized during the war owing to the establishment of industries producing substitutes for imports that were in short supply because of the disruption to normal shipping.[107] As it was envisaged that these demands were likely to continue, if not escalate, in the post-war period, the bank in September 1942 launched an essay competition among its staff, who were required to write on the subject "The Bank in Relation to Post-War Colonial Development", to generate ideas.[108] The idea of a development corporation evolved out of suggestions that were put forward in some of the essays.[109] In January 1946, Barclays Overseas Development

Corporation (hereafter BODC), a subsidiary of Barclays Bank (DCO), was established with an authorized capital of £5,000,000, of which £1,000,000 was issued in "A" shares of £10 each, and a subscribed and paid-up capital of £2,000,000 each. The corporation had its own board of directors under the chairmanship of Geoffrey Cockayne Gibbs, who was also a vice chairman in the parent bank. Julian Crossley, who was deputy chairman of Barclays Bank (DCO) at the time, sat on the board as deputy chairman.[110] The administrative structure of the corporation was kept minimal, consisting of a London manager, an assistant manager and a secretary. The branches of Barclays Bank (DCO) acted as agents for the corporation, and all propositions that were garnered through them were submitted to the BODC board in London for consideration and approval.[111]

It may be argued that Barclays Bank (DCO)'s willingness to sponsor a competition to generate ideas regarding colonial development was evidence of its readiness to consider fresh approaches to long-term finance. The idea of establishing a subsidiary company specifically for the purpose of providing medium- and long-term financing represented significant innovation and spoke of the bank's ability to adapt to the changed circumstances in which it was operating.[112] Nonetheless, the BODC was generally conservative in its approach, not only in terms of its customers but also in the types of businesses it was willing to provide financing for. The level of loans it made was initially low, with just £500,000 being approved during its first nine months of operation, though there was steady growth afterwards.[113] In 1949 the number of projects which received financing stood at 103 and accounted for £2.5 million.[114] By 1950 this had grown to 180 with total financing amounting to £4.5 million. In 1951 the loans made by the BODC totalled £5.252 million, and between that year and 1961 they rose to £14.274 million. The number of projects receiving financing had also grown during this period, from 212 in 1951 to 427 in 1957, though there was a decrease afterwards, to 382 in 1961 (see Table 8.7).

The West Indies and East Africa received the highest proportion of loans from the BODC, averaging 28 per cent and 26.6 per cent respectively of the total loans made between 1951 and 1961. The Rhodesias and Nyasaland received an average 19.4 per cent, while other territories – Swaziland, Cyprus, Malta, Gibraltar and Mauritius – received 14.2 per

Table 8.7 Barclays Overseas Development Corporation, Loans (Thousands of Pounds Sterling) by Region, 1951, 1957 and 1961

Region	1951			1957			1961		
	No.	Amount	%	No.	Amount	%	No.	Amount	%
East Africa	70	1,332	25.40	122	3,437	27.53	125	3,860	27.04
West Africa	13	588	11.20	22	1,416	11.35	39	1,787	12.51
Rhodesia/ Nyasaland	15	732	14.20	68	3,043	24.36	58	2,824	19.78
West Indies	83	1,755	33.40	117	2,967	23.78	94	3,830	26.84
Other	31	845	15.80	98	1,625	12.98	66	1,973	13.83
Total	**212**	**5,252**	**100.00**	**427**	**12,488**	**100.00**	**382**	**14,274**	**100.00**
Type									
Agriculture/ forestry	49	1,329	25.30	58	1,732	13.87	49	2,178	15.26
Industrial	31	1,345	25.60	56	3,013	24.13	74	3,865	27.08
Building & development	61	1,278	24.30	153	2,812	22.52	119	2,452	17.17
Commercial	31	479	9.10	80	2,724	21.82	61	1,834	12.85
Other	40	821	15.60	80	2,207	17.66	79	3,945	27.64
Total	**212**	**5,252**	**100.00**	**427**	**12,488**	**100.00**	**382**	**14,274**	**100.00**
By Amount									
0–£5,000	48	155	2.90	103	278	2.23	88	246	1.72
Over £5,000–£25,000	111	1,445	27.50	203	2,673	21.41	173	2,350	16.47
Over £25,000–£50,000	28	1,038	19.80	60	2,309	18.49	53	2,087	14.62
Over £50,000–£100,000	19	1,412	26.90	37	2,860	22.90	37	2,936	20.57
Over £100,000	6	1,202	22.90	24	4,368	34.97	31	6,655	46.62
Total	**212**	**5,252**	**100.00**	**427**	**12,488**	**100.00**	**382**	**14,274**	**100.00**
By Period									
0–5 years	50	999	19.00	167	2,325	18.62	166	2,464	17.27
6–10 years	104	2,033	38.70	205	7,048	56.45	162	7,631	53.45
11–15 years	39	1,407	26.80	35	1,810	14.50	32	2,398	17.31
16–25 years	12	453	8.60	4	384	3.08	2	407	2.34
Undated	7	360	6.90	16	921	7.35	20	1,374	9.63
Total	**212**	**5,252**	**100.00**	**427**	**12,488**	**100.00**	**382**	**14,274**	**100.00**

Source: Accounts and Board Meeting Papers, BBA 38/251.

Note: There are minor discrepancies in the returns for the West Indies in the BODC accounting papers.

cent. West Africa received the lowest proportion of loans, averaging 11.6 per cent of the total (see Table 8.7).

Overall for the period 1951–61, an average of 48.3 per cent of the total number of loans, representing 21.7 per cent of the total financing, fell within the category £5,001 to £25,000. Another 13.6 per cent of the total number of loans, representing 17.6 per cent of the total financing, were for amounts between £25,001 and £50,000. A significant number of small loans under £5,000, some 23.2 per cent, received 2.2 per cent of the total financing. Large loans of between £50,001 and £100,000 accounted for 9 per cent of the total number of loans, representing 23.4 per cent of total financing. Those of over £100,000 accounted for 5.5 per cent of the total number, representing 34.83 per cent of total financing (see Table 8.7).

At the same time, the BODC exercised caution in the time given for repayment. First, most of the loans, 46.4 per cent, representing nearly 50 per cent of the total financing, were repayable within ten years, and of those a significant number, 35.4 per cent, representing 18.29 per cent of the total financing, had a term of five years or less. Taken together, 82 per cent of the total number of loans, representing 68 per cent of the total financing provided by the BODC for the period 1951–61, were repayable within ten years (see Table 8.7). Of the total number, 11.3 per cent, representing 19.5 per cent of the total financing, had terms of between eleven and fifteen years, and 2.3 per cent of the total number, representing 4.6 per cent of the total amount, were repayable between sixteen and twenty-five years. Loans with an unspecified repayment date accounted for 4 per cent of the total number and represented 7.96 per cent of the total financing (see Table 8.7).

As innovative as it was, the establishment of BODC to provide long-term financing did not represent a radical alteration of the bank's lending policies and services, as is clear from the terms and conditions laid down for the approval of investment loans by the corporation. One of its stipulations was that applicants were expected to be in a position to contribute their share of their capital requirements and to have enlisted reasonable financial support before approaching BODC.[115] This requirement put constraints on persons from territories that were economically underdeveloped and therefore lacking in the capital requirements necessary to qualify for a loan. So, while the corporation's stated objective was to foster the development of local industry in the colonies, there was clearly a bias in favour of the more economically advanced colonial territories.[116] The geographic spread of its investments bore this out. A relatively high proportion of BODC's total loans was made to the West Indies and East Africa, and other areas, particularly West Africa, received much less (see Table 8.7).

In the West Indies the distribution of BODC's investment loans was clearly skewed in favour of the more economically advanced territories, as the highest proportion was made to Jamaica and Trinidad and Tobago. Together they accounted for 80 per cent and 71 per cent of total loans made to the region in 1951 and 1957. Jamaica alone accounted for nearly 50 per cent of the total loans made to the region in 1957 (see Table 8.8).

The stipulated terms and conditions meant that a significant proportion of the borrowers were private and public companies whose organizational structures put them in a good position in terms of the necessary

Table 8.8 Barclays Overseas Development Corporation, Loans in the West Indies (Thousands of Pounds Sterling), 1951 and 1957

Territory	1951			1957		
	No.	Amount	%	No.	Amount	%
Antigua	3	21	1.35	6	75	2.58
Barbados	0	0	0.00	2	23	0.79
British Guiana	3	68	4.39	0	0	0.00
Honduras	3	84	5.42	6	198	6.81
Bahamas	1	4	0.26	6	385	13.24
Dominica	1	4	0.26	1	40	1.38
Grenada	2	36	2.32	3	26	0.89
Jamaica	26	554	35.77	47	1,400	48.14
Montserrat	1	1	0.06	0	0	0.00
St Kitts	2	11	0.71	0	0	0.00
St Lucia	0	0	0.00	3	30	1.03
St Vincent	6	82	5.30	5	61	2.10
Trinidad & Tobago	34	684	44.16	34	670	23.04
Total	82	1,549	100.00	113	2,908	100.00

Source: Accounts and Board Meeting Papers, BBA 38/251.

capital requirements and made them creditworthy clients. Over 70 per cent of the loans made by the BODC in 1957 and 1961 were to such companies, which represented more than half of the total number of applicants in both years. In contrast, individual applicants – numbering 111 and 78 in 1957 and 1961 respectively – accounted for 10 per cent and 7 per cent respectively of the total amount of BODC loans. Partnerships accounted for only 4.32 per cent and 1.74 per cent of total loans in 1957 and 1961 respectively (see Table 8.9.).

Cooperatives, governments and semi-government bodies received a relatively small proportion of the loans. Cooperative bodies accounted for 1.71 per cent and a mere 0.94 per cent of the loans in 1957 and 1961 respectively. In 1957 colonial governments accounted for 2.87 per cent of the loans made, though this proportion was increased to 10.84 per cent in 1961. Colonial municipalities and quasi-government concerns accounted for 7.69 per cent in 1957 and 8 per cent in 1961 (see Table 8.9).

The corporation made relatively few loans to these bodies because it did not regard the kind of development projects that they promoted as economically viable. This was borne out in the BODC's response to a proposal from the Jamaica government in 1946 regarding long-term

Table 8.9 Barclays Overseas Development Corporation, Loans by Applicant (Thousands of Pounds Sterling), 1957 and 1961

Applicant	1957			1961		
	No.	Amount	%	No.	Amount	%
Individual	111	1,249	10.00	78	986	6.91
Partnership	40	539	4.32	32	249	1.74
Private company	186	6,143	49.19	188	6,892	48.28
Public company	41	3,023	24.22	36	3,323	23.28
Cooperative	28	214	1.71	19	134	0.94
Colonial municipality	8	365	2.92	9	284	1.99
Quasi-government	8	595	4.77	10	859	6.02
Colonial government	5	359	2.87	10	1,547	10.84
Total	427	12,487	100.00	382	14,274	100.00

Source: Accounts and Board Meeting Papers, BBA 38/251.

financing for food production among the peasant farming community through the Jamaica Agricultural Loan Securities Board.[117] The bank had always shied away from providing any financing of this nature, believing that

> It [was] inevitable that some finance for development will be required in each year, and if this proves to be the case, we may well be placed in the awkward position of either having to insist on the government adhering to the scheme laid down or of having to provide more or less permanent finance. Even if the government's proposals were carried out, the scheme as it stands is not attractive as money would not be repaid until the twenty-fourth year.[118]

The Jamaica government had been pursuing a programme of improving local food production that it had begun in 1940, and which it hoped to expand after the hurricane of August 1944 did considerable damage to peasant cultivations and housing. Much of Kingston had become congested with rural people seeking employment, and, in an effort to relieve this situation, the government sought to increase the loans available through cooperative banks.[119]

Overall, agricultural development projects did not receive a high proportion of loans from the BODC. Initially, in 1951, business proposals in this category accounted for a relatively high proportion, representing 23 per cent of the total number of projects and receiving 25.3 per cent of the total financing. This share later fell, however, accounting for 14 per cent and 13 per cent of the total number of projects and receiving 14 per cent and 15 per cent of the total financing made by the BODC in 1957 and 1961 respectively (see Table 8.7). Overall, for the period 1951–61, agriculture and forestry accounted for 16 per cent of the total number of projects and 18 per cent of the total amount of loans made by BODC. Building development companies were the most numerous businesses receiving loans, accounting for 32 per cent of the total number and receiving 21 per cent of the total amount of loans. Industrial businesses, while accounting for just 15 per cent of the total number, received the largest proportion of loans, accounting for an average of 26 per cent of the total (see Table 8.7). This suggests that fairly large businesses in this category received substantial loans during this period. Commercial businesses represented an average of 16 per cent of the total number, receiving 15 per cent of the total amount of loans. Businesses which fell into the category "other" accounted for 19 per cent of the total number and 20 per cent of the total loans made. Such businesses included hotels, shipping companies, educational institutions, cooperatives, public works, mining companies and cinemas (see Table 8.7).

It is difficult to say whether the lending pattern of the BODC in the West Indies was similar to its pattern worldwide, as the breakdown of these data for the region exists only for 1951. It has been possible to identify fifty of the eighty-two businesses in the West Indies which received financing in that year. Only five, representing 10 per cent of the total, were agricultural, and these accounted for 16 per cent of BODC's total financing to the region in 1951 (see Table 8.10). This contrasted sharply with the overall pattern for that year. Industrial businesses received a substantial proportion of the loans made to the West Indies. Businesses of this type numbered eleven, or 22 per cent of the total, and accounted for 30 per cent of the total loans (see Table 8.10). In contrast to the larger pattern, development companies in the West Indies received a relatively small proportion in 1951: there were six of them, or 12 per cent of the total, and they accounted for 11 per cent of the total amount of loans (see Table 8.10).

Businesses in the category "other" numbered twenty-two, or 44 per cent of the total number, accounting for 36 per cent of the total loans. It was difficult to identify commercial businesses from other types, as the

Table 8.10 Barclays Overseas Development Corporation, Loans (Thousands of Pounds Sterling) by Category in the West Indies, 1951

Category	Number	Amount	%
Development company	6	158	10.69
Shipping company	2	29	1.96
Agricultural	5	236	15.97
Industrial	11	438	29.65
Church	2	32	2.16
Trust companies & clubs	2	48	3.29
Other	22	536	36.28
Total	50	1,477	100.00

Source: Accounts and Board Meeting Papers, BBA 38/251.

names do not readily suggest the nature of the business. However, we do know that of the twenty-two, four were a law firm, a hotel enterprise, a publishing company and a cinema company. Given the expansion of the wholesale and retail sectors in the West Indies during this period, it is reasonable to assume that a significant portion of those unidentifiable businesses classified under "other" represented commercial businesses.

It therefore appears that commercial businesses in the West Indies in 1951 were the recipients of the highest proportion of medium- and long-term credit facilities from the corporation. This is in contrast to the 9.1 per cent recorded overall in the world for that year. Shipping, churches, trust companies and clubs numbered six, or 12 per cent of the total number, and accounted for 7 per cent of the total amount (see Table 8.10). It appears, then, that after five years of existence, the BODC in the West Indies tended to favour businesses that were non-industrial, given the high number of individual projects and the level of loans granted which fell in this category, in contrast with the other categories.

Summary

Barclays Bank (DCO) adopted certain strategies to respond to the changed economic conditions in the West Indies in the period 1940–62. These included a major expansion of its branch network throughout the region in response to new business opportunities, some of them in new territories, namely the Bahamas and British Honduras. The expansion of its branch network was also an important aspect of Barclays Bank (DCO)'s competitive strategy in the region. The bank established agencies, linked to branches and sub-branches, which were used to establish first-mover advantages within territories and to stake out a niche in an area already occupied by a competitor bank. This was particularly evident in Jamaica, where the British bank's main rival was the BNS. Other competitive strategies adopted by the bank included luring customers from competitor banks by offering better terms for services, soliciting new clients through established clients and acting as agents for banks not established in the region. It also wooed customers by offering specialized convenience services, particularly to the American bauxite companies whose exchange transactions were valuable to the bank. Barclays Bank (DCO) also used the advantages arising out of the legacy of British colonialism, particularly in its pursuit of savings deposits. Competition even manifested itself in the provision of amenities such as parking facilities, and in the design and decor of buildings. The effective competitive strategy pursued by Barclays Bank (DCO) in the region meant that, despite liquidity problems towards the end of the period, it was able to maintain the substantial market share it had staked out for itself. Aiding in this was the maintenance of collusive agreements between Barclays Bank (DCO) and the other banks which minimized price competition.

In another response to the changes in the region's economy, Barclays Bank (DCO) undertook a certain amount of diversification in its products and services, evident in the shift from financing primarily agricultural production and trade to financing the expanding commercial and industrial sectors. It was during this period that one can mark Barclays Bank (DCO)'s further transformation in the region, from essentially a trade bank to a full retail banking institution. The bank also undertook product innovation by establishing a subsidiary, BODC, to provide medium- and long-term credit facilities, demand for which was growing. As innovative as this was, the creation of a development corporation did not signify any radical alteration in the bank's lending policy. Barclays Bank (DCO)'s core customer base in the West Indies continued to be members of the elite class who had expanded into manufacturing and other industrial enterprises, and the foreign multinational firms which had been attracted to the region by the incentive policies implemented by the various governments.

Chapter Nine

Towards Independence
Staffing and Decentralization, 1940–1962

The branch expansion and product diversification undertaken by Barclays Bank (DCO) in response to increased business opportunities arising out of the post-1940 economic expansion and diversification were accompanied by other strategic changes. These included modifications in the bank's recruitment practices and in its organizational control of operations in the region, which form the focus of this chapter.

In addition to being important strategies for improving the resource capabilities of the bank, the changes in its recruitment practices and organizational control of its regional operations were reflective of the bank's awareness of the markedly different sociopolitical climate accompanying the nationalism which pervaded the region after 1940.[1] As the region was set on the road to political independence, questions were raised which challenged the old social order. Despite the perceptible social changes dating back to the late nineteenth century, which included the emergence of a black middle class, mid-twentieth-century West Indian society remained highly segregated along racial and class lines, with preference accorded to the white and propertied classes. And even though members of the black intelligentsia, and popular movements such as that led by the Jamaican Marcus Mosiah Garvey and the Rastafarian faith, challenged notions of black inferiority and white superiority in the early decades of the twentieth century, not much had changed by the 1950s and 1960s. As noted by Douglas Hall, in the early twentieth century in the West Indies,

> to be someone with unchallengeable social credentials, it was necessary to be white, wealthy, and educated . . . Whites [saw] nothing wrong with this. They would accept the occasional and exceptionally qualified black or coloured person into their social class, provided it was understood that they were the favoured exceptions.

As far as whites were concerned, "the black man's proper place was in the service of the white man".[2] Nevertheless, as decolonization proceeded, these notions were again challenged, particularly by the newly emerging political elite and the trade unions and from civil society.

In the context of political decolonization, these new voices had added resonance, which Barclays Bank (DCO) – given its long association with British imperialism in the region – could hardly afford to ignore. The bank would have been patently aware of its status as a British organization and would have been anxious not to be regarded as a symbol of continued British imperialism. Tellingly, in 1954 the bank's official name was changed from Barclays Bank (Dominion, Colonial and Overseas) to simply Barclays Bank DCO – though one may well question whether merely abbreviating the three words removed the imperialistic connotations associated with the name. Nevertheless, it was an obvious recognition of the unsuitability of the old name in the sociopolitical climate then permeating throughout much of the British empire.[3]

Staffing

The increase in business conducted by Barclays Bank (DCO) along with the establishment of its extensive West Indian branch network necessitated a commensurate increase in the number of staff employed. The increase was particularly rapid between 1952 and 1962, when the number of persons employed by the bank increased by 111 per cent, from 726 to 1,533.[4] Quite a few of the newly recruited staff were West Indians and a significant proportion were women, all of which marked a radical departure from earlier employment practices by Barclays Bank (DCO) in the West Indies.

The recruitment practices of British overseas banks throughout the nineteenth century centred on the development of a socially and culturally homogeneous cadre of staff that was British, middle-class and invariably male, with most recruited from fee-paying public schools. Emphasis was placed on an outgoing personality and the possession of good social and sporting skills, which were considered more important for a successful banking career than the possession of strong formal academic qualifications.[5] As part of their preparation for overseas service, new recruits generally began their career with a brief spell as juniors in the London office, where they underwent training and socialization. The objective was to inculcate attitudes of dependability, loyalty and conformity with standard banking procedure, all regarded as important elements in the matter of corporate control. Such socialization continued after staff were sent overseas. For example, when young bachelors were sent overseas, they were generally housed together to encourage male bonding and thereby foster and strengthen corporate cultural feeling, and to watch over each other so as to prevent what was considered inappropriate behaviour.[6]

In effect, the recruitment and socialization strategies led to the development of a specific corporate culture in the nineteenth century, lasting well into the twentieth, that was identifiable not only with British multinational banking but with Canadian banking as well.[7] This culture was invariably British or Canadian and male, imbued with a strong sense of loyalty which was underscored by lifetime employment and reasonable remuneration extended with an air of paternalism.[8]

Nevertheless, it was evident that change was occurring, as some banks had begun to employ locals towards the end of the nineteenth century. This practice was generally restricted to regions where a relatively high proportion of the population was of British descent, including Australia, New Zealand and South Africa.[9] The argument has been made that, since the recruitment and socialization strategies were based on judgements about character and type rather than on formal qualifications, it would have been difficult and costly to apply them to a culturally heterogeneous staff, thus explaining the banks' reluctance to employ locals whose cultures were vastly different from their own.[10] This argument was tested in the early twentieth century when both the Bank of British West Africa and Barclays Bank (DCO) began employing black Africans to clerical positions during the inter-war years. Those who showed promise were sent to the Barclays' London office for further socialization and training for managerial positions. The explanation for this early recruitment of black Africans was the difficulty of getting and keeping suitable British staff owing to the unhealthy and unappealing environment on the West African coast at that time.[11] Within banking circles, in fact, an appointment to a post in West Africa was regarded as being assigned to "dirty service", an unfortunate and unflattering term used to connote the hardship and discomfiture that was associated with the area.[12]

In East Africa, employment opportunities in banking were restricted to Africans of Asian ancestry. George Money, who was to become the local director of the bank in the West Indies, suggests that this had to do with the insufficient number of black Africans with secondary education, at least until the late 1940s, and that Barclays Bank (DCO) had no official policy of racial discrimination in its recruitment of staff. Notwithstanding, this does not explain the continued recruitment of only white West Indians, who, by the beginning of the 1950s, made up as much as 70 per cent of the total staff complement in the region (the rest being British), despite the emergence, as early as the late nineteenth century, of a noticeable black middle class with all the required academic and other qualifications.[13]

In essence, the recruitment practices of Barclays Bank (DCO) reflected the racial and class divisions prevalent in West Indian colonial societies in the nineteenth and early twentieth centuries. British colonial societies naturally bore the social legacies of British imperial and colonial rule and, as a result, were highly stratified along racial and class lines. This was evident in many of the region's territories. As Brereton has pointed out, territories like Barbados and the Bahamas, which had large white creole populations, were overtly racist in spite of the absence of an official system of segregation. In Jamaica and in Trinidad and Tobago, blacks and browns were considered socially inferior to whites and others considered near white. The average black Jamaican considered those ethnic groups white since they "looked white", even while recognizing their distinction from the "other whites". And while not regarded by whites as their social equals, they were considered more "equal" than blacks and browns by virtue of both their race and their economic status, derived from their dominance of the agricultural and mercantile sectors. In Trinidad and Tobago, the "French creoles", who were really descendants of early French, Spanish, Italian, German and Irish settlers, formed the planter and mercantile elite. Similarly in British Guiana, the planter and mercantile elite was dominated by the white minority group which was essentially of British and Portuguese ancestry.[14] In other words, in all the West Indies, the elite which formed the core of the bank's clientele was invariably white, or considered white by the general population, since they were not black and were rarely brown in complexion. Given the context of the period, this clientele, according to the social expectations of the time, would have expected the bank's staff to at least look like them, and would certainly have objected to black and brown personnel in positions which allowed them access to knowledge of their financial status.[15]

These attitudes about race and class would have reinforced the recruitment policy of many of the branch managers in the West Indies who, if not West Indian, had their own social prejudices and assumptions about West Indians in general and about non-white West Indians in particular. Many of them clearly exhibited a reluctance to engage black and brown locals on their staff, even after it was becoming more politic to start doing so.[16] George Money noted upon his arrival in the region in 1952:

> The reasons the managers gave for not recruiting black staff of their own volition [before] were not very convincing. Most of them made the point that no blacks ever applied, but this was a case of the chicken and the egg. As long as people knew they would be rebuffed, none but the most insensitive or belligerent would be likely to apply.[17]

Plate 9.1 Jim Whiting. *Jamaican Eagle*, Barclays Bank Staff Newsletter 2, no. 7 (1975).

So before 1950 the recruitment of locals in the West Indies was generally restricted to whites, or to persons who could "pass" for white. For example, the Jamaican P.E.N. Mortimer was one of the earliest local recruits, entering the service of the Colonial Bank before its reconstitution as Barclays Bank (DCO) in the West Indies. Mortimer eventually became the manager of the main branch at King Street. Similarly, Jim Whiting, originally from the parish of Trelawny in Jamaica, came to Kingston upon hearing of an opening in the Colonial Bank and was hired as a clerk in 1916 in the Harbour Street branch. Arthur Piercy Gardiner

Plate 9.2 Barclays Bank (DCO) staff (with their wives) in Jamaica, 1926, gathered to welcome Charles Hewitt, general manager (third row, central figure). *Courtesy of the National Library of Jamaica.*

Austin, who was born in Barbados and educated at Harrison's College, the top boys' school in the colony, rose to the position of manager of the Barbados branch before retiring.[18] Another early local recruit, Cecil Harold Abraham, a Jamaican, began working for the bank in 1920, serving as branch manager in several parishes before being appointed manager of the Harbour Street branch in 1957. Abraham would have been considered an ideal recruit because of his links with the planter and mercantile class, being the son of a planter from the parish of St Mary. Born in 1903, he was schooled at the Jamaica College for boys, which was modelled after English public schools and was the most prestigious secondary educational institution in Jamaica at the time. An Anglican, he was also a member of the exclusive Jamaica, Liguanea, St Andrew and Morgan Harbour Beach clubs, all catering to the white elite in Jamaican society.[19]

Not all local recruits fitted the profile of Abraham, but were nevertheless suitable candidates for the job, given their race and class status in colonial society. Noel Dennis Silvera, a Jamaican who joined the staff in

Plate 9.3 Barclays Bank (DCO) staff (and wives) Barbados, 1926. *Quarterly Magazine* (October 1955).

1930, later rose to the position of accountant in the King Street branch in 1955. Silvera, while not from a business family, would have been seen as an important link with the flourishing Jewish commercial community that practically dominated the wholesale and retail trade in Kingston. Evidently middle-class, Silvera was born in 1913 to a government officer and his wife and was educated at the Calabar High School, which, while not as prestigious as the Jamaica College, was nonetheless a well-respected institution.[20]

While British multinational banks in the nineteenth and early twentieth centuries normally rotated their staff among the different countries in which they maintained a branch network, it appeared that this practice was restricted to their British staff. Barclays Bank (DCO) apparently did not rotate its locally recruited staff out of the West Indies. For example, Whiting, who served the bank mostly in Jamaica at various postings throughout the island, was in 1947 sent to Dominica where he spent four and a half years. He was to expand his banking experience in other West Indian territories before being sent to Trinidad in 1952.[21] In contrast, it was more common for British staff who had served at various overseas locations to be brought into the region to hold the top managerial positions at the principal branch. A clear example is John V. Basford, who was appointed manager of the King Street branch in Jamaica in 1957, arriving from Nassau, where he had been manager. Basford had previously served as acting assistant manager to W.A. Bertram in Jamaica between 1946 and 1947. He had also been a travelling inspector to the West Indies, Africa, the United States and Canada and had held appointments in London, San Francisco and New York.[22]

It was not until 1951 that black West Indians were employed in the commercial banks in positions other than janitor, chauffeur or messenger. The change first occurred in Jamaica, probably brought about by the vocal criticism of discriminatory recruitment practices in the business and banking sectors that sensitized the public to the issue. It was kept alive in the newspapers by citizens' associations in the corporate area and the Kingston and St Andrew Corporation (hereafter the KSAC), led by the Kingston mayor, Cleveland G. Walker. The commercial banks were singled out for criticism, and in 1950 the KSAC councillors passed a resolution urging them to employ black Jamaicans in clerical positions.[23] The resolution read, in part:

Plate 9.4 John Basford and his wife upon arrival in Jamaica to assume duties as manager of the King Street branch, 1955. *Courtesy of the National Library of Jamaica.*

> The Council is also of the opinion that with the aspirations of the inhabitants of the island toward nationhood, the policy which has always existed in your bank in this respect should be changed and that qualified black men and women be appointed to senior posts in your service as, it is submitted, there are a great number of black persons who possess the necessary qualifications to fill these posts.[24]

Shortly thereafter the BNS employed Edna Ffrench (now Ramsey), placing her at its King Street branch. Her employment created quite a stir. The sight of a black person performing clerical duties in the collections department, which was located in full view of the main banking hall of the branch, was so uncommon that scores of ordinary Jamaicans felt compelled to visit the branch. "Some even opened small savings accounts with deposits of 10s to provide them with an excuse to enter the bank." Ramsey herself noted, "The bank was very crowded with civil servants who all beamed their satisfaction of seeing a black face working in a clerical position in the bank. It was even mentioned in the papers."[25]

Plate 9.5 Barclays Bank (DCO) branch managers in Kingston: *(left to right)*: C.H. Pratt (manager, Cross Roads); C.H. Abraham (acting manager, Harbour Street); J.V. Basford (manager, King Street); Field-Marshal the Rt. Hon. The Earl Alexander of Tunis (director, Barclays Bank Ltd); A.E.V. Oliver (assistant manager, King Street); J.F. Simmers (acting manager, West Queen Street). *Courtesy of the National Library of Jamaica.*

Barclays Bank (DCO) followed in January 1951 with the employment of Roy McFarlane.[26] Crossley, in reference to this impending appointment, noted, "Apparently, we have an almost ideal candidate now of the requisite colour, and I hope we shall make the experiment. I believe it is all a question of careful selection".[27] Evidently, the appointment of McFarlane, who was of black complexion, was a response to the criticisms being levelled at the banking community. But it could also be argued that McFarlane's appointment by Barclays Bank (DCO) at that particular time occurred in reaction to the BNS's appointment of Ffrench. It could not have been coincidental that McFarlane was placed at the bank's branch on the same street as the branch of its most ardent competitor, where Ffrench had drawn so much attention. Evidently, the rivalry between the two banks in Jamaica gained greater resonance within the sociopolitical circumstances in which both appointments were made.

Other locals of colour employed to Barclays Bank (DCO) in this early period included Donald Banks in January 1952 and Eldon Forrest in August of that year. Both were employed in the Harbour Street branch in Kingston, Jamaica. Augusta Payne (nee Cools-Lartigue) was also employed in August 1952, at the Kingstown branch, St Vincent, as a clerk in the foreign exchange department; she later joined the staff at the Harbour Street branch in Kingston in 1953 when her family immigrated to Jamaica.[28] Barbara Duhaney joined the staff in 1962 at the Montego Bay branch.[29]

Plate 9.6 Don Banks in 1956. NCB The National Banker (March 1992).

Plate 9.7 Eldon Forrest, c. 1951. Courtesy of Eldon Forrest.

Plate 9.8 Barbara Duhaney. Daily Gleaner, 19 August 1967. Courtesy of the National Library of Jamaica.

Plate 9.9 Augusta Payne in 1974. Jamaican Eagle, Barclay's Bank Staff Newsletter 1, no. 19 (1974).

Nevertheless, very few black West Indians were employed in the banking industry in the 1950s and 1960s. The vast majority of non-white West Indian employees were persons of mixed racial composition or of Chinese ancestry, with darker-complexioned recruits confined to persons regarded as "brown" in West Indian parlance – all of whom were presumably socially more acceptable than their black counterparts. The other commercial banks followed the same practice. The BNS in Jamaica was noted for preferring Jamaicans of Chinese extraction. Its Princess Street branch was so dominated by this ethnic group that it led to the passing of a most unsavoury remark by a white American tourist upon entering the branch.[30] Indeed, the "sprinkling" of a few black and brown personnel in the commercial banking sector in the 1950s led Banks to recall, most descriptively, that he and his compatriots were "the few 'flies' in the bowl of milk all over the place".[31] The other commercial banks in Jamaica were less inclined than Barclays Bank (DCO) and the BNS to hire persons of colour, which may be explained by their more limited market share in the island in that period.[32]

Elsewhere in the region there was even less inclination among the commercial banks to hire black West Indians. In British Guiana and Trinidad and Tobago, most of the newly recruited local staff of Barclays Bank (DCO) were persons of Chinese ancestry.[33] Many of the branch

Plate 9.10 Barclays Bank (DCO) staff in Jamaica, 1952. *NCB: The National Banker* (October 1962).

managers expressed their scepticism regarding the hiring of blacks, predicting that not only would local white staff object but their white clientele would move their business to other banks. Money, who had encouraged the hiring of blacks and browns, was accused by the Barbadian white community of "blackening the face" of banking in the West Indies. Money, in commenting on these accusations, noted that those customers "were for a while longer able to go on dealing with an all white bank, by transferring their accounts to one of the Canadian banks who were our only competitors, and who (except, I think, in Jamaica and Belize) continued to employ only white staff for about another two years".[34]

While Money did not identify the bank and territory, he was more than likely referring to the RBC in the Bahamas, which at the time was the only other bank operating in that part of the region and Belize.

White clients' hostility towards the hiring of black personnel continued into the early 1960s; Payne recalls the venomous attitude of members of the French creole community who were resentful of having to see her first in her role as assistant to the manager in the Bank of Trinidad, which Barclays Bank (DCO) acquired in 1963.[35] These racist attitudes undoubtedly influenced bank supervisors' decision to limit the contact between their coloured employees and their customers at certain branches. Payne recalls that when she first arrived at the Harbour Street branch in Kingston, no coloured person was to be found on the

Plate 9.11 Barclays Bank (DCO) staff in Barbados in 1952. *Barclays International Quarterly* (May 1972).

front line where they would, of necessity, interact with customers. She explained the situation as it was then:

> The situation was, when we arrived [there], most of the staff were white, and those of us who were coloured ... we created a little problem for them. So they put us to work facing the wall, with our backs to the banking hall where the customers were ... where we posted those big Burrough ledgers ... boom! ... boom! ... boom![36]

This was not the standard practice throughout the bank's branch network in the region. In the smaller, less socially and racially stratified societies of the Eastern Caribbean such as St Vincent, where the only white residents were the Anglican and Catholic priests and perhaps the doctor and magistrate, even in the 1950s there was no concern about offending the sensibilities of the clients of the bank where Payne had worked before moving to Jamaica. At any rate, Payne would have been considered as part of the middle class in St Vincent, particularly as her father was then the Supreme Court judge for the Windward Islands.[37] In contrast, Jamaica was much more stratified by both race and class, and the Harbour Street branch, considered the premier Barclays branch in the region, controlled the largest and most important clientele, who would naturally have been drawn from the white planter and business elite.

As much as the social and political circumstances of the period influenced the recruitment of non-white West Indians, and greater numbers of West Indians overall, economic considerations were just as important. The weaker financial performance of British multinational banks during the inter-war years had encouraged many of them to adopt cost-saving measures, one of which was to replace expensive expatriate staff with less expensive nationals wherever possible. This rationale remained relevant in the post-1945 period, as with the significant increase in the number of branches, it would have been even more costly to employ expatriates at the executive level at every location, given the differences in salaries and allowances between the two categories of staff.[38] In 1958 concern was expressed about the failure of Barclays Bank (DCO) to recruit a fair number of local staff in the Bahamas, where, it was noted, the bank's operations were "most expensive, not only in salaries, but in providing living accommodation as well".[39] The strategy then was to "make a more determined effort to recruit staff locally on a temporary basis without pensions if we are prepared to offer local rates of say £20 per week".[40]

The savings in salary and emoluments were significant as more West Indians were employed. For example in 1946, a seventeen-year-old West Indian male employee would only after the first five years of service enter onto the same salary scale as his British counterpart serving in the region (see Table 9.1). In addition to their salaries, British staff were paid dislocation allowances and return fares for leaves of absence, as well as receiving higher territorial allowances. For instance, in 1951 married West Indian staff were given £150 per annum in territorial allowances, while married British covenanted staff received £200.[41]

In addition to the prudential advantage, it was judicious to hire more West Indian staff as the bank became more involved in the region's domestic economies. There was now a greater need for information, which was more readily available from West Indians than from British staff, who were less familiar with the society and economy. The bank had by this time extended its representation into the rural areas of many of the territories in which it was located. As banking involved interpersonal relationships, it was important for the staff, and particularly

Table 9.1 Barclays Bank (DCO), Annual Salary Scales for British and West Indian Male Staff, 1946

British Staff Recruited in UK		West Indian Staff		
Age	£	Age	Years' Service	£
20	240	17	–	150
21	260	18	1	170
22	280	19	2	190
23	300	20	3	210
24	330	21	4	235
25	360	22	5	260
26	385	23	6	300
27	410	24	7	330
28	435	25	8	360
29	460	26	9	385
30	485	27	10	410
31	510	28	11	435

Source: Board Minutes, 2 December 1946, Barclays Bank (DCO) Board Minute Book no. 8, BBA 38/507.

managers, to be familiar with and understanding of local idiosyncrasies peculiar to certain territories or locales within territories, about which a lack of knowledge could be costly to the bank.

As it was in the 1920s and 1930s, the strong need for economy in the 1950s also encouraged Barclays Bank (DCO) to employ more women in clerical positions. This marked perhaps an even more radical change in the bank's recruitment practices, since it fundamentally altered the male-dominated corporate culture that was associated with the banking industry. Throughout the world, banking had always been a male-dominated industry. As McDowall notes, women had traditionally played a peripheral role in bank life, if not merely as wives of branch managers, then as stenographers, typists and filing clerks, usually working behind the scenes.[42] Discrimination against women as potential employees was not peculiar to the banking industry, of course; it informed general attitudes towards women in the working world in the nineteenth and early twentieth centuries. In banking, apart from being regarded as not "having a head for money" and business, women were not seen as being suited for an industry which required of its staff both mobility and loyalty. Since women were deemed to be primarily homemakers and mothers, it was not expected that they would remain within the service for long or be available for assignment in the bank's various branch locations.[43] While their services were needed during wartime, they were hired only for shorthand and typing "where [it was] believed [that they were] better than a man", and only for a temporary period, after which it was expected that they would go back to their prescribed role in society.[44]

Nevertheless, perhaps in the interest of economy, Barclays Bank (DCO) hired a few women as "lady clerks" from as early as the 1920s: Sybil Chenery has the distinction of being the first lady clerk to join the bank, in Barbados in 1920. A few women were hired in that position in St Lucia in 1922. More were hired during the Depression years, when the view was expressed that more lady clerks should be employed, as the "strong need for economy . . . justified our doing so".[45] Evidently, the recruitment of white West Indian women became fairly standard, as by 1952 they made up 45 per cent of the bank's staff in the region.[46]

The savings were significant because of the huge disparity in salaries paid to male and female staff. In the 1920s, local female staff could expect to earn £80 per annum, compared with the £120 paid to their male counterparts.[47] In the 1940s the starting salary per annum for female staff in the West Indies was as follows: in Trinidad and Jamaica, £135; in Barbados and British Guiana, £115; and for the other islands, £100. In the twelfth year of employment, female staff could expect to earn in Jamaica and Trinidad, £300; in Barbados and British Guiana, £280; and in the other islands, £265.[48] For the same period, West Indian male staff were being offered a starting salary of £150 and could expect twice that amount by their sixth year in the service (see Table 9.1). By 1952, a newly recruited West Indian male entering at the level of a junior clerk could expect a starting salary of £210 along with a temporary special allowance of £135 per annum.[49]

The lower salaries paid to women reflected the general attitude towards them in the banking industry. As a general rule, married women were not employed by the banks; when a single woman changed her

Plate 9.12 Barclays Bank (DCO) staff at the San Fernando branch, Trinidad and Tobago, 1952. Republic Bank Ltd, *From Colonial to Republic*, 120.

marital status, she had to resign. For example, when Augusta Payne married in 1955, she was required to resign and was then rehired only on a temporary basis. If rehired on a temporary basis, women who became pregnant were required to terminate their contracts before their pregnancy became evident. This meant that none of the married women could qualify for long leave or pension benefits since qualification was based on working for the bank for ten consecutive years.[50]

The deliberate policy of employing more women was partially responsible for their making up just over half of the staff in the West Indies in the late 1950s and early 1960s.[51] A similar revolution for the same reasons occurred within the bank's parent bank, Barclays Bank Ltd, where "from less than one fifth of the bank's work force before World War II, women employees almost equalled men in the 1950s".[52] The high proportion of females on the staff in the West Indies was also a result of the difficulty the bank was experiencing in hiring qualified male staff because the civil service offered more attractive careers at the time. Of the fifty-four clerical staff recruited in 1954, only fifteen were men.[53] The situation was no different in 1958, when only twelve of the seventy-eight new recruits were male.[54] Given the prevailing attitudes towards women in banking during this period, this situation caused some consternation within the top management of Barclays Bank (DCO), as indicated in comments by A.C. Barnes:

Plate 9.13 Barclays Bank (DCO) staff at Half Way Tree branch, Kingston, Jamaica, 1957. *From left:*
Y. Humphries, M. Sadler, V. Curling; *Back:* P. Rimmer, J. Tomlinson, R. Catchpole, C. Mace.
DCO Quarterly Magazine (October 1957). National Library of Jamaica.

I was somewhat doubtful whether we had enough young men of the right calibre who could take positions of responsibility later on . . . Where we are working with a large proportion of women, it is essential that the men we engage should be of high quality as we shall need practically all of them for senior positions later on, and we cannot afford to have passengers.[55]

Owing to the insufficient number of "men of the right calibre" for positions of senior responsibility, within a relatively short period the bank had to make concessions to its policy regarding the positions that could be held by women. Accordingly, the decision was taken to begin appointing members of its female staff to supervisory positions. This it did for the first time in 1954, with the granting of signatory powers to female staff at two of its main branches in the region.[56]

Evidently, some of these women were being recognized for their talents and identified for future managerial positions, as the career paths of both Payne and Ena Evadne Leung-Walker (now Thompson) demonstrate. After resigning from the bank in 1957, Payne rejoined it in 1959 and was assigned to the Advances Department in the King Street branch, where her talents were noted. Between 1964 and 1968 she was the manager's assistant in the Bank of Trinidad, which Barclays Bank (DCO) acquired in 1963. Following stints as treasury officer, assistant accountant and manager's assistant in the Antigua branch, she came back to Jamaica as assistant to the manager in the West Queen Street branch in Kingston for three months. She then went to the West Caribbean Head Office in Jamaica, in the King Street branch, to work in the advances section, during which time she acted for a short spell as manager of the Duke Street branch. Thereafter, she returned to the West Caribbean Head Office and was made advances supervisor, a position which was later retitled advances manager. Eventually, Payne went on to become the first woman in the Barclays organization to be appointed local director's assistant, in the Barbados office. Following the acquisition of the bank's assets in Jamaica by the government in 1977, Payne was appointed deputy managing director of the National Commercial Bank in 1978, the first woman in the region to attain such a high position.[57]

Leung-Walker joined Barclays Bank (DCO) in 1953 as a general clerk and typist in the Water Street branch in British Guiana. She was put on the path to a managerial position when, after four years, she was sent to the Gracechurch Street head office in London for further training. During her London stint she was successful in three of the Part I Institute of the Bankers Examinations, which she completed in 1963, receiving the AIB following her return to British Guiana. In 1960 she worked in the foreign exchange department and was placed in charge of it two years later.

Plate 9.14 Ena Evadne Leung-Walker. *Barclays Caribbean Bulletin* (Summer 1968).

In 1964, at the age of thirty-four, Leung-Walker was appointed accountant in the Main Street branch, Georgetown, Guyana, for three years, being the first woman in the region to hold this position. During this period, she was seconded to the Advances Department in the Caribbean Head Office in Barbados. This was followed by her participation in the junior managers' six-week course in London before being appointed acting manager of the Main Street branch, and then manager in 1968. The latter appointment made Walker the first woman in the DCO organization to be appointed manager of a full branch anywhere in the world.[58]

Meanwhile, Dorothy Eve Reid, who had joined the Barclays Bank (DCO) staff as a typist in the St Ann's Bay branch in 1949, was to become Jamaica's first female manager of a commercial bank when she was so appointed in 1969 to the Manor Park branch in Kingston.[59]

Plate 9.15 Dorothy Eve Reid. *NCB: The National Banker* (March 1989).

Decentralization: The Establishment of a Local Directorship

An important aspect of Barclays Bank (DCO)'s strategy during this period included decentralization of its West Indian operations, which was accomplished with the establishment of a local regional head office in 1952 at Bridgetown, Barbados. George G. Money was appointed local director, and Henry Dale joined him a year later.[60]

The establishment of a local directorship in the West Indies was part of an evolutionary approach to the control of the bank's overseas operations that was adopted very early in its history. Following the amalgamation in 1925, the organizational structure of the three constituent banks, with their respective boards or committees, was initially retained, thereby retaining their separate identities. However, in 1929 the regulations governing the local and sectional boards of the three constituent banks stipulated that they be combined in a weekly meeting attended by the sectional board general manager, the deputy and/or assistant manager, or by the next senior administrative officer. This gathering constituted the London Committee, and it was this body which exercised control over lending policy with powers delegated to it from the Central Board, and which effectively facilitated the fusion of the operations of the bank as a whole.[61]

It was at these meetings that all requests involving credit facilities over a certain amount that had been forwarded by the branch managers were submitted for approval. For example, in 1927 facilities of £10,000 and over had to be submitted to the London Committee for approval.[62] In cases where it was anticipated that a delay in the approval of a particular facility would be prejudicial to the business of the bank, the section could go ahead and sanction the facility but had to seek confirmation at the following weekly meeting.[63] The regulations also specified that the particulars of all facilities of £10,000 and over had to be submitted to the local sectional boards every three months; they, along with the sectional boards' comments, were forwarded to the Central Board every six months for review.[64] Any excess over the sanctioned amount had to be reported at the next full meeting of the local sectional boards. In addition, the returns on all advances and the particulars relating to other administrative matters had to be submitted to the local sectional boards and, in turn, forwarded with the sectional boards' comments to the Central Board for review each week.[65]

At the same time, considerable power remained below the level of head office in Barclays Bank (DCO)'s organizational structure, and in fact the regional management system which was applied to the West Indian operations in 1952 was part of the bank's organizational structure from the beginning. For example, the bank's operations in South Africa were controlled directly through a local regional board that was established in Johannesburg prior to the amalgamation and which continued thereafter. This board had considerable discretionary powers over lending within limits set by head office.[66] Local regional boards were established in Egypt and then in Palestine. Generally, these regional boards were granted discretionary limits up to £25,000. Business ranging between £25,000 and £50,000 had to be sanctioned by the local board and by the general manager for the particular section at head office. Any difference of opinion regarding the accommodation being granted was referred to the chairman. Business involving £50,000 and over had to be submitted to the Central Board with a recommendation from the sectional board and the general managers at head office.[67]

It was only in the former Colonial Bank regions – that is, in the West Indies and West Africa – that the regional management concept was not immediately applied following the amalgamation of the constituent banks in 1926. This was because the primary focus of the bank's operations in these regions continued to be that of providing trade finance for agricultural exports. As noted by Jones, the organizational structure that centralized discretionary powers over lending and administration in the London head office was ideal for a bank whose business was essentially trade-related. A London-based board had better access to information about market conditions for commodities, essential for a bank whose primary interest was in the provision of financing for British colonial trade. As well, a London-based board provided vital contacts with British mercantile firms involved in overseas trade. Also, close contact with the diplomatic and colonial administrative bodies, such as the Colonial Office, enabled the bank to be more readily responsive to policy changes affecting banking and trade with respect to the colonies.[68]

Circumstances which influenced the implementation of a regional management system within a particular area included the extent to which the bank had become involved in the domestic economy, providing retail banking services. Such an organizational structure was more capable of assessing domestic risk than a structure in which the decision-making was centralized in London. However, with regard to the bank's West Indian operations, other factors were equally important. One was the level of development of communications within the region and between the region and London. In 1946, when the question of whether to establish a local controlling office in the West Indies was being consid-

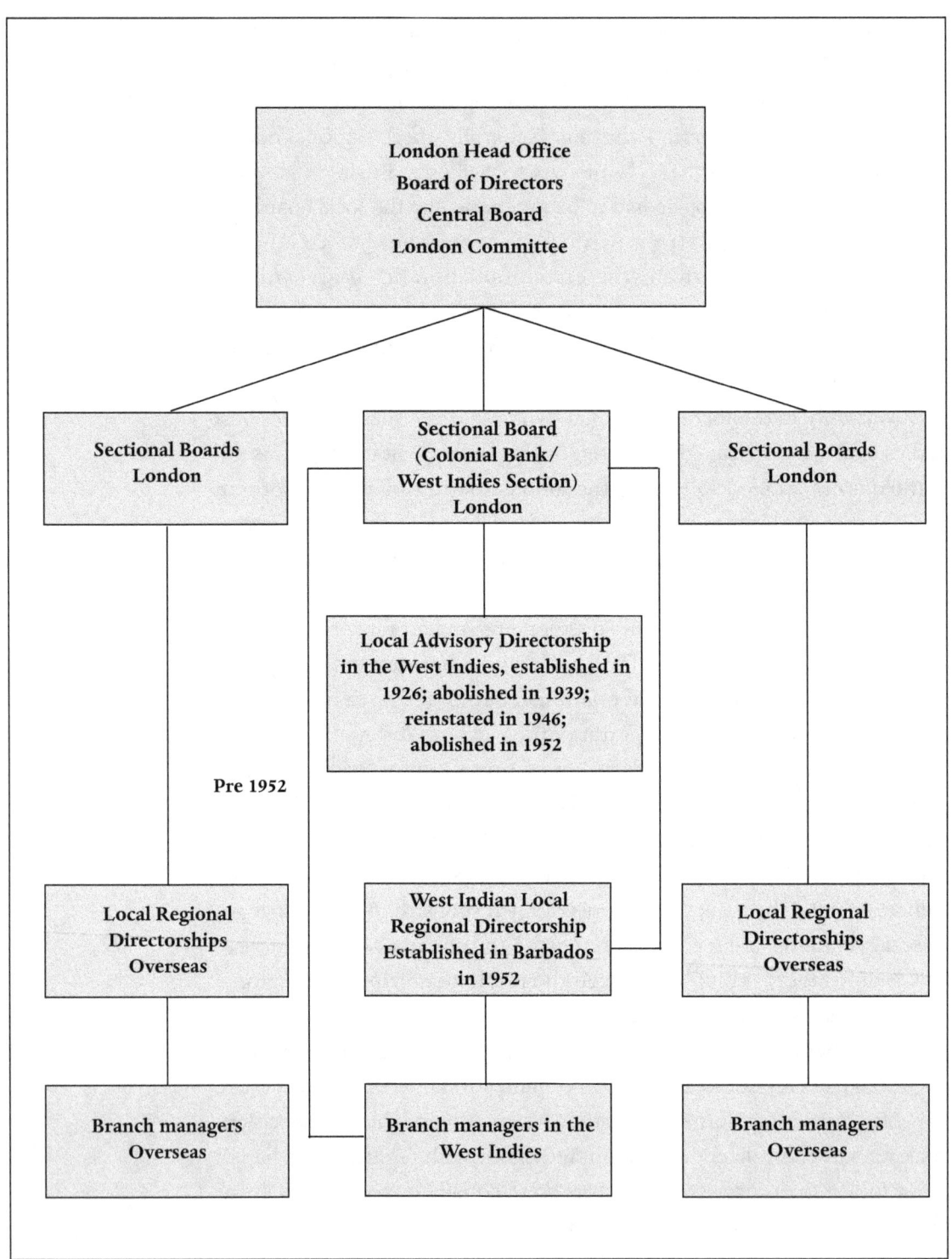

Figure 9.1 Management structure of Barclays Bank (DCO), 1952

ered, it was acknowledged that the considerable improvements in communications within the region had made it easier for a local control to make contact with the branches. It was also contended, however, that communications with London were easier than before. In addition, it was pointed out that at that particular time, the absence of a local control had not caused the loss of any business because the bank's business in the region was still primarily concerned with the provision of trade finance for the region's export crops. To further argue that point, it was noted that the RBC had established a local controlling office at Port of Spain in Trinidad and Tobago, which had "not prevented our making far greater progress in Trinidad itself despite our remote control".[69] Nevertheless, it was accepted that a "watch" was necessary on potential developments in the region of which it needed to keep abreast, considering the Colonial Office plan to launch the Colonial Development Corporation, along with the bank's own recently established development corporation. As a consequence, it was decided to reinstate the former local advisory directorship that it had adopted in 1926 and abandoned in 1939.[70]

The local advisory director was normally a retired senior branch manager with fairly long experience in the region. His assignment was essentially a watching brief over the bank's operations. The first to hold the post was E.W. Lucie-Smith, who was appointed in 1926. His area of jurisdiction was restricted to Jamaica. A.P.G. Austin, who had been a senior manager at the Barbados branch, was appointed in a similar capacity in 1934 for the rest of the branches in the region. Austin's supervisory powers were extended to include Jamaica in 1935, following Lucie-Smith's full retirement. In essence, the local advisory position was informal and did not involve the maintenance of an office or staff, and West Indian branch managers remained directly accountable to the London head office.

After Austin's retirement, the post was allowed to lapse, on the understanding that more frequent visits would be paid to the region by members of the board and other senior officials. The position was resuscitated in 1946 with the appointment of C.C. George, who had been senior manager of the main branch at Port of Spain, Trinidad and Tobago, for some fifteen years. Whereas the previous local advisory directors' duties had been broad and general in nature, George was given specific terms of reference. He was required to keep in close touch with the general economic and social conditions of the islands and to report any significant developments, particularly with regard to business associated with the bank's development corporation. He was also required to make frequent visits to the various territories, visiting each branch at least once every six months. Administrative matters continued to be handled by the head office in London, though the position carried with it some authority to override decisions made by a branch manager if warranted. In addition, George was charged with the responsibility of investigating any difficult problems that might arise at any of the branches and was to be available to head office for consultation on such matters. He was also to keep a close watch on matters pertaining to the staff, with a view to ensuring that any problems which arose were to be brought to the notice of the head office immediately before they became difficult or acute.[71]

Clearly then, Barclays Bank (DCO) had adopted an evolutionary approach to the administrative control of its branch network in the region, and the establishment of the more permanent local directorship in 1952 can be viewed as a natural progression. The gradual political decolonization of the region obviously would have had a compelling influence on the decision to decentralize in that year. Indeed, several of the islands, beginning with the larger economies of Jamaica and Trinidad and Tobago, attained internal self-government by 1957 and 1961 respectively, with full political independence imminent by 1962. In addition, many of them had implemented a version of the Puerto Rican economic model discussed in the previous chapter, which led to quickened economic activity in the 1950s. All of this had implications for the bank's operations, and required a structure which would allow it to be immediately informed of new economic, fiscal and banking policy and to respond accordingly. Therefore, considerable discretionary powers with regard to lending and administration were transferred from the head office in London to the local office in the West Indies.[72] Initially, the local director could sanction a loan of up to £15,000 without consulting head office. This was later increased to £25,000, secured or unsecured, with the sanction being agreed to by both directors. In the event of one of the local directors being absent, the director who was present was allowed to sanction the loan but was duty-bound to report to his colleague on his return. The local directors were also charged with the power to sanction staff recruitment, branch expansion and development.[73]

Summary

Barclays Bank (DCO) was sufficiently aware of changed social and political developments in the West Indies during the period 1940–62 to modify its previous employment practices, and it began recruiting non-white West Indians for the first time. However, the bank was constrained to some extent by the prevailing racial and class divisions inherent in West Indian societies, and consequently, rather than take the lead in making social change, it preferred to make adjustments to suit the existing status quo.

The increased recruitment of West Indians was also in the interest of keeping operational costs down, as was the recruitment of more women in this period. Later on, however, the bank's top management experienced difficulty in recruiting sufficient suitable male staff to fill managerial posts. Despite the prevailing bias against women in such posts, the bank eventually had to make some concession, and accordingly, women were appointed to supervisory posts for the first time in the bank's history in the region.

An important aspect of the bank's strategy included the adoption of a decentralized system of administration in the West Indies, with the establishment of a local directorship in Barbados in 1952. The intent was to be more readily responsive to increased business opportunities. The establishment of a local controlling office was also a response to the impending political independence of territories in the region. The bank's ability to implement such a change in response to these developments was evidence of the adaptability of its administrative structure, which had been in place from its inception in December 1925.

Conclusion

The formation of Barclays Bank (DCO) in 1925 represented one of the strategies adopted by the British overseas multinational banks that had first appeared in the 1830s, in response to the economic and political instability which many of them had begun to experience in the late nineteenth and early twentieth centuries. Faced with a decline in their original competitive advantages, many of these banks sought equity shareholding from well-established British domestic banks, a number of which had grown in size and dominance by that time. Barclays Bank Ltd, which had invested extensively in the Colonial Bank, also acquired shareholding in two other overseas banks, the National Bank of South Africa and the Anglo-Egyptian Bank. The three banks were amalgamated to form Barclays Bank (Dominion, Colonial and Overseas), resulting in the creation of the largest multinational bank in the world at that time.

The infusion of capital and its eventual reconstitution were strategically important for the survival of the Colonial Bank in the West Indies, albeit under a new name. The Colonial Bank, a much smaller entity than its Canadian rivals, which were vertical outgrowths of well-established domestic banking entities in Canada, had suffered extensive losses as a result of sharp falls in the price for cane sugar on the international market in the 1880s and 1890s. And although some rebound was experienced in 1914 with the outbreak of World War I, which disrupted production and trade in European beet sugar, it was apparent that the Colonial Bank as it existed then would have found it difficult to cope with the new challenges which lay ahead in the early twentieth century.

As the original competitive advantages available to the British overseas banks began to wane in the late nineteenth and early twentieth centuries, strategies were devised which enabled them to survive. At the same time, obvious nation-specific advantages still existed that were associated with banking operations within the empire. This book has argued that the "factor endowments" associated with colonialism – in terms of British fiscal, social and economic policy – were to some extent important to the operations of Barclays Bank (DCO) in the West Indies between 1926 and 1962. Nevertheless, the bank's own business strategy contributed equally to its ability to operate effectively.

Certainly, demand conditions in the West Indies for Barclays Bank (DCO) continued to be favourable in the period 1926–62. For much of the period, the region's economies continued to be structured around plantation agriculture for export, characterized by heavy investment in the dominant sugar industry by British corporate entities, which owned and controlled vast amounts of property. Other British firms concentrated on the business of procuring and exporting agricultural crops and importing a wide variety of manufactured goods for the wholesale and retail trade in the region. The bank found another valuable customer base among the local merchant/planter elite, who had by the late nineteenth century displaced the traditional planter class which had dominated plantation agriculture for centuries. Both British and local firms had reorganized properties they had acquired, infusing them with capital and increasing their productivity, thereby making them more creditworthy.

It is evident that British imperial policy towards colonial economies was instrumental in safeguarding the demand conditions and therefore the operations of Barclays Bank (DCO) in the West Indies. This was clearly borne out during the inter-war period, when the sugar industry in the region was threatened with collapse as a consequence of the Great Depression of the 1930s. As the bank was extensively involved in financing the production and marketing of West Indian agricultural crops – particularly sugar – for export, it was affected by the severe decline in the world market prices in that period. Indeed, the drastic fall in the world price of sugar resulted in many of the region's producers finding it difficult to cover their costs of production. Consequently, many were unable to repay loans when they became due. A contraction in the commercial centres of the region followed, including a drop in the demand for consumer items because the decline in money wages paid to the labouring population meant that there was less money in circulation. Naturally, this led to a general contraction in the bank's business, adversely affecting its performance in the early years of the Depression. This was evident in the decline in profits registered by the branches in the region and in the contributions of the West Indian Section to the bank as a whole.

Nonetheless, it was apparent that some degree of recovery occurred during the period, as by 1933 profits at both branch and sectional levels began to show an increase. An important factor in this recovery was support from the British government in the form of the loan-guarantee scheme, which helped to minimize the risks involved in the bank's provision of credit to the sugar industry. The British government's concern for maintaining the stability of the region's sugar industry led it to devise a scheme in which the government undertook to share the loss on loans made by the bank to the industry. Even more helpful was the extension of the imperial preferential tariff rate on colonial produce entering the British market in 1932. This had the immediate effect of increasing the returns on production and export of sugar from the West Indies, since the commodity was assured of an expanded market and a profitable price under the cover of preferential rates of duty. The result was a tremendous growth in exports to the British market, which meant more profitable business for the bank.

The provision of special marketing arrangements for the West Indian sugar crop throughout World War II and after also benefited the regional operations of Barclays Bank (DCO) in the period 1940–62. Such arrangements, by guaranteeing a market for the West Indian sugar crop at remunerative prices, ensured the sustained profitability of the region's most important export crop. Considering the level of advances to the agricultural sector, and particularly to sugar production and export, the marketing arrangements were an added boon for the bank.

The preferential marketing arrangements, by facilitating the viability of the sugar industry in the West Indies, also facilitated continued British foreign investment in that industry and helped to ensure that the major proportion of the region's exports continued to be directed to Britain. Indeed, West Indian trade on the whole stayed primarily with Britain, even as the various territories' economies experienced structural changes owing to the infusion of American capital that accompanied developments in manufacturing, mining and tourism. As a result, Barclays Bank (DCO) did not face significant pressure with regard to the demand for dollars to finance trade in the West Indies, in contrast to many of its counterparts in South America.

That the West Indies was part of the British empire during this period meant that Barclays Bank (DCO) was to a large extent guaranteed a high level of receptivity as far as government regulation of the commercial banking industry was concerned. The laissez-faire policy of successive British governments left commercial banks in the colonies virtually free of restrictions on their activities. The focus of government regulation as it pertained to banking was on the protection of depositors and holders of banknotes, and there was virtually nothing in the legislation to restrict the banks in their movement of funds and in their allocation of credit. That did not change until a central bank was established in Jamaica in 1961.

Nevertheless, the reform of the currency system in the West Indies introduced changes which negatively affected certain aspects of the bank's operations, including the withdrawal of its note-issuing privileges. Even then, the British government's permissive attitude towards commercial banking was evident in its approach, as during the currency-reform process the Colonial Office exhibited a reluctance to interfere with the banks' note-issuing privileges. This was in the interest of maintaining stability, as some officials in the Colonial Office were of the view that a significant part of the West Indian note issue was better off under the management of the commercial banks. Certainly, this belief informed the Colonial Office decision to support Barclays Bank (DCO)'s request for a temporary increase in its circulatory limit, which seemed to contradict the ultimate objective of replacing the banknote circulation with a government currency note issue.

This ambiguity on the part of the Colonial Office encouraged the Jamaica government to take steps to make the banknote issue unprofitable in that colony. It did this by imposing an oppressive rate of taxation on all banknotes in circulation, to which Barclays Bank (DCO) strenuously objected. This raises the question of the extent to which

British colonialism guaranteed receptivity in the West Indies in this period. Theoretically, one could argue that it was so; however, given a degree of ambiguity in the Colonial Bank Act 1925, and the fact that it was the ultimate objective of the reform process to withdraw the note-issuing rights from the commercial banks in the region, it would have been incongruous for the Colonial Office to insist that the Jamaica government amend the law pertaining to the banknote issue. As Barclays Bank (DCO) wished to avoid a court battle with the colonial government, possibly for fear of damage to its public image, the matter was dropped.

The establishment of government currency notes as the principal medium of exchange also had implications for the banks' foreign exchange business. The banks were now obliged to conduct their trade finance business using government currency notes, for which they had to provide the required amount of sterling. For this they were charged a commission rate, which was set by the currency boards. Because the currency boards dealt only with transactions of £5,000 and over, however, the banks' foreign exchange business was not adversely affected by the new arrangements.

As important as British colonialism was to Barclays Bank (DCO)'s operations in the region, it does not fully account for the bank's relatively good performance in the period 1926–62. The adoption of appropriate business strategies was also important to the bank's success. First, it generally adhered to conventional lending practices, which helped to minimize risk. As a result, loans and advances were generally short-term and made against relatively safe security. At the same time, the bank exhibited a degree of flexibility, occasionally allowing roll-overs on the repayment of loans. This occurred particularly during World War II, when wartime conditions disrupted the shipment of produce, causing delays in the repayment of loans. In addition, the bank was prepared to provide unsecured loans to creditworthy customers whose business it valued highly.

But deviation from conventional lending practices was not common, and the bank generally maintained a conservative approach to lending in the West Indies. It lent only to customers it thought to be creditworthy, and there are indications that the assessment was based not only on economic criteria but also on race and ethnicity. Its products and services were for the most part restricted to British and other foreign companies, as well as West Indian planter and commercial interests – the groups that formed the elite in these societies. In general, the provision of credit was not extended to the peasantry, small farmers and small-business enterprises in the region, since the bank considered these groups far too risky. What was available to these groups were savings account facilities, which became more widespread in the 1950s, when the bank embarked upon a concentrated effort to increase its level of deposits. These groups had to rely on government institutions, credit arrangements with merchants or informal credit arrangements made amongst themselves.

Barclays Bank (DCO)'s business strategy in the West Indies also included establishing and maintaining collusive agreements with other commercial banks in the region. These agreements covered rates charged for business and were designed to minimize price competition, with a view to protecting profit margins. The collusion among the commercial banks functioned as an effective barrier against entry by institutions with limited capital. In this regard, collusive agreements served as an effective safeguard against the development of instability, since they prevented excessive price competition within the industry.

Although the objective of such agreements was to minimize competition, their terms allowed some degree of price competition. Too, although the agreements were generally binding, they were sometimes broken, which led to price competition being engaged in during the hiatus while terms were renegotiated. In other words, the rigidity that is assumed to be characteristic of collusive agreements among the commercial banks of the period was not present in the West Indies. Despite the presence of a long-standing collusive agreement which limited price competition among the banks, in fact, the West Indian commercial banking market in this period was fairly competitive. Barclays Bank (DCO) bank faced very keen competition from the Canadian banks, which were prepared to use a variety of non-price-competitive strategies to undermine the position of the British bank. Among these strategies was flexibility, with regard to both the terms for loan facilities and the types of business for which they would provide financial accommodation. This brought into sharp focus the more conservative practices of Barclays Bank (DCO), which contributed to a loss of business by the British bank, particularly during the inter-war period. During those years Barclays exhibited inflexibility and insufficient sagacity, both of which contributed to a poor image in the eyes of the public – particularly in Jamaica in the 1930s – which the Canadian banks, particularly the BNS, were only too willing to exploit. Indeed, it was in Jamaica that Barclays Bank (DCO) faced its greatest competitive threat, which was attributed largely to the presence of the BNS there.

The existence of a competitive environment made an effective strategy extremely important to Barclays Bank (DCO)'s survival in the region. The expansion of its branch network in the region was a significant aspect of this strategy, particularly after World War II. It increased its representation through the establishment of agencies, thereby establishing first-mover advantages within territories and staking out a niche in areas already occupied by a competitor bank. Other competitive strategies included luring customers by offering better terms for services, soliciting new clients through established clients and acting as an agent for banks not established in the region. The British bank also wooed customers, particularly the American bauxite companies, to gain valuable foreign exchange business, by offering specialized convenience services. Barclays Bank (DCO) found the advantages arising out of the legacy of British colonialism useful, particularly in its pursuit of savings deposits. The provision of amenities, such as parking facilities and attractive building design and decor, was another aspect of the bank's competitive strategy.

Barclays Bank (DCO) was able to adapt to changing circumstances in the region between 1940 and 1962. One indication was its response to the growth in business opportunities which resulted from the expansion of other sectors of the region's economy after 1940. The expansion stemmed primarily from the policy of "industrialization by invitation" which was pursued by various governments with a view to fostering economic growth and development. The result was a substantial increase in American investment, which boosted the manufacturing, mining, commercial and service sectors.

The bank's business strategy in response to this development included the broad expansion of its branch network. Branches were extended into new territories, namely the Bahamas and British Honduras, to take advantage of new business opportunities developing there. Branches were also extended to the burgeoning new commercial centres and rural townships. Barclays Bank (DCO) facilitated its branch expansion programme through the establishment of agencies, which were particularly useful for areas in which sufficient business had yet to emerge to warrant the establishment of a more permanent office. Agencies kept transaction costs to a minimum while garnering what business was available.

Barclays Bank (DCO) also diversified its products and services in response to the structural changes in the region's economy. It undertook a shift from primarily financing agricultural production and trade to financing the expanding commercial and industrial sectors. In so doing, the bank met the increased demands for working capital from local commercial and manufacturing firms.

To meet the increased demand for credit in the 1950s, the bank had to embark upon an intensive campaign to increase its level of savings and other deposit accounts, especially since it was during this period – particularly after 1957 – that it experienced low liquidity. In addition, there was a significant decline in the level of deposits remitted to London, which was a reflection of the growth in demand for credit. Indeed, Barclays Bank (DCO), instead of being a net exporter of capital, had become a net importer, as substantial amounts were drawn on its overseas resources to finance advances.

Diversification was also evident in the bank's provision of securities-management services and stocks and shares arbitration facilities, which it offered through trustee departments that it established in a number of branches. Some of these departments later evolved into nominees companies, as this aspect of the business expanded. The greatest development of this service was witnessed in the Bahamas and encouraged the establishment of the subsidiary BITCO.

Product innovation came with the establishment of the subsidiary BODC to provide medium- and long-term credit facilities. The decision to establish the BODC, while partly a response to the growth in demand for such facilities after 1940, was also a reaction to sharp criticism of British multinational banks operating in the empire. During the 1940s, British multinational banks were criticized for neglecting the developmental needs of their host countries by concentrating on short-term finance. In response, Barclays Bank (DCO) established the BODC specifically to provide medium- and long-term credit for development projects in the territories in which it operated.

As innovative as this development was, however, it did not imply any radical alteration in the bank's lending policy. For one thing, the terms and conditions for making loans meant that lending by the BODC was skewed in favour of the more advanced territories in the region. As well, even though the stated objective was to finance development projects, commercial-type businesses in the West Indies appeared to be most favoured by the BODC, which generally shunned government-sponsored development projects.

Barclays Bank (DCO) was aware of the changed social and political environment in the period after 1945 and made modifications accordingly. These included changes in its previous employment practices, which had resulted in an all-white, predominantly male and mostly expatriate staff. On account of a heightened sense of nationalism pervading the region and the consequent steps towards political independence, banks and other commercial businesses in the region were criticized for employment policies which excluded black and coloured West Indians from clerical positions in their organizations. It was during the 1950s that non-white West Indians were recruited to the bank for the first time; however, the bank was constrained to some extent by the racial and class divisions inherent in a colonial society in which the legacies of slavery still persisted.

The increased recruitment of locally born personnel by the bank was also in the interest of keeping operational costs down. As a consequence, a significant proportion of the newly recruited staff were women. This later presented a problem for the bank's top management, when it became difficult to attract suitable male staff for managerial posts and the bias against women in such posts still prevailed. Eventually the bank had to make some concessions, and it was then that women were appointed to supervisory posts for the first time.

An important aspect of Barclays Bank (DCO)'s strategy included the adoption of a decentralized system of administration, beginning with the establishment of a local directorship in Barbados in 1952. This was done to enable quicker decision-making about loan applications, thereby increasing the bank's responsiveness to the business opportunities associated with the period. These changes were also a response to the region's impending political independence. The bank's management recognized that political independence would bring changes in regulations pertaining to the banking sector, and that modifications in administrative control over its branch network would enable the bank to respond quickly to local developments.

Barclays Bank (DCO)'s operations in the West Indies between 1926 and 1962 represented an important part of the bank's operations as a whole. This was clearly evident in the level of profits contributed by the West Indian Section to the total profits of the bank. Its general performance was one of increase throughout the period, with the section contributing an average of 7.5 per cent of the total profit. While this percentage represented a relatively small proportion of the total, its significance is apparent when viewed in relation to the performance of the other sections of the bank's operations. In the period 1926–62, the section contributed, on average, the fourth-highest level of profits of the fourteen sections then in existence. Nevertheless, the operational costs of the bank's branch network in the region accounted for a substantial proportion of its gross profits. In this regard, the bank's performance in the West Indies, particularly in the period 1952–62, was not as impressive as its profit levels might have suggested.

Clearly, the operations of Barclays Bank (DCO) between 1926 and 1962 represented an integral part of the commercial banking sector in the West Indies. Along with the other commercial banks, especially the Canadians, Barclays Bank (DCO) contributed to the development of modern banking there. As a commercial banking institution engaged in financing foreign trade and providing working capital for the commercial and industrial sectors, the bank facilitated the redirection of existing tangible wealth into productive channels. As a commercial banking entity, it did not see its role as that of promoting investment opportunities, and so it did not help to generate new industries and enterprises. Instead, it responded to business opportunities as they arose in the societies in which it functioned. Its interaction with the various sectors of the economies in the West Indies was mainly permissive, in that it accommodated those whom it considered creditworthy borrowers rather than actively promoting new investment opportunities or encouraging applicants to come forward for advice and extra services. Nevertheless, the bank helped in the spread and use of financial instruments, such as bills of exchange, currency notes and overdraft and deposit facilities. By providing opportunities for saving, which encouraged a proportion of current income to be saved over a period of time, the bank facilitated the reallocation of current savings for alternative investments, and, in general, the spread of a banking habit in the region's economies. This was accomplished through the vast branch network which it established throughout the region. Very significantly, through its changed employment practices in the post-war period, the bank facilitated the training of a cadre of West Indian bankers and therefore the development of an efficient banking sector in the region. This efficiency was aided by the regulatory control that was established from the nineteenth century and which continued to evolve into the twentieth. The result was that a fairly modern system and tradition of bank regulation was in place in the period immediately preceding independence.

Appendix A

Bank Exchange Quotations for the West Indies, 1942

Bank Exchange Quotations (US$)

	Selling		Buying
	TT*	Demand	Demand
Antigua & St Lucia			
Below $2,500	20 3/8% prm*	20 1/8% prm	18 1/2% prm
$2,500–4,999	20 1/4%	20%	18 1/4%
$5,000–9,999	20 3/16%	19 15/16%	18 5/16%
$10,000 and over	20 1/8%	19 7/8%	18 3/8%
St Kitts & St Vincent			
Below $2,500	20 3/8% prm	20 1/2% prm	18 1/8%
$2,500–4,999	20 1/4%	20%	18 1/4%
$5,000 and over	20 3/16%	19 15/16%	18 5/16%
Jamaica	$4.00	$4.01	$4.05
Grenada			
Below $2,500	19 7/8% prm	19 5/8% prm	17 5/8% prm
$2,500–4,999	19 3/4%	19 1/2%	17 3/4%
$5,000 and over	19 11/16%	19 7/16%	17 13/16%
Dominica			
Below $2,500	19 3/4% prm	19 1/2% prm	17 1/2%
$2,500–4,999	19 5/8%	19 3/8%	17 5/8%
$5000 and over	19 9/16%	19 5/16%	17 11/16%

Barbados Drafts	Selling		Buying	
	TT*	Demand	Bankers' Cheques	Demand Draft
Below $5,000	20 3/8% prm	20 1/2% prm	18 1/2% prm	18% prm
$5,000–9,999	20 3/4% prm	19 15/16% prm	18 5/16% prm	18 3/16% prm
$10,000 and over	20 1/2% prm	19 7/8% prm	18 3/8% prm	18 1/4% prm

Appendix A continues

Appendix A

	Selling		Buying
	TT*	Demand	Demand
Trinidad & Tobago			
Below $5,000	$20^3/_8$% prm	$20^1/_8$% prm	$18^1/_8$% prm
$5,000–9,999	$20^3/_{16}$%	$19^{15}/_{16}$%	$18^5/_{16}$%
$10,000 and over	$20^1/_8$%	$19^7/_8$%	$18^3/_8$%
Demerara			
Below $5,000	$20^5/_8$% prm	$20^1/_8$% prm	$18^1/_8$% prm
$5,000–9,999	$20^7/_{16}$%	$19^{15}/_{16}$%	$18^5/_{16}$%
$10,000 and over	$20^3/_8$%	$19^7/_8$%	$18^3/_8$%

Bank Exchange Quotations (per £100)

	Selling		Buying
	TT*	Demand	Demand
Trinidad, Barbados, Demerara	$7/_{16}$% prm	$5/_{16}$% prm	$1^5/_8$% disct*
Windward & Leeward Islands	$1/_2$% prm	$3/_8$% prm	$1^3/_4$% disct
Jamaica	$7/_{16}$% prm	$5/_{16}$% prm	$1^1/_8$% disct.
Trinidad & Barbados			
Below £1,000	$484	$482.50	$477.50
£1,000–1,999	483.62^1/_2$	482.12^1/_2$	477.87^1/_2$
£2,000–2,999	$483.50	$482	$478
£3000 and upwards	$483.25	$481.75	$478.25
Demerara			
Below £1,000	$484.50	$482.50	$477.50
£1,000–1,999	484.12^1/_2$	482.12^1/_2$	477.87^1/_2$
£2,000–2,999	$484	$482	$478
£3,000 and upwards	$483.75	$481.75	$478.25
Windward & Leeward Islands	$485	$483	$477
Jamaica	$1/_2$% prm	$1/_4$% prm	$9/_{16}$% disct

*TT = telegraphic transfer; prm = premium; disct = discount.

Source: British West Indies and British Guiana Exchange Quotations, 14 January 1942, CO 852/359/2.

Appendix B

Barclays Bank (DCO)'s West Indian Sectional Performance (£ sterling) in Relation to the Bank as a Whole, 1940–1962

Year	West Indian Section	Whole Bank	Percent
1940	54,538	917,926	6
1941	65,949	1,137,908	6
1942	80,053	1,242,469	6
1943	94,492	1,427,707	6
1944	97,723	1,503,779	6
1945	89,208	1,712,938	5
1946	107,446	1,980,481	5
1947	172,069	2,752,398	6
1948	181,095	3,045,999	6
1949	177,876	3,052,387	6
1950	158,644	2,871,015	5
1951	255,794	4,052,684	6
1952	298,551	4,295,170	7
1953	271,488	3,811,918	7
1954	225,004	4,585,002	5
1955	309,639	5,667,711	5
1956	623,587	11,328,329	5
1957	714,801	9,978,330	7
1958	952,498	10,963,434	9
1959	861,010	9,346,420	9
1960	1,301,563	12,581,618	10
1961	1,159,701	13,810,326	8
1962	851,829	13,480,075	6

Source: Accounts and Board Meeting Papers, 1940–1962, BBA 38/251.

Appendix C

West Indian Sugar Production and Exports (Thousands of Tons), 1940–1962

Year	Production	Exports
1940	550	441
1941	631	547
1942	636	456
1943	607	509
1944	656	508
1945	623	482
1946	660	558
1947	614	555
1948	802	492
1949	859	701
1950	891	745
1951	890	746
1952	1,000	797
1953	1,049	846
1954	1,119	934
1955	1,044	989
1956	1,132	968
1957	1,097	964
1958	1,132	931
1959	1,224	954
1960	1,276	1,050
1961	1,232	1,114
1962	1,120	1,054

Source: Compiled from statistics from Commonwealth Economic Committee, *Plantation Crops* (1950), 7, 4; (1952), 4, 8; (1955), 12, 18; (1956), 20, 26; (1960), 21, 26; (1963), 24, 29.

Appendix D

Accounts of the Antigua Sugar Factory Ltd, 1938–1947

Year	Sugar Produced (tons)	Gross receipts[a]	Profit before Tax	Dividends	Balance to Credit of Shareholders
1938	18,921	180,938	11,408	9,686	39,272
1939	19,226	204,198	18,717	9,687	40,802
1940	14,113	177,153	15,798	9,686	39,914
1941	17,584	238,672	21,850	11,624	41,140
1942	21,979	301,957	24,672	11,624	42,188
1943	21,867	323,724	28,794	11,624	47,358
1944	16,280	258,339	15,464	9,687	47,435
1945	20,663	369,376	26,020	11,624	49,831
1946	26,023	516,543	44,355	11,624	53,562
1947	22,736	499,303	34,177	9,687	54,052

[a] For sugar and molasses sales.

Source: *Report of the Commission appointed to enquire into the Organization of the Sugar Industry in Antigua* (London: Crown Agents of the Colonies on behalf of the Government of Antigua, 1949), 97.

Appendix E

Profits and Return on Capital Expenditure (£) on Sugar Estates and Factories in Jamaica 1939–1943

	1939	1940	1941	1942	1943
Net profit on cane and sugar production	109,420	48,950	138,535	84,262	49,602
Net profit on rum production	67,289	88,941	87,408	150,733	172,571
Net profit on cane, sugar and rum production	176,709	137,891	225,943	234,995	222,173
Return on capital investment	3.40%	2.66%	4.37%	4.54%	4.29%

Source: Report of the Sugar Industry Commission: Jamaica, 1944–45, 141.

Appendix F

Consolidated Balance Sheet of Four Trinidad Sugar Companies,[a] 1944–1947 (£ sterling)

	1944	1945	1946	1947
Assets				
Land, buildings, plant, railways, etc.	1,771,831	1,709,417	1,685,931	1,689,982
Stores on hand	421,975	398,835	426,054	643,858
Expenditure on future crops	110,133	136,734	173,914	201,715
Subtotal	**2,303,939**	**2,244,986**	**2,285,899**	**2,535,555**
Produce on hand	485,143	457,133	666,981	597,663
Sundry debtors and advances	306,418	127,345	188,784	151,936
Cash in hand and at bankers	55,602	163,025	58,312	125,869
Subtotal	**847,163**	**747,503**	**914,077**	**875,468**
British government securities	141,873	96,193	96,095	84,988
Invested in subsidiary company	0	10,000	37,435	91,171
Subtotal	**141,873**	**106,193**	**133,530**	**176,159**
Total Assets	**3,292,975**	**3,098,682**	**3,333,506**	**3,587,182**

Appendix F continues

Appendix F

	1944	1945	1946	1947
Capital, Reserves & Liabilities				
Stock	1,964,585	1,964,785	1,964,985	1,964,985
General reserves	176,454	172,116	179,604	228,458
Profit and loss accounts	101,979	112,484	146,055	142,590
Subtotal	**2,243,018**	**2,249,385**	**2,290,644**	**2,336,033**
Liabilities				
(a) General	1,007,481	759,745	909,602	982,046
(b) Income tax	42,476	89,552	133,260	278,103
Subtotal	**1,049,957**	**849,297**	**1,042,862**	**1,260,149**
Total	**3,292,975**	**3,098,682**	**3,333,506**	**3,596,182**

[a]Ste Madeleine Sugar Company, Woodford Lodge Estates Ltd, Caroni Ltd, Trinidad Sugar Estates Ltd.

Source: Report of the Commission Appointed to Enquire into the Working of the Sugar Industry in Trinidad, 69.

Appendix G

Value of West Indian Trade (Thousands of Pounds Sterling), 1940–1962[a]

Year	Imports	Exports	Total Trade
1940	17,748	13,795	31,543
1941	20,659	14,015	34,674
1942	18,878	14,142	33,020
1943	27,636	18,856	46,492
1944	31,271	22,152	53,423
1945	30,995	23,574	54,569
1946	38,658	29,309	67,967
1947	58,556	38,145	96,701
1948	63,374	48,347	111,721
1949	68,773	53,589	122,362
1950	77,147	66,069	143,216
1951	100,560	79,446	180,006
1952	115,703	90,693	206,396
1953	108,981	104,019	213,000
1954	116,202	110,830	227,032
1955	138,107	119,251	257,358
1956	154,829	133,021	287,850
1957	180,129	164,372	344,501
1958	174,740	155,413	330,153

Appendix G continues

Appendix G

Year	Imports	Exports	Total Trade
1959	200,743	169,895	370,638
1960	230,728	193,273	424,001
1961	244,313	225,152	469,465
1962	250,704	229,564	480,268

[a]These sources yield a disparity in the availability of statistics for the period for the various territories. For Barbados, statistics are absent for only 1958. For Trinidad and Tobago, none are available for the years before 1939. For British Guiana, statistics are available for 1938 and for 1943–62.

Sources: The West Indies Year Book, 1937; The West Indies Year Book, 1947–48; The West Indies and Caribbean Year Book (for the years 1951, 1952, 1955, 56, 1960–64 and 1966); Colonial Office, *An Economic Survey of the Colonial Territories, 1951;* Barbados, *Report for the Years 1956 and 1957; Handbook of Jamaica* (for the years 1947–48, 1950, 1953, 1957, 1959 and 1963); *Colonial Reports. Annual: Jamaica, 1938; Annual Report on Jamaica, for the Year 1947; Colonial Reports. Annual: British Guiana, 1938.*

Notes

Introduction

1. Geoffrey Jones, *Banking and Empire in Iran* (Cambridge: Cambridge University Press, 1986); Geoffrey Jones, *Banking and Oil* (Cambridge: Cambridge University Press, 1987); Geoffrey Jones, *British Multinational Banking, 1830–1990* (Oxford: Clarendon Press, 1993); F.H.H. King, *History of the Hong Kong Shanghai Banking Corporation* (Cambridge: Cambridge University Press, 1987–1991); David Merrett, *ANZ Bank: An Official History* (Sydney: Allen and Unwin, 1985).
2. Jones, *British Multinational Banking*, 13–62. See also Geoffrey Jones, "The Legacy of the Past: British Multinational Banking Strategies since the Nineteenth Century", in *Multinational Enterprises in the World Economy*, ed. Peter J. Buckley and Mark Casson (Aldershot: Edward Elgar, 1992), 156–60.
3. Jones, *British Multinational Banking*, 58; see also Geoffrey Jones, "Competitive Advantages in British Multinational Banking since 1890", in *Banks as Multinationals*, ed. Geoffrey Jones (London: Routledge, 1990), 38.
4. Jones, "Competitive Advantages", 42–48; Jones, *British Multinational Banking*, 136–84.
5. Jones, "Competitive Advantages", 48–51.
6. Jones, "Competitive Advantages", 48–54; Jones, "Legacy of the Past", 170–74.
7. Jones, *British Multinational Banking*, 200–201.
8. P.J. Cain and A.G. Hopkins, *British Imperialism: Crisis and Deconstruction, 1914–1990* (Harlow, UK: Pearson, 1993), 285–86; James Millette, "Decolonization, Populist Movements, and the Formation of New Nations, 1945–1970", in *General History of the Caribbean*, vol. 5, *The Caribbean in the Twentieth Century*, ed. Bridget Brereton (Paris and London: UNESCO and Macmillan, 2004), 181–83; W. David McIntyre, *The Commonwealth of Nations: Origins and Impact, 1869–1971* (Minneapolis: University of Minnesota Press, 1977), 315–16.
9. See Patrick Bryan, *The Jamaican People, 1880–1902* (London: Macmillan, 1991), 216–65; also Bridget Brereton, *A History of Modern Trinidad, 1783–1962* (Kingston: Heinemann, 1981), 127–30; Bridget Brereton, "Society and Culture in the Caribbean: The British and French West Indies, 1870–1980", in *The*

Modern Caribbean, ed. Franklin W. Knight and Colin A. Palmer (Chapel Hill: University of North Carolina Press, 1989), 90–92.

10. Deryck Brown, *History of Money and Banking in Trinidad and Tobago from 1789 to 1989* (Port of Spain: Paria, 1989), 183–86, 193; Republic Bank Ltd, *From Colonial to Republic: One Hundred and Fifty Years of Business and Banking in Trinidad and Tobago, 1837–1987* (Port of Spain: Republic Bank, n.d.), 153–54; Barclays Bank plc, *Barclays Bank in the Caribbean* (London: Barclays Bank plc, 1991), 27; Donald Banks, interview by author, Kingston, Jamaica, 18 January 1995.
11. A.S.J. Baster, *The Imperial Banks* (London: King, 1929); A.S.J. Baster, *The International Banks* (London: King, 1935).
12. Barclays Bank Ltd, *A Banking Centenary: A History of Barclays Bank (Dominion, Colonial and Overseas) 1836–1936* (Plymouth: W. Brendon and Sons, 1938).
13. Barclays Bank Ltd, *A Bank in Battledress: Being the Story of Barclays Bank (Dominion, Colonial and Overseas) during the Second World War, 1939–1945* (London: Williams, Lea and Co., 1948).
14. Sir Julian Crossley and John Blandford, *The DCO Story: A History of Banking in Many Countries, 1925–1971* (London: Barclays Bank International Ltd, 1975).
15. Barclays Bank plc, *Barclays Bank in the Caribbean*, 27; Carl C. Campbell, review of *From Colonial to Republic*, *Journal of Caribbean History* 23, no. 1 (1990): 111–14.
16. Brown, *History of Money and Banking*.
17. Maurice Odle, *Multinational Banks and Underdevelopment* (New York: Pergamon Press, 1981).
18. Norman Girvan, *Foreign Capital and Economic Underdevelopment in Jamaica* (Kingston: Institute of Social and Economic Research, University of the West Indies, Mona, 1971); Owen Jefferson, *The Post-War Economic Development of Jamaica* (Kingston: Institute of Social and Economic Research, University of the West Indies, Mona, 1972).
19. See Rondo Cameron, Olga Crisp, Hugh T. Patrick and Richard Tilly, eds., *Banking in the Early Stages of Industrialization: A Study in Comparative Economic History* (New York: Oxford University Press, 1967), 6–8; and Richard Tilly, *Financial Institutions and Industrialization in the Rhineland, 1815–1870* (Wisconsin: University of Wisconsin Press, 1966), 4–6. See also Rondo Cameron, *Banking and Economic Development: Some Lessons of History* (New York: Oxford University Press, 1972), 7.

Chapter 1

1. Geoffrey Jones, *The Evolution of International Business: An Introduction* (London: Routledge, 1996), 34.
2. Ibid. See also Mira Wilkins, "The Free-Standing Company, 1870–1914: An Important Type of British Foreign Direct Investment", *Economic History Review*, 2nd ser., 61, no. 2 (1988): 259–82. Also see Mark Casson, "Institutional

Diversity in Overseas Enterprise: Explaining the Free–Standing Company", *Business History* 36, no. 4 (1994): 95–108. For a brief but worthwhile discussion of this issue, see P.J. Cain and A.G. Hopkins, *British Imperialism: Innovation and Expansion, 1688–1914* (Harlow, UK: Pearson, 1993), 173–77; and Geoffrey Jones, *Merchants to Multinationals: British Trading Companies in the Nineteenth and Twentieth Centuries* (Oxford: Oxford University Press, 2000), 8.

3. Wilkins, "The Free-Standing Company", 261.
4. Jones, *Evolution of International Business*, 26; Jones, *Merchants to Multinationals*, 8; Jones, *British Multinational Banking*, 13–16.
5. Jones, *Evolution of International Business*, 152; Geoffrey Jones, ed., *Multinational and International Banking* (Aldershot: Edward Elgar, 1992), xiii.
6. Jones, "Competitive Advantages", 36–37; Jones, *British Multinational Banking*, 13–16. See also Baster, *The Imperial Banks*, 1–2; Cain and Hopkins, *British Imperialism: Innovation and Expansion*, 172.
7. Jones, *British Multinational Banking*, 17.
8. Herbert Grubel, "A Theory of Multinational Banking", *Banca Nazionale del Lavoro Quarterly Review* 123 (December 1977): 349–63, reprinted in Jones, *Multinational and International Banking*, 3–17. Also, Jean M. Gray and H. Peter Gray, "The Multinational Bank: A Financial MNC?", *Journal of Banking and Finance* 5 (1981): 33–63, reprinted in Jones, *Multinational and International Banking*, 18–48; and Adrian E. Tschoegl, "International Retail Banking as a Strategy: An Assessment", *Journal of International Business Studies* 18, no. 2 (Summer 1987): 67–88, reprinted in Jones, *Multinational and International Banking*, 70–71.
9. Jones, *British Multinational Banking*, 58.
10. Cain and Hopkins, *British Imperialism: Innovation and Expansion*, 120. See also S.D. Chapman, *The Rise of Merchant Banking* (London: Unwin Hyman, 1988), 209.
11. W.M. Clarke, *The City in the World Economy* (London: The Institute of Economic Affairs, 1965), 7, 8; Cain and Hopkins, *British Imperialism: Innovation and Expansion*, 171–73.
12. Jones, *British Multinational Banking*, 28–30.
13. Cain and Hopkins, *British Imperialism: Innovation and Expansion*, 177.
14. Jones, *British Multinational Banking*, 60; also Jones, "Competitive Advantages", 38, 40.
15. Jones, "The Legacy of the Past", in *Multinational Enterprises in the World Economy*, ed. Peter Buckley and Mark Cason (Aldershot: Edward Elgar, 1992), 157–58; Jones, *British Multinational Banking*, 15–16.
16. Jones, "Competitive Advantages", 38.
17. Jones, *British Multinational Banking*, 13–14; Barclays Bank Ltd, *A Banking Centenary*, 25–26.
18. Barclays Bank plc, *Barclays Bank in the Caribbean*, 31; Republic Bank Ltd, *From Colonial to Republic*, 3, 4.

19. The West India Committee, formed in the eighteenth century when it functioned as an extremely influential lobby group, was composed of London merchants and other businessmen with interests in the West Indian–metropolitan trade, and absentee owners of West Indian estates who lived in London and its environs. The committee's business was mainly concerned with safeguarding their commercial interests. See Douglas Hall, *A Brief History of the West India Committee* (Barbados: Caribbean Universities Press, 1971), 1, 17.
20. Baster, *The Imperial Banks*, 67–68; Hall, *West India Committee*, 1, 17.
21. The Act for the Abolition of Slavery in the West Indies came into effect in 1834 and was followed by a period of "apprenticeship", under which ex-slaves ("apprentices") were required to work for a specified number of hours per week, without wages, for their former masters. This system came to an end on 1 August 1838.
22. Republic Bank Ltd, *From Colonial to Republic*, 2n4.
23. William A. Green, *British Slave Emancipation: The Sugar Colonies and the Great Experiment, 1830–1865* (Oxford: Clarendon Press, 1976, 1991), 180.
24. Douglas Hall, *Free Jamaica, 1838–1865: An Economic History* (Aylesbury: Ginn, 1959, 1976), 111.
25. Ibid., 224; C.V. Callender, *The Development of Capital Market Institutions in Jamaica* (Kingston: Institute of Social and Economic Research, University of the West Indies, Mona, 1965), 6.
26. Douglas Hall, *Five of the Leewards, 1834–1870: The Major Problems of the Post-Emancipation Period in Antigua, Barbuda, Montserrat, Nevis, and St Kitts* (Aylesbury: Ginn, 1977), 135.
27. Hall, *Free Jamaica*, 11, 209, 223; Hall, *Five of the Leewards*, 135.
28. Michael Moohr, "The Economic Impact of Slave Emancipation in British Guiana, 1832–1852", *Economic History Review* 25 (1972): 595.
29. R.M. Martin, *The British Colonies* (London: J. Tallis and Co., 1853), 120.
30. Ibid., 183.
31. Alan Adamson, *Sugar without Slaves: The Political Economy of British Guiana, 1838–1900* (New Haven: Yale University Press, 1972), 238–39; see also Moohr, "The Economic Impact", 592.
32. Callender, *Capital Market Institutions*, 7. Callender asserts that "the compensation payments received by planters upon freeing their slaves provided huge sums in search of temporary investment outlets or adequate strong boxes and consequently proved to be the motivating stimulus for the establishment of not one but three banks". See also Deryck R. Brown, "The Response of the Banking Sector to the General Crisis: Trinidad, 1836–56", *Journal of Caribbean History* 24, no. 1 (1990): 31.
33. Richard A. Lobdell, "Patterns of Investment and Sources of Credit in the British West Indian Sugar Industry, 1838–1897", *Journal of Caribbean History* 4

(1972): 31–53, reprinted in *Caribbean Freedom: Economy and Society from Emancipation to the Present*, ed. Hilary Beckles and Verene Shepherd (Kingston: Ian Randle, 1993), 321–22. See also Richard Pares, *Merchants and Planters* (Cambridge: Cambridge University Press, 1960, 1970), 49; Hall, *Free Jamaica*, 87–88; Green, *British Slave Emancipation*, 218; Gisela Eisner, *Jamaica 1830–1930: A Study in Economic Growth* (Manchester: Manchester University Press, 1961), 196.

34. Kathleen Mary Butler, *The Economics of Emancipation: Jamaica and Barbados, 1823–1843* (Chapel Hill: University of North Carolina Press, 1995) 44, 52–54.
35. Hall, *Free Jamaica*, 87–88; Eisner, *Jamaica 1830–1930*, 196.
36. Philip Curtin, "The British Sugar Duties and West Indian Prosperity", *Journal of Economic History* 14 (1954): 157–64, reprinted in Beckles and Shepherd, *Caribbean Freedom*, 314–18.
37. Jones, *British Multinational Banking*, 104.
38. Baster, *Imperial Banks*, 70.
39. Ibid., 70–71.
40. Ibid., 71, 72–73.
41. Brown, "The Response of the Banking Sector", 35.
42. Lobdell, "Patterns of Investment", 321–27; Baster, *Imperial Banks*, 70, 75.
43. Barclays Bank plc, *Barclays Bank in the Caribbean*, 10; Brown, "Response of the Banking Sector"; Hall, *Five of the Leewards*, 141; Baster, *Imperial Banks*, 37. Baster mentions the establishment of the Union Bank of Jamaica in 1839 and the St Vincent Commercial Bank in 1840, but there is no further reference to these banks in the records, and the assumption is that they never got off the ground.
44. Callender, *Capital Market Institutions*, 19, 20; Barclays Bank plc, *Barclays Bank in the Caribbean*, 10; Baster, *Imperial Banks*, 74.
45. Richard B. Sheridan, *Sugar and Slavery: The Economic History of the British West Indies, 1623–1775* (Kingston: Canoe Press, University of the West Indies, 1974, 1994), 40–44; see also Cain and Hopkins, *British Imperialism: Innovation and Expansion*, 84–88.
46. Curtin, "British Sugar Duties", 314.
47. Lobdell, "Patterns of Investment", 322–23. Beginning in 1846, British West Indian muscovado entered the British market with only a seven-shilling tariff advantage over foreign-grown muscovado. Even after 1854, sugars of differing quality were taxed differently when imported into the United Kingdom. The British government, anxious to protect its home sugar-refining industry, introduced a progressive tariff that increased as the quality of sugar rose. Hence, the highest duties were paid on refined sugar, and successively lower duties were charged on partially refined and muscovado sugar. This advantage disappeared in 1874, when all sugar could enter Britain free of any duties.
48. Brown, "Response of the Banking Sector", 44.

49. B.W. Higman, *Abstract of Caribbean Historical Statistics* (Kingston: Department of History, University of the West Indies, Mona, 1985), table 19/1: Metropolitan Raw Sugar Prices, 1623–1972; Curtin, "British Sugar Duties", 316; Brereton, *A History of Modern Trinidad*, 82.
50. Hall, *Five of the Leewards*, 97; Green, *British Slave Emancipation*, 234; Brown, "Response of the Banking Sector", 48; Brereton, *A History of Modern Trinidad*, 82; Eisner, *Jamaica 1830–1930*, 198–99.
51. Brown, *History of Money and Banking*, 35.
52. Republic Bank Ltd, *From Colonial to Republic*, 21.
53. Ibid., 22; Green, *British Slave Emancipation*, 234–35.
54. Hall, *Free Jamaica*, 113.
55. Ibid; Callender, *Capital Market Institutions*, 15, 19.
56. Jones, *British Multinational Banking*, 47.
57. Brown, "Response of the Banking Sector", 45.
58. Republic Bank Ltd, *From Colonial to Republic*, 23.
59. Jones, *British Multinational Banking*, 47–48.
60. Brown, "Response of the Banking Sector", 48.
61. See Brown, *History of Money and Banking*, 50–52.
62. Barclays Bank Ltd, *A Banking Centenary*, 69. See also Eisner, *Jamaica 1830–1930*, 250–52; Woodville Marshall, "Nineteenth-century Crises in the Barbadian Sugar Industry", in *Emancipation II: Aspects of the Post-Slavery Experience in Barbados*, ed. Woodville Marshall (Cave Hill: Department of History, University of the West Indies, 1987), 92–94; Higman, *Abstract of Caribbean Historical Statistics*, table 19/1.
63. Higman, *Abstract of Caribbean Historical Statistics*, table 19/1.
64. Barclays Bank Ltd, *A Banking Centenary*, 69. See also Eisner, *Jamaica 1830–1930*, 250–52.
65. Jones, *British Multinational Banking*, table A5.1; Barclays Bank Ltd, *A Banking Centenary*, 57.
66. Jones, *British Multinational Banking*, table A5.1. Real profit figures are not available for the period in question.
67. See chapter 3.
68. Eisner, *Jamaica 1830–1930*, 275, 276; E.F. Nash, "Trading Problems of the British West Indies", in *The Economy of the West Indies*, ed. George E. Cumper (Westport, CT: Greenwood, 1960, 1974), 235.
69. Eisner, *Jamaica 1830–1930*, 272, 273; Brereton, *A History of Modern Trinidad*, 88.
70. Jones, *British Multinational Banking*, 95–96. In 1916, the Colonial Bank Act was amended to allow it to "establish and carry on the business of banker in the United Kingdom or in any colony, state or dependency of the British Empire".
71. Brown, *History of Money and Banking*, 89; Jones, *British Multinational Banking*, 148; Margaret Ackrill and Leslie Hannah, *Barclays: The Business of Banking, 1690–1996* (Cambridge: Cambridge University Press, 2001), 81.

72. Jones, *British Multinational Banking*, 138–39, 148.
73. Jones, *British Multinational Banking*, 139, 147–50; Crossley and Blandford, *DCO Story*, 1–19; Edward Nevin and E.W. Davis, *The London Clearing Banks* (London: Elek Books, 1970), 82–83. The "Big Five" consisted of Midland Bank Ltd, Barclays Bank Ltd, Lloyds Bank Ltd, Westminster Bank Ltd and National Provincial Bank Ltd. Together they controlled some £2,012 million in deposits, representing almost 90 per cent of the total deposits held among all London clearing banks in 1936. Barclays Bank Ltd held the second largest amount of deposits, totalling approximately £430 million.
74. Ibid., 149–50; Crossley and Blandford, *DCO Story*, 1–19; Ackrill and Hannah, *Barclays*, 82.
75. Jones, *British Multinational Banking*, 150; Ackrill and Hannah, *Barclays*, 82.

Chapter 2

1. Richard S. Grossman, "The Shoe That Didn't Drop: Explaining Banking Stability during the Great Depression", *Journal of Economic History* 54, no. 3 (September 1994): 654, 657–74.
2. Jones, *British Multinational Banking*, 181–84.
3. Ibid., 152.
4. Ibid.
5. Ibid., 153.
6. Republic Bank Ltd, *From Colonial to Republic*, 107.
7. Crossley and Blandford, *DCO Story*, 2.
8. Ibid., 71, 72.
9. Thomas B. Birnberg and Stephen A. Resnick, *Colonial Development: An Econometric Study* (New Haven: Yale University Press, 1975), 3; Report presented at Ordinary General Meeting, 21 January 1932, Report of the Directors with Statement of Accounts presented at Ordinary General Meetings of Stockholders, 1926–1962, BBA 38/351.
10. Kathleen Stahl, *The Metropolitan Organisation of British Colonial Trade* (London: Faber and Faber, 1951), 32.
11. Crossley and Blandford, *DCO Story*, 81.
12. O. Barritt, manager of the Colonial Bank Section, Barclays Bank (DCO), to G.E.A. Grindle, Colonial Office, 8 March 1930, CO 323/1113/21.
13. Report of the Directors with Statement of Accounts presented at Ordinary General Meetings of Stockholders held December 1929 and December 1930, BBA 38/351.
14. Cabinet Paper, February 1930, CO 323/1113/21; Eisner, *Jamaica 1830–1930*, 251–52; Brereton, *A History of Modern Trinidad*, 205; Bill Albert and Adrian Graves, eds., *The World Sugar Economy in War and Depression, 1914–1940* (London: Routledge, 1988), 6–7. Before 1926, the price of sugar was in decline

as a result of the return to the market of beet sugar following the end of World War I. Prices fell sharply from 58s per hundredweight in 1920 to 18s 3d in 1921. A temporary recovery was registered between 1922 and 1924, after which the price was in continuous decline.

15. Sugar Commission Report. Part 1, CO 318/398/1. Between 1913 and 1914 sugar produced from cane and beet were imported in almost equal proportions (54 per cent cane and 45 per cent beet). The production of beet fell during World War I to almost one-third of what it was in 1913–14, which in turn stimulated the production of cane sugar, so that in 1919–20, 79 per cent of the world's supply was cane sugar and 20.1 per cent of the supply was beet sugar.

16. The Jamaica Imperial Association to the Antigua Chamber of Commerce, 18 July 1929, CO 318/394/8; *Report of the Sugar Industry Commission, Jamaica, 1944–1945* (Kingston, Jamaica, 1945), 5.

17. JIA to ACC, 18 July 1929, CO 318/394/8; Sugar Commission Report, Part 1, CO 319/398/1; Eisner, *Jamaica 1830–1930*, 252.

18. JIA to the ACC, 18 July 1929, CO 318/394/8; Sugar Commission Report Part 1, CO 319/398/1.

19. Cabinet Paper, February 1930, CO 323/1113/21; *Report of the Sugar Industry Commission, Jamaica, 1944–1945*, 5.

20. British Guiana Sugar Planters Association to Private Secretary, Government House, Georgetown, 10 May and 13 June 1929, CO 318/394/8; *Bookers Sugar* (n.p., 1954), 106. The BGSPA comprised the British firms Bookers Sugar Estates Ltd, Bookers Demerara Sugar Estates Ltd, S. Davson and Co., Sandbach, Parker and Co. Ltd, Port Morant Ltd, and West Bank Estates Ltd.

21. Sugar Commission Report. Part 1, CO 319/398/1.

22. *Report of the Sugar Industry Commission, Jamaica, 1944–1945*, 5.

23. Ibid., 6, 7, 13. Before 1931, rum stocks in Jamaica and abroad had been steadily increasing owing to the ever widening gap between consumption and production. Consumption in Britain had decreased as a result of increased import duty on spirits, while rum production had increased as a result of increases in sugar production. Consequently, the world rum market had become depressed, and the price was falling. There was nonetheless a sustained demand for Jamaica-produced rum, and prices were remunerative so long as Jamaica did not over-supply the market. To monitor production, in 1932 the sugar manufacturers formed a Rum Pool.

24. Crossley and Blandford, *DCO Story*, 46–47.

25. G. Grindle, memorandum, 6 March 1930, "Sugar Industry in the Colonies", Proposals Arising from Report of West Indian Sugar Commission 1930, CO 323/1113/21.

26. F.C. Goodenough, chairman, Barclays Bank (DCO), to Lord Passfield, 7 March 1930, CO 323/1113/21.

27. Despatch no. 549, Governor Edward Denham, British Guiana, November 1930, CO 318/401/9.
28. Michael Craton and James Walvin, *A Jamaican Plantation: The History of Worthy Park, 1670–1970* (London, New York: W. H. Allen, 1970), 275–76.
29. Despatch no. 549, Governor Edward Denham.
30. Tim Rooth, *British Protectionism and the International Economy: Overseas Commercial Policy in the 1930s* (Cambridge: Cambridge University Press, 1992), 48–54, 59, 60.
31. G.E.A. Grindle to Stockdale, Secretary of State for the Colonies, 16 July 1929, CO 318/394/8.
32. G.E.A. Grindle, Colonial Office, memorandum on short-term advances, 8 March 1930, CO 323/1113/21.
33. Ibid; Cabinet Paper, February 1930, CO 323/1113/21; Draft telegram to Mauritius, Barbados, British Guiana, Jamaica, Trinidad, Leeward Islands and the Windward Islands, 8 March 1930, CO 323/1113/21.
34. Draft telegram to Mauritius et al., 8 March 1930; Grindle, memorandum, 6 March 1930.
35. Grindle, memorandum on short-term advances, 8 March 1930; Barritt to Grindle, 8 March 1930.
36. Goodenough to Lord Passfield, 7 March 1930.
37. Ibid.
38. Barritt to Grindle, 8 March 1930.
39. Ibid.
40. Government Loan Guarantees, CO 323/1113/21. In the official history of the bank, the figure of £250,000 is given. See Crossley and Blandford, *DCO Story*, 47.
41. Goodenough to Lord Passfield, 7 March 1930. As an illustration, if the bank were to make a crop advance of £10,000 and only £5,000 were repaid, the bank would be responsible for 70 per cent of the £10,000, or £7,000, less what had been repaid, so £2,000. The bank and the government would share equal responsibility for the next £2,000, making it £1,000 each, and the government would be solely responsible for the final £1,000. Thus the bank's total share of the loss would amount to £3,000 and the government's to £2,000.
42. Ibid.
43. Ibid.; Upcott, Treasury, to G.E.A. Grindle, Colonial Office, 7 March 1930, CO 323/1113/21.
44. Ian Drummond, *British Economic Policy and the Empire, 1919–1939* (London: Allen and Unwin, 1972), 36.
45. Ibid; Rory Miller, *Britain and Latin America in the Nineteenth and Twentieth Centuries* (London: Longman, 1993), 184–203, 205–32; C.P. Hill, *British Economic and Social History, 1700–1982* (London: Hodder and Stoughton, 1957, 1985), 244–45.

46. Tim Rooth, *British Protectionism*, 24; A.G. Kenwood and A.L. Lougheed, *The Growth of the International Economy 1820–2000: An Introductory Text* (London: Unwin, Hyman, 1971), 210, 215–16, 225; F.V. Meyer, *Britain's Colonies in World Trade* (London: Oxford University Press, 1948), 90–91. See also Hill, *British Economic and Social History*, 244–45; Michael Haviden and David Meredith, *Colonialism and Development: Britain and its Tropical Colonies, 1850–1960* (London: Routledge, 1993, 1996), 187.
47. The McKenna Duties (1915 onwards) had been levied on some goods to restrict imports and save shipping space, and the Safeguarding of Industries Act (1921) taxed some imports. See Hill, *British Economic and Social History*, 245; Drummond, *British Economic Policy*, 52.
48. Meyer, *Britain's Colonies*, 92–94; *Trade Regulations and Commercial Policies of the United Kingdom* (London: Cambridge University Press, 1943) 26–30, 31, 32. See also Nash, "Trading Problems", 235–36; *Report of the Sugar Industry Commission, Jamaica*, 9.
49. Stahl, *The Metropolitan Organization*, 36; Brereton, *A History of Modern Trinidad*, 206.
50. Crossley and Blandford, *DCO Story*, 81.
51. Reports of the Directors with Statement of Accounts presented at Ordinary General Meetings, 24 January 1935 and 12 December 1935, BBA 38/351.
52. Crossley and Blandford, *DCO Story*, 81.
53. Board minutes, 12 November 1936 and 6 May 1937, Barclays Bank (DCO) Board Minute Book no. 3, April 1935–March 1939, BBA 38/505 ; Crossley and Blandford, *DCO Story*, 81.
54. Craton and Walvin, *A Jamaican Plantation*, 276, 280.
55. Jones, *British Multinational Banking*, 186.
56. Meyer, *Britain's Colonies*, 93–94; *Trade Regulations and Commercial Policies*, 26–30, 32; Nash, "Trading Problems", 235–36.
57. Cain and Hopkins, *British Imperialism: Crisis and Deconstruction*, 58. By the 1930s, American investment in Cuba amounted to $166 million; in the Dominican Republic, $41 million; and in Haiti, $10 million. See Isaac Dookhan, *A Post-Emancipation History of the West Indies* (London: Longman, 1988, 1989), 167.
58. M. Shahabuddeen, *From Plantocracy to Nationalisation: A Profile of Sugar in Guyana* (Georgetown: University of Guyana, 1983), 45.
59. Brereton, *A History of Modern Trinidad*, 206; Higman, *Caribbean Historical Statistics*, table 6.
60. O. Nigel Bolland, *On the March: Labour Rebellions in the British Caribbean, 1934–39* (Kingston: Ian Randle, 1995), 64–65, 190–94; Kelvin Singh, *Race and Class Struggles in a Colonial State: Trinidad 1917–1945* (Kingston: The Press, University of the West Indies, 1994), 172; Brereton, *A History of Modern Trinidad*, 206; Clem Seecharan, *Sweetening Bitter Sugar: Jock Campbell, The*

Booker Reformer in British Guiana, 1934–1966 (Kingston: Ian Randle, 2005), 62–65.
61. Singh, *Race and Class*, 172.

Chapter 3

1. Maurice Odle, *Multinational Banks and Underdevelopment* (New York: Pergamon Press), 29–30; Nugent Miller, *Organization and Structure of Commercial Banking in Jamaica* (Kingston: Institute of Social and Economic Research, University of the West Indies, Mona, 1971), 4–7, 184–207.
2. Jones, *British Multinational Banking*, 203; see also Geoffrey Jones, "Competition and Competitiveness in British Banking, 1918–1971", in *Competitiveness and the State: Government and Business in Twentieth-century Britain*, ed. Geoffrey Jones and Maurice Kirby (Manchester: Manchester University Press, 1991), 121.
3. Mark Casson, "Multinational Monopolies and International Cartels", in *The Economic Theory of the Multinational Firm*, ed. Peter Buckley and Mark Casson (London: Macmillan, 1985), 74, 77; Kenneth D. George, Caroline Joll and E.L. Lynk, *Industrial Organization: Competition, Growth, and Structural Change* (London: Routledge, 1971), 204; W. J. Baumol, John C. Panzar and Robert D. Willig, *Contestable Markets and the Theory of Industry Structure* (San Diego: Harcourt Brace Jovanovich, 1982, 1988), 4–5, 7.
4. Jones, "Competition and Competitiveness", 127.
5. Ibid., 121.
6. Paul Geroski, Richard J. Gilbert and Alexis Jacquemin, eds., *Barriers to Entry and Strategic Competition* (Chur, Switzerland: Harwood Academic, 1990), 1; Jones, *British Multinational Banking*, 203.
7. Jones, *British Multinational Banking*, 202–5.
8. Ibid., 202, 203.
9. Results, Statistics and Review of the Period Ending 30 September 1953, Nassau, Bahamas, BBA 29/173; Miller, *Commercial Banking in Jamaica*, 184–86.
10. Manager, Kingston branch, Jamaica, to general manager, Barclays Bank (DCO), 17 September 1929, West Indian Business, 1926–1934, BBA 11/197.
11. Ibid.
12. Sir Julian Crossley Diaries, 1942–1951, 20 January 1943, BBA 38/209.
13. Ibid., 16 February 1943; James L. Darroch, *Canadian Banks and Global Competitiveness* (Montreal: McGill-Queen's University Press, 1994), 129.
14. Darroch, *Canadian Banks*, 129.
15. Crossley Diaries, 20 January 1943, 29 January 1943 and February 16, 1943, BBA 38/209.
16. Ibid., 22 February 1943; Crossley and Blandford, *DCO Story*, 107.
17. Crossley Diaries, 22 February 1943, BBA 38/209.

18. Ibid., 18 March 1943.
19. Ibid., 17 February 1943.
20. Ibid., 18 March 1943.
21. Ibid., 25 March 1943.
22. Ibid., 25 October 1943.
23. Ibid., 30 November 1944.
24. Ibid., 20 December 1944.
25. Ernest Sykes, *Banking and Currency* (London: Butterworth, 1937), 112–13.
26. The RBC's interest in the region was clearly expressed in its initial overtures to take over the Colonial Bank in 1911. However, because of concerns about risks involved in some of the accounts, the matter was dropped. See Neil C. Quigley, "The Bank of Nova Scotia in the Caribbean, 1889–1940: The Establishment of an International Branch Banking Network", *Business History Review* 63 (1989): 797–838; Callender, *Capital Market Institutions*, 49; Daniel Jay Baum, *The Banks of Canada in the Commonwealth Caribbean: Economic Nationalism and Multinational Enterprises of a Medium Power* (New York: Praeger, 1974), 21–22; Republic Bank Ltd, *From Colonial to Republic*, 76. See also Duncan McDowall, *Quick to the Frontier: Canada's Royal Bank* (Toronto: McClelland and Stewart, 1993), 163–202.
27. Baum, *The Banks of Canada*, 22; Darroch, *Canadian Banks*, 68.
28. Miller, *Commercial Banking in Jamaica*, 6.
29. *Handbook of Jamaica 1929*, 268 (hereafter cited as *HBJ*).
30. McDowall, *Quick to the Frontier*, 250.
31. Jones, *British Multinational Banking* 201–5; Eisner, *Jamaica 1830–1930*, 163–76; *Production and Trade of the British West Indies, British Guiana, Bermuda, and British Honduras* (London: His Majesty's Stationery Office, 1934) 21; *An Economic Survey of the Colonial Empire (1932)* (London: His Majesty's Stationery Office, 1934).
32. Board minutes, 20 July 1933, Barclays Bank (Dominion, Colonial and Overseas) Board Minute Book no. 2, BBA 38/504.
33. Board minutes, 15 December 1938, Barclays Bank (Dominion, Colonial and Overseas) Board Minute Book no. 3, BBA 38/505; West Indian Branches, 1926–1934, BBA 38/202.
34. *Daily Gleaner*, 5 January 1926, 24 November 1926. See Bank of Nova Scotia (Jamaica) Ltd, *Scotiabank in Jamaica: A Century of Progress, 1889–1989* (Kingston: Bank of Nova Scotia (Jamaica) Ltd, 1989).
35. Quigley, "The Bank of Nova Scotia", 812–13, 830–38.
36. Patrick Bryan, "The Creolisation of the Chinese Community in Jamaica" (seminar paper, Department of History, University of the West Indies, Mona, 1993), 37.
37. *Daily Gleaner*, 25 January 1926, 1 March 1926.
38. Ibid., 1 September 1926.

39. Ibid., 27 September 1926, 4 October 1926.
40. E. Gittens Knight, *The Grenada Handbook and Directory 1946* (n.p., n.d.), 140.
41. Quigley, "The Bank of Nova Scotia", 830–38.
42. Nash, "Trading Problems", 235. See also Hilary Beckles, *A History of Barbados: From Amerindian Settlement to Nation-State* (Cambridge: Cambridge University Press, 1990), 141.
43. Nash, "Trading Problems", 235.
44. *Production and Trade*, 21.
45. Ibid., 21, 25.
46. *An Economic Survey (1932)*, 260.
47. See Michael Sleeman, "The Agri-Business Bourgeoisie of Barbados and Martinique", in *Rural Development in the Caribbean*, ed. P.I. Gomes (London: C. Hurst and Co., 1985), 19.
48. Ibid.
49. Higman, *Abstract of Caribbean Historical Statistics*, table 13/12.
50. *The West Indies Year Book, 1936* (Montreal: Thomas Skinner, 1936), 124.
51. Certainly, its predecessor, the Colonial Bank, in 1915 had considered establishing a branch in Canada to facilitate this interest, and an application had been made to the Canadian government to this end. See Barclays Bank Ltd, *A Banking Centenary*, 58–59; Kenneth Mackenzie, *The Banking Systems of Great Britain, France, Germany, and the United States of America* (London: Macmillan, 1947), 45; Robert Anderson, ed., *The St Vincent Handbook 1938* (Kingstown: The Vincentian, 1938), advertisement in back; Jones, *British Multinational Banking*, 154; *HBJ 1930* (Kingston: Government Printing Office, 1930), 270.
52. Jones, *British Multinational Banking*, 154–55.
53. Memorandum re Jamaica–Canada Business, 26 May 1933, West Indian Business, 1926–34, BBA 11/197.
54. I.H. Dickson, Barclays Bank (Canada), to H.P. Sheldon, Barclays Bank (DCO), 28 June 1933, London, BBA 11/197.
55. Darroch, *Canadian Banks*, 180. Up to 1920 the CBC, as a result of its connection with the Halifax Banking Company, had acted as an agent for the Colonial Bank in Canada; when this relationship ended, the Bank of Montreal was appointed.
56. J. Caulcutt, general manager, Barclays Bank (DCO), to H.A. Stevenson, general manager, Barclays Bank (Canada), 18 June 1934, West Indian Business, 1926–34, BBA 11/197.
57. Crossley Diaries, 30 June 1943, BBA 38/209. See also McDowall, *Quick to the Frontier*, 300.
58. McDowall, *Quick to the Frontier*, 166, 191; see also Darroch, *Canadian Banks*, 88.
59. *HBJ 1920*, 333. The BNS had an office in London in 1920. Its agents in the UK were the London Joint and City, the Midland Bank and the Royal Bank of Scotland.

60. Douglas Hall, "Scotiabank in Jamaica, 1889–1989" (manuscript, 1989) 28–30; Quigley, "The Bank of Nova Scotia", 810–11.
61. Memorandum to Mr Bradfield, assistant general manager, Barclays Bank (DCO), 14 June 1933, West Indian Business, 1926–34, BBA 11/197.
62. Ibid.
63. Michael Collins, *Money and Banking in the UK: A History* (London: Routledge, 1988), 79–80, 211.
64. H. Richardson, inspector, head office, to H.R. Bradfield, assistant general manager, 23 November 1934, 26 November 1934, West Indian Business, 1926–1934, BBA 11/197. Reference to this early competition can be found in Hall's "Scotiabank", 55–56.
65. R.V. Butt, manager, Jamaica Branch, to general manager's office, Barclays Bank (Dominion, Colonial and Overseas), 17 September 1929, West Indian Business, 1926–34, BBA 11/197.
66. Ibid; Allister MacMillan, *The Red Book of the West Indies: Historical and Descriptive Commercial and Industrial Facts, Figures, and Resources* (London: W.H. and L. Collingridge, 1922), 70, 78.
67. Ibid.
68. Ken Post, *Arise Ye Starvelings: The Jamaican Labour Rebellion of 1938 and Its Aftermath* (The Hague: Martinus Nijhoff, 1978), 37, 90, 117, 298–99.
69. H.R. Bradfield, assistant general manager, to O. Barritt, manager, Colonial Bank Section, 19 November 1934, West Indian Business, 1926–34, BBA 11/197.
70. O. Barritt, manager, Colonial Bank Section, to H. Bradfield, assistant general manager, Barclays Bank (DCO), 28 December 1934, West Indian Business, 1926–1934, BBA 11/197.
71. Bradfield to Barritt, 19 November 1934.
72. Barritt to Bradfield, 28 December 1934.
73. Ibid.; Bradfield to Barritt, 19 November 1934.
74. Butt to general manager's office, 17 September 1929.
75. Bradfield to Barritt, 19 November 1934; Richardson to Bradfield, 23 November 1934.
76. Richardson to Bradfield, 23 November 1934; Post, *Arise Ye Starvelings*, 89.
77. Bradfield to Barritt, 19 November 1934.
78. Ibid.
79. Ibid.
80. Richardson to Bradfield, 23 November 1934.
81. Ibid.
82. Crossley Diaries, 17 March 1943, BBA 38/209.
83. Ibid., 28 March 1943.
84. Bradfield to Barritt, 19 November 1934.

Chapter 4

1. Jones, *British Multinational Banking*, 83–92; 188, 210.
2. Ibid., 35.
3. Chibuike Ugochukwu Uche, "Credit Discrimination Controversy in British West Africa: Evidence from Barclays Bank (DCO)", *African Review: Money, Finance, and Banking* 20 (1996): 90–91; see also Chibuike Ugochukwu Uche, "Foreign Banks, Africans, and Credit in Colonial Nigeria, c. 1890–1912", *Economic History Review* 52, no. 4 (November 1999): 669.
4. W.T. Newlyn and D.C. Rowan, *Money and Banking in British Colonial Africa: A Study of the Monetary and Banking System of Eight British African Territories* (Oxford: Clarendon Press, 1954), 72–95.
5. Uche, "Credit Discrimination", 90–91.
6. M.H.Y. Kaniki, "The Colonial Economy: The Former British Zones", in *General History of Africa, 7: Africa under Colonial Domination, 1880–1935*, ed. A.H. Boahen (Paris: UNESCO; Ibadan, Nairobi: Heinemann; California: University of California Press, 1985), 382; P. Kennedy, *African Capitalism: The Struggle for Ascendancy* (Cambridge: Cambridge University Press, n.d.).
7. G.O. Nwankwo, "The British Overseas Banks in the Developing Countries, 1 – Until 1945", *Journal of the Institute of Bankers* 93, part 3 (June 1972): 153–54; Uche, "Foreign Banks", 669.
8. Uche, "Foreign Banks", 669.
9. Jones, *British Multinational Banking*, 305.
10. Baster, *The Imperial Banks*, 49–77; Clarke, *The City*, 9; R.J. Truptil, *British Banks and the London Money Market* (London: Jonathan Cape, 1936), 165–80; Barclays Bank plc, *Barclays Bank in the Caribbean*, 9; Jones, *British Multinational Banking*, 32.
11. Brown, "The Response of the Banking Sector", 28–64; see also Brown, *History of Money and Banking*, 25–26.
12. K.G. Davis, "The Origins of the Commission System in the West India Trade", *Transactions of the Royal Historical Society* (London, 5th ser., 001–2, 1952), reprinted in *Caribbean Slavery in the Atlantic World*, ed. Verene Shepherd and Hilary Beckles (Kingston: Ian Randle, 2001), 326–34.
13. Ibid., 328; Douglas Hall, "Incalculability as a Feature of Sugar Production during the Eighteenth Century", *Social and Economic Studies* 10, pt. 3 (September 1961), 340–52. See also Pares, *Merchants and Planters*, 5; Lobdell, "Patterns of Investment", 319–29.
14. Jones, *British Multinational Banking*, 33.
15. Ibid., 32–33; Truptil, *British Banks*, 253; Clarke, *The City*, 8–9.
16. Jones, *British Multinational Banking*, 32–33; Truptil, *British Banks*, 251–53.
17. Brown, "The Response of the Banking Sector", 56.
18. O. Barritt, manager, Colonial Bank Section, Barclays Bank (DCO), to G.E.A.

Grindle, Colonial and Dominions Office, 8 March 1930, CO 323/1113/21.

19. Phillipe Chalmin, *The Making of a Sugar Giant: Tate and Lyle, 1859–1989* (Chur, Switzerland: Harwood Academic, 1990), 309–10. In the 1930s approximately 75 per cent of Jamaica's sugar production was from cane cultivated by independent cane farmers. In Trinidad, approximately 40 per cent of sugar-cane cultivation was in the hands of 18,000 tenant farmers, two-thirds of whom were of East Indian ancestry, and who cultivated lands owned by sugar factory companies, or on properties of major landowners.

20. George L. Beckford, *Persistent Poverty: Underdevelopment in Plantation Economies of the Third World* (New York: Oxford University Press, 1972). See also Veront Satchell, *From Plots to Plantations: Land Transactions in Jamaica, 1866–1900* (Kingston: Institute of Social and Economic Research, University of the West Indies, Mona, 1990); J.H. Galloway, *The Sugar Cane Industry: An Historical Geography from Its Origins to 1914* (Cambridge: Cambridge University Press, 1989).

21. Stahl, *The Metropolitan Organization*, 39.

22. Barritt to Grindle, 8 March 1930.

23. Ibid; Lobdell, "Patterns of Investment", 322–26; Eisner, *Jamaica 1830–1930*, 198–200. The process of transfer was facilitated by the West India Encumbered Estates Act, passed in 1854 by the British government, which enabled owners or creditors to apply for estates to be sold by judicial decree. In addition to courts in the various colonies, the act provided for a central court in London, to ensure equal protection of all litigants. Estates processed through the London court were generally sold to British merchant firms, to which many of them had become indebted. See also Hall, *Five of the Leewards*, 96–127; Sleeman, "The Agri-Business Bourgeoisie", 15–33.

24. Eisner, *Jamaica 1830–1930*, 198–200; Hall, *Five of the Leewards*, 96–127; Sleeman, "The Agri-Business Bourgeoisie", 15–33; Beckford, *Persistent Poverty*, 102–3; Shahabuddeen, *From Plantocracy to Nationalisation*, 90.

25. Eisner, *Jamaica 1830–1930*, 198–99. Lobdell, "Patterns of Investment", 326–27; Galloway, *The Sugar Cane Industry*, 147–48; Christine Barrow, "Ownership and Control of Resources in Barbados: 1834 to the Present", *Social and Economic Studies* 32, no. 3 (September 1983): 83–120; Walter Rodney, *A History of the Guyanese Working People, 1881–1905* (Baltimore: Johns Hopkins University Press, 1981), 26. Rodney notes Quintin Hogg's decision to redeploy his investments to the tea and coffee industries in Ceylon from British Guiana, St Kitts, St Lucia and Jamaica as a result of low returns in the 1890s.

26. Norton Breton, *Henckell, Du Buisson and Co. 1697–1947* (London: Henckell, Du Buisson and Co., n.d.), 19. See Craton and Walvin, *A Jamaican Plantation*, 272–75, for extracts from Fred Clarke's diaries of 1920 and 1922, indicating this method of selling sugar for export.

27. S.D. Chapman, "British-based Investment Groups before 1914", *Economic*

History Review, 2nd ser., 38 (1985): 231–33; Jones, *Merchants to Multinationals*, 11.
28. R.W. Beachy, *The British West Indian Sugar Industry in the Late Nineteenth Century* (Cambridge: Cambridge University Press, 1957); also Galloway, *The Sugar Cane Industry*, 155–79; Wilkins, "The Free-Standing Company", 259–82; Jones, *Merchants to Multinationals*, 48–51.
29. Stahl, *The Metropolitan Organization*, 39; Shahabuddeen, *From Plantocracy to Nationalisation*, 108; MacMillan, *The Red Book*, 281–83.
30. Stahl, *The Metropolitan Organization*, 39; Shahabuddeen, *From Plantocracy to Nationalisation*, 93.
31. Stahl, *The Metropolitan Organization*, 44.
32. Chalmin, *The Making of a Sugar Giant*, 314–15.
33. Shahabuddeen, *From Plantocracy to Nationalisation*, 108.
34. MacMillan, *The Red Book*, 402.
35. Stahl, *The Metropolitan Organization*, 39, 44.
36. Chalmin, *The Making of a Sugar Giant*, 311; Brereton, *A History of Modern Trinidad*, 20.
37. Chalmin, *The Making of a Sugar Giant*, 314–15.
38. Stahl, *The Metropolitan Organization* 41; Brereton, *A History of Modern Trinidad*, 20.
39. Chalmin, *The Making of a Sugar Giant*, 312; Kleinwort, Sons and Co., a merchant banking firm, was founded in Cuba in 1792 and transferred to London in 1830. See Truptil, *British Banks*, 150. Furness, Withy and Co. Ltd acted as agents for Trinidad Estates Co. Ltd, of Glasgow.
40. MacMillan, *The Red Book*, 179.
41. O. Barritt, manager, Colonial Bank Section, Barclays Bank (DCO) to G.E.A. Grindle, Colonial and Dominions Office, 8 March 1930, CO 323/1113/21.
42. Chalmin, *The Making of a Sugar Giant*, 314.
43. Ibid.
44. Stahl, *The Metropolitan Organization*, 39; Chalmin, *The Making of a Sugar Giant*, 315.
45. Board minutes, 6 May 1937, Barclays Bank (Dominion, Colonial and Overseas), Board Minute Book no. 3, 25 April 1935–23 March 1939, BBA 38/505; Chalmin, *The Making of a Sugar Giant*, 314–15. The British firm United Molasses had a minority share in WISCo; Post, *Arise Ye Starvelings*, 88–89.
46. Chalmin, *The Making of a Sugar Giant*, 315.
47. Stahl, *The Metropolitan Organization*, 41; Wyatt Bryce, ed., *Reference Book of Jamaica* (Kingston: n.p., 1946), 224.
48. N. Girvan, "Foreign Investment and Economic Development in Jamaica" (PhD diss., University of London, 1966), 218.
49. Beckford, *Persistent Poverty*, 102–3.
50. Ibid., 43–44.
51. Allister MacMillan, *The West Indies, Past and Present, with British Guiana and*

Bermuda (London: W.H. and L. Collingridge, 1938), 372–73. See also Shahabuddeen, *From Plantocracy to Nationalisation*, 93, who notes that because of the apparent dominance by Bookers, McConnell and Co. Ltd of the agricultural and commercial sector, "which extended to the social and political life of the country at large", British Guiana was often disparagingly referred to by locals as "Booker's Guiana".

52. MacMillan, *The West Indies*, 402.
53. Brereton, *A History of Modern Trinidad*, 200–201; Geoffrey Jones, *The State and the Emergence of the British Oil Industry* (London: Macmillan, 1981), 105–20; Fitzroy Baptiste, "The Exploitation of Caribbean Bauxite and Petroleum, 1914–1945", *Social and Economic Studies* 37, nos. 1 and 2, (March–June 1988): 107–42.
54. Stahl, *The Metropolitan Organization*, 29. See also MacMillan, *The West Indies*, 125.
55. MacMillan, *The West Indies*, 125; Brereton, *A History of Modern Trinidad*, 204.
56. Brereton, *A History of Modern Trinidad*, 204.
57. Hall, *Five of the Leewards*, 97, 102–3, 119, 120, 132.
58. MacMillan, *The West Indies*, 259–60.
59. Ibid., 373.
60. Returns £10,000 and Over, 31 October 1929, Colonial Bank, Customer Liabilities of £10,000, BBA 11/84; Central Board Register. Colonial Advances, BBA 80/700; Barclays Bank (Dominion, Colonial and Overseas), London Committee, Colonial Bank Section, BBA 80/698.
61. Eisner, *Jamaica 1830–1930*, 200; Sleeman, "The Agri-Business Bourgeoisie", 18.
62. Sleeman, "The Agri-Business Bourgeoisie", 18–19.
63. Brown, *History of Money and Banking*, 90.
64. Republic Bank Ltd, *From Colonial to Republic*, 72. Chalmin, in *The Making of a Sugar Giant*, incorrectly states (p. 315) that Gordon, Grant and Co. Ltd was a British company.
65. Chalmin, *The Making of a Sugar Giant*, 311.
66. MacMillan, *The Red Book*, 67.
67. Ibid., 327–28; *HBJ 1931*; *HBJ 1936*.
68. Barclays Bank (Dominion, Colonial and Overseas), Colonial Bank Section, 8 March 1939, Applications for limits of £20,000 and over, and over £500,000, BBA 80/668; MacMillan, *The Red Book*, 89; Swithin Wilmot, Department of History and Archaeology, University of the West Indies, Mona, Kingston, Jamaica, personal communication.
69. See Douglas Hall, *Grace, Kennedy and Company Ltd: A Story of Jamaican Enterprise* (Kingston: Grace, Kennedy and Co. Ltd, 1992), 6–8. W.R. Grace and Co. was founded in Peru in 1851 by an Irishman, James Grace. The company owned the chief shipping agencies in that country and, as sole agent for the Government of Peru, controlled the entire export trade in nitrates. In 1890,

the firm opened in London. The company also operated in New York, Hawaii and New Zealand, conducting an extensive trade in fertilizers, beer and dairy produce.

70. For an informative discussion on the origins of these firms in Barbados, see Sleeman, "The Agri-Business Bourgeoisie", 19–20.
71. MacMillan, *The Red Book*, 194.
72. Ibid., 283.
73. Colonial Bank Section, 6 September 1938, Central Board Register, 9 August 1938 to 22 August 1939, BBA 80/669.
74. F.E. Perry, *A Dictionary of Banking* (Plymouth: MacDonald and Evans, 1979), 75.
75. Ibid., 44.
76. Ibid., 26.
77. Ibid., 26, 27.
78. Ibid., 2.
79. Barclays Bank (Dominion, Colonial and Overseas) Anglo–Egyptian and Colonial Bank Section, Advances, Assistant General Manager's Office, BBA 80/767.
80. G. Grindle, Short-Term Advances, 8 March 1930, CO 323/1113/21.
81. S. Evelyn Thomas, *Banking and Exchange* (St Albans: Donnington Press, 1930), 208. A "lien" is defined as the right of one person to retain property which belongs to another until certain legal demands against the owner of the property by the person in possession are satisfied.
82. Returns of £10,000 and over, Colonial Bank Section, Customer liabilities of £10,000 and over as of 31 October 1929, BBA 11/84; Thomas, *Banking and Exchange*, 206–10.
83. Returns of £10,000 and over. Colonial Bank Section, Customer liabilities of £10,000 and over as of 31 October 1929, BBA 11/84.
84. Ibid.
85. Colonial Bank Section, December 1936, Applications for limits of £20,000 and over, Sanction for which is required in anticipation of the approval of the London Committee and or the Central Board, BBA 80/668.
86. R.K.S. Gonsalves (Port of Spain, Trinidad), Essay no. 11, Bank Essay Competition 1943, BBA 38/983:1.
87. Ibid.
88. Central Board Register, Colonial Advances, 11 July 1940, BBA 80/700.
89. Central Board Register, Colonial Advances, 11 September 1937, Applications for Limits £20,000 and Over, BBA 80/668.
90. Central Board Register, Colonial Advances, 16 September 1937, Applications for Limits £20,000 and Over, BBA 80/668.
91. Central Board Register, Colonial Advances, July 1940, BBA 80/668.
92. At its first directors' meeting on 15 February 1922, the company appointed the Colonial Bank as its banker. See Hall, *Grace, Kennedy*, 10.

93. Central Board Register, Colonial Advances, 25 August 1939, BBA 80/668.
94. Central Board Register, Colonial Advances, 9 July 1937, Applications for Limits £20,000 and Over, BBA 80/668.
95. Central Board Register, Colonial Advances, 23 March 1939, BBA 80/668.
96. London Committee, Colonial Bank Section, 20 May 1941, BBA 80/698.
97. MacMillan, *The Red Book*, 86.
98. Central Board Register, Colonial Advances, 9 July 1937, Applications for Limits £20,000 and Over, BBA 80/668.
99. MacMillan, *The Red Book*, 362, 364; *The Barbados Year Book and Who's Who, 1934* (Barbados: Advocate Press, 1934), 243; Sleeman, "The Agri-Business Bourgeoisie", 21; Beckles, *A History of Barbados*, 149, 187.
100. Barclays Bank (Dominion, Colonial and Overseas) Central Board, 1933, BBA 80/743.
101. Central Board Register, Colonial Advances, 25 August 1939, Applications for Limits £20,000 and Over, BBA 80/668.
102. Central Board Register, Colonial Advances, 20 April 1936, Applications for Limits £20,000 and Over, BBA 80/668.
103. Barclays Bank (Dominion, Colonial and Overseas), 31 January 1935, Central Board Register, Colonial Bank Advances, Anglo–Egyptian Advances, and East African Advances, 10 January 1935–11 July 1935, BBA 80/787.
104. Barclays Bank (Dominion, Colonial and Overseas), Central Board Register, 13 June 1935, Colonial Bank Advances, Anglo–Egyptian Advances, and East African Advances, 10 January 1935–11 July 1935, BBA 80/787.
105. Central Board Register, 26 September 1935, Anglo–Egyptian Advances, Colonial Bank Advances, and East African Advances, BBA 80/783.
106. Colonial and Anglo–Egyptian Advances, 26 January 1932, Assistant General Manager's office, BBA 80/768.
107. Report for 1942, Barbados, Administration Reports, 1942–1945, CO 31/132. In 1942, some 477 vessels with a net tonnage of 324,562 tons arrived in Barbados, compared with 770 vessels with a tonnage of 1,091,144 in 1941.
108. Ibid; Gonsalves, Essay no. 11.
109. Hall, *Grace, Kennedy*, 33–34; Administration Report, 1939, Barbados Administration Reports, 1942–1945, CO 31/132; Jamaica. Administration Reports, 1942–1945, CO 140/298; Central Board Register, 13 June 1940, Colonial Advances, BBA 80/700; Crossley Diaries, 29 December 1942, BBA 38/209.
110. Central Board Register, 13 June 1940, Colonial Advances, BBA 80/700.
111. Crossley Diaries, 29 December 1942 and 16 March 1943, BBA 38/209.
112. Sugar Commission Report, Part 1, CO 318/398/1.
113. Marshall, "Nineteenth Century Crises", 95. As plantations were acquired by British merchant firms through the Encumbered Estate Court in other West Indian territories, local proprietors of Barbadian estates recognized the

necessity of defending their property against a similar fate. Through the Barbados Association for the Protection of Liens Against the Plantations, local planters successfully argued that the consignee's lien was damaging to investment and to confidence in the viability of Barbadian estates. Consequently, the Colonial Office advised that if Barbados so desired, it could legislate against the consignee's lien, which the legislature did in 1882. In addition, in 1887 the Agricultural Aids Act was passed, through which funds for the ailing industry were provided out of the colony's budget, in response to the credit squeeze following the depression in 1884.

114. Pares, *Merchants and Planters*, 33; Sleeman, "The Agri-Business Bourgeoisie", 18–19. Much of the financing of the Barbadian sugar industry was locally based, in contrast to the other West Indian territories where the British merchant company played the principal role. This had a lot to do with the demography of Barbados, which always had a relatively high proportion of British settlers compared with other West Indian territories. As Sleeman points out, in the post-emancipation period the Barbados Mutual Life Assurance Society (BMLA) was established by a group of local merchants and supplied credit to the industry, and from then on the BMLA and the Barbados Savings Bank were the primary financial institutions supplying credit to the sugar industry.

115. Barrow, "Ownership and Control", 89–90; Sleeman, "The Agri-Business Bourgeoisie", 18–19; see also *Barbados Year Book and Who's Who, 1934*, 243–48. In contrast, the West Indian–owned sugar estates in Jamaica, through a process of amalgamation in the 1920s, averaged 661 cultivated acres by the early 1930s. This enabled the necessary technical improvements to be made, helped along by the passing of Law 31 of 1902, guaranteeing government backing for interest payments on loans used to establish modern sugar factories; see Eisner, *Jamaica 1830–1930*, 204, 207–8; *HBJ 1931*, 364–67.

116. *Report of the Banks' Committee of the Local Government Board and on the Cooperative Credit Banks established in the Colony: For the Year 1927* (Georgetown: Argosy Co. Ltd, 1928), 2.

117. H.R.J. Smith (Port of Spain, Trinidad), Essay no. 27, Bank Essay Competition 1943, BBA 38/983.

118. Ibid.

119. Ibid.

120. *Report of the Banks' Committee of the Local Government Board and on the Cooperative Credit Banks established in the Colony: For the Year 1934* (Georgetown: Argosy Co. Ltd, 1935), 3.

121. *Report of the Banks' Committee of the Local Government Board and on the Cooperative Credit Banks established in the Colony: For the Year 1938* (Georgetown: Argosy Co. Ltd, 1939), 3; *Annual Report of the Cooperative Credit Banks for the Year 1945* (Georgetown: Argosy Co. Ltd, 1946), 1.

122. *Report of the Banks' Committee 1927*, 2.
123. *Annual Report on the Cooperative Credit Banks, 1945*, 1.
124. Ibid.
125. *Report of the Banks' Committee of the Local Government Board and on the Cooperative Credit Banks established in the Colony: For the Year 1933* (Georgetown: Argosy Co. Ltd, 1934), 5.
126. Ibid., 3–4.
127. Ibid., 6; *Report of the Banks' Committee, 1938*, 4.
128. *HBJ 1928*, 411; Board minutes, 12 April 1926, 28 July 1926, 25 August 1926, Barclays Bank (Dominion, Colonial and Overseas) Board Minute Book no. 1, BBA 38/503.
129. Butt to general manager's office, 17 September 1929.
130. Brereton, "Society and Culture", 92.
131. Brian Moore, "Ethnicity and Economic Behaviour in Nineteenth-century Guyana", in *Working Slavery, Pricing Freedom: Perspectives from the Caribbean, Africa, and the Diaspora*, ed. Verene Shepherd (Kingston: Ian Randle, 2001), 378.
132. R.N. Escolme (Barbados), Essay no. 34, Bank Essay Competition, 1943, BBA 38/983.
133. Ibid.
134. Sugar Commission Report, Part 1, CO 318/398/1; Barbados Enclosure no. 210, 18 October 1930, CO 318/398/1; see Barrow, "Ownership And Control", 89–90; Sleeman, "The Agri-Business Bourgeoisie", 18–19; see also *Barbados Year Book and Who's Who, 1934*, 243–48.
135. Marshall, "Nineteenth Century Crises", 96–97; Singh, *Race and Class Struggles*, 69–70. The establishment of this bank was a further extension of the local government's assistance under the Agricultural Aids Act; the bank provided short-term financing to sugar planters in Barbados.
136. Singh, *Race and Class Struggles*, 80–82; Brereton, *A History of Modern Trinidad*, 208.
137. Brown, *History of Money and Banking*, 93–96.
138. Barritt to Grindle, 8 March 1930.
139. Singh, *Race and Class Struggles*, 72.
140. Ibid.
141. Trinidad, Administration Reports, 1939–45, CO 298/183.
142. See Kathleen Phillips Lewis, "The Trinidad Cocoa Peasants and their Struggle for Acceptance, 1890–1939" (paper presented at UNESCO/University of the West Indies Conference on Slavery, Emancipation and the Shaping of Society, St Augustine, Trinidad and Tobago, 8–10 December 1988), and "The Poor and the Powerful: The Cocoa Contracts Crisis in Trinidad, 1884–1890", *Journal of Caribbean History* 32, nos. 1 and 2 (1998): 22. See also Selwyn Ryan and Lou Anne Barclay, *Sharks and Sardines: Blacks in Business in Trinidad and Tobago* (St Augustine, Trinidad: Institute of Social and Economic Research, University of the West Indies, 1992), 8, 10.

143. *Caribbean Commission* (Port of Spain: Central Secretariat, 1957), 80; see also Anderson, *St Vincent Handbook*, 345.
144. G.F. Sharp, ed., *The Barbados Year Book, 1937* (Barbados: Advocate Press, 1937), 111.
145. *HBJ 1928*, 411.
146. Ibid.; Callender, *Capital Market Institutions*, 55. The banks were also used as instruments through which land was purchased by the government under the land settlement scheme which was begun in 1920. The Agricultural Loan Societies Board advanced money to the banks at a certain rate of interest; the banks in turn lent out sums at a slightly higher rate of interest to small landowners for the purpose of purchasing portions of the estates which had been cut up into smaller lots. In addition to the amount loaned by the banks under the land settlement scheme, the board advanced a total of over £114,000 to thirty-five of the fifty-one banks in existence in 1923.
147. Brown, *History of Money and Banking*, 90; Christine Barrow, "Meetings: Group Savings Arrangement in Barbados", *African Studies Association of the West Indies Bulletin* 8: 32–40. This type of credit arrangement was not peculiar to the West Indies but was practised in many African communities in the early twentieth century. See Grietjie Verhoef, "Stokvels and Economic Empowerment: The Case of African Women in South Africa, c. 1930–1998" in *Women and Credit: Researching the Past, Refiguring the Future*, ed. Beverly Lemire, Ruth Pearson, and Gail Campbell (Oxford: Berg, 2001), 91–114.

Chapter 5

1. Jones, *British Multinational Banking*, 19.
2. Richard Kesner, *Economic Control and Colonial Development: Crown Colony Financial Management in the Age of Joseph Chamberlain* (Oxford: Clio, 1981), 147.
3. Jones, *British Multinational Banking*, 19.
4. Ibid; Crossley and Blandford, *DCO Story*, Illustrations, p. vii.
5. Jones, *British Multinational Banking*, 41; Kenwood and Lougheed, *The Growth of the International Economy, 1820–2000*, 13–15.
6. Hall, *Free Jamaica*, 225; see also Green, *British Slave Emancipation*, 180–81.
7. Brown, "The Response of the Banking Sector", 38. See chapter 1 for a discussion of the establishment and failure of these banks.
8. See W.E. Armstrong, "Island 'Checks' and the Advent of Commercial Banks in Jamaica, 1819–1888", seminar paper, University of the West Indies, Cave Hill, 1982), 25–26.
9. Ibid.
10. Brown, "The Response of the Banking Sector", 39.
11. Ibid.
12. The Planters' Bank began operations in Jamaica in 1839 under a Deed of

Settlement, but was subsequently incorporated for twenty-one years by the Act 4 Vict. Cap.17 of 19 December 1840. In its prospectus, the bank stated that its business would include that of "advancing loans against crops, produce, lands, houses and other property". See Armstrong, "Island 'Checks'", 22.

13. Brown, "The Response of the Banking Sector", 39.
14. Ibid., 40, 54; Lobdell, "Patterns of Investment", 37.
15. Brown, "The Response of the Banking Sector", 54.
16. Lobdell, "Patterns of Investment", 36.
17. The shareholders of the Colonial Bank met at a special general meeting on 24 May 1855 to frame a petition for a supplementary charter. The original charter made provision for the winding up of the business after twenty years – or earlier, should it be deemed expedient – but none for extending the period. It was thought that the difficulty might be overcome by assent, but two of the shareholders were not in agreement, and unanimous agreement could not be reached. The law officers of the Crown stated that the only way out was through the legislature, and suggested that it would be easier to get a private bill passed as an Act of Parliament than to petition for a supplementary charter, with royal assent being given to the Colonial Bank Act, 1856. See Republic Bank Ltd, *From Colonial to Republic*, 30.
18. Cain and Hopkins, *British Imperialism: Innovation and Expansion*, 78–84. See also Kenwood and Lougheed, *Growth of the International Economy*, 62–64.
19. Jones, *British Multinational Banking*, 104.
20. Armstrong, "Island 'Checks'", 9.
21. Brown, "The Response of the Banking Sector", 56.
22. W. Evan Nelson, "The Hongkong and Shanghai Banking Corporation Factor in the Progress toward a Straits Settlements Government Note Issue, 1881–1889", in *Eastern Banking*, ed. F.H.H. King (London: Athlone, 1983), 156, 163–64; See also Kesner, *Economic Control*, 148.
23. Callender, *Capital Market Institutions*, 72; *Report of the West Indian Currency Committee* (London: His Majesty's Stationery Office, 1923), 9.
24. Currency, West Indies, Note Issues of the various Banks, CO 323/1312/9; Colonial Bank Act, 1925, BBA 38/76, 17.
25. Currency, West Indies, Note Issues of the various Banks, CO 323/1312/9; Colonial Bank Act, 1925, 16.
26. Colonial Bank Act, 1925, 16–18.
27. Ibid., 19–20.
28. See chapter 1 for discussion of the Canadian banks' entry to the region. A.B. Jamieson, *Chartered Banking in Canada* (Toronto: Ryerson Press, 1953), 33; Donald Bailey Marsh, "Canada", in *Banking Systems*, ed. B.H. Beckhart (Toronto: Ryerson Press, 1953), 133, 137; Quigley, "The Bank of Nova Scotia", 797–838.
29. Baum, *The Banks of Canada*, 30.
30. Jamieson, *Chartered Banking*, 33.

31. *Report of the West Indian Currency Committee*, 9; Memorandum on Issues of Notes by Banks in Jamaica, CO 852/284/9; Governor of Jamaica, Stubbs, to Secretary of State for the Colonies, MacDonald, 28 April 1939, West Indian Note Issue CO 852/214/8; Jamieson, *Chartered Banking*, 33; Marsh, "Canada", 138; Callender, *Capital Market Institutions*, 72.
32. See *Report of the West Indian Currency Committee*, 10; Currency, West Indies, CO 323/1312/9. References are made to the following in the memo: For Barbados, see the Bank Notes Act, No. 5 of 1911; for British Guiana, the Bank Notes Ordinance, No. 1 of 1914; for Trinidad, the Bank Notes Ordinance, Cap. 214 of the 1925 revision; for the Leeward Islands, the Bank Notes Act Cap. 115; for Grenada, the Bank Notes Ordinance, No. 2 of 1914; for St Lucia, the Bank Notes Ordinance, No. 24 of 1920, the Bank Notes Amendment Ordinance, No. 17 of 1922, and the Bank Notes Amendment Ordinance, No. 3 of 1923; and for Jamaica, the Bank Notes Law, No. 20 of 1904.
33. Callender, *Capital Market Institutions*, 73; *Report of the West Indian Currency Committee*, 10–11; Memorandum by Sydney Caine, Colonial Office, on Canadian banks' note issue, Currency, West Indies, Note Issues of Various Banks, 1935, CO 323/1312/9. In 1924, the RBC's circulatory limit was increased to $700,000 with the approval of the secretary of state for the colonies, for which the bank was required to deposit with the Crown Agents a quarter of the value of the additional note issue as security; Hemmings to Chamberlain, 6 January 1900, despatch no. 16, CO 884/6; Hemmings to Chamberlain, 24 February 1900, despatch no. 88, CO 137/609; Hemmings to Chamberlain, 20 March 1900, CO 137/610 ; Governor Richards to Malcolm MacDonald, Barclays Bank (DCO), 28 April 1939, British West Indian Note Issue, 1939–1940, CO 852/214/8; Brown, *History of Money and Banking*, 101.
34. Governor of the Windward Islands to the Secretary of State, CO 852/214/8; Governor of the Windward Islands to the Secretary of State, 25 January 1939, CO 852/214/8; Governor of the Leeward Islands to the Secretary of State, CO 852/214/8.
35. Memorandum on issue of notes by banks in Jamaica, 5 June 1940, sent with Despatch No. 237 from Colonial Office to Jamaica, Currency Reserves, Barclays Bank (DCO) British West Indian note issue, 1940, CO 852/284/9.
36. S. Caine, Memorandum on Canadian banks' note issues, Currency, West Indies, Note Issues of Various Banks, 1935, CO 323/1312/9.
37. Boyse, Memorandum, 12 December 1938, Currency reserves in the Colonies, Barclays Bank (DCO), British West Indian Note Issue 1939–1940, CO 852/214/8.
38. Colonial Banking Legislation, CO 852/767/4.
39. Powell, Bank of England, to the Colonial Office, 22 October 1948, CO 852/767/4; see also H.M. Allen, S.R. Cope and H.J. Witheridge, *Commercial Banking Legislation and Control* (London: Macmillan, 1938), 236.

40. Boyse, Memorandum, 12 December 1938, Currency reserves in the Colonies, CO 852/214/8; Caine, Memorandum on Canadian banks' note issues, Currency, West Indies, Note Issues of Various Banks, CO 323/1312/9. Included in the memo were the following references: Jamaica Law 20, 1904, Vic 7 Cap. 47, the amending Act Vic. 7 Cap. 52, and the Jamaica Bank Notes Law No. 36 of 1914; Barbados Bank Notes Act No. 5, 1911; British Guiana, Bank Notes Ordinance No. 1, 1914; Leeward Islands, the Bank Notes Act (Cap. 115); Trinidad Bank Notes Ordinance Cap. 214 of 1925 for the Windward Islands; Grenada, Bank Notes Ordinance No. 2 of 1914; and St Lucia Bank Notes Ordinance No. 24 of 1920 as amended by the Bank Notes Amendment Ordinance No. 17 of 1922 and the Bank Notes Amendment Ordinance No. 3 of 1923.
41. *Report of the West Indian Currency Committee,* 11; Governor of the Windward Islands to the Secretary of State, CO 852/214/8; Governor of the Windward Islands to the Secretary of State, 25 January 1939, CO 852/214/8 ; Despatch from the Governor of the Leeward Islands to the Secretary of State, CO 852/214/8.
42. *Report of the West Indian Currency Committee,* 11.
43. Governor of Jamaica to the Secretary of State, 6 April 1939, CO 852/214/8.
44. Ibid.
45. Powell, Bank of England, 22 October 1948, CO 852/767/4.
46. A. Creech-Jones, Secretary of State for the Colonies, to colonial governments, 6 May 1949, CO 852/767/5.
47. Powell, 22 October 1948.
48. Ibid; Colonial Banking Legislation, CO 852/767/4.
49. A. Creech-Jones to colonial governments, 6 May 1949.
50. Colonial Banking Legislation, CO 852/767/4.
51. Ibid.
52. Powell, 22 October 1948.
53. Colonial Banking Legislation, CO 852/767/4.
54. The Banking Law, No. 31, 1960, *Jamaica Gazette Supplement: Proclamations, Rules, and Regulations* 84, no. 35 (May 1961).
55. Ibid.
56. Ibid.
57. Crossley and Blandford, *DCO Story,* 208; Jones, *British Multinational Banking,* table A5.1, appendix.
58. The Overseas Incorporated Banks (Exemption) Order nos. 185, 186, 134, 135, 136, 137, *Jamaica Gazette Supplement: Proclamations, Rules, and Regulations* 84, no. 66 (20 July 1961). Also see chapter 9.
59. The Bank of Jamaica Law, No. 32, 1960, Section 5, *Jamaica Gazette Supplement: Proclamations, Rules, and Regulations* 84, no. 35 (1 May 1961).
60. The Bank of Jamaica Law, No. 32, 1960, Section 30 and Section 31, *Jamaica*

Gazette Supplement: Proclamations, Rules, and Regulations 84, no. 35. (1 May 1961). The central bank also had the power to request from any commercial bank any information for the purpose of ascertaining whether that bank was complying with the provisions of Section 11 of the law.

61. The Bank of Jamaica Law, No. 32, 1960, Sections 25, 27, 32, *Jamaica Gazette Supplement: Proclamations, Rules, and Regulations* 84, no. 35 (1 May 1961).
62. See Part IV, Section 13 (2) of the Bank of Jamaica Act, 1960, *Jamaica Gazette Supplement: Proclamations, Rules, and Regulations* 84, no. 35 (1 May 1961); see chapter 6.
63. W.F. Crick, "The Framework of Inter-Relations", in *Commonwealth Banking Systems*, ed. W.F. Crick (Oxford: Clarendon Press, 1965), 14–15; D.J. Morgan, "The West Indies", in *Commonwealth Banking Systems*, ed. W.F. Crick (Oxford: Clarendon Press, 1965), 473.
64. Ida Greaves, *Colonial Monetary Conditions* (London: Her Majesty's Stationery Office, 1953), 27.

Chapter 6

1. Analyst, "Currency and Banking In Jamaica", *Social and Economic Studies* 1, no. 4 (August 1953): 41–53; G.L.M. Clauson, "The British Colonial Currency System", *Economic Journal* 54, no. 213 (April 1944): 1–23; Arthur Hazlewood, "The Economics of Colonial Monetary Arrangements", *Social and Economic Studies* 3, nos. 1–4 (1954): 291–315; Clive Y. Thomas, *Monetary and Financial Arrangements in a Dependent Monetary Economy: A Study of British Guiana, 1945–1962* (Kingston: Institute of Social and Economic Research, University of the West Indies, Mona, 1965).
2. Charles Goodhart, *The Evolution of Central Banks* (Cambridge, MA: MIT Press, 1988), 4–5.
3. Kenwood and Lougheed, *The Growth of the International Economy, 1820–2000*, 198–205. Similar developments also occurred in the British Commonwealth; see Forrest Capie, "The Evolving Regulatory Framework In British Banking", in *Government, Industries, and Markets: Aspects of Government-Industry Relations in the UK, Japan, West Germany, and the USA since 1945*, ed. Martin Chick, 127–41 (Aldershot: Edward Elgar, 1990).
4. Ibid; Crick, "The Framework of Inter-Relations", 11–13; Newlyn and Rowan, *Money and Banking*, 51.
5. Crick, "The Framework of Inter-Relations", 15–21; Jefferson, *The Post-War Economic Development of Jamaica*, 9; Brown, *History of Money and Banking*, 166–79; Callender, *Capital Market Institutions*, 148–60; Girvan, *Foreign Capital and Economic Underdevelopment in Jamaica*, 119.
6. Sykes, *Banking and Currency*, 274–81; William Ashworth, *A Short History of the International Economy since 1850* (London: Longman, 1987), 235–38, 246–53; Cain and Hopkins, *British Imperialism: Crisis and Deconstruction*, 76–79; Derek H.

Aldcroft, *From Versailles to Wall Street, 1919–1929* (Harmondsworth: Penguin Books, 1977, 1987), 125–51, 168–86; Kenwood and Lougheed, *The Growth of the International Economy*, 193–98; James Foreman-Peck, *A History of the World Economy: International Economic Relations since 1850* (Hertfordshire: Wheatsheaf, 1983), 244–46.

7. Canada and British Honduras were not part of the Sterling Area. See Cain and Hopkins, *British Imperialism: Crisis and Deconstruction*, 79–81; Paul Bareau, "The Sterling Area", in *Banking in the British Commonwealth*, ed. R.S. Sayers (Oxford: Clarendon Press, 1952), 465; Kenwood and Lougheed, *The Growth of the International Economy*, 208–11; David Williams, "The Evolution of the Sterling System", in *Money and Banking in Honour of R.S. Sayers,* ed. E.R. Whittlesey and J.S.G. Wilson (Oxford: Clarendon Press, 1968), 273.

8. Crick, "The Framework of Inter-Relations", 5–8; Cain and Hopkins, *British Imperialism: Crisis and Deconstruction*, 36–39, 79; Rooth, *British Protectionism*, 24–25, 29–33; Kenwood and Lougheed, *The Growth of the International Economy*, 26–27.

9. Ibid; *Report of the West Indian Currency Committee*, 8. See also Callender, *Capital Market Institutions*, 73.

10. Callender, *Capital Market Institutions*, 72; *Report of the West Indian Currency Committee*, 4–6; Secretary of State for the Colonies P. Cunliffe-Lister to Governor of British Guiana, 27 March 1935, CO 323/1312/3 .

11. Cunliffe-Lister to Governor of British Guiana, 27 March 1935.

12. Ibid; *British Guiana, Report of the Commissioners of Currency for the Year 1937* (Georgetown: Demerara, 1937), 1. For British Guiana, the Currency Notes Ordinance, Chapter 50, was repealed by Ordinance No. 14 of 1937, which came into effect on 1 June 1937; Currency Returns, Barbados, No. 38, 1937, Act No. 12 of 1937, CO 852/153/1; Callender, *Capital Market Institutions*, 74. In Jamaica, Laws 9 and 21 of 1937 provided for the establishment of government currency notes on a sterling exchange standard. Currency notes were to be exchanged for the equivalent values of sterling, either with the board in Jamaica or with the Crown Agents in London; Crick, "The Framework of Inter-Relations", 8.

13. *Report of the West Indian Currency Committee*, 11–12, 20.

14. Ibid., 6; the West African Currency Board was established in 1913. See Williams, "Sterling System", 274; and Newlyn and Rowan, *Money and Banking in British Colonial Africa*, 43–44, 46.

15. Stubbs, Governor of Jamaica, to Sydney Webb, Secretary of State for the Colonies, 25 June 1929, CO 323/1034/7; Trinidad to the Colonial Office, 9 August 1929, CO 323/1034/7; Millbank to Caine, 19 April 1933, CO 323/1207/1; Caine, 27 April 1933, CO 323/1207/1; Caine, 20 March 1934, CO 323/1250/2 .

16. Stubbs, Governor of Jamaica, to P. Cunliffe-Lister, Secretary of State for the Colonies, 10 May 1932, CO 323/1165/3.

17. Caine, 20 March 1934, CO 323/1250/2.
18. Special Correspondent, "Monetary Systems of the Colonies: The West Indies", *Banker* 88, no. 27 (November 1948): 163.
19. Richard Kesner, *Economic Control and Colonial Development: Crown Colony Financial Management in the Age of Joseph Chamberlain* (Oxford: Clio, 1981),148.
20. Callender, *Capital Market Institutions*, 73–74; G.C. Wainwright, Reginald Butt, W.A. Clarke, William Alexander per A. Watson to Governor Stubbs, 12 February 1929, Currency Reorganization, CO 323/1030/14; *Report of the West Indian Currency Committee*, 4, 5.
21. *Report of the West Indian Currency Committee*, 4, 5. In Barbados, which did not have a government issue at the time, banknotes were in the denominations of $5, $10, $50 and $100.
22. Ibid; Callender, *Capital Market Institutions*, 73–74; Wainwright et al. to Stubbs, 12 February 1929.
23. Despatch no. 198, 22 August 1929, Barbados, CO 323/1030/14.
24. Caine, 20 March 1934.
25. Governor of British Guiana to Secretary of State, 3 March 1937, CO 323/1122/9.
26. Ibid. The memo noted that Section 15 (2) of the Bank Notes Ordinance, Chapter 51, prescribed a period of five years before the RBC's right to issue notes could be terminated, but thereafter, twelve months was considered sufficient notice for the governor to recall and redeem the entire amount of the bank's notes.
27. Caine, 9 April 1937, CO 323/1411/1.
28. R. Burns, 30 April 1937, CO 323/1411/1.
29. R.V. Vernon, 1 May 1937, CO 323/1411/1.
30. *Report of the West Indian Currency Committee*, 9; R. Burns, 6 April 1937, CO 323/1411/1; Young, Treasury Chambers, to Clauson, Colonial Office, 31 December 1938, CO 852/214/8.
31. Burns, 30 April 1937; Vernon, 1 May 1937; Ormsby-Gore to Governor of British Guiana, 21 May 1937, CO 323/1411/1.
32. Burns, 30 April 1937.
33. Ormsby-Gore to Governor of British Guiana, 21 May 1937.
34. Vernon, 1 May 1937.
35. Susan Estabrook, *The Banking Crisis of 1933* (Kentucky: University of Kentucky Press, 1973), 5, 19–20; Benjamin J. Klebaner, *American Commercial Banking: A History* (Boston: Twayne, 1990), 147.
36. Colonial Office to Governor of Jamaica, 22 August 1941, CO 852/359/1; Governor Richards to Secretary of State for the Colonies, 29 August 1941, CO 852/359/1.
37. Colonial Office to Governor of Jamaica, 26 September 1941, CO 852/359/1.
38. Callender, *Capital Market Institutions*, 75.
39. Ibid.

40. Young, Treasury Chambers, to Clauson, 31 December 1938, CO 852/214/8.
41. Ibid.
42. J. Fisher, Bank of England, to T. Bewley, 15 June 1939, CO 852/214/8; J. Caulcutt, Barclays Bank (DCO), to Young, Treasury, 29 December 1938, CO 852/214/8.
43. Young, Treasury Chambers, to Clauson, 31 December 1938, CO 852/214/8; J. Fisher, Bank of England, to T. Bewley, 15 June 1939, CO 852/214/8; Secretary of State of the Colonies to the Governor of Jamaica, 5 June 1940, CO 852/284/9; General managers, Barclays Bank (DCO), to Treasury, 9 October 1941, CO 852/359/1; Treasury to Barclays Bank (DCO), 20 October 1941, CO 852/359/1; Secretary of State to Governors of Jamaica, Trinidad, Barbados, Leewards, Windwards and British Guiana, 31 October 1941, CO 852/359/1; J. Caulcutt, Barclays Bank (DCO), to Forrest, Colonial Office, 27 May 1942, CO 852/359/2; Grant, Treasury, to Forrest, Colonial Office, 4 June 1942, CO 852/359/2.
44. J. Fisher, Bank of England, to T. Bewley, Colonial Office, 15 June 1939, CO 852/214/8.
45. Moyne, Colonial Office, to Richards, Governor of Jamaica, 21 February 1941, CO 852/359/1.
46. Richards, Governor of Jamaica, to Lloyd, Secretary of State for the Colonies, 16 December 1940, CO 852/359/1.
47. Richards, Governor of Jamaica, to Lloyd, Secretary of State for the Colonies, 27 August 1940, CO 852/284/9.
48. Ibid; P.E.N. Mortimer, Kingston branch manager, Barclays Bank (DCO), to the general managers, Barclays Bank (DCO), London, 24 June 1941, CO 852/359/1.
49. Wainwright et al. to Stubbs, 12 February 1929; From the attorney general's chambers, Jamaica, Report on Law entitled "A Law to Amend the Stamp Duty Law, 1903 (Law 40 of 1903)", Currency Reorganization, 14 June 1929, CO 323/1030/14. This was following a petition from the managers of the commercial banks in 1928 about the proposed currency reforms. They argued that, if the tax was reduced, the bankers would be able to issue their own notes freely and the issue of £1 notes by the local commissioners would be unnecessary.
50. John Caulcutt, Barclays Bank (DCO), to Downes, Colonial Office, 21 August 1941, Memorandum re Barclays Bank (DCO) Note Issue, Jamaica, CO 852/359/1; Colonial Office to Jamaica, 22 August 1941, CO 852/359/1; Richards, Governor of Jamaica, to Moyne, Colonial Office, 29 August 1941, CO 852/359/1.
51. Kesner, *Economic Control and Colonial Development*, 147n7.
52. Forrest to E.W. Playfair, 26 July 1941, CO 852/359/1; Colonial Office to the Governor of Jamaica, 26 September 1941, CO 852/359/1.

53. Mortimer to the general managers, 24 June 1941.
54. Minute Book no. 2, 13 October 1932, Board Minutes, Barclays Bank (DCO), BBA 38/504; Minute Book no. 4, 11 March 1943, Board Minutes, Barclays Bank (DCO), BBA 38/506.
55. Board Minutes, 11 March 1943, Barclays Bank (DCO).
56. Moyne, Colonial Office, to Richards, Governor of Jamaica, 26 September 1941, CO 852/359/1.
57. Caulcutt to Downes, 21 August 1941.
58. Moyne, Colonial Office, to Richards, Governor of Jamaica, 14 January 1942, CO 852/359/1.
59. Colonial Bank Act, 1925, BBA 38/76.
60. Clauson, 13 December 1939, CO 852/153/3.
61. H. Duncan, 15 December 1939, CO 852/154/3; H. Duncan to Sir K. Poyser, 10 October 1942, CO 852/359/2.
62. Duncan to Poyser, 10 October 1942; Somervell to Poyser, 7 April 1943, CO 852/359/4.
63. Somervell to Poyser, 7 April 1943. Gater, a Colonial Office official, in a personal letter to Governor Richards, in an apparent attempt to have the matter resolved in favour of the bank, had stated that "apart from the legal position which was not entirely free from doubt, there were certain considerations of a general equitable character which led them to wonder whether the tax ought to be continued". See Gater to Richards, 20 May 1943, CO 852/359/4. Governor Richards responded that although he would have liked to remove the tax, he was unable to do so since it would mean the loss of revenue which the colony could not afford. In addition, the argument that special favours were shown to outside concerns would be used to stir up popular feeling and secure the rejection of any bill in the Legislative Council for this purpose. See Richards to Gater, 27 July 1943, CO 852/359/4.
64. Caine, 12 October 1942, CO 852/359/2.
65. Board Minute Book no. 4, 14 October 1942, Board Minute Books, Barclays Bank (Dominion, Colonial and Overseas), BBA 38/506.
66. Secretary of State to Governors of Bahamas, Barbados, Bermuda, British Guiana, Jamaica, Trinidad, 15 January 1942, CO 852/359/2; Fisher, Bank of England, to Forrest, Colonial Office, 10 April 1942, CO 852/359/2.
67. Fisher to Forrest, 10 April 1942; Fisher, Bank of England, to Forrest, Colonial Office, 28 July 1942, CO 852/359/2; Fisher, Bank of England, to Forrest, Colonial Office, 12 August 1942, CO 852/359/2.
68. Fisher to Forrest, 12 August 1942. The initial proposal put forward by the Colonial Office was to base the reduction in circulation on Barclays Bank (DCO)'s previous three years' quarterly averages in banknote circulation. As that bank's average circulation for the period July 1939 to June 1942 amounted to £1,033,957, a reduction of approximately 42 per cent would have been

required to bring it down to the £600,000 limit. If a 42 per cent cut had been applied to the Canadian banks, the limits would have been as follows: CBC, from an average of $498,221 to $288,968; the BNS, from an average of $751,076 to $435,624; and the RBC, from an average of $2,283,515 to $1,324,439. In other words, both the CBC and the RBC would have secured a larger circulatory limit had the first proposal been adopted. Only the BNS would have fared worse.

69. Ibid.
70. Fisher, Bank of England, to Forrest, Colonial Office, 17 August 1942, CO 852/359/2; Bank of Canada to Bank of England, 25 September 1942, CO 852/359/2.
71. Bank of Canada to Bank of England, 25 September 1942; Colonial Office to the West Indies, September 1942, CO 852/359/2.
72. Bank of Canada to Bank of England, 25 September 1942. This issue had come up during the discussions in the Colonial Office on how to arrive at the circulatory limits for the Canadian banks. One arrangement that had been considered would have subjected Barclays Bank (DCO) to a limit in each colony. Apparently, this was put to the British bank, which indicated its preference for a global limit. See Fisher to Forrest, 10 April 1942.
73. Bank of England to Bank of Canada, 9 October 1942, CO 852/359/2; Fisher, Bank of England, to Forrest, Colonial Office, 10 October 1942, CO 852/359/2; Fisher, Bank of England, to Forrest, Colonial Office, 15 October 1942, CO 852/359/2 ; Towers, Bank of Canada, to Bank of England, 9 November 1942, CO 852/359/2; Forrest, Colonial Office, to Fisher, Bank of England, 19 November 1942, CO 852/359/2.
74. Bank of Canada to Bank of England, 25 September 1942; Colonial Office to the West Indies, September 1942.
75. Bank of England to Colonial Office, 20 May 1943, CO 852/359/3; Crossley to Caine, 15 June 1943, CO 852/359/3. Barclays Bank (DCO)'s circulation in the West Indies on 31 May 1943 was approximately £830,000. A temporary limit of £850,000 was applied for to cover the position from 30 June 1943 until 31 December 1943, when the existing limit of £1,500,000 expired. The BNS also had to apply for a temporary limit of £140,000 for a period of six months because on 31 May 1943 its circulation stood at £108,831. Chairman of the commissioners of currency to BNS manager, Kingston, 25 May 1943, CO 852/359/3.
76. Bank of Canada to Bank of England, 25 November 1943, CO 852/359/3; Fisher, Bank of England, to Myers, Treasury, 23 November 1943, CO 852/359/3. By November 1943, the BNS was able to report that its circulation in Jamaica had been reduced to £84,000, well within its limit of £100,000. At the end of October 1943, the RBC's outstanding circulation in the West Indies totalled $1,506,773, and it was estimated that approximately $1,425,000 would

be in circulation on 31 December 1943. At that time, the CBC's outstanding circulation amounted to $408,600, and it was estimated that it would only be able to reduce this figure to $390,000 by 31 December 1943.

77. Fisher to Forrest, 12 August 1942.
78. Sir D. Jardine, Governor of the Leeward Islands, to Secretary of State for the Colonies, 25 February 1942, CO 852/359/2.
79. Bank of England to Forrest, Colonial Office, 7 July 1942, CO 852/359/2; Norman, Bank of England, to Towers, Bank of Canada, 10 July 1942, CO 852/359/2; Towers to Bank of England, 9 November 1942. See Lester D. Langley, *The United States and the Caribbean in the Twentieth Century* (Athens: University of Georgia Press, 1989), 155. To deter German intrusion into the Caribbean, ninety-nine-year leases on bases were established in Jamaica, St Lucia, Trinidad, British Guiana and Antigua, as well as in the Bahamas and Bermuda. Jobs in Trinidad, Antigua and British Guiana became available on the US bases, where "tens of thousands of West Indians, many sailing from nearby islands aboard schooners, worked on airplane runways, harbors, constructed military barracks and worked as messengers, cooks and maids". See also Bonham C. Richardson, "Caribbean Migrations, 1838–1965", in Knight and Palmer, *The Modern Caribbean*, 215–16.
80. Young to Governor of Trinidad, 27 January 1942, CO 852/359/2.
81. Bank of England to Towers, Bank of Canada, 7 July 1942, CO 852/359/2; Towers, Bank of Canada, to Bank of England, 7 July 1942, CO 852/359/2; Bank of Canada to Bank of England, 25 September 1942. In July 1942, Trinidad had large orders outstanding with the printers for government currency notes, but none included notes of $20 denomination. In the same month, the RBC in Trinidad reported that there was an acute shortage of government currency notes and that demand was expected to rise by September, for the army's payroll requirements, to a figure in excess of the existing circulation figure. The local currency commissioners had stated that they would not have sufficient notes to meet this demand until October, and that even then there would be a shortage of $20 notes.
82. Towers, Bank of Canada, 9 July 1942, CO 852/359/2; Bank of England to Towers, 7 July 1942; Towers to Bank of England, 7 July 1942; Bank of Canada to Bank of England, 25 September 1942.
83. Colonial Office (draft cable to be sent) to West Indies, 3 June 1943, CO 852/359/2; Sir G. Bushe, Governor of Barbados, to Secretary of State for the Colonies, 4 January 1943, CO 852/359/2. British Guiana reported in February of that year that almost the whole initial supply of $750,000 in $10 government currency notes and the small supply of $20 government currency notes were exhausted shortly after their arrival. See Sir G. Lethem, Governor of British Guiana, to Secretary of State for the Colonies, 23 February 1943, CO 852/359/3. In Jamaica, the BNS manager in Kingston noted in May 1943 that

"unless £5 notes of the government of Jamaica arrived in the very near future, I would be unable to reduce this bank's circulation to within the limit of £100,000"; see Torrie, BNS Kingston branch manager, to chairman of the commissioners of currency, Kingston, 19 May 1943, CO 852/359/3. At the end of June 1943, Barclays Bank (DCO) reported that the Trinidad government was very short of $20 notes, although there were some on order. The bank noted that "it may be that they will request us to use some of our notes ($20) if it becomes urgent. We shall of course continue not to issue any of our notes except at the request of the local government." See Crossley to Caine, 30 June 1943, CO 852/359/3.

84. Bank of Canada to Bank of England, 25 September 1942; Towers, Bank of Canada, to Bank of England, 9 November 1942, CO 852/359/2.
85. Lethem to Secretary of State for the Colonies, 23 February 1943.
86. Bank of Canada to Bank of England, 25 November 1943, CO 852/359/3. The problem was especially acute in Trinidad where the construction of the naval bases was the most extensive, at Chaguaramas and Wallerfield. See Brereton, *A History of Modern Trinidad*, 191–92.
87. *British Caribbean Currency Board. Report of the Executive Commissioner for 1957* (Port of Spain: Government Printing Office, 1957), 7; *Colonial Annual Reports. Barbados, 1947* (London: His Majesty's Stationery Office, 1947) 20–21; Brown, *History of Money and Banking*, 157–58.
88. Thomas, *Monetary and Financial Arrangements*, 15.
89. *British Caribbean Currency Board Report for 1957*, 7; Marsh, "Canada", 138.
90. *British Caribbean Currency Board Report for 1957*, 7–8.
91. Crick, "The Framework of Inter-Relations", 9.
92. *British Caribbean Currency Board Report for 1957*, 7. See Law No. 51 of 1954, *Jamaica Gazette Supplement: Bills and Laws*, 81, no. 10 (13 March 1958).
93. Law No. 9 of 1954, *Jamaica Gazette Supplement: Bills and Laws*, 81, no. 10 (13 March 1958).
94. Ibid; *British Caribbean Currency Board, 1957*, 7. The Canadian Bank Act Revision, 1934, had called for a gradual curtailment of the banks' note-issuing powers over a period of fifteen years, so that after 31 January 1950, each bank was required to pay to the Bank of Canada an amount equal to the face value of its notes outstanding on that date. Thereafter the Bank of Canada assumed responsibility for redemption. As late as 1958 Canadian banks could still issue notes outside of Canada for circulation abroad in any British dominion, colony or possession in which the local government allowed private banknote issues.
95. *Report on Jamaica, 1958* (Kingston: Government Public Relations Dept., 1958), 75.
96. Minute Book No. 7, Board Minutes, 23 November 1950, Barclays Bank (DCO) Board Minute Books, BBA 38/509; *British Caribbean Currency Board. Report for 1957*, 7. Following this agreement, in 1957, £61,000 non-issued West Indian

Barclays Bank (DCO) currency notes which had been printed as a wartime measure were destroyed.
97. W.T. Newlyn, "The Colonial Empire", in *Banking in the British Commonwealth*, ed. R.S. Sayers (Oxford: Clarendon Press, 1952), 421–28.
98. Special Correspondent, "Monetary Systems of the Colonies", 165–66.
99. Marsh, "Canada", 138.
100. Wainwright et al. to Stubbs, 12 February 1929.
101. Letham to Secretary of State for the Colonies, 23 February 1943. See also a note summarizing commission charges for the issue and redemption of currency, 8 March 1943, CO 852/359/3; Colonial Office to Caulcutt, 26 March 1943, re Currency commission charges in the West Indies, CO 852/359/3.
102. Jones, *British Multinational Banking*, 33.
103. Caulcutt to Caine, 1 January 1942, British West Indian and British Guiana Exchange Quotations (per £100), CO 852/359/2.
104. Initially, charges in Jamaica had been set at 0.5 per cent for both the issue and redemption of currency by the Currency Board. See Cranborne to Richards, 13 November 1942, CO 852/359/2; Richards to Stanley, 3 December 1942, CO 852/359/2; Stanley to Richards, 2 January 1943, CO 852/359/2, no. 10; Richards to Stanley, 21 January 1943, CO 852/359/3; Stanley to Richards, 17 May 1943, CO 852/359/3; Richards to Stanley, 17 June 1943, CO 852/359/3.
105. Colonial Office to Trinidad, 26 November 1942, CO 852/359/2.
106. Analyst, "Currency and Banking In Jamaica", 43–44.

Chapter 7

1. Statement in Report for 30 September 1953 by Chairman Crossley, BBA 38/251; Barclays Bank (DCO), *Overseas Trade, 1958: Covering the Trade and Economic Conditions Which Prevailed in the Year 1957 in the Overseas Territories in Which the Barclays Group of Banks Is Represented* (London: Barclays Bank DCO, 1958), 18, 28, 30, 73. A world surplus in maize during 1957 drove prices to decline significantly. The price of copper had declined from a peak of £437 per ton in March 1956 to £180–190 per ton by the end of 1957. The total value of minerals had fallen from £118,511,000 to £89,123,000 between 1956 and 1957. The fall in price for wool was the result of financial difficulties in the United Kingdom and France: the credit squeeze and the rise in the bank rate in the former had led to a reduction in the stocks carried by British manufacturers, while the devaluation of the franc by 20 per cent raised the cost of wool to France.
2. The Anglo-Egyptian Section, later renamed the Egyptian Control, contributed an average of 6 per cent between 1946 and 1951. Its contribution thereafter averaged 4 per cent between 1953 and 1956.

3. Crossley and Blandford, *DCO Story*, 185–86.
4. Ibid. In 1946, a bomb explosion in the Haifa branch resulted in extensive damage. In 1948 Barclays Bank (DCO) suffered the largest cash loss by a bank in Palestine, of £P.195,409, when the Tel Aviv branch was raided by eighty bandits. Following this incident, the branch was closed for five weeks while security measures were put in place. See Nikshoy C. Chatterji, *A History of the Modern Middle East* (New York: Envoy Press, 1987), 77. In 1956 and 1957, the Israeli Section recorded losses of £40,513 and £93,418, respectively.
5. The number of sections in the bank's multinational network increased during this period mainly because of decolonization in the British empire and the decentralization of operations by the bank.
6. Michael Havinden and David Meredith, *Colonialism and Development: Britain and Its Tropical Colonies, 1850–1960* (London: Routledge, 1993), 206, 208–9.
7. *Annual Report on Jamaica for the Year 1947* (London: His Majesty's Stationery Office, 1948); Brereton, *A History of Modern Trinidad*, 211.
8. Higman, *Abstract of Caribbean Historical Statistics*, table 6/1, Sugar Production, 1700–1983; *Colonial Annual Report: British Guiana, 1946* (London: His Majesty's Stationery Office, 1948), 4–5.
9. Brereton, *A History of Modern Trinidad*, 211–12.
10. Ibid., 211.
11. *Colonial Report, Annual, British Guiana, 1938* (London: His Majesty's Stationery Office, 1940), 29; *Colonial Annual Report: British Guiana, 1946*, 17.
12. Commonwealth Economic Committee, *Plantation Crops: A Summary of Figures of Production, Trade, and Consumption Relating to Sugar, Tea, Coffee, Cocoa, Spices, Tobacco, and Rubber* (London: Her Majesty's Stationery Office, 1950, 1952, 1955, 1956, 1960, 1963).
13. Chalmin, *The Making of a Sugar Giant*, 217–20.
14. David Meredith, "State-Controlled Marketing and Economic Development: The Case of West African Produce during the Second World War", *Economic History Review*, 2nd ser., 39, no. 1 (February 1986): 89. See also Kenneth M. Wright, "Dollar Policy in the Sterling Area, 1939–1952", *American Economic Historical Review* 64 (1954): 569; Gerold Krozewksi, *Money and the End of Empire: British International Economic Policy and the Colonies, 1947–1958* (Houndmills: Palgrave, 2001), 25, 30.
15. Wright, "Dollar Policy", 569.
16. See chapter 2, which discusses the impact of the Great Depression on the bank's operations in the West Indies. See Stahl, *The Metropolitan Organization*, 27.
17. Crossley and Blandford, *DCO Story*, 103–4.
18. *Report of the Commission appointed to Enquire into the Organization of the Sugar Industry in Antigua* (London: Crown Agents of the Colonies on behalf of the Government of Antigua, 1949) 5.
19. Craton and Walvin, *A Jamaican Plantation*, 292.

20. Brereton, *A History of Modern Trinidad*, 211.
21. Colonial Office, *An Economic Survey of the Colonial Territories, 1951* (London: Her Majesty's Stationery Office, 1953), 69.
22. Havinden and Meredith, *Colonialism and Development*, 207.
23. Higman, *Abstract of Caribbean Historical Statistics*, table 12/1, Barbados Shipping.
24. Hall, *Grace, Kennedy*, 31, 32–33, 38.
25. Havinden and Meredith, *Colonialism and Development*, 209.
26. G.B. Hagelberg, *The Caribbean Sugar Industries: Constraints and Opportunities* (New Haven: Yale University Press, 1974) 22–23.
27. Craton and Walvin, *A Jamaican Plantation*, 287–88.
28. *Commission of Enquiry on the Sugar Industry of Jamaica, 1959–1960* (Kingston: Government Printing Office, 1961), 3.
29. Jefferson, *Post-War Economic Development*, 95; Hagelberg, *The Caribbean Sugar Industries*, 23. In the following years, the NPQ fluctuated within a range of 10 per cent above this figure, until it was fixed at 725,000 in 1965.
30. *Commission of Enquiry on the Sugar Industry of Jamaica, 1959–1960*, 6, 23. Price negotiations later occurred at triennial reviews.
31. Ibid., 3.
32. Ibid., 5.
33. *Barclays Bank Review* 26, no. 2 (May 1951): 32.
34. Higman, *Abstract of Caribbean Historical Statistics*, table 6/1: Sugar Production.
35. *The Booker Group: Review of the Year 1962* (London: Booker Brothers, McConnell and Co. Ltd, 1962), 36; *Handbook of the British West Indian Sugar Association (Inc.), 1961* (n.p., n.d.), 117. See also Jefferson, *Post-War Economic Development*, 93.
36. George Beckford, *The West Indian Banana Industry* (Kingston: Institute of Social and Economic Research, University of the West Indies, Mona, 1967), 4; D.W. Rodriquez, *Bananas: An Outline of the Economic History of Production and Trade with Special Reference to Jamaica* (Kingston: Department of Agriculture, 1955), 47. Under the Ottawa agreement of 1932, Britain had granted a preference of £2 10/- per ton on empire-produced bananas.
37. Higman, *Abstract of Caribbean Historical Statistics*, table 13/12: Jamaica: Major Agricultural Exports, 1788–1982.
38. See *The Windward Islands (Annual, 1959–1960)* (n.p., n.d.), 40.
39. Central Board, Analysis of Loans and Advances, September 1948 and 1949, BBA 11/556.
40. See chapter 8, table 8.4.
41. Jay R. Mandle, "British Caribbean Economic History: An Interpretation", in Knight and Palmer, *The Modern Caribbean*, 245.
42. Jefferson, *Post-War Economic Development*, 129. See also Colin Clarke, *Kingston,*

Jamaica: Urban Growth and Social Change, 1692–1962 (Berkeley: University of California Press, 1975), 39–40; Wyatt Bryce, ed., *Reference Book of Jamaica* (Kingston, 1946), 82–83.

43. Jefferson, *Post-War Economic Development*, 133.
44. Republic Bank Ltd, *From Colonial to Republic*, 131.
45. Brereton, *A History of Modern Trinidad*, 218–20.
46. Jefferson, *Post-War Economic Development*, 11, 16, 151–52; Western Hemisphere Exports Council, *Trade and Industrial Mission to the Caribbean, 1962* (London: Western Hemisphere Exports Council, 1962), 11.
47. Brereton, *A History of Modern Trinidad*, 214–15; Iserdeo Jainarain, *Trade and Development: A Study of the Small Caribbean Countries and Large Multinational Corporations* (Georgetown: Institute of Development Studies, University of Guyana, 1976), 136.
48. Western Hemisphere Exports Council, *Trade and Industrial Mission*, 20.
49. Ibid.
50. Barclays Bank DCO, *The Bahamas: An Economic Survey, 1962* (Bridgetown: Local Head Office, Barclays Bank DCO, 1962), 23–25.
51. Western Hemisphere Exports Council, *Trade and Industrial Mission*, 63.
52. Barclays Bank DCO, *The Cayman Islands: An Economic Survey, 1960* (Bridgetown: Local Head Office, Barclays Bank DCO, 1960), 11–12.
53. Barclays Bank DCO, *Trinidad: An Economic Survey, 1962* (Bridgetown: Local Head Office, Barclays Bank DCO, 1962), 20–21; Barclays Bank DCO, *Barbados: An Economic Survey, 1958* (Bridgetown: Local Head Office, Barclays Bank DCO, 1958), 8.
54. Colonial Office, *An Economic Survey*, 28; *Barbados: Report for the Years 1956 and 1957* (London: Her Majesty's Stationery Office, 1959), 32; *Barbados: Report for the Years 1960 and 1961* (London: Her Majesty's Stationery Office, 1962), 3, 45.
55. Western Hemisphere Exports Council, *Trade and Industrial Mission*, 44–48, 50, 54.
56. Ibid., 28.
57. Amalgamated Results, Statistics, and Review for all Branches in the Caribbean of the period Ending 30 September 1954, BBA 29/173; Amalgamated Results, Statistics, and Review for all Branches in the Caribbean of the period Ending 30 September 1961, BBA 29/193; F.R. Augier, S.C. Gordon, D.G. Hall and M. Reckord, *The Making of the West Indies* (London: Longman, 1960, 2002), 286.
58. Western Hemisphere Exports Council, *Trade and Industrial Mission*, 11.
59. Ibid.
60. Ibid., 28, 37, 44–48, 50.
61. Amalgamated Results, Statistics, and Review for all Branches in the Caribbean for the Period Ending, September 30, 1955, for 1956, for 1958, for 1960, for 1961, BBA 29/173.

62. Accounts and Board Meeting Papers, Report of the Directors, Barclays Bank (DCO), Chairman's Statement, 35th Ordinary General Meeting, 30 September 1960, BBA 38/251.
63. Ackrill and Hannah, *Barclays*, 115.
64. Barclays Bank DCO, Chairman's Statement, 35th Ordinary General Meeting, 30 September 1960.
65. Accounts and Board Meeting Papers, Report of the Directors, Barclays Bank (DCO), Chairman's Statement, 26th Ordinary General Meeting, 30 September 1951, BBA 38/251.
66. See also Girvan, *Foreign Capital*, 176–77.
67. Ibid., 177. The decline would also have been partly attributable to the imposition of a statutory minimum ratio of deposits at the central bank in Jamaica as of 1961. See chapters 5 and 6.
68. Girvan, *Foreign Capital*, 177.
69. Ibid; see *Bank of Jamaica Report and Statement of Accounts for the Year Ended 31 December 1961* (Kingston: Bank of Jamaica, 1962), 21.
70. Thomas, *Banking and Exchange*, 361.
71. Nash, "Trading Problems", 227–29; see also Miguel Alvarez Uriarte, "World and Hemisphere Trade Policies Affecting the Caribbean Area", in *Western Hemisphere International Relations and the Caribbean Area*, vol. 2, ed. Maurice Waters (Kingston: University of the West Indies, Mona, 1968), 24.
72. Amalgamated Results, Statistics and Review, 30 September 1953, BBA 29/173.
73. Results, Statistics, and Review of the Period Ending 31 March 1958, Port Maria Branch, Jamaica, BBA 29/175.
74. Results, Statistics, and Review of the Period Ending 30 September 1961, May Pen Branch, Jamaica, BBA 29/175.
75. Results, Statistics, and Review of the Period Ending 30 September 1958, Harbour Street Branch, Kingston, Jamaica, BBA 29/173; Results, Statistics, and Review of the Period Ending 30 September 1962, Grenada Branch, BBA 29/192.
76. Results, Statistics, and Review of the Period Ending 31 March 1961, Harbour Street Branch, Kingston, Jamaica, BBA 29/173.
77. Street transactions are known today as black market transactions.
78. Results, Statistics, and Review of the Period Ending 31 March 1958, Savanna–la–Mar Branch, Jamaica, BBA 29/173.
79. Results, Statistics, and Review of the Period Ending 30 September 1958, Savanna–la–Mar branch, Jamaica, BBA 29/173.
80. Amalgamated Results, Statistics, and Review for all Branches in the Caribbean for the Period Ending 31 March 1958, BBA 29/171.
81. Results, Statistics, and Review of the Period Ending 30 September 1961, Savanna-la-Mar branch, Jamaica, BBA 29/173.

82. Results, Statistics, and Review of the Period Ending 31 March 1961, Harbour Street Branch, Kingston, Jamaica, BBA 29/173.
83. Memorandum Outlining Suggestions for Increasing Revenue, 25 April 1962, BBA 38/252.
84. Board Minutes, 10 April 1958 and 9 October 1958, Board Minute Book no. 9, Barclays Bank (DCO), Board Minute Books, BBA 38/511; Board Minutes, 9 June 1960, 23 March 1961, and 23 August 1962, Board Minute Book no. 10, Barclays Bank DCO, BBA 38/512.
85. Amalgamated Results, Statistics, and Review of the Period Ending 30 September 1962, BBA 29/155.
86. This issue is discussed in chapter 8.
87. Amalgamated Results, Statistics and Review, September 1955, BBA 29/173.

Chapter 8

1. These figures refer only to the number of branches and sub-branches operated by the bank. The number of offices was higher in 1962, since the bank also maintained temporary offices, referred to as agencies. As these offices could be closed and opened whenever circumstances demanded, they are not included in this table. Board Minutes, 27 July 1961, Barclays Bank (DCO) Board Minute Book no. 10, BBA 38/512.
2. Diary of Tours, 28 February 1946, the West Indies and the Bahamas, January to March 1946, BBA 38/907.
3. Results, Statistics, and Review of the Period Ending 31 March 1959, Nassau Branch, Bahamas, BBA 29/175.
4. Board Minutes, 13 August 1953, Barclays Bank (DCO) Board Minute Book no. 8, BBA 38/510; Board Minutes, 6 December 1956, Barclays Bank (DCO) Board Minute Book no. 9, BBA 38/511.
5. Crossley and Blandford, *DCO Story*, 312–14; Board Minutes, 26 February 1953, Barclays Bank (DCO) Board Minute Book no. 7, BBA 38/509.
6. Amalgamated Results, Statistics, and Review for all Branches in the Caribbean Area, for the Period Ending 30 September 1957, BBA 29/171.
7. Barclays Bank (DCO), *The British Caribbean* (London: Barclays Bank (DCO), 1958), 103; Amalgamated Results, Statistics and Review for all Branches in the Caribbean Area for the Period Ending 30 September 1953, BBA 29/173; Board Minutes, 8 November 1951, Barclays Bank (DCO) Board Minute Book no. 7, BBA 38/509; Results, Statistics, and Review of the Period Ending 30 September 1954, Stann Creek Sub-branch, British Honduras, BBA 29/173; Results, Statistics, and Review of the Period Ending 30 September 1959, Belize Branch, British Honduras, BBA 29/175.
8. Board Minutes, 12 April 1951, 25 August 1952, 12 February 1953, Barclays Bank (DCO) Board Minute Book no. 7, BBA 38/509; Amalgamated Results,

Statistics and Review of all the Branches in the Caribbean Area for the Period Ending 30 September 1953, BBA 29/173; Diary of Tours 1957–1960, 17 February 1959, Visit to the West Indies, 9 February to 10 March 1959, BBA 277/2.

9. Brereton, *A History of Modern Trinidad,* 201–4, 216; Diary of Tours January 1946 to February 1949, 23 January 1946, West Indies and Bahamas, January to March 1946, BBA 38/907; Diary of Tours, 17 February 1959, Visit to the West Indies, 9 February to 10 March 1959, BBA 277/2.
10. Board Minutes, 26 March 1953, Barclays Bank (DCO) Board Minute Book no. 7, BBA 38/509.
11. Clarke, *Kingston, Jamaica,* 69–71, 109.
12. *HBJ 1959,* 453; Results, Statistics, and Review of the Period Ending 31 March 1958, Linstead Sub-branch, Jamaica, BBA 29/175.
13. Diary of Tours 1957–1960, 6 March 1959, Visit to the West Indies, 9 February to 10 March 1959, BBA 277/2.
14. *HBJ 1959,* 463.
15. Ibid., 450, 460–64.
16. Diary of Tours 1957–1960, 7 and 8 March 1959, Visit to the West Indies, 9 February to 10 March 1959, BBA 277/2.
17. Amalgamated Results, Statistics, and Review for all Branches in the Caribbean for the Period Ending 30 September 1961, BBA 29/173.
18. Amalgamated Results, Statistics, and Review for all Branches in the Caribbean for the Period Ending 30 September 1954, BBA 29/173; Amalgamated Results, Statistics, and Review for all Branches in the Caribbean for the Period Ending 30 September 1961, BBA 29/173; Augier et al., *The Making of the West Indies,* 286.
19. Brian L. Moore, formerly of the Department of History and Archaeology, University of the West Indies, Mona, now at Colgate University, provided the description of these areas in Guyana in the 1950s.
20. Board Minutes, 25 October 1956, 10 January 1957, Barclays Bank (DCO) Board Minute Book no. 9, BBA 38/511.
21. Board Minutes, 14 March 1957, 13 June 1957, 10 April 1958, Barclays Bank (DCO) Board Minute Book no. 9, BBA 38/511.
22. Results, Statistics, and Review of the Period Ending 30 September 1962, St Kitts branch, BBA 29/192.
23. See Republic Bank Ltd, *From Colonial to Republic,* 121. The agencies established by Barclays Bank (DCO) actually fitted Perry's definition of a sub-branch, which he noted was a small agency operated by a branch; Perry, *A Dictionary of Banking,* 238.
24. See Republic Bank Ltd, *From Colonial to Republic,* 88.
25. Ibid.
26. Results, Statistics, and Review for the Period Ending 30 September 1962, St Kitts branch, BBA 29/192.

27. Board Minutes, 23 July 1953, 8 April 1954, Barclays Bank (DCO) Board Minute Book no. 8, BBA 38/510.
28. See Republic Bank Ltd, *From Colonial to Republic,* 88; Hall "Scotiabank", 27. See also Perry, *A Dictionary of Banking,* 7; Jones, *British Multinational Banking,* 5, 16, 18, 30.
29. Board Minutes, 29 June 1950, 12 April 1951, 14 August 1952, 25 August 1952, 22 October 1953, Barclays Bank (DCO) Board Minute Book no. 7, BBA 38/509; Board Minutes, 22 December 1955, Barclays Bank (DCO) Board Minute Book no. 8, BBA 38/510; Board Minutes, 27 September 1956, 25 October 1956, 22 November 1956, 9 May 1957, 13 June 1957, 26 June 1958, Barclays Bank (DCO) Board Minute Book no. 9, BBA 38/511.
30. Republic Bank Ltd, *From Colonial to Republic,* 121.
31. Results, Statistics and Review for the Period Ending 30 September 1960, St Lucia Branch, BBA 29/193; Results, Statistics and Review for the Period Ending 31 March 1960, St Vincent Branch, BBA 29/193. An agency was established at St Vincent in September 1959, and a branch was re-opened in April 1960.
32. Amalgamated Results, Statistics, and Review for all Branches in the Caribbean for the Period Ending 30 September 1962, BBA 29/173.
33. Amalgamated Results, Statistics, and Review for all Branches in the Caribbean for the Period Ending 30 September 1961, BBA 29/173; Results, Statistics, and Review of the Period Ending 30 September 1958, Half Way Tree Branch, BBA 29/155.
34. Ramesh F. Ramsaran, *The Monetary and Financial System of the Bahamas: Growth, Structure, and Operation* (Kingston: Institute of Social and Economic Research, University of the West Indies, Mona, 1978), 54; Minutes of a discussion held 12 April 1946, West Indies and the Bahamas tour, January to March 1946, Diary of Tours January 1946 to February 1949, BBA 38/907; Bank Surveys, BBA 38/743: 2.
35. Bank Surveys, BBA 38/743: 2.
36. Results, Statistics, and Review of the Period Ending 31 March 1958, Montego Bay Branch, Jamaica, BBA 29/173; Minutes of a discussion held 12 April 1946, West Indies and the Bahamas tour, January to March 1946.
37. Results, Statistics, and Review of the Period Ending 30 September 1959, Nassau Branch, the Bahamas, BBA 29/173; Amalgamated Results, Statistics, and Review for all Branches in the Caribbean for the Period Ending 30 September 1961, BBA 29/173; Ramsaran, *The Monetary and Financial System of the Bahamas,* 54.
38. Ramsaran, *Monetary and Financial System of the Bahamas,* 54.
39. Results, Statistics, and Review of the Period Ending 30 September 1958, Port Maria sub-branch, Jamaica, BBA 29/173.
40. Barclays Bank (Canada) was sold to the Imperial Bank in 1955. See *Daily Gleaner,* 14 October 1955; see also Ackrill and Hannah, *Barclays,* 309.

41. Board Minutes, 26 October 1961, Barclays Bank (DCO) Minute Book no. 11, BBA 38/513. Nevertheless, the link with the CIBC continued, as Barclays Bank (DCO) continued to act as its agent in other overseas territories. See Ackrill and Hannah, *Barclays*, 310.
42. Jones, *British Multinational Banking*, 246–55; 264–65; Results, Statistics, and Review of the Period Ending 30 September 1959, Nassau Branch, the Bahamas, BBA 29/175; Ramsaran, *The Monetary and Financial System of the Bahamas*, 17–25, 54.
43. Amalgamated Results, Statistics, and Review for all the Caribbean Branches for the Period Ending 30 September 1960, BBA 29/155.
44. First National City Bank later became Citibank, and then Citicorp. Results, Statistics, and Review of the Period Ending 30 September 1959, Nassau Branch, the Bahamas, BBA 29/173; Ramsaran, *The Monetary and Financial System of the Bahamas*, 54.
45. Amalgamated Results, Statistics, and Review for all the Caribbean Branches for the Period Ending 30 June 1961, BBA 29/90; Amalgamated Results, Statistics, and Review for all the Caribbean Branches for the Period Ending 31 March 1959, BBA 29/90; Amalgamated Results, Statistics and Review for all the Caribbean Branches for the Period Ending 30 September 1960, BBA 29/155; Harold van B. Cleveland and Thomas F. Huertas, *Citibank 1812–1970* (Cambridge: Harvard University Press, 1985), 264.
46. Results, Statistics, and Review of the Period Ending 30 September 1959, Nassau Branch, the Bahamas, BBA 29/173; Ramsaran, *The Monetary and Financial System of the Bahamas*, 54.
47. Jones, *Evolution of International Business*, 189–90; Jones, *Multinational and International Banking*, xvii.
48. Jones, *British Multinational Banking*, 290.
49. See Thomas F. Huertas, "US Multinational Banking: History and Prospects", in *Banks as Multinationals*, ed. Geoffrey Jones (London: Routledge, 1990), 249–50; Jones, *Multinational and International Banking*, xvi.
50. Diary of Tours, 19 January 1961, BBA 277/2.
51. Huertas, "US Multinational Banking", 250; Cleveland and Huertas, *Citibank*, 264.
52. Results, Statistics, and Review of the Period Ending 31 March 1960, Marsh Harbour, Abaco, Sub-branch, the Bahamas, BBA 29/175; Diary of Tours, 18 January 1960, BBA 38/277.
53. Results, Statistics and Review for the Period Ending 30 September 1958, Brown's Town Sub-branch, Jamaica, BBA 29/173.
54. Results, Statistics and Review for the Period Ending 30 September 1961, Mandeville Branch, Jamaica, BBA 29/173.
55. General Comments by A.C. Barnes, Visit to the Bahamas, Jamaica, Grand Cayman, and British Honduras, December 1957 to January 1958, BBA 38/907.

56. Bank Surveys, BBA 38/743: 2.
57. Crossley Diaries, 23 March 1948, BBA 38/209.
58. Bank Surveys, BBA 38/743: 2, 3. The other banks in the Bahamas also utilized this strategy, routing their business through Guaranty Trust Co. of New York, Hanover Bank, the Hong Kong and Shanghai Banking Corporation, Manufacturers Trust Co., Martin's Bank Ltd, Midland Bank Ltd, the National Provincial Bank Ltd, Westminster Bank Ltd, and the William Deacon's Bank Ltd.
59. General Comments by A.C. Barnes, Visit to the Bahamas, Jamaica, Grand Cayman, and British Honduras, December 1957 to January 1958, BBA 38/907.
60. Richardson, "Caribbean Migrations", 216; Results, Statistics, and Review of the Period Ending 30 September 1961, Mandeville Branch, BBA 29/173.
61. Results, Statistics, and Review of the Period Ending 30 September, Savanna-la-Mar Branch, Jamaica, BBA 29/173; Results, Statistics, and Review of the Period Ending 30 September 1958, Port Maria Sub-branch, Jamaica, BBA 29/173; Results, Statistics, and Review of the Period Ending 30 September 1958, Spanish Town Sub-branch, Jamaica, BBA 29/173; Results, Statistics, and Review of the Period Ending 30 September 1960, St Lucia Branch, BBA 29/173; Results, Statistics, and Review of the Period Ending 30 September 1960, St Vincent Branch, BBA 29/173.
62. Bank Surveys, BBA 38/742: 3; Diary of Tours 1957–1960, 25 February 1959, Visit to New Amsterdam Branch, British Guiana, BBA 277/2.
63. Results, Statistics, and Review for the Period Ending 31 March 1961 and 30 September 1961, Mandeville Branch, Jamaica, BBA 29/173.
64. Results, Statistics, and Review for the Period Ending, 31 March 1961, Cross Roads Branch, Jamaica, BBA 29/173.
65. Board Minutes, 11 January 1951, 12 April 1951, 10 May 1951, Barclays Bank (DCO) Board Minute Book no. 7, BBA 38/509; Board Minutes, 14 May 1953, 25 June 1953, 13 August 1953, 10 September 1953, 11 March 1954, 24 June 1954, 22 July 1954, 12 August 1954, 11 November 1954, 23 December 1954, Barclays Bank (DCO) Board Minute Book no. 8, BBA 38/510; Board Minutes, 12 June 1956, Barclays Bank (DCO) Board Minute Book no. 9, BBA 38/511.
66. Results, Statistics, and Review for the Period Ending 31 March 1961, Half Way Tree Branch, Jamaica, BBA 29/173.
67. Diary of Tours 1957–1960, 4 March 1959, BBA 277/2.
68. *Daily Gleaner*, 31 March 1955.
69. Republic Bank Ltd, *From Colonial to Republic,* 125; Amalgamated Results, Statistics, and Review for all Branches in the Caribbean for the Period Ending 31 March 1962, BBA 29/90.
70. The parent bank, Barclays Bank Ltd, had introduced adding machines in its Lombard Street office in London as early as 1914 and had expanded their use during the 1920s. Nevertheless, as pointed out by Ackrill and Hannah, in

terms of mechanization, Barclays even then was far behind its counterparts in Germany and America. See Ackrill and Hannah, *Barclays*, 77.
71. Amalgamated Results, Statistics, and Review of all the Caribbean Branches for the Period Ending 30 September 1962, BBA 29/155.
72. Results, Statistics and Review of the Period Ending 30 September 1961, King Street Branch, Jamaica, BBA 29/155.
73. Ibid.; Results, Statistics, and Review of the Period Ending 31 March 1961, Half Way Tree Branch, Jamaica, BBA 29/155.
74. Results, Statistics, and Review of the Period Ending 31 March 1961, King Street branch, Jamaica, BBA 29/155.
75. Diary of Tours, 17 January 1961, BBA 277/2.
76. Results, Statistics, and Review of the Period Ending 31 March 1961, Linstead Sub-branch, Jamaica, BBA 29/155.
77. Results, Statistics, and Review of the Period Ending 30 September 1953, Nassau Branch, the Bahamas, BBA 29/173 .
78. Miller, *Commercial Banking in Jamaica*, 184–86.
79. Results, Statistics, and Review of the Period Ending 30 September 1953, Nassau Branch, the Bahamas, BBA 29/173.
80. Miller, *Commercial Banking in Jamaica*, 184–86.
81. Amalgamated Results, Statistics, and Review for the Period Ending 30 September 1957, BBA 29/192.
82. *Bank of Jamaica, Report and Statement of Accounts for the Year Ended 31 December, 1963* (Kingston: Government of Jamaica, 1964), 6; Miller, *Commercial Banking in Jamaica*, 186–87. The Bankers' Committee consisted of the representatives of all the commercial banks and was chaired by the governor of the central bank. The stated function of the committee was to facilitate the exchange of views on general banking policy.
83. Girvan, *Foreign Capital*, 186.
84. Results, Statistics, and Review of the Period Ending September 30, 1954, Springlands Sub-branch, British Guiana, BBA 29/173.
85. Survey of the Bank's Business, BBA 38/743: 4.
86. Ibid.
87. See table 7.8 in chapter 7.
88. International Departments, general managers' office, BBA 11/551.
89. Callender, *Capital Market Institutions*, 133, 141, 165.
90. Board Minutes, 26 February 1953, Barclays Bank (DCO) Board Minute Book no. 7, BBA 38/509; Board Minutes, 9 July 1953, 8 December 1955, Barclays Bank (DCO) Board Minute Book no. 8, BBA 38/510.
91. Board Minutes, 24 May 1962, Barclays Bank (DCO) Board Minute Book no. 11, BBA 38/513. Barclays (Trinidad) Nominees Co. Ltd was established in 1960; Board Minutes, 8 June 1950, 24 January 1952, Barclays Bank (DCO) Board Minute Book no. 7, BBA 38/509; Crossley and Blandford, *DCO Story*, 312.

92. Perry, *A Dictionary of Banking*, 164.
93. Ramsaran, *The Monetary and Financial System of the Bahamas*, 251.
94. Board Minutes, 12 July 1956, Barclays Bank (DCO) Board Minute Book no. 9, BBA 38/511.
95. Board Minutes, 10 January 1957, 24 January 1957, Barclays Bank (DCO) Board Minute Book no. 9, BBA 38/511. H. Dale, a local director for the West Indies, and R.K.S. Gonsalves, manager of the Nassau branch, were made directors of the BITCO Ltd. D.A. Wright and H. Rivington, who were appointed managers in BITCO Ltd, were previously assistant manager in the King Street branch in Jamaica, and manager of the trustee department in the main branch at Port of Spain, Trinidad, respectively.
96. Board Minutes, 27 February 1958, Barclays Bank (DCO) Board Minute Book no. 9, BBA 38/511.
97. Ramsaran, *The Monetary and Financial System of the Bahamas*, 251–53.
98. Board Minutes, 24 January 1957, Barclays Bank (DCO) Board Minute Book no. 9, BBA 38/511.
99. Frances Bostock, "The British Overseas Banks and Development Finance in Africa after 1945", *Business History* 33, no. 3 (July 1991): 160.
100. See Post, *Arise Ye Starvelings*, 325–42.
101. D.J. Morgan, *The Official History of Colonial Development*, vol. 1, *The Origins of British Aid Policy 1924–1945* (London: Macmillan, 1980), 30–31.
102. In 1942 a Colonial Research Committee was established in the Colonial Office to examine colonial economic development. This was followed by the establishment, in 1943, of the Colonial Economic Advisory Committee, whose function it was to advise the Secretary of State for the Colonies on matters of general economic policy, particularly with regard to programmes of economic development. See Bostock, "The British Overseas Banks", 160.
103. Ibid; Jones, *British Multinational Banking*, 302; W.A. Lewis, 1 June 1946, 16 August 1944, CO 852/554/1.
104. Bostock, "The British Overseas Banks", 161; A. Emmanuel, 5 October 1944, reporting on a meeting attended by Julian Crossley, S. Caine, W.A. Lewis, G. Lamb and other officials in the Colonial Office, CO 852/554/1.
105. Emmanuel, 5 October 1944, CO 852/554/1.
106. Bostock, "The British Overseas Banks", 161.
107. Jefferson, *The Post-War Economic Development of Jamaica*, 126.
108. Crossley and Blandford, *DCO Story*, 140.
109. Essays submitted by G.G. Money, LHO, Nairobi; R.G. Dyson, Nairobi branch, and T. Basset, Palestine, BBA 28/196. See Ackrill and Hannah, *Barclays*, 279.
110. Bostock, "The British Overseas Banks", 163; Report of the Directors with Statement of Accounts Presented at Ordinary General Meeting, 28 December 1945, Accounts and Board Meeting Papers, BBA 38/251; Report of

111. Bostock, "The British Overseas Banks", 163.
112. Ibid., 162.
113. Ibid., 167.
114. Report of the Directors with Statement of Accounts Presented at Ordinary General Meeting, 30 September 1949, Accounts and Board Meeting Papers, BBA 251.
115. Bostock, "The British Overseas Banks", 167.
116. Report of the Directors with Statement of Accounts Presented at Ordinary General Meeting, 28 December 1945, Accounts and Board Meeting Papers, BBA 38/251.
117. The Jamaica Agricultural Loan Societies Board was appointed in 1912 to encourage the formation and work of agricultural loan societies, which were registered as the People's Cooperative Banks. The board made advances available through the cooperative banks from the Agricultural Credit Revolving Fund that was created in 1944. See *HBJ 1946*, 299.
118. Diary of Tours 1946–1949, 11 April 1946, 15 April 1946, Visits to the West Indies and the Bahamas, BBA 38/907.
119. Ibid.

Chapter 9

1. Patrick Bryan, "Proletarian Movements (1940–90)" in Brereton, *The Caribbean in the Twentieth Century*, 141–73, 150; Millette, "Decolonization", 185–88.
2. Douglas Hall, *The Caribbean Experience: An Historical Survey 1450–1960* (Kingston: Heinemann, 1982), 124; Millette, "Decolonization", 185. See also Fe Iglesias Garcia, "Demographic and Social Structural Changes in the Contemporary Caribbean", in Brereton, *The Caribbean in the Twentieth Century*, 411.
3. Crossley and Blandford, *DCO Story*, 179–80. In addition to the humorous phrases "Debits, Credits and Overdrafts" and "Don't Come and Overdraw" coined by both customers and bank staff, the abbreviation featured in a political demonstration outside the bank's London offices in 1971, in the phrase "Defenders of Colonial Oppression". The name was eventually changed in 1972 to Barclays Bank International Ltd. See George Money, *Nine Lives of a Bush Banker* (London: Merlin Books, 1990), 13.
4. The figures after 1954 do not include the staff employed in the Bahamas, as that section was placed under the direct control of the London head office in 1955. Amalgamated Results, Statistics, and Review of all the Branches in the Caribbean for the Period Ending 30 September 1956, BBA 29/155.

5. Jones, *British Multinational Banking*, 49–50, 171; Ackrill and Hannah, *Barclays*, 74–76.
6. Jones, *British Multinational Banking*, 51.
7. Ibid., 315–19; McDowall, *Quick to the Frontier*, 89–91.
8. Jones, *British Multinational Banking*, 51; McDowall, *Quick to the Frontier*, 89–91.
9. Jones, *British Multinational Banking*, 52.
10. Ibid., 316.
11. Ibid., 218.
12. Maurice Clarke, interview by author, Kingston, Jamaica, 9 January 1995. Clarke, a Jamaican, was employed at Barclays Bank (DCO) in 1959. Between 1973 and 1975 he was manager of Barclays Finance Corporation. Following the Jamaica government's acquisition of the bank, in 1977 he was appointed general manager of the renamed National Commercial Bank.
13. Money, *Nine Lives*, 268; See Brereton, *A History of Modern Trinidad*, 126–30; Brereton, "Society and Culture", 90–91; Bryan, *The Jamaican People*, 216–38.
14. Brereton, "Society and Culture", 93–94.
15. Ibid.
16. Money, *Nine Lives*, 268; Eldon Forrest, interview by author, Kingston, Jamaica, 26 November 2003; Crossley Diaries, 3 January 1951, BBA38/209.
17. Money, *Nine Lives*, 268–69. Money's appointments before the West Indies included those in Libya and Ethiopia. His father, Sir Arthur Money, was a former director of the Anglo-Egyptian Bank. Crossley and Blandford, *DCO Story*, 181.
18. Money, *Nine Lives*, 268; Barclays Bank International, *Barclays Bank in the Caribbean*, 17, 21, 24; Bank of Nova Scotia (Jamaica) Ltd, *Scotiabank in Jamaica*. See also *Who's Who In Jamaica, 1951* (Kingston: Who's Who [Jamaica] Ltd, 1951); G. F. Sharp, comp., *Barbados Year Book Who's Who, 1935* (Barbados: Advocate Press, 1935), 335; "Jim Whiting: A Career Began in 1916", *Jamaican Eagle*, Barclays Bank Staff Newsletter 2, no. 7 (1975): 6.
19. *Who's Who: Jamaica, West Indies, 1957* (Kingston: Who's Who [Jamaica] Ltd, 1957), 17, 425.
20. Ibid., 425.
21. "Jim Whiting", 6. Whiting began his banking career in the Harbour Street branch in 1916. Seven months later he was transferred to the Port Maria branch in the parish of St Mary, where he was located for three years. In 1919, after being officially "put on staff", he was sent to the Port Antonio branch as acting manager, and later to the May Pen branch to relieve the manager there who was ill for a week. In 1931, after being promoted to sub-accountant, he was appointed as the Receiver of James Charley's Estates. In 1936 he was appointed accountant in the Harbour Street branch, before being sent to Dominica in 1947 and Trinidad in 1952, returning to Kingston in 1955, and retiring two and a half years later.

22. *Daily Gleaner*, 31 March 1955.
23. Colin A. Palmer, "Identity, Race, and Black Power in Independent Jamaica", in Knight and Palmer, *The Modern Caribbean*, 114; Augusta Payne, interview by author, Kingston, Jamaica, 11 January 1995; Hartley Neita, "Emancipating Ourselves from Colour Inferiority", *Sunday Gleaner*, 23 February 1997.
24. *Daily Gleaner*, 13 May 1950.
25. Edna Ramsey, interview by author, Kingston, Jamaica, 7 July 2003; "Remarks by Eldon Forrest at Long Service Awards Function, National Commercial Bank, Kingston Jamaica", Forest's personal files.
26. Forrest, interview.
27. Crossley Diaries, 3 January 1951, BBA 38/209
28. Payne, interview; Donald Banks, interview by author, Kingston, Jamaica, 18 January 1995; Forrest, interview.
29. *Daily Gleaner*, 19 August 1967.
30. Banks, interview. The remark was "Am I in a f——g laundry?!!"
31. Ibid; see also *The Jamaica Directory of Personalities, 1992–93* (Kingston: Selecto Publications, 1993), 15–16. Donald A. Banks, a Jamaican, joined the staff as a junior "waste clerk" at the Harbour Street branch in January 1952, shortly after leaving the Wolmer's Boys School in Kingston. As a waste clerk, he was responsible for the posting of the savings ledgers and the preparation of ledger sheets and statements. While still at Harbour Street in 1954, he did short stints as the cashier at an agency run by the bank at Linstead three times a week. In 1955, he was assigned to the King Street branch, where he worked in various departments. While there he did short stints as the relief accountant at the West Queen Street branch. In 1962 he was made a supervisor of junior staff before receiving his first managerial post in the Duke Street branch in Kingston in 1964. Between 1968 and 1969 he was appointed as assistant to the local director in the Eastern Caribbean Local Head Office in Barbados, and then between 1969 and 1970 as local director's assistant in the Western Caribbean Local Head Office in Jamaica. In 1970 he was appointed manager of the King Street branch, following which he became the director of the Western Caribbean Local Head Office in 1972. In the same year Banks was appointed deputy managing director of Barclays Bank (Jamaica) Ltd. He subsequently became managing director in 1977, following the sale of the bank's assets in Jamaica to the Jamaican government, whereupon it was renamed the National Commercial Bank, or the NCB, as it is often called. Banks held this post until his retirement in 1990.
32. Forrest, interview. Forrest recalls that of the Royal Bank of Canada in Jamaica in the 1950s. After a series of interviews Eldon Forrest, a graduate of Kingston College, was engaged to Barclays Bank (DCO) on 7 August 1952. He entered at the position of junior clerk with his main duties being "outdoor" – going to the post office three times a day, as well as filing and clearing, before

being elevated to cashiering. He received his "B" signature on 27 August 1956 and the "A" signature on 11 March 1960. Forrest was also posted in the United Kingdom as the bank's liaison officer for eighteen months to encourage the opening of accounts by West Indian immigrants, and sent on training courses to branches in the United Kingdom and Hamburg, Germany. In 1964, Forrest was appointed to the position of supervisor of junior staff, and assistant resident instructor, Jamaica. In this new role, Forrest was responsible for recruiting all staff to the Kingston branches and for their welfare and training during the first two years of their appointment. He was also responsible for organizing and instructing on all courses held in Jamaica. Forrest also acted in several positions within the bank: sub-manager for several branches; accountant at the Harbour Street branch in 1970; manager at the Windward Road branch in 1973; manager at the Newport West branch in 1974; credit officer in the head office in 1975. Forrest also worked in the business advisory service of the National Commercial Bank. In 1986, he was appointed senior assistant inspector in the Inspection Department, and later appointed inspector. In April 1991 he was appointed assistant general manager of personnel. *NCB: The National Banker*, National Commercial Bank Newsletter (October 1992); appointment letter, 14 May 1964, from Henry Dale, local director, Barbados, to Eldon Forrest, Kings Street branch, Forrest's personal files.

33. Diary of Tours December 1957 to January 1961, Visits to the West Indies, 9 February to 10 March 1959, BBA 277/2.
34. Money, *Nine Lives*, 269; George Money, interview by author, Hastings, Barbados, 21 July 2003.
35. Payne, interview; Money, interview.
36. Ibid. See also *Jamaican Eagle*, Barclays Bank Staff Newsletter 1, no. 19 (1974): 2.
37. Ibid; See Brereton, "Society and Culture", 90, 91.
38. Jones, *British Multinational Banking*, 218–19, 315–16.
39. General Comments by A.C. Barnes, BBA 38/907.
40. Ibid.
41. Board Minutes, 26 July 1951, Barclays Bank (DCO) Board Minute Book no. 7, BBA 38/509.
42. McDowall, *Quick to the Frontier*, 121; Ackrill and Hannah, *Barclays*, 77.
43. McDowall, *Quick to the Frontier*, 100–101; A.W. Tuke, chairman of Barclays Bank Ltd, addressing shareholders in 1954, commented that "no self-respecting man likes to think his wife is obliged to work outside the home to help keep the home together". See Ackrill and Hannah, *Barclays*, 345.
44. Barclays Bank International, *Barclays Bank in the Caribbean*, 17–19.
45. Ibid., 19.
46. Money, *Nine Lives*, 268.
47. Barclays Bank International, *Barclays Bank in the Caribbean*, 17.

48. Board Minutes, 11 July 1946, Barclays Bank (DCO) Board Minute Book no. 5, BBA 38/507.
49. Confirmation Letter of Appointment from manager, Barclays Bank (Dominion, Colonial and Overseas), to Eldon Forest, 7 August 1952, Forrest's personal file.
50. Payne, interview.
51. General Comments by A.C. Barnes, BBA 38/907; Amalgamated Results, Statistics, and Review of all the Branches in the Caribbean for the Periods Ending 30 September 1954, 1961, and 1962, BBA 29/155.
52. Ackrill and Hannah, *Barclays*, 344.
53. Amalgamated Results, Statistics, and Review of all the Branches in the Caribbean for the Period Ending 30 September 1954, BBA 29/155.
54. General Comments by A.C. Barnes, BBA 38/907.
55. Ibid.
56. Amalgamated Results, Statistics, and Review of all the Branches in the Caribbean for the Periods Ending 30 September 1954 and 30 September 1955, BBA 29/155.
57. Payne, interview. See also *Jamaican Eagle,* Barclays Bank Staff Newsletter 1, no. 19 (1974): 2.
58. "The First DCO", *Barclays Caribbean Bulletin* (Summer 1968): 502–3.
59. Eldon Forrest, "Au Revoir: Mrs. Dorothy Eve Reid, Pace Setter", *NCB: The National Banker* (March 1989): 16.
60. Money assumed the more senior position in the directorship following Dale's appointment. Report of the Directors with Statement of Accounts presented at Ordinary General Meeting, 30 September 1952, Accounts and Board Meeting Papers, BBA 38/251; Crossley and Blandford, *DCO Story,* 180–81.
61. Report of the Directors with Statement of Accounts presented at Ordinary General Meeting, 30 September 1952, Accounts and Board Meeting Papers, BBA 38/251; Crossley and Blandford, *DCO Story,* 30, 180–81.
62. Board Minutes, 24 February 1927, Barclays Bank (Dominion, Colonial and Overseas) Board Minute Book no. 1, BBA 38/503.
63. Board Minutes, 26 November 1925, Barclays Bank (Dominion, Colonial and Overseas) Board Minute Book no. 1, BBA 38/503.
64. Ibid.
65. Ibid.
66. Jones, *British Multinational Banking,* 151. For example, the South African local board was permitted to sanction proposals for renewals of existing limits for direct facilities in excess of £50,000, but proposals for new business involving direct facilities in excess of that amount had to be referred to London except in cases of emergency.
67. Board Minutes, 26 November 1925, Barclays Bank (DCO) Board Minute Book no. 1, BBA 38/503.

68. Jones, *British Multinational Banking*, 48; Jones, "The Legacy of the Past", 163.
69. Minutes of a discussion held in the chairman's room re A.C. Barnes's notes on his visit to the West Indies, 12 April 1946, Diary of Tours January to March 1946 West Indies and the Bahamas, BBA 38/907.
70. Ibid.
71. Ibid.
72. Board Minutes, 27 August 1953, Barclays Bank (DCO) Board Minute Book no. 8, BBA 38/510.
73. Ibid; Report of the Directors with Statement of Accounts presented at Ordinary General Meeting, 30 September 1952, Accounts and Board Meeting Papers, BBA 38/251; Crossley and Blandford, *DCO Story*, 180–81.

Bibliography

Barclays Bank Plc. Archives, Manchester, UK

Barclays Bank (Dominion, Colonial and Overseas) Records

The main primary sources for this book are the Barclays Bank (Dominion, Colonial and Overseas) records. A work such as this would have benefited from the Canadian banks' archives, but numerous requests went unheeded. The reliance on a single company source does impose some degree of limitation. Nevertheless, a fair amount of the Barclays Bank (DCO) records do throw light on the position and operations of the Canadian banks, while the secondary literature on these banks and the Colonial Office records provide for a balanced assessment.

The bank records used are varied and include the asset and liability records for branches in the West Indies for the period 1926–34. These provide useful information on the operations of individual branches, agencies and sub-branches, and reflect much of the business transactions and performance of the bank in British Guiana, Jamaica, Trinidad and Tobago, and Barbados. Unfortunately, they do not extend beyond 1934 or to the other territories in the region.

The Profit and (Loss) Account papers relate to the worldwide territorial sections of the bank's operations, and cover the period 1926 to 1962. This account is basically a ledger account to which balances reflecting revenue and expenses are periodically transferred. It is therefore a repository of any gain or loss. In the case of banks, these accounts reflect the gross profits made from the normal course of banking transactions, along with unusual items of gain from sources other than those associated with the normal course of business. Therefore, these accounts are essentially the operating profits and losses of the bank. In this book, the profit and loss accounts for the period ending 30 September of each year were used, since that date marked the end of the bank's financial year. These records are useful, as they provide an indication of the overall profitability of the various territorial sections for each year, allowing for a long-term perspective on the West Indian Section's performance in relation to the other territorial sections and the bank as a whole. Other accounting papers include those of the Barclays Overseas Development Corporation Ltd. Unfortunately, detailed records begin in 1951 and continue through to 1961, with the exception of 1958 and 1959.

Bibliography

The bank's board minute books are also very informative and cover the entire period, affording a fair perspective of the evolution of operations of the bank in the region from 1926 to 1962. The Loans and Advances registers also cover the entire period.

BBA 11/84 Returns of £10,000 and Over, Colonial Bank.

BBA 11/197 West Indian Business, 1926–1934.

BBA 11/551 International Departments. General Managers' Office.

BBA 11/556 Central Board. Analysis of Loans and Advances, September 1948 and 1949.

BBA 28/196 Essays Submitted by G.G. Money, LHO, Nairobi, R.G. Dyson, Nairobi Branch and T. Basset, Palestine.

BBA 29/192; BBA 29/193; BBA 29/173; BBA 29/175 Results, Statistics, and Review of the Period Ending March 31, and September 30 Branch Reports (for the years 1953 to 1962).

BBA 29/90; BBA 29/192; BBA 29/193; BBA 29/171; BBA 29/173; BBB 29/155 Amalgamated Results, Statistics, and Review for all Branches in the Caribbean of the Period Ending September 30 (for the years 1953 to 1962).

BBA 38/76 Colonial Bank Act, 1925.

BBA 38/202 West Indian Branches, 1926–1934.

BBA 38/209 Sir Julian Crossley Diaries, 1942–1951.

BBA 38/251 Accounts and Board Meeting Papers, Boxes A, B, and C.

BBA 38/252 Memorandum Outlining Suggestions for Increasing Revenue, 1962.

BBA 38/351 Report of the Directors with Statement of Accounts Presented at Ordinary General Meeting of Stockholders, 1926–1962.

BBA 38/503–BBA 38/513 Barclays Bank (Dominion, Colonial and Overseas) Board Minute Books, nos. 1–11.

BBA 38/742 Bank Surveys.

BBA 38/743 Survey of the Bank's Business.

BBA 38/907 Diary of Tours. Visits to the West Indies and the Bahamas, January 1946 to February 1949; Visits to the Bahamas, Jamaica, Grand Cayman, and British Honduras by A.C. Barnes, December 1957–January 1958.

BBA 38/983 Bank Essay Competition, 1943.

BBA 80/668 Central Board Register. Colonial Advances. Applications for Limits of £20,000 and Over.

BBA 80/689 Barclays Bank (Dominion, Colonial and Overseas) London Committee, Colonial Bank Register.

BBA 80/700 Central Board Register. Colonial Advances.

BBA 80/743 Barclays Bank (Dominion, Colonial and Overseas) Central Board, 1933.

BBA 80/767 Colonial and Anglo-Egyptian Advances. Assistant General Managers Office.

BBA 80/783 Barclays Bank (Dominion, Colonial and Overseas). Central Board Register. Colonial Bank Advances, Anglo-Egyptian Advances, and East African Advances.

BBA 80/787 Barclays Bank (Dominion, Colonial and Overseas). Central Board Register. Colonial Bank Advances, Anglo-Egyptian Advances, and East African Advances, 10 January–11 July 1935.

BBA 277/2 Diary of Tours. Visits to the West Indies, December 1957 to January 1961.

Colonial Office Records

Public Records Office, London

CO 318, CO 319 West Indian Files.
CO 137, CO 323 General Files.
CO 852 Economic Files.
CO 31/132, CO 31/128 Barbados. Administration Reports, 1942–1945.
CO 140/298 Jamaica. Administration Reports, 1942–1945.
CO 298/183 Trinidad. Administration Reports, 1939–1945.
CO 852, CO 884 Economic Files.

Government Publications

Annual Report on the Cooperative Credit Banks for the Year 1945 (Georgetown: Argosy Co. Ltd, 1946).

Annual Report on Jamaica. For the Year 1947. London: His Majesty's Stationery Office, 1948.

Bank of Jamaica, Report and Statement of Accounts for the Year Ended 31 December 1961. Kingston: Bank of Jamaica, 1962.

Bank of Jamaica, Report and Statement of Accounts for the Year ended 31 December, 1963. Kingston: Bank of Jamaica, 1964.

Barbados. Report for the Years 1956 and 1957. London: Her Majesty's Stationery Office, 1959.

Barbados. Report for the Years 1960 and 1961. London: Her Majesty's Stationery Office, 1962.

British Caribbean Currency Board. Report of the Executive Commissioner for 1957. Port of Spain: Government Printing Office, 1957.

British Guiana, Report of the Commissioners of Currency for the Year 1937. Georgetown, Demerara, 1937.

Caribbean Commission. Port of Spain: Central Secretariat, 1957.

Central Statistical Office. *Annual Statistical Digest no. 12, 1962.* Government of Trinidad and Tobago, 1962.

Colonial Annual Reports. Barbados, 1947. London: His Majesty's Stationery Office, 1947.

Colonial Report. Annual. British Guiana. 1938. London: His Majesty's Stationery Office, 1940.

Colonial Annual Report. British Guiana, 1946. London: His Majesty's Stationery Office, 1948.

Colonial Office. *An Economic Survey of the Colonial Territories, 1951.* London: Her Majesty's Stationery Office, 1952.

Commission of Enquiry on the Sugar Industry of Jamaica, 1959–1960. Kingston: Government Printing Office, 1961.

Commonwealth Economic Committee. *Plantation Crops. A Summary of Figures of Production, Trade, and Consumption relating to Sugar, Tea, Coffee, Cocoa, Spices, Tobacco, and Rubber.* (For various years between 1950 and 1963). London: Her Majesty's Stationery Office.

An Economic Survey of the Colonial Empire (1932). London: His Majesty's Stationery Office, 1933.

Handbook of Jamaica (for various years between 1910 and 1963). Kingston: Government Printing Office.

Jamaica Gazette Supplement. Proclamations, Rules, and Regulations 84, no. 35 (1 May 1961).

Jamaica Gazette Supplement. Proclamations, Rules, and Regulations 84, no. 66 (20 July 1961).

The Jamaica Gazette Supplement. Bills and Laws 81, no. 10 (13 March 1958).

Production and Trade of the British West Indies, British Guiana, Bermuda, and British Honduras. London: His Majesty's Stationery Office, 1934.

Report of the Banks' Committee of the Local Government Board on the Cooperative Credit Banks Established in the Colony (for various years between 1927 and 1938). Georgetown: Argosy Co. Ltd.

Report on Jamaica (Annual) (for years 1939 to 1959). Kingston: Government Printer.

Report on Jamaica, 1961. Kingston: Government Public Relations Department.

Report of the Sugar Industry Commission, Jamaica, 1944–1945. Kingston, Jamaica, 1945.

Report of the Commission Appointed to Enquire into the Organization of the Sugar Industry in Antigua. London: Crown Agents of the Colonies on behalf of the Government of Antigua, 1949.

Report of the Commission Appointed to Enquire into the Working of the Sugar Industry in Trinidad. Trinidad: Government Printer, 1948.

Report of the West Indies Currency Committee. London: His Majesty's Stationery Office, 1923.

Trade Regulations and Commercial Policies of the United Kingdom. London: Cambridge University Press, 1943.

Newspapers and Magazines

Daily Gleaner, January–December 1926; 13 May 1950; March 1955; October 1955.
Sunday Gleaner, 23 February 1997.

Barclays Bank Review 26, no. 2 (May 1951).
Barclays Caribbean Bulletin (Summer 1968).
Jamaican Eagle. Barclays Bank Staff Newsletter 2, no. 7 (1975).
NCB: The National Banker. National Commercial Bank Newsletter, March 1989.

Annuals

Barclays Bank DCO. *The Bahamas. An Economic Survey, 1960.* Bridgetown: Local Head Office, Barclays Bank DCO, 1960.
———. *The Bahamas. An Economic Survey, 1962.* Bridgetown: Local Head Office, Barclays Bank DCO, 1962.
———. *Barbados. An Economic Survey, 1958.* Bridgetown: Local Head Office, Barclays Bank DCO, 1958.
———. *Barbados. An Economic Survey, 1960.* Bridgetown: Local Head Office, Barclays Bank DCO, 1960.
———. *The British Caribbean.* London: Barclays Bank (DCO), 1958. *Barclays Bank Review* 26, no. 2 (May 1951).
———. *The Cayman Islands. An Economic Survey, 1960.* Bridgetown: Local Head Office, Barclays Bank DCO, 1960.
———. *Trinidad. An Economic Survey, 1962.* Bridgetown: Local Head Office, Barclays Bank DCO, 1962.
The Booker Group. Review of the Year 1962. London: Booker Brothers, McConnell and Co. Ltd, 1962.
The Jamaica Directory of Personalities, 1992–93. Kingston: Selecto Publications, 1993.
Royal Bank of Canada. Annual Report. Report of The Proceedings at Annual General Meetings of Shareholders, 1953–1962. Montreal: Royal Bank of Canada.
The West Indies and Caribbean Year Book (for various years between 1951 and 1956). London: Thomas Skinner.
The West Indies Year Book, 1936. Montreal: Thomas Skinner, 1936.
The West Indies Year Book, 1947–48. London: Thomas Skinner, 1948.
Who's Who in Jamaica, 1951. Kingston: Who's Who (Jamaica) Ltd, 1951.
Who's Who. Jamaica, West Indies, 1957. Kingston: Who's Who (Jamaica) Ltd, 1957.
The Yearbook of the Bermudas, the Bahamas, British Guiana, and the British West Indies (for various years between 1922 and 1963). London: Thomas Skinner.
The Windward Islands (for various years between 1954 and 1961).

Books and Articles

Ackrill, Margaret, and Leslie Hannah. *Barclays: The Business of Banking, 1690–1996.* Cambridge: Cambridge University Press, 2001.
Adamson, Alan. *Sugar without Slaves: The Political Economy of British Guiana, 1838–1900.* New Haven: Yale University Press, 1972.

Allen, H.M., S.R. Cope and H.J. Witheridge. *Commercial Banking Legislation and Control*. London: Macmillan, 1938.

Albert, Bill, and Adrian Graves, eds. *The World Sugar Economy in War and Depression 1914–1940*. London: Routledge, 1988.

Aldcroft, Derek H. *From Versailles to Wall Street, 1919–1929*. London: Penguin Books, 1977, 1987.

Analyst. "Currency And Banking In Jamaica". *Social and Economic Studies* 1, no. 4 (August 1953): 41–53.

Anderson, Robert, ed. *The St Vincent Handbook, 1938*. Kingstown: The Vincentian, 1938.

Armstrong, W.E. "Island 'Checks' and the Advent of Commercial Banks in Jamaica, 1819–1888". Seminar paper, University of the West Indies, Cave Hill, 1982.

Ashworth, William. *A Short History of the International Economy since 1850*. London: Longman, 1987.

Augier, F.R., S.C. Gordon, D.G. Hall and M. Reckord. *The Making of the West Indies*. London: Longman, 1960, 2002.

Bank of Nova Scotia (Jamaica) Ltd. *Scotiabank in Jamaica: A Century of Progress 1889–1989*. Kingston: Bank of Nova Scotia (Jamaica) Ltd, 1989.

Baptiste, Fitzroy. "The Exploitation of Caribbean Bauxite and Petroleum, 1914–1945". *Social and Economic Studies* 37, nos. 1 and 2 (March–June 1988): 107–42.

Barbados Year Book and Who's Who, 1934. Barbados: Advocate Press, 1934.

Barclays Bank (Dominion, Colonial and Overseas). *Report of Ordinary General Meeting, 1929–1936*. London: Barclays Bank (Dominion, Colonial and Overseas), 1937.

Barclays Bank DCO. *Overseas Trade, 1958: Covering the Trade and Economic Conditions Which Prevailed in the Year 1957 in the Overseas Territories in Which the Barclays Group of Banks Is Represented*. Barclays Bank DCO, 1958.

———. *The British Caribbean*. London: Barclays Bank DCO, 1958.

Barclays Bank Ltd. *A Banking Centenary: A History of Barclays Bank (Dominion, Colonial and Overseas) 1836–1936*. Plymouth: W. Brendon and Sons, 1938.

———. *A Bank in Battledress: Being the Story of Barclays Bank (Dominion, Colonial and Overseas) during the Second World War, 1939–1945*. London: Williams, Lea and Co., 1948.

Barclays Bank Plc. *Barclays Bank in the Caribbean*. London: Barclays Bank Plc, 1991.

Bareau, Paul. "The Sterling Area". In *Banking in the British Commonwealth*, edited by R.S. Sayers, 460–75. Oxford: Clarendon Press, 1952.

Barrow, Christine. "Ownership and Control of Resources in Barbados: 1834 to the Present". *Social and Economic Studies* 32, no. 3 (September 1983): 83–120.

———. "Meetings: Group Savings Arrangement in Barbados". *African Studies Association of the West Indies Bulletin* 8: 32–40.

Baster, A.S.J. *The Imperial Banks*. London: King, 1929.
———. *The International Banks*. London: King, 1935.
Baum, Daniel Jay. *The Banks of Canada in the Commonwealth Caribbean: Economic Nationalism and Multinational Enterprises of a Medium Power*. New York: Praeger, 1974.
Baumol, William, John C. Panzar and Robert D. Willig, eds. *Contestable Markets and the Theory of Industry Structure*. San Diego: Harcourt Brace Jovanovich, 1982, 1988.
Beachy, R.W. *The British West Indian Sugar Industry in the Late Nineteenth Century*. Cambridge: Cambridge University Press, 1957.
Beckford, George. *The West Indian Banana Industry*. Kingston: Institute of Social and Economic Research, University of the West Indies, Mona, 1967.
———. *Persistent Poverty: Underdevelopment in Plantation Economies of the Third World*. New York: Oxford University Press, 1972.
Beckles, Hilary. *A History of Barbados: From Amerindian Settlement to Nation-State*. Cambridge: Cambridge University Press, 1990.
Birnberg, T., and S.A. Resnick. *Colonial Development: An Econometric Study*. New Haven: Yale University Press, 1975.
Boahen, A., ed. *General History of Africa 7: Africa under Colonial Domination, 1880–1935*. Paris: UNESCO; Ibadan, Nairobi: Heinemann; California: University of California Press, 1985.
Bolland, O. Nigel. *On the March: Labour Rebellions in the British Caribbean, 1934–39*. Kingston: Ian Randle, 1995.
Bookers Sugar. N.p., 1954.
Bostock, Frances. "The British Overseas Banks and Development Finance in Africa after 1945". *Business History* 33, no. 3 (July 1991): 157–76.
Breton, Norton. *Henckell, Du Buisson and Company, 1697–1947*. London: Henckell, Du Buisson and Co., n.d.
Brereton, Bridget. *A History of Modern Trinidad 1783–1962*. Kingston: Heinemann, 1981.
———. "Society and Culture in the Caribbean. The British and French West Indies, 1870–1980". In *The Modern Caribbean*, edited by Franklin Knight and Colin Palmer, 85–110. Chapel Hill: University of North Carolina Press, 1989.
———, ed. *General History of the Caribbean*. Vol. 5, *The Caribbean in the Twentieth Century*. Paris and London: UNESCO and Macmillan, 2004.
Brown, Deryck. *History of Money and Banking in Trinidad and Tobago from 1789 to 1989*. Port of Spain: Paria, 1989.
———. "The Response of the Banking Sector to the General Crisis: Trinidad, 1836–56". *Journal of Caribbean History* 24, no. 1 (1990): 28–64.
Bryan, Patrick. *The Jamaican People, 1880–1902*. London: Macmillan, 1991.
———. "The Creolisation of the Chinese Community in Jamaica". Seminar paper, University of the West Indies, Mona, 1993.

———. "Proletarian Movements (1940–90)". In *General History of the Caribbean*. Vol. 5, *The Caribbean in the Twentieth Century*, edited by Bridget Brereton. Paris and London: UNESCO and Macmillan, 2004.

Bryce, Wyatt, ed. *Reference Book of Jamaica*. Kingston: n.p., 1946.

Buckley, Peter J., and Mark Casson, eds. *The Economic Theory of the Multinational Firm*. London: Macmillan, 1985.

———, eds. *Multinational Enterprises in the World Economy*. Aldershot: Edward Elgar, 1992.

Butler, Kathleen Mary. *The Economics of Emancipation: Jamaica and Barbados, 1823–1843*. Chapel Hill: University of North Carolina Press, 1995.

Cain, P.J., and A.G. Hopkins. *British Imperialism: Innovation and Expansion, 1688–1914*. Harlow, UK: Pearson, 1993.

———. *British Imperialism: Crisis and Deconstruction, 1914–1990*. Harlow, UK: Pearson, 1993.

Callender, C.V. *The Development of the Capital Market Institutions of Jamaica*. Kingston: Institute of Social and Economic Research, University of the West Indies, Mona, 1965.

Cameron, Rondo, ed. *Banking and Economic Development: Some Lessons of History*. New York: Oxford University Press, 1972.

Cameron, Rondo, Olga Crisp, Hugh T. Patrick, and Richard Tilly, eds. *Banking in the Early Stages of Industrialization: A Study in Comparative Economic History*. New York: Oxford University Press, 1967.

Campbell, Carl C. Review of *From Colonial to Republic: One Hundred and Fifty Years of Business and Banking in Trinidad and Tobago, 1837–1987*. *Journal of Caribbean History* 23, no. 1 (1990): 111–14.

Capie, Forrest. "The Evolving Regulatory Framework In British Banking". In *Government, Industries, and Markets: Aspects of Government-Industry Relations in the UK, Japan, West Germany, and the USA since 1945*, edited by Martin Chick, 127–41. Aldershot: Edward Elgar, 1990.

Caribbean Commission. Port of Spain: Central Secretariat, 1957.

Casson, Mark. "Institutional Diversity in Overseas Enterprise: Explaining the Free-Standing Company". *Business History* 36, no. 4 (1994): 95–108.

———. "Multinational Monopolies and International Cartels". In *The Economic Theory of the Multinational Firm*, edited by Peter J. Buckley and Mark Casson, 60–97. London: Macmillan, 1985.

Chalmin, Phillipe. *The Making of a Sugar Giant: Tate and Lyle, 1859–1989*. Chur, Switzerland: Harwood Academic, 1990.

Chapman, S.D. *The Rise of Merchant Banking*. London: Unwin Hyman, 1988.

———. "British-Based Investment Groups before 1914". *Economic History Review*, 2nd ser., 38 (1985): 230–51.

Chatterji, Nikshoy C. *A History of Modern Middle East*. New York: Envoy Press, 1987.

Clarke, Colin. *Kingston, Jamaica: Urban Growth and Social Change 1692–1962*. Berkeley: University of California Press, 1975.

Clarke, W.M. *The City in the World Economy*. London: The Institute of Economic Affairs, 1965.

Clauson, G.L.M. "The British Colonial Currency System". *Economic Journal* 54, no. 213 (April 1944): 1–23.

Cleveland, Harold van B., and Thomas F. Huertas. *Citibank 1812–1970*. Cambridge, MA: Harvard University Press, 1985.

Collins, Michael. *Money and Banking in the UK: A History*. London: Routledge, 1988.

Craton, Michael, and James Walvin. *A Jamaican Plantation: The History of Worthy Park, 1670–1970*. London: W.H. Allen, 1970.

Crick, W.F. "The Framework of Inter-Relations". In *Commonwealth Banking Systems*, edited by W.F. Crick, 1–53. Oxford: Clarendon Press, 1965.

Crossley, Sir Julian, and John Blandford. *The DCO Story: A History of Banking in Many Countries 1925–1971*. London: Barclays Bank International Ltd, 1975.

Curtin, Philip. "The British Sugar Duties and West Indian Prosperity". *Journal of Economic History* 14 (1954). Reprinted in *Caribbean Freedom: Economy and Society From Emancipation to the Present*, edited by Hilary Beckles and Verene Shepherd, 314–18. Kingston: Ian Randle, 1993.

Darroch, James L. *Canadian Banks and Global Competitiveness*. Montreal: McGill-Queen's University Press, 1994.

Davis, K.G. "The Origins of the Commission System in the West India Trade". *Transactions of the Royal Historical Society*. London, 5th ser., 001–2, 1952. Reprinted in *Caribbean Slavery in the Atlantic World*, edited by Verene Shepherd and Hilary Beckles, 326–34. Kingston: Ian Randle, 2001.

Dookhan, Isaac. *A Post-Emancipation History of the West Indies*. London: Longman, 1988, 1989.

Drummond, Ian. *British Economic Policy and the Empire, 1919–1939*. London: Allen and Unwin, 1972.

Eisner, Gisela. *Jamaica 1830–1930: A Study in Economic Growth*. Manchester: Manchester University Press, 1961.

Estabrook, Susan. *The Banking Crisis of 1933*. Kentucky: University of Kentucky Press, 1973.

Foreman-Peck, James. *A History of the World Economy: International Economic Relations since 1850*. Hertfordshire: Wheatsheaf, 1983.

Galloway, J.H. *The Sugar Cane Industry: An Historical Geography from Its Origins to 1914*. Cambridge: Cambridge University Press, 1989.

Garcia, Fe Iglesias. "Demographic and Social Structural Changes in the Contemporary Caribbean". In *General History of the Caribbean*. Vol. 5, *The Caribbean in the Twentieth Century*, edited by Bridget Brereton, 401–33. Paris and London: UNESCO and Macmillan, 2004.

George, Kenneth D., Caroline Joll and E.L. Lynk. *Industrial Organization: Competition, Growth, and Structural Change.* London: Routledge, 1992.

Geroski, Paul, Richard J. Gilbert and Alexis Jacquemin eds., *Barriers to Entry and Strategic Competition.* Chur, Switzerland: Harwood Academic, 1990.

Girvan, Norman. "Foreign Investment and Economic Development in Jamaica". PhD diss., University of London, 1966.

———. *Foreign Capital and Economic Underdevelopment in Jamaica.* Kingston: Institute of Social and Economic Research, University of the West Indies, Mona, 1971.

Gomes, P.I., ed. *Rural Development in the Caribbean.* London: C. Hurst and Co., 1985.

Goodhart, Charles. *The Evolution of Central Banks.* Cambridge, MA: MIT Press, 1988.

Gray, Jean M., and H. Peter Gray. "The Multinational Bank: A Financial MNC?" *Journal of Banking and Finance* 5 (1981): 33–63. Reprinted in *Multinational and International Banking,* edited by Geoffrey Jones, 18–48. Aldershot: Edward Elgar, 1992.

Greaves, Ida. *Colonial Monetary Conditions.* London: Her Majesty's Stationery Office, 1953.

Green, William A. *British Slave Emancipation: The Sugar Colonies and the Great Experiment 1830–1865.* Oxford: Clarendon Press, 1976, 1991.

Grossman, Richard. "The Shoe That Didn't Drop: Explaining Banking Stability during the Great Depression". *Journal of Economic History* 54, no. 3 (September 1994): 654–82.

Grubel, Herbert. "A Theory of Multinational Banking". *Banca Nazionale del Lavoro Quarterly Review* 123 (December 1977): 349–63. Reprinted in *Multinational and International Banking,* edited by Geoffrey Jones, 3–17. Aldershot: Edward Elgar, 1992.

Hagelberg, G.B. *The Caribbean Sugar Industries: Constraints and Opportunities.* New Haven: Yale University Press, 1974.

Hall, Douglas. "Incalculability as a Feature of Sugar Production during the Eighteenth Century". *Social and Economic Studies* 10, no. 3 (September 1961): 340–52.

———. *A Brief History of the West India Committee.* Barbados: Caribbean Universities Press, 1971.

———. *Free Jamaica 1838–1865: An Economic History.* Aylesbury: Ginn, 1959, 1976.

———. *Five of the Leewards 1834–1870: The Major Problems of the Post-Emancipation Period in Antigua, Barbuda, Montserrat, Nevis, and St Kitts.* Aylesbury: Ginn, 1977.

———. *The Caribbean Experience: An Historical Survey 1450–1960.* Kingston: Heinemann, 1982.

———. "Scotiabank in Jamaica, 1889–1989". Manuscript, 1989.

———. *Grace, Kennedy and Company Limited: A Story of Jamaican Enterprise.* Kingston: Grace, Kennedy and Co. Ltd, 1992.

Handbook of the British West Indian Sugar Association (Inc.), 1961. N.p., n.d.

Havinden, Michael, and David Meredith. *Colonialism and Development: Britain and Its Tropical Colonies, 1850–1960*. London: Routledge, 1993.

Hazlewood, Arthur. "The Economics of Colonial Monetary Arrangements". *Social and Economic Studies* 3, nos. 1–4 (1954): 291–315.

Higman, B.W. *Abstract of Caribbean Historical Statistics*. Kingston: Department of History, University of the West Indies, Mona, 1985.

Hill, C.P. *British Economic and Social History, 1700–1982*. London: Hodder and Stoughton, 1957, 1985.

Huertas, Thomas F. "US Multinational Banking: History and Prospects". In *Banks as Multinationals*, edited by Geoffrey Jones, 248–67. London: Routledge, 1990.

Jainarain, Iserdeo. *Trade and Development: A Study of the Small Caribbean Countries and Large Multinational Corporations*. Georgetown: Institute of Development Studies, University of Guyana, 1976.

Jamieson, A.B. *Chartered Banking in Canada*. Toronto: Ryerson Press, 1953.

Jefferson, Owen. *The Post-War Economic Development of Jamaica*. Kingston: Institute of Social and Economic Research, University of the West Indies, Mona, 1972.

Jones, Geoffrey. *The State and the Emergence of the British Oil Industry*. London: Macmillan, 1981.

———. *Banking and Empire in Iran*. Cambridge: Cambridge University Press, 1986.

———. *Banking and Oil*. Cambridge: Cambridge University Press, 1987.

———, ed. *Banks as Multinationals*. London: Routledge, 1990.

———. *British Multinational Banking, 1830-1990*. Oxford: Clarendon Press, 1993.

———. "Competitive Advantages in British Multinational Banking since 1890". In *Banks as Multinationals*, edited by Geoffrey Jones, 30–61. London: Routledge, 1990.

———. "Competition and Competitiveness in British Banking, 1918–1971". In *Competitiveness and the State*, edited by Geoffrey Jones and Maurice Kirby, 120–40. Manchester: Manchester University Press, 1991.

———. ed. *Multinational and International Banking*. Aldershot: Edward Elgar, 1992.

———. *The Evolution of International Business: An Introduction*. London: Routledge, 1996.

———. "The Legacy of the Past: British Multinational Banking Strategies since the Nineteenth Century". In *Multinational Enterprises in the World Economy*, edited by Peter Buckley and Mark Casson, 153–75. Aldershot: Edward Elgar, 1992.

———. *Merchants to Multinationals. British Trading Companies in the Nineteenth and Twentieth Centuries*. Oxford: Oxford University Press, 2000.

Jones, Geoffrey, and Maurice Kirby, eds. *Competitiveness and the State: Government and Business in Twentieth-century Britain*. Manchester: Manchester University Press, 1991.

Kaniki, M.H.Y. "The Colonial Economy: The Former British Zones". In *General History of Africa 7: Africa Under Colonial Domination, 1880–1935*, edited by A.H.

Boahen, 382–419. Paris: UNESCO; Ibadan, Nairobi: Heinemann; California: University of California Press, 1985.

Kennedy, P. *African Capitalism: The Struggle for Ascendancy*. Cambridge: Cambridge University Press, n.d.

Kenwood, A.G., and A.L. Lougheed. *The Growth of the International Economy 1820–2000: An Introductory Text*. London: Unwin, Hyman, 1971.

Kesner, Richard. *Economic Control and Colonial Development: Crown Colony Financial Management in the Age of Joseph Chamberlain*. Oxford: Clio, 1981.

King, F.H.H. *History of the Hong Kong Shanghai Banking Corporation*. Cambridge: Cambridge University Press, 1987–1991.

Klebaner, Benjamin J. *American Commercial Banking: A History*. Boston: Twayne, 1990.

Knight, E. Gittens. *The Grenada Handbook and Directory 1946*. N.p., n.d.

Knight, Franklin W., and Colin A. Palmer, eds. *The Modern Caribbean*. Chapel Hill: University of North Carolina Press, 1989.

Krozewksi, Gerold. *Money and the End of Empire: British International Economic Policy and the Colonies, 1947–1958*. Houndmills: Palgrave, 2001.

Langley, Lester. *The United States and the Caribbean in the Twentieth Century*. Athens: University of Georgia Press, 1989.

Lewis, Kathleen Phillips. "The Trinidad Cocoa Peasants and their Struggle for Acceptance, 1890–1939". Paper presented at UNESCO/University of the West Indies Conference on Slavery, Emancipation and the Shaping of Society, St Augustine, Trinidad and Tobago, 8–10 December 1988.

———. "The Poor and the Powerful: The Cocoa Contracts Crisis in Trinidad, 1884–1890". *Journal of Caribbean History* 32, nos. 1 and 2 (1998).

Lobdell, Richard. "Patterns of Investment and Sources of Credit in the British West Indian Sugar Industry, 1838–1897". *Journal of Caribbean History* 4 (May 1972). Reprinted in *Caribbean Freedom: Economy and Society From Emancipation to the Present*, edited by Hilary Beckles and Verene Shepherd, 319–25. Kingston: Ian Randle, 1993.

Mackenzie, Kenneth. *The Banking Systems of Great Britain, France, Germany, and the United States of America*. London: Macmillan, 1947.

MacMillan, Allistair. *The Red Book of the West Indies: Historical and Descriptive Commercial and Industrial Facts, Figures, and Resources*. London: W.H. and L. Collingridge, 1922.

———. *The West Indies, Past and Present, with British Guiana and Bermuda*. London: W.H. and L. Collingridge, 1938.

Mandle, Jay R. "British Caribbean Economic History. An Interpretation". In *The Modern Caribbean*, edited by Franklin W. Knight and Colin A. Palmer, 229–58. Chapel Hill: University of North Carolina Press, 1989.

Marsh, Donald Bailey. "Canada". In *Banking Systems*, edited by B.H. Beckhart. Toronto: Ryerson Press, 1953.

Marshall, Woodville. "Nineteenth Century Crises in the Barbadian Sugar Industry". In *Emancipation II: Aspects of the Post-Slavery Experience in Barbados*, edited by Woodville Marshall, 85–101. Cave Hill: Department of History, University of the West Indies, 1987.

Martin, R.M. *The British Colonies*. London: J. Tallis and Co., 1853.

McDowall, Duncan. *Quick to the Frontier: Canada's Royal Bank*. Toronto: McClelland and Stewart, 1993.

McIntyre, W. David. *The Commonwealth of Nations: Origins and Impact, 1869–1971*. Minneapolis: University of Minnesota Press, 1977.

Meredith, David. "State-Controlled Marketing and Economic Development: The Case of West African Produce during the Second World War", *Economic History Review*, 2nd ser., 39, no. 1 (February 1986): 77–91.

Merret, David. *ANZ Bank: An Official History*. Sydney: Allen and Unwin, 1985.

Meyer, F.V. *Britain's Colonies in World Trade*. London: Oxford University Press, 1948.

Miller, Nugent. *Organisation and Structure of Commercial Banking in Jamaica*. Kingston: Institute of Social and Economic Research, University of the West Indies, Mona, 1971.

Miller, Rory. *Britain and Latin America in the Nineteenth and Twentieth Centuries*. London: Longman, 1993.

Millette, James. "Decolonization, Populist Movements, and the Formation of New Nations, 1945–1970". In *General History of the Caribbean*. Vol. 5, *The Caribbean in the Twentieth Century*, 174–223, edited by Bridget Brereton. Paris and London: UNESCO and Macmillan, 2004.

Money, George. *Nine Lives of a Bush Banker*. London: Merlin Books, 1990.

Moohr, Michael. "The Economic Impact of Slave Emancipation in British Guiana, 1832–1852". *Economic History Review* 25 (1972): 588–607.

Moore, Brian. "Ethnicity and Economic Behaviour in Nineteenth-century Guyana". In *Working Slavery, Pricing Freedom: Perspectives from the Caribbean, Africa, and the Diaspora*, edited by Verene Shepherd, 377–95. Kingston: Ian Randle, 2001.

Morgan, D.J. *The Official History of Colonial Development*. Vol. 1, *The Origins of British Aid Policy 1924–1945*. London: Macmillan, 1980.

———. "The West Indies". In *Commonwealth Banking Systems*, edited by W.F. Crick, 463–94. Oxford: Clarendon Press, 1965.

Nash, E.F. "Trading Problems of the British West Indies". In *The Economy of the West Indies*, edited by George E. Cumper, 223–42. Westport, CT: Greenwood, 1960, 1974.

Nelson, W. Evan. "The Hongkong and Shanghai Banking Corporation Factor in the Progress toward a Straits Settlements Government Note Issue, 1881–1889". In *Eastern Banking*, edited by F.H.H. King, 155–79. London: Athlone, 1983.

Nevin, Edward, and E.W. Davis. *The London Clearing Banks*. London: Elek Books, 1970.

Newlyn, W.T. "The Colonial Empire". In *Banking in the British Commonwealth*, edited by R.S. Sayers, 425–60. Oxford: Clarendon Press, 1952.

Newlyn, W.T., and D.C. Rowan. *Money and Banking in British Colonial Africa: A Study of the Monetary and Banking System of Eight British African Territories*. Oxford: Clarendon Press, 1954.

Nwankwo, G.O. "The British Overseas Banks in the Developing Countries. 1 – Until 1945". *Journal of the Institute of Bankers* 93, part 3 (June 1972): 148–58.

Odle, Maurice. *Multinational Banks and Underdevelopment*. New York: Pergamon Press, 1981.

Palmer, Colin A. "Identity, Race, and Black Power in Independent Jamaica". In *The Modern Caribbean*, edited by Franklin W. Knight and Colin A. Palmer, 111–28. Chapel Hill: University of North Carolina Press, 1989.

Pares, Richard. *Merchants and Planters*. Cambridge: Cambridge University Press, 1960, 1970.

Perry, F.E. *A Dictionary of Banking*. Plymouth: MacDonalds and Evans, 1979.

Post, Ken. *Arise Ye Starvelings: The Jamaican Labour Rebellion of 1938 and Its Aftermath*. The Hague: Martinuss Nijhoff, 1978.

Quigley, Neil, C. "The Bank of Nova Scotia in the Caribbean, 1889–1940: The Establishment of an International Branch Banking Network". *Business History Review* 63 (1989): 797–838.

Ramsaran, Ramesh. *The Monetary and Financial System of the Bahamas: Growth, Structure, and Operation*. Kingston: Institute of Social and Economic Research, University of the West Indies, Mona, 1978.

Republic Bank Ltd. *From Colonial to Republic: One Hundred and Fifty Years of Business and Banking in Trinidad and Tobago, 1837–1987*. Port of Spain: Republic Bank, n.d.

Richardson, Bonham C. "Caribbean Migrations, 1838–1965". In *The Modern Caribbean*, edited by Franklin W. Knight and Colin A. Palmer, 203–28. Chapel Hill: University of North Carolina Press, 1989.

Rodney, Walter. *A History of the Guyanese Working People, 1881–1905*. Baltimore: Johns Hopkins University Press, 1981.

Rodriquez, D.W. *Bananas: An Outline of the Economic History of Production and Trade with Special Reference to Jamaica*. Kingston: Department of Agriculture, 1955.

Rooth, Tim. *British Protectionism and the International Economy: Overseas Commercial Policy in the 1930s*. Cambridge: Cambridge University Press, 1992.

Ryan, Selwyn, and Lou Anne Barclay. *Sharks and Sardines: Blacks in Business in Trinidad and Tobago*. St Augustine, Trinidad: Institute of Social and Economic Research, University of the West Indies, 1992.

Satchell, Veront. *From Plots to Plantations: Land Transactions in Jamaica, 1866–1900*. Kingston: Institute of Social and Economic Research, University of the West Indies, Mona, 1990.

Seecharan, Clem. *Sweetening Bitter Sugar: Jock Campbell, the Booker Reformer in British Guiana, 1934–1966*. Kingston: Ian Randle, 2005.

Shahabuddeen, M. *From Plantocracy to Nationalisation: A Profile of Sugar in Guyana.* Georgetown: University of Guyana, 1983.

Sharp, G.F., compiler. *Barbados Year Book Who's Who, 1935.* Barbados: Advocate Press, 1935.

———, ed. *The Barbados Year Book, 1937.* Barbados: Advocate Press, 1937.

Sheridan, Richard. *Sugar and Slavery: The Economic History of the British West Indies, 1627–1775.* Kingston: Canoe Press, University of the West Indies, 1974, 1994.

Singh, Kelvin. *Race and Class Struggles in a Colonial State: Trinidad, 1917–1945.* Kingston: The Press, University of the West Indies, Mona, 1994.

Sleeman, Michael. "The Agri-Business Bourgeoisie of Barbados and Martinique". In *Rural Development in the Caribbean*, edited by P.I. Gomes, 15–33. London: C. Hurst and Co., 1985.

Special Correspondent. "Monetary Systems of the Colonies: The West Indies". *The Banker* 88, no. 27 (November 1948): 161–67.

Stahl, Kathleen. *The Metropolitan Organisation of British Colonial Trade.* London: Faber and Faber, 1951.

Sykes, Ernest. *Banking and Currency.* London: Butterworth, 1937.

Thomas, Clive. *Monetary and Financial Arrangements in a Dependent Monetary Economy. A Study of British Guiana 1945–1962.* Kingston: Institute of Social and Economic Research, University of the West Indies, Mona, 1965.

Thomas, S. Evelyn. *Banking and Exchange.* St Albans: Donnington Press, 1930.

Tilly, Richard. *Financial Institutions and Industrialization in the Rhineland, 1815–1870.* Wisconsin: University of Wisconsin Press, 1966.

Trade Regulations and Commercial Policy of the United Kingdom. London: Cambridge University Press, 1943.

Truptil, R.J. *British Banks and the London Money Market.* London: Jonathan Cape, 1936.

Tschoegl, Adrian E. "International Retail Banking as a Strategy: An Assessment". *Journal of International Business* 18, no. 2 (Summer 1987): 67–88. Reprinted in *Multinational and International Banking*, edited by Geoffrey Jones. England: Edward Elgar, 1992.

Uche, Chibuike Ugochukwu. "Credit Discrimination Controversy in British West Africa: Evidence from Barclays Bank (DCO)". *African Review: Money, Finance, and Banking* 20 (1996): 87–106.

———. "Foreign Banks, Africans, and Credit in Colonial Nigeria, c. 1890–1912". *Economic History Review* 52, no. 4 (November 1999): 669–91.

Uriarte, Miguel Alvarez. "World and Hemisphere Trade Policies Affecting the Caribbean Area". In *Western Hemisphere International Relations and the Caribbean Area*. Vol. 2, edited by Maurice Waters, 10–30. Kingston: University of the West Indies, Mona, 1968.

Verhoef, Grietjie. "Stokvels and Economic Empowerment: The Case of African Women in South Africa, c. 1930–1998". In *Women and Credit: Researching the Past,*

Refiguring the Future, edited by Beverly Lemire, Ruth Pearson, and Gail Campbell, 91–114. Oxford: Berg, 2001.

Western Hemisphere Exports Council. *Trade and Industrial Mission to the Caribbean, 1962.* London: Western Hemisphere Exports Council, 1962.

Wilkins, Mira. "The Free-Standing Company, 1870–1914: An Important Type of British Foreign Direct Investment". *Economic History Review,* 2nd ser., 61, no. 2 (1988): 259–82.

Williams, David. "The Evolution of the Sterling System". In *Money and Banking in Honour of R.S. Sayers,* edited by E.R. Whittlesey and J.S.G. Wilson, 266–97. Oxford: Clarendon Press, 1968.

Wright, Kenneth M. "Dollar Policy in the Sterling Area, 1939–1952". *American Economic Historical Review* 64 (1954).

Interviews

Banks, Donald. Interview by author. Kingston, Jamaica, 18 January 1995.
Clarke, Maurice. Interview by author. Kingston, Jamaica, 9 January 1995.
Forrest, Eldon. Interview by author. Kingston, Jamaica, 26 November 2003.
Money, George C. Interview by author. Hastings, Barbados, 21 July 2003.
Payne, Augusta. Interview by author. Kingston, Jamaica, 11 January 1995.
Ramsey, Edna. Interview by author. Kingston, Jamaica, 7 July 2003.

Personal Files

Eldon Forrest's personal files.

Index

Note: General terms related to banking refer to Barclays Bank (DCO) unless otherwise specified.

abolition of slavery. *See* emancipation
Abraham, Cecil Harold, 237, 240
agencies, compared with branches, 196–98, 316n1
agricultural banks, 103–4
agricultural credit societies, 105
Agricultural Loan Board, 106
Agricultural Loan Societies Law, 1912, 106
Aitken, William Maxwell (Lord Beaverbrook), 25
American imperialism: growth of, in West Indies, 51
Anglo-Egyptian Bank, 26
Antigua, 16, 19, 40
   sugar industry in, 84, 167, 271
   US bases in, 149
Antigua Sugar Factory Company Ltd, 84, 105, 271
arbitration facilities, for stocks and shares, 219–20, 263
Austin, Arthur Piercy Gardiner, 236–37, 253
Austin, John Gardiner, 66

Bahamas
   Barclays Bank (DCO) in, 189–90
   tourism in, 175
Bahamas International Trust Co. (BITCO) Ltd, 220–21, 263
Bahamas International Trust Co. (Freeport) Ltd, 220
banana industry, West Indian, 172–73

Bank in Battle Dress, A: Being the Story of Barclays Bank (Dominion, Colonial and Overseas) during the Second World War, 1939–1945, 8
Banking Centenary, A: A History of Barclays Bank (Dominion, Colonial and Overseas), 1836–1946, 7–8
banking histories, commemorative, 7–8
Bank Notes (Demonetization and Redemption) Law, 1958, 151
banknotes, commercial, 131
   British, government control over, 115, 116–17
   Canadian: circulation limits on, 147–50, 308n68, 308n72, 308nn75–76, 310n94; legislation regarding, 117–18, 119–20
   hoarding of, in 1940s, 150
   increase in, for Barclays Bank (DCO), 139–41
   issuing privileges, withdrawal of, 150–53, 259–60
   security of, 111, 121, 148
Bank of British Guiana, 19–23, 61
Bank of Jamaica, 23, 112
   collusion policy of, 214
   establishment of, 19, 124–25
Bank of British Honduras, 61
Bank of British Guiana, 19, 61
Bank of British West Africa, 56, 76
Bank of Jamaica Act, no. 32, 1960, provisions of, 124–25

Bank of London and Montreal (BOLAM), 124, 203, 212
Bank of Nova Scotia (BNS), 24–25, 58, 68
    black employee, first, 239
    branch expansion by, in West Indies, 199–200, 202–3
    competitive strategies of, 68, 69
    exemption of, from security requirements, 118–19, 148
    regional policies of, 64
    success of, in Jamaica, 60, 61
Banks, Donald, 241, 325n31
Barbados
    Barclays Bank (DCO) in, 65–66
    government currency notes, attitude towards, 135
    local firms in, 90
    Peasants' Loan Bank, 106
    sugar industry: local financing of, 18, 297n114; local ownership in, 98–99, 297n113
    West India Bank in, 19
    white community in, 242
Barbados Agricultural Bank, 103
Barbados Shipping and Trading Co. Ltd, 66
Barclay, David, 15
Barclays (Jamaica) Nominees Co. Ltd, 220
Barclays (Nassau) Nominees Co. Ltd, 220
Barclays Bank (Canada), 66–67
Barclays Bank (DCO)
    dominance of, in West Indies, 59–60
    evolution of, into retail bank, 81–82, 214–30
    formation of, 26, 27, 256
    local regional head office (*see* decentralization of operations)
    sectional performance, 30–34, 157–62, 164

Barclays Bank (Jamaica), 7
Barclays Bank in the Caribbean, 8
Barclays Bank Ltd: multinational branch network, 26, 66
Barclays Bank of Trinidad and Tobago, 7
Barclays Overseas Development Corporation (BODC), 222–30, 253, 263–64
    formation of, 222–23
    lending patterns of, 223–26; in West Indies, 226–30
Barnes, A.C., 190, 207, 247–48
Barritt, O., 46, 80
Basford, John V., 238–39
Baster, A.S.J., 7, 15
Bath sugar estate, 84
Bertram, W.A., 239
"Big Six", 96
bills of exchange
    clean credit, 92
    documentary bills, 92
    use of, in financing trade, 78–80, 91, 113, 265
black market in foreign exchange. *See* street transactions
black West Indians, employment of, 234–35, 239–45, 264
    hostility of white clients towards, 236, 241, 242–43
    salary differentials, 244
Blairmont, 84, 86
Booker Bros., McConnell and Co. Ltd, 83–84, 86
Bookers Demerara Sugar Estates Ltd, 83, 284
branch expansion, 60–61, 189–98, 232, 262–263
    by Canadian banks, 198–202
British and American Exchange Bank, 23

British Caribbean Currency Board, 150–51
British colonial Africa, banking in, 75–76
British corporate ownership, emergence of, in West Indies, 82–88
British Guiana
  banking in, 18–23, 99–100, 120, 195–96
  bauxite industry in, 168, 176
  British investment groups in, 83–84
  exports from, 176
  government currency notes, attitude towards, 135–36
  labour: expenditure on, 1927–30, 42; shortage of, 1937–45, 164–65
  socialist government in, 176, 195
  sugar industry in, growth of, 1929–38, 51
  Sugar Producers Association, 37–38
British Honduras, 189–90, 191
British Ministry of Food, 172
  "sugar division", 166
British Multinational Banking, 1830–1990 (Jones), 9
British overseas banks. *See* multinational banking
British silver coins, 131–32
  surplus of, in West Indies, 132
British Treasury, 103, 110, 112, 115, 116, 135
British West Indian Sugar Association, 170
Brown, Deryck (*History of Money and Banking in Trinidad and Tobago from 1789 to 1989*), 8–9, 22, 111–12, 113–14
bulk purchasing arrangements, 165–66, 170–71
Butt, R.V., 69, 101

Caine, Sydney, 136–37
Calabar High School, 238
Calvert, C.A., 19, 21
Cameron, Alister, 66, 90
Canada–West Indies trade, 65–67, 289n51
Canadian Bank Act, 117
Canadian Bank Circulation Redemption Fund, 117–18
Canadian Bank of Commerce (CBC), 24, 40, 58, 68, 203, 289n55
Canadian Imperial Bank of Commerce (CIBC), 203
Canadian multinational banks
  Barclays Bank (DCO): collusion with, 54–58; competition with, 59–73, 198–212, 261
  branch expansion by, 198–202
  competitive advantage of, 65, 66–67
  corporate culture in, 234
  distribution of, in West Indies, 59
  regulatory regime for, 117–20
  security requirements, inconsistent application of, 118–19
  success of, in Jamaica, 60, 68
Caroni Sugar Estates (Trinidad) Ltd, 85
cartelization
  Bahamas, in, 56
  Jamaica Inter-Bank Agreement of 1959, 213
Caulcutt, John, 67
Cavan, James, 15
Cayman Islands, 175, 189–90, 191
central banking, evolution of, 121, 129
Charley, James, 50
Charley estates, 49–50, 85–86, 324
charters, royal, 109–11, 115
Chase Manhattan Bank, 203–4
Chenery, Sybil, 246
citizens' associations, 239
citrus industry
  in British Honduras, 191
  Jamaica, exports from, 66
  in Trinidad and Tobago, 174

347

Index

City Bank, 124, 203, 204
Clarke, Fred, 40–41, 50
clientele, bank, 80–91, 236, 241, 242–43
collusion, 54, 69, 212–14, 261
    advantages of, perceived, 55–58, 212, 277
    in exchange business, 153–54, 213
    collusive agreements
    evidence of, in West Indies, 56, 277
    See also cartelization, collusion
Colonial Bank, 1, 11, 18, 109, 289n51
    advantages of, over local banks, 22, 27
    Barclays Bank Ltd, linkage with, 25–26
    charter, stipulations of, 110–11
    directors of, first, 15
    domination of commercial sector by, 23
    establishment of, in West Indies, 15–19
    evolution of, to retail bank, 80
    opposition to, among local merchants, 18–19
    sugar industry, dependence on, 23–24, 256–57
    trade financing, emphasis on, 77
Colonial Bank Act, 1856, 115, 300n17
Colonial Bank Act, 1925, 116–17, 145–46, 260
    interpretation of, by attorney general, 146
Colonial Banking Regulations, 109–15
colonial development, bank's role in, 222–30
Colonial Development Corporation, 253
colonial governments, bank relations with, 141–46
colonialism, advantages of, to bank, 43, 207
Colonial Laws Validity Act, 1865, 145–46

Colonial Office
    banking legislation, attitude towards, 121
    colonial development, role in, 253, 322n102
    government note issues, ambivalence towards, 134–35, 136–38, 140–41, 146–47, 259–60
    sugar production, financing proposal for, 45
    West Indies, British obligation to, 44, 46
Colonial Sugar Preference Certificates, 49
commercial banks, regulation of, 108–27, 259
commission system, 77
Commonwealth Sugar Agreement, 1951 (CSA), 156, 170–72
common West Indian note issue, 133–34
Companies Acts, 120, 121
compensation. See emancipation
competition
    between Barclays Bank (DCO) and Canadian banks, 59–73, 198–212, 261
    non-price competition, 69, 74
    price competition, control of, 55–56, 73–74, 212, 231, 261
consignee lien system, 98
cooperative banks, 99–101
Corentyne Sugar Co. Ltd, 83
Corn Laws, 20
corporate culture
    creation of, 14, 234
    male-dominated, 245, 264
credit
    alternatives, for smallholders, 103–7
    contraction of, during Depression, 41

crop production loans, flexible terms for, 94–103
   increased demand for, post-war, 177–81, 263
   informal arrangements, 106–7
credit facilities, 91–103, 218–19
   approval required for, 250
   medium- and long-term, 221–22
Crossley, Julian, 56, 57–58, 73, 203, 223, 240
Cuba
   "Black Pact", 170
   effect of revolution on West Indian sugar industry, 172
currency-board system, 128–30
   effect of, on exchange business, 154–55, 260
   West Indian note issue, proposal for, 133
currency notes, government
   introduction of, 131, 134, 259
   Note Guarantee Fund, 138–39
   relationship of, to commercial banknotes, 133–50
currency of trade, 14, 110–11
   coins in circulation, exchange value of, 111–12,
Cyprus, Central Cooperative Bank, 99
Czarnikows, 67

DaCosta and Co. Ltd, 90
Dale, Henry, 249
DCO Story, The: A History of Banking in Many Countries, 1925–1971, 8
decentralization of banking operations, 249–54, 264, 312n5
decolonization, British, 4, 232, 233, 254, 255, 312n5
Demerara Company Holdings, 84
deposits
   interest rates paid on, 178–79, 186, 188, 213

invested in colonial regions, 222
remitted for investment, 180–81, 221, 263
solicitation of, 63–64, 69, 74, 192, 207, 247, 261, 262
Depression. *See* Great Depression
Diamond sugar estate, 84
discriminatory lending practices, 75, 76, 101–3
Dudley, A.T., 57
Duhaney, Barbara, 241

Earl T. Robinson Ltd, 67
East Africa, 210, 223, 226
East African Section (*see* Barclays Bank [DCO]: sectional performance)
   employment opportunities in banking, 235
emancipation, 15, 280n21
   compensation paid to slave owners, 17–18, 280n32
   consequences of, in Leeward Islands, 16
   public administration following, 17
Encumbered Estates Act, 1854, 98–99, 292n23
English Chancery Court System, 66, 98
Enmore Estates Ltd, 83
Escolme, R.N., 102–3
exchange business, 181–85, 267–68
   collusion in, 153–54, 213
   commissions, effect on, 153–55
   street transactions, effect on, 183–84, 213–14
exports, colonial: British control of, 166–67

Farquaharson, W.N., 89
Ffrench, Edna (now Ramsey), 239

First National City Bank of New York. *See* City Bank
Fisher, J., 141, 147
Fogarty, William, 90–91
Foreign Capital and Economic Underdevelopment in Jamaica (Girvan), 10
foreign direct investment (FDI), 11
    British, compared with American, 12
    incentive legislation for, 174–77
    investment groups, 83–88
foreign exchange. *See* exchange business
Forrest, Eldon, 241, 325n32
Free Quota sugar, 170–71
free trade policy, British, 20, 48–49
From Colonial to Republic: One Hundred and Fifty Years of Business and Banking in Trinidad and Tobago, 1837–1987, 8
Frome estate, 86
Furness, Withy and Co. Ltd, 85, 293n39

Gardiner, Austin and Co. Ltd, 66
Geo. F. Huggins and Co., 105
George, C.C., 253–54
Gibbs, Geoffrey Cockayne, 223
Girvan, Norman (*Foreign Capital and Economic Underdevelopment in Jamaica*), 10
gold standard, 3, 48, 130
Goodenough, F.C., 26, 40
Gordon, Grant and Co. Ltd, 88, 105, 294n64
government securities, 29, 57
Grace, Kennedy and Co. Ltd, 89–90, 294n69
Gray's Inn (Jamaica) Central Factory Ltd, 84
Great Depression, 4
    effect of, on Barclays Bank (DCO) performance, 29–53, 258
    effect of, on sugar industry, 28, 35–53, 257–58
    impact of, British resistance to, 48–49
Grindle, G.E.A., 44, 46
guarantees, 184, 213, 215, 219
    See also loan guarantees, government
Gurney, Samuel, 15

Hall, Douglas, 16, 233
Hankey, J.A., 15
Harbour Street branch, 236, 237, 241, 243, 324n21, 325–26nn31–32
Harrison's College, 237
Henckell, Du Buisson and Co., 84, 167
History of Money and Banking in Trinidad and Tobago from 1789 to 1989 (Brown), 8–9
Hoare, John Gurney, 15
Holland estate, 89

Imperial Economic Conference, 131
Import Duties Act of 1932, 49
import-export trade, 87–88, 164–72, 183
    West Indian firms in, 89–91
imports, post-emancipation increase in, 16–17
indigenous banks
    disadvantages of, 22, 27
    multinationals, relations with, 54, 99–101, 261
    imprudent practices of, 20–23
    regulatory framework for, 111–115
    See also under specific territories
industrial development
    incentive legislation for, 174–77
Inswood sugar estates, 84, 194
International Bank, 23

International Sugar Agreement (ISA), 171
investment groups, British, 83–88
Irving, John, 15

Jagan, Cheddi, 176, 195
Jamaica
    Agricultural Loan Societies Board, 101, 106, 299n146, 323n117
    banana industry in, 70, 71, 95, 164, 172, 194,
    banking in, 19–23, 63–64, 106, 120–21
    Banking Law, No. 31, 1960, 123–25, 193–95
    bauxite production in, 174–75, 193–94
    Canadian banks in, 24–25, 56–57, 60, 68
    economy of, foreign banks' role in, 10
    industrial development in, 173–74
    migration from, to United Kingdom, 207–8
    money-lending, by local merchants, 16
    rum production in, 284n23
    sugar industry in, 38, 51, 272; independent farmers, 292n19
    taxation of banknotes by, 141–45, 259, 307n63
    tourism in, 175, 194–95
    unified currency, rejection of, 151
    World War II, economic effects on, 167–68
Jamaica College, 237, 238
Jamaica Import and Export Co., 89
Jamaica Inter-Bank Agreement of 1959, 213
Jefferson, Owen (*The Post-War Economic Development of Jamaica*), 10
Joaquim Ribiero Ltd., 90
Jones Estates Ltd, 83–84

Jones, Geoffrey, 1, 2, 22, 115
    British Multinational Banking, 1830–1990, 9
    racial stereotyping by multinational banks, 76

Kaniki, M.H.Y., 76
Kennedy, P., 76
Kingston and St Andrew Corporation (KSAC), 239
Kleinwort, Sons and Co., 84–85

labour disturbances
    factors underlying, 173
    potential, British fear of, 44
    widespread, 52
Lascelles, DeMercado and Co., Ltd, 41, 88–89
legal tender: varieties of, in West Indies, 131
lending practices, inflexibility of, 69–73, 261–62
Leonora estates, 84
Leung-Walker, Ena Evadne, 249
Lewis, W. Arthur, 173
licence fees, for commercial banks, 120–21
Lindo, H.V., 89
loan guarantees, government, 43–48, 52, 53, 258, 285nn40–41
Lobdell, Richard, 113–14
London and Colonial Bank, 23
London Clearing House, 69
London Committee, 250
London Provincial and South Western Bank, 25
Lucie-Smith, E.W., 101, 253

management structure, 249–50, 252
    Central Board, 95, 96, 98, 250, 251
    local advisory directorship, 253–54, 264

management structure *(cont'd)*
    London Committee, 96, 97, 250, 295n85
    regional management system, 250–54
    sectional boards, 250
Manning and Co., 99
Martin's Bank, 68–69
McFarlane, Roy, 240
McGarel, Charles, 15
Michael Cavan and Co. Ltd, 66
Miller, J. Stephen, 89
Miller, Nugent, 54
Money, George, 210, 211–12, 235, 236, 242, 249
Monymusk estate, 85
Moore, Brian, 102
Morgan, D.J., 221
mortgages, 80, 83, 92, 93, 104, 106, 116, 218, 219
Mortimer, P.E.N., 236
Moyne Commission, 173
multinational banking
    American: handicaps of, in West Indies, 204–5
    British dominance of, 1–2, 13–14, 27, 59–60
    Canadian (*see* Canadian multinational banks)
    competitive advantages, 1–2, 13–15, 27, 43, 259
    decline in, 3, 256, 257
    definition of, 12
    director–branch manager relations, 23
    discriminatory practices in, 75, 101–3
    emergence of, 1, 12–13
    lending practices: principles underlying, 77–80, 113–15, 260
    products and services, 75–107
    quality of service among, 69–73

Multinational Banks and Underdevelopment (Odle), 9–10
multinational enterprise, 11, 85
"mushroom banks", 122–23
Mutual Brokers (Montreal) Ltd, 67

National Commercial Bank, 326n32
nationalism: growth of, 3, 4, 232
Negotiated Price Quota (NPQ), 170–71, 313n29
New Store, The, 90
Noble, Ran, 67
nominees companies, 219–20
North Shore Mills Ltd, 68
note circulation, significance of, 59–60
Note Guarantee Fund, 132, 138

Odle, Maurice (*Multinational Banks and Underdevelopment*), 9–10, 54
oligopoly theory, 55
Olivier Commission, 43
operational costs, post-war, 185–87
organizational structure. *See* management structure
Ottawa Agreement of 1932, 49, 50

Palestine
    Agricultural Mortgage Corporation, 99, 100
    Barclays Bank (DCO), raid of, 312n4
    mushroom banks in, 122
    regional boards in, 251
Payne, Augusta, 241, 242–43, 247, 248–49
People's Cooperative Loan Banks, 106
Philharmonic, The, 90
plantation agriculture
    British control of, 80, 82–88, 257
    West Indian firms' ownership, 88–90
Planters Bank, 19, 21–22, 112

political independence. *See* decolonization

Post-War Economic Development of Jamaica, The (Jefferson), 10

preferential agreements, 25, 65–67
    See also protectionist policies, British

price competition, 54, 55–58, 212–13, 261

product diversification, post-war, 214–18, 232, 263

protectionist policies, British, 43–49, 166–67, 170–72, 258–59, 281n47

Providence sugar estates, 84

public administration: expansion of, after emancipation, 17

Puerto Rican economic model, 173, 188, 254

R. & G. Challenor Ltd, 99

racial stereotyping, 102–3, 233
    See also discriminatory practices; social stratification

Ramsey, Edna. *See* Ffrench, Edna

Rasheen estate, 89

real estate, as collateral, 113–15

recruitment practices, 14, 234–36, 255
    changes in, 232, 233, 234–49, 264
    criticism of, 239

Regulations for the Incorporation of Banking Companies in the Colonies, 112–15

regulatory regime, British, 18, 108–17, 120–27, 259

Reid, Dorothy Eve, 249

Rennie, William, 21

Ressouvenir Estates Ltd, 83

Richardson, H., 72

Robarts, Abraham George, 15

Rowan, D.C., 76

Royal Bank of Canada (RBC), 19, 24–25, 57, 67, 288n26
    branch expansion by, 61, 198
    exemption of, from security requirements, 119
    London branch of, 68
    success of, in Leeward Islands, 65

Ruimveldt estate, 84

Rum Pool, 284n23

Sandbach, Parker and Co. Ltd, 84

Sandbach, Tinne and Co. Ltd, 83, 84

S. Davson and Co. Ltd, 83, 84, 86

securities management, 219–21, 263

silver exchange standard: problems with, 131–32

Silvera, Noel Dennis, 237–38

Singh, Kelvin, 105

Smith, H.R., 100

social stratification, by race and class, 232, 235–36
    See also discriminatory practices; racial stereotyping

South Africa
    Barclays Bank (DCO) operations in, 30, 34, 55, 121, 234
    local regional board in, 250–51, 327n66

South African Section, 157, 163,

sterling
    dominance of, in world trade, 14
    exchange standard, establishment of, 130–33

Sterling Area, 130

Stevenson, H.A., 67

St Kitts, 16, 19

St Kitts (Basseterre) Sugar Factory Company Ltd, 84, 105

street transactions, 183–84, 213–14

St Vincent Agricultural Credit and Loan Bank Ltd, 105–6

Subsidiary Coinage Fund, 138–39

Sugar Duties (Equalization) Act of 1846, 19–20, 23

sugar industry, West Indian, 16, 18
- beet sugar, effect on, 24, 25, 37, 284n15
- British control of, 80, 82–88, 257
- Canada, preferential agreements with, 25, 65–67
- Cuban revolution, effect on, 172
- Great Depression, effects on, 28, 35–53
- loan-guarantee scheme, 43–48, 258
- United States, exports to, 25
- West Indian firms' role in, 88–90
- World War II, effects on, 156, 165–67

Tate and Lyle Ltd, 50, 85–86
Thom and Cameron Ltd, 88
Thomas Daniels and Sons, 66, 90
Thomson, Hankey and Co., 87–88
tourism, emergence of, 175–76
trade financing
- currency of, 2, 14, 110–11
- emphasis on, by British overseas banks, 77–80
- exchange business, linkage with, 153–55
- lending policy for, 251

Trinidad and Tobago, 23
- Agricultural Loan Bank, 104
- banking in, 19, 192–93
- British investment groups in, 84–85
- Canadian banks in, 56–57
- cocoa industry in, 104, 164
- government currency notes, attitude towards, 135
- industrial development in, 174
- oil industry of, 87, 175
- sugar industry in, 51, 164, 273–74
- tenant farmers in, 292n19
- World War II, economic effects on, 168

Trinidad Shipping and Trading Co. Ltd, 85
trust companies, 220–21
trustee business, development of, 219–21, 263

Uche, Chuibuike U., 76
Union Bank of Halifax, 61
United Estates, 89
United Fruit Company, 68, 85
United Molasses, 85
United Nations Sugar Conference, 171
US naval bases, effects of
- on currency policy, 140, 149, 150, 309n81, 309n83
- on labour market, 165, 309n79

Vere Estates Co. Ltd, 88–89

Walker, Cleveland G., 239
Waterloo estates, 84, 85
West Africa
- Barclays Bank (DCO) operations in, 25, 26, 33, 55–56, 225, 226,
- employment of black Africans in, 234–35
- indigenous banks in, 76
- West African Section, 33
West Bank Estates Ltd, 83
West Caribbean Head Office, 248
West India Bank, 19–21
West India Committee, 15, 280n19
West Indian currency boards, 151, 154, 155, 260
West Indian Section performance, 269
- during Depression, 29, 30–53, 258
- post–World War II, 156–88, 265
West Indies
- currency reform in, 128–57, 259
- decolonization: effect of, on bank organization, 254, 255

economic expansion in, post-war, 156, 169–77; bank business, effect on, 177–88; bank response to, 189–231, 262

exports from, 50, 81, 164–65, 168–70, 172, 270

imports to, 16–17, 50, 168–69

industrialization policies in, 173–77

inflation in, 169

per capita incomes, regional, 177

trade, value of, 275–76

trade with Canada, 25, 37, 50, 65–67, 74, 170

trade with United States, 25, 37, 50, 51, 172

West Indies Sugar Co. Ltd (WISCo), 86

Whiting, Jim, 236, 238, 324n21

Wilkinson and Gaviller, 90

Wilkinson and Haynes Co. Ltd, 90, 99

Wilkinson, John Hadely, 90

William Fogarty Ltd, 90–91

Williamsfield Trading Co., 89

women, employment of, 245–49, 264
    salary disparity with men, 246–47

world trade, British dominance in, 13–14

World War II
    as catalyst for change in West Indies, 4
    repercussions of, on overseas trade, 97–98, 156

Worthy Park, 40–41, 50, 168

W.R. Grace and Co. *See* Grace, Kennedy and Co. Ltd

www.ingramcontent.com/pod-product-compliance
Lightning Source LLC
Chambersburg PA
CBHW080724300426
44114CB00019B/2486